D1094522

18964   B
821
Spitz   S75

The religious Renaissance of the
  German humanists

Date Due

NOV 2 7 '69			
NOV 8 1988			
NOV 22 '88			

CHABOT
COLLEGE
LIBRARY

bff   PRINTED IN U.S.A.

The
Religious Renaissance
of the
German Humanists

The

Religious Renaissance

of the

German Humanists

✢ ✢ ✢

LEWIS W. SPITZ

HARVARD UNIVERSITY PRESS

Cambridge, Massachusetts

1963

Distributed in Great Britain by Oxford University Press, London

Publication of this book has been aided by a grant from the Ford Foundation

Library of Congress Catalog Card Number 63-9563

Printed in the United States of America

To My Parents

Acknowledgments

The author wishes to express his deepest appreciation to a number of people whose inspiration, good will, and assistance have made the completion of this work possible. In correspondence and conversation he has received suggestions and encouragement from several historians and Reformation scholars. Among these he must mention especially Dr. Hans Baron of the Newberry Library, Dr. Richard Douglas of the Massachusetts Institute of Technology, Dr. Eli Sobel of the University of California at Los Angeles, Dr. Robert Kingdon of the State University of Iowa, Dr. Hans Rupprich of the University of Vienna, Dr. Quirinus Breen of the University of Oregon, and Dr. Charles Mullett of the University of Missouri. In addition to contributions of this kind Dr. Harold J. Grimm of Ohio State University read various chapters and made a number of valuable suggestions. Special thanks are due Dr. Myron P. Gilmore of Harvard University who read the entire manuscript and gave it the benefit of his criticism. Moreover, he initially inspired the author with an interest in that line of inquiry which has resulted in this book.

Without the generous award of a fellowship by the Guggenheim Foundation, 1956–1957, which provided sustained time and access to European libraries, the appearance of this book would have been long delayed. A subvention from the American Council of Learned Societies further facilitated the research done abroad. The Research Council of the University of Missouri provided a summer research grant. Dean Albert H. Bowker of the Graduate Division of Stanford University supplied a supplementary research grant for secretarial help. The Henry E. Huntington Library awarded a research grant which made it possible for the author in 1959 to spend a delightful summer with Erasmus and his friends in San Marino. For all of this very substantial assistance the author is deeply grateful.

Parts of this volume were presented in lecture form at the *Institut für Europäische Geschichte*, Mainz, Germany, during the academic year 1960–1961, while the author was a Fulbright professor at the Institute. While there he enjoyed a friendly and scholarly association with Professor Joseph Lortz, distinguished church historian and head of the division for religious history at the Institute. Count and Countess Páli Esterházy extended their generous hospitality to the author and his family during his year of research in Vienna.

Chapter IV was published substantially in its present form under the title: "Reuchlin's Philosophy: Pythagoras and Cabala for Christ," *Archiv für Reformationsgeschichte*, XLVII (1956), 1–20. Chapter VII appeared previously as "The Conflict of Ideals in Mutianus Rufus," *Journal of the Warburg and Courtauld Institutes*, XVI, nos. 1–2 (1953), 121–143. They are included here with the kind permission of the respective editors.

The author is grateful also to Mrs. Wilbert Rosin, to Miss Goldie Sweaney, to Mrs. Francine Long and to his wife for doing various parts of the typescript. Once again he owes to his wife gratitude and thanks for her patience, her many sacrifices, and her help.

Stanford University   L.W.S.
Stanford, California

Contents

Illustrations

The
Religious Renaissance
of the
German Humanists

INTRODUCTION

O NE of the most famous and best loved pictures by the great Renaissance artist Albrecht Dürer is his engraving of "St. Jerome in His Cell" (figure 1). Jerome, the perfect example of the Christian scholar and thinker, is seated undisturbed at his desk in the peaceful seclusion of his well-ordered study. The scene idealizes the *vita contemplativa*, life in the service of God, and the learned tradition, for Jerome, who once dreamt that he heard a voice declare him more a Ciceronian than a Christian, has his books near at hand and is writing another. The room may very well have been the study room of the Nuremberg humanist Willibald Pirckheimer, Dürer's closest friend, or the library room of the sanctuary which Conrad Mutian named his *beata tranquillitas*. In fact, it would be possible to substitute for Jerome almost any one of the German humanists and he would fit perfectly into the scene — except for Hutten for whom the *miles Christianus* in Dürer's "Knight, Death and Devil" would seem more appropriate. Later in the century, in fact, the Protestant artist Wolfgang Stuber, a Nuremberg engraver, did a mirror-image reproduction of Dürer's cozy scene and substituted for Jerome that renowned Augustinian, Martin Luther (figure 12), as though he wished to emphasize the continuity of the learned tradition from humanism through the Reformation.

Few decades have been so portentous for the history of the Christian church as those falling in the first half of the sixteenth century. Those years witnessed intellectual and religious developments which have determined much of the thought and the structure of Christendom down to the present time. In Germany, the homeland of the Reformation, Renaissance humanism became a significant force among the intellectual classes and played a very important role in the dramatic events of the Reformation era. Two major themes dominated the concerns of the German humanists, romantic cultural nationalism and religious enlightenment, and both were of tremendous importance to the Reformation movement itself. This book is a study of the leading men and their ideas about ecclesiastical reform and religious renewal. It has to do with the time-honored theme *de spiritu et littera*.

There is a danger in making an arbitrary and artificial distinction between church history and secular history. This generation of Christian humanists illustrates perfectly the truth that the history of the church can be understood only within the framework of the history of the world and that Western history is unintelligible apart from the history of the church. Étienne Gilson's formula is in the case of Christian humanism singularly apropos. Gilson speaks of man "who without Christianity cannot redeem himself, but without whom Christianity would have nothing to redeem." The historian's purpose in the first instance should be neither to condemn, with Kierkegaard, those false manifestations which parade as Christian humanism, nor to applaud, with Hegel, those thinkers who assumed the cultural burden of Christianity, but to understand as best he can the nature of their ecclesiastical conceptions and religious thought in order to see more clearly the role which they played in Western intellectual history and in the history of the Christian Church.

The problems of Christian humanism are rooted in the dual origins of Western culture in classical and Christian antiquity, problems which have at no time come into such a sharp focus as during the age of the Renaissance and Reformation and in the land where the Reformation began. The interpretation of Northern humanism has been dominated by two major points of view. The first of these is the "reception" theory, that humanism in the North resulted primarily from the reception of Italian Renaissance influences. For this theory the presuppositions of Jacob Burckhardt's magnificent essay on the Renaissance in Italy were decisive. His picture of Renaissance Italy as the incubus of modern individualism, of the rediscovery of the world and of man, naturally led to the portrayal of septentrional humanism as the result of a process of Italianization in the North. Nineteenth-century militant liberals like David Friedrich Strauss, lacking Burckhardt's pessimistic realism and historical sense, projected their own noisome battles with ultramontanism and orthodoxy backward in time and described the German humanists as men of freedom and enlightenment. They tried to fit Roman togas on German patricians and build marble forums in the market places of Gothic cities. They criticized the humanists unfairly for having arrived at only half-solutions for man's basic problems. The great intellectual historian Wilhelm Dilthey in his well-known essay on the analysis and interpretation of man in the fifteenth and sixteenth centuries saw the Reformation as the religious expression of the Renaissance and interpreted German humanism and the Lutheran Reformation as together constituting the decisive step on the way from medieval scholasticism to modern idealism and liberty.[1] The "reception" theory dominated many of the older books, notably Ludwig Geiger's classic, *Renaissance und Humanismus in Italien und Deutschland* (Berlin, 1882), in which he practically used the "parallel lives" approach. The primacy of Italy was the basic assumption also of Paul Wernle's *Die Renaissance des Christentums im 16. Jahrhundert* (Tübingen, 1904). Wernle saw the Italian-dominated Renaissance as highly important for the reformers such as Calvin and Zwingli, and held the Renaissance and Reformation to be kindred movements.

The second interpretation was very naturally that of the revisionists who held to the autochthonous nature of Northern humanism and its continuous development out of the medieval past. Albert Hyma, for example, in *The Christian Renaissance, a History of the "Devotio Moderna"* (New York, 1924), attributed the Northern Renaissance fundamentally to the work of the Brethren of the Common Life. This approach led to some very curious results, particularly where a Catholic apologetic leitmotiv came into play. Johannes Janssen's voluminous history of the German people at the end of the Middle Ages, for instance, glorified German culture just prior to the Reformation.[2] He was obliged to make a sharp distinction between the good humanists, who owed their cultural achievements and religious philosophy to their medieval inheritance, and the bad humanists, whose skepticism and eudemonistic hedonism was largely the product of classic and Italianesque influences. Luther, he charged, destroyed the aristocratic culture of the German Renaissance and brought to an end a splendid era. The revisionists, too, have been found by critical historians to have presented too one-sided a picture of German humanism. To say that the truth lies somewhere in between these two extremes may be accurate, but it is not very meaningful without an examination of the historical realities involved.

Renaissance historiography has struggled manfully with conceptual problems, particularly with the meaning of the central term humanism in a sixteenth-century context. The word humanism means many things to many people, but two uses of the term are particularly apt to produce confusion in the present historical context. The one is humanism as a philosophical point of view which refers all truth and all knowledge to man who is made the absolute center of all reality. Such anthropocentrism, while not irrelevant to a certain tendency in Renaissance humanism, cannot be applied very generally to Italian much less to German humanism. The second is humanism as an interest in classical antiquity. Clearly there have been many intellectuals in both medieval and modern times who have been theologically, aesthetically, historically, philologically, or merely pedantically interested in antiquity who can in no way be considered humanists. Humanism was not merely an interest in classical and Christian antiquity; it was a certain way of looking at antiquity.

The humanists were all concerned with the *humaniora*, the humane studies. The concept of the *studia humanitatis* was taken over from Cicero, who believed the orator or poet to be their best-suited protagonist. The Italian humanist Leonardo Bruni believed that, as he expressed it in his well-known letter to Niccolò Strozzi, these studies were best designed to perfect and ornament man — *propterea humanitatis studia nuncupantur, quod hominem perficiant et exornent*. The wandering apostle of humanism in Germany, Peter Luder, in 1456 announced at Heidelberg that he would "deliver a public lecture on the *studia humanitatis*, that is, the books of the poets, orators, and historians." In the Germanies the term *humanista* was first used in the *Epistolae Obscurorum Virorum*, 1515–1517, but it is clear that with humanist the Germans as well as the Italians meant something quite specific, if not always carefully defined.

Like the Italian Politian, who decried subordinating one's own personality to the outward forms of Ciceronianism, the German humanists, too, were concerned with the humane content of antique letters and their relevance for life, not merely with outward form. Paul Joachimsen was, therefore, quite right in defining humanism as a spiritual movement rooted in a desire for the rebirth of classical antiquity. This had to be a rebirth in the strictest sense of the word, for it presupposed that antiquity was once dead but could be revitalized and made useful to men. It was necessary for the humanists to see a chasm between themselves and antiquity and for them to view antiquity as a closed unity. As such it was unique and unrepeatable, but it must contain the principles of forming and providing the norms for their own culture and way of life. In the case both of the romantic longing and desire for the palingenesis of antiquity and of the classical approach of using antiquity to justify one's own cultural standards, antiquity becomes the criterion of form and norm.[3] As a matter of form humanism was primarily aesthetic, but as a matter of norm it included ethical and spiritual values of fundamental importance. It is in viewing antiquity as norm that Renaissance humanism tended to deviate from the humanism of the Middle Ages. In Germany humanism retained more of a literary-philological character than in Italy, for there was a less well-developed Renaissance society and culture to support it and give it shape. It was more a matter of schools and universities, somewhat less of princely courts and public life. But it became an important spiritual force and precisely in its religious reform efforts helped to make history. Some waspish and inflexible critic in the tradition of Pierre Bayle might hold the idea of a religious renaissance of humanists or the term Christian humanism to be self-contradictory, but scholarship, except for rare throwbacks, has long since transcended that negative level and appreciates the fact that beginning with anthropology the Christian religion and classical humanism have many areas of common concern and some areas of agreement.

The course of German humanism may be roughly divided into three phases. First of all, there was a brief blossoming of humanist interest in Prague under Emperor Charles IV, who founded the University in 1348 and reformed the imperial chancellery. His chancellor, Johann von Neumarkt, produced a new book of forms for documents and letters which improved both the Latin and German style of public writings. The notary Johann von Tepl's *Ackermann aus Böhmen*, a dialogue between a plowman and death who has just taken his wife, reflects the influence of Petrarch and shows a familiarity with Plato, Seneca, and Boethius, but it had medieval roots. This chancellery humanism lasted until the time of Wenceslaus in Bohemia and was transplanted to the court in Vienna by Albert of Austria, the son-in-law of Sigismund, the last Luxemburger. But the importance attached to this earlier bloom and to the influence of Cola di Rienzo in the North by historians like Conrad Burdach and Karl Brandi has now been greatly revised downward. Secondly, there was the phase of frankly avowed inspiration from and enthusiasm for the Italian Renaissance. Beginning with the reform councils of Constance and Basel and the visits in Germany of Poggio, Vergerio, and Aeneas Silvius, it was continued by the wandering prophets of humanism such as Peter Luder and Samuel Karoch, the translators and folkish narrators such as Albrecht von Eyb, Heinrich Steinhöwel, and Nicholas von Wyle, and patricians and lawyers such as Sigismund Gossembrot and Gregor Heimburg. This phase lasted to the end of the third quarter of the *quattrocento*. There followed then in the final phase the high tide of German humanism carried to its climax and denouement by three generations of humanists. In the last quarter of the century there was a greater development of emphasis more distinctly Northern in nature, a more serious concern for religious reform and a growing feeling of romantic patriotism. The second part of this final phase which we may arbitrarily equate with the reign of Maximilian, 1493–1519, witnessed the maturation of the leading generation of German humanists, men who made a determined effort to free German intellectual life from subservience to the Italians. The third and in many ways historically the most important part of this final phase was the rise of the new young generation of humanists who rallied around Luther and became the defenders and builders of the Protestant church. The renewal of religious life within Catholicism produced also within the old church a third generation of humanists who were more successful than their elders had been in uniting antique culture with the scholastic tradition.

These three generations of German humanists parallel in an interesting way the three generations of English and French humanism. In the case of England the pioneers like Grocyn and Linacre were succeeded by the great generation of Pole, Colet, and More, who in turn were pushed aside by Starkey, Morrison, and the makers of Tudor policy in the days of the Henrican reformation. In France, Gaguin's generation was followed by men of the stature of Budé and Lefèvre d'Étaples who were superseded in due course by Farel and Calvin.

Although the German humanists and reformers represent a wide diversity of types, they were all concerned in one way or another with certain common problems and subject to certain common influences. Among the problems were their relation to scholasticism, their reaction against the formalization of religious life and the loss of existential immediacy, their criticism of church practices, of rote sacramentalism, of the hierarchy, and of sacerdotalism. Among the important influences were the *Devotio Moderna* and German mysticism, particularly significant for the Nuremberg group, which conditioned their piety, their inner spirituality, and the direction of their learning, and the Italian intellectual currents, especially Platonism, which affected the humanists' church relations and their religious thought.

The theory advanced by Heinrich Hermelink that the scholastic *via antiqua*, revived in Germany during the mid-fifteenth century, served as the incubus for Northern humanism has long since been proved to be untenable.[4] Thanks largely to Gerhart Ritter's studies in late scholasticism it is now understood that the scholastic *via moderna* itself was not so hopelessly negative or desiccated as was once thought.[5] Neither anti-metaphysical skepticism nor this-worldliness caused the decline of scholasticism. Occamism never fully developed into an epistemological positivism, which could well have been its logical extreme and final consequence, especially not in the German universities, where it by and large prevailed. Humanism was not a system of thought designed to challenge scholasticism on its own metaphysical grounds. Rather, it directed attention away from the speculative concerns of scholasticism toward immediate problems arising out of life and experience. The attacks of the humanists upon scholasticism were often upon the dialectical form, the academic monopoly of teaching positions, and the neglect of vital areas of experience, not a philosophical payment in kind. What the relation of humanism to scholasticism meant in the case of individual humanists clearly merits exploration.

One of the essential influences upon nearly all the German humanists either directly or indirectly was the *Devotio Moderna* of the Brethren of the Common Life. Founded by Gerard Groote (d. 1384), the Brethren pressed for a deepening inwardness of faith. They stressed self-knowledge and practical Christian living. Their spiritualist emphasis and their almost Stoical ethical standards quite unintentionally led to a minimizing of the sacraments as a channel for grace and of the church as an apparatus for salvation. The Brethren spread from Deventer and Zwolle in the Netherlands along the Rhine through Westphalia, Hessia, and Württemberg and along the North and Baltic seas into Saxony and as far as Kulm. They established schools, hospices for poor students in university towns, and printing presses for constructive devotional literature. Among the famous men of the time directly educated or supported by them were Cusanus, Agricola, Celtis, Mutian, Johannes Murmellius, Hermann von dem Busche, Erasmus, and Luther. Their importance for German humanism was great indeed, even though that importance has been greatly exaggerated by some historians.

German mysticism, primarily of the voluntaristic rather than of a speculative type, was closely related to the *Devotio Moderna*. This mysticism placed man immediately before the ineffable God and stressed the inwardness of religious experience. It was not merely a negative reaction against the formalization of faith into dogma and personal piety into an ecclesiastical mold, but was itself a positive force and the expression of a widespread religiosity especially among the laity. It sought the fulfillment of human striving for perfection through divine grace and the example of Christ. The stress of the mystics was not upon sin and redemption but upon practical piety. The three leading German mystics of the fifteenth century, Pupper von Goch, Johann Wesel, and Wessel Gansfort, stood in the Dominican Neoplatonic tradition. Wessel Gansfort, the most significant of the three for the German humanists, had been educated by the Brethren of the Common Life. He lived for a time in Rome and visited Venice and Florence, and thus had come into contact with Italian humanism. But he did not take over the critical methods of Valla or the religious ideas of the Florentine Platonists. There is not a trace in him of Florentine universal theism, for example, such as the idea of the *communis religionis veritas* inspired in the pre-Christian philosophers by the Logos. He speaks of Christ as the incarnation of God and as Redeemer, not merely as a teacher of Platonic wisdom or as an example for man to imitate. What was Platonic in Wessel was in the medieval Neoplatonic tradition. Similarly his criticisms of ecclesiastical abuses were expressions of the general late medieval opposition to the papacy and the hierarchy familiar from the days of the reform councils and articulated in the *gravamina* or grievances of the diets. He was a late medieval reforming type quite different from more distinctively "Renaissance personalities." Yet his friendship with such humanists as Agricola and Reuchlin demonstrates all the more clearly the community of interests and the spiritual bonds uniting the German mystics and the more pious humanists.[6] The legacy of German mysticism to the reformers had even more fateful consequences.

One giant figure among the German intellectuals of the fifteenth century towered high above the others, Cardinal Nicholas Cusanus (d. 1464), a man variously described as the last of the scholastics, the first of the modern philosophers, a mystic, and a humanist. Cusanus was the kind of universal man who might very well appeal to the humanists. He, too, was educated by the Brethren of the Common Life. He was the discoverer of several classic manuscripts, a jurist and theologian, a speculative thinker and an observer of nature. As a critical historian he exposed the fraudulent nature of the Donation of Constantine. As a churchman he belonged at first to the conciliar reform party, then turned to the papal side and worked for the unity of the Eastern and Western churches. He was conciliatory and pacific also toward Mohammedanism and other non-Christian religions. Error seemed to him to be merely insufficient truth. The scholastics mistrusted him and the humanists seem not to have fully understood him. Nevertheless, Cusanus was important for the German humanists both as a cultural symbol and for certain emphases in his thought which were particularly meaningful to them.

Without summarizing Cusanus' whole system, for as system it meant little to most of the humanists, it might be useful to point out aspects of his thought which were apt to intrigue the humanists. His thought was very dependent upon Proclus, Dionysius the Areopagite, and the mystics, especially Meister Eckhardt. It received from them its Neoplatonic character and the method of the *theologia negativa*, arriving at what God is through an ascending series of demonstrations of what God is not. The basic problem for Cusanus was the search for unity, seeking to find the infinite which individualizes and reveals itself in the finite. In his *De quaerendo Deum* Cusanus asserted that "man has actually come into this world in order to seek God." Because they are necessitated only by the finiteness of all creaturely things, all differences and opposites coincide in the infinity of God. God is the coincidence of opposites, *coincidentia oppositorum*, which in the world unfold themselves as the revelation of the invisible. The heart of Cusanus' *docta ignorantia*, learned ignorance, is the insight that the very deepest reason with its rational principles is unable to grasp this identity. God is the *complicatio* or nexus of all things, which in turn are the *explicatio* or unfolding of God and participate in Him even in their unique condition of being something "other." Thus for Cusanus the world becomes *deus visibilis* or *deus creatus*, expressions which drew upon him charges of pantheism. Cusanus was concerned with the universe in its living totality. The created world had for him a dignity and value not known to medieval ascetics. Mathematics and geometric abstractions, such as the straight line coinciding with the infinitely enlarged angle or straightened curve or the coinciding of the center and periphery of a circle, provided him with illustrations of his metaphysical theories. The Spirit alone made the laws of the universe and alone can reveal them. Learning results primarily from receptivity to the Spirit's truth. Cusanus introduced the idea of relativity by denying the centrality of the earth in the universe, taught the rotation of the world on its axis, drew the first map of central Europe, and in other ways indicated an interest in the cosmos which made him important for Copernicus and Giordano Bruno in the following century.

In the Platonic tradition, moreover, his philosophy tended to glorify man. Man at the midpoint in the universe is at one and the same time *humanatus deus* and *humanus mundus*, containing within himself the entire macrocosm. His task is to unfold the power of his intellectual nature, the most valuable thing there is next to God himself. In learning to know and in mastering the world man participates in the creative work of God himself and thereby wins for himself his true status as a son of God. Christ, as the perfect Son of God, is the mediator between God and men and the model for mankind. In his sermons, *Excitationum libri decem*, Cusanus speaks as orthodox priest and at the same time as mystic, seeking as had Eckhardt in his sermons to make his thought and beliefs religiously available to his hearers. The humanists did not hear all that he had to say. After all Cusanus in his *Idiota* had himself mocked dependence upon authorities. But some of the humanists were influenced by his conception of God, his interest in cosmology, natural philosophy, and mathematics, and by his anthropology.

A preliminary comment is also in order on the nature of the Italian influence, if for no other reason than to make the author's understanding of this difficult subject explicit and to reveal his prejudices, for there are sure to be some. The general tendency of recent scholarship has been to emphasize more strongly the religious element in the Italian Renaissance.[7] Most scholarly opinion has moved far from Jacob Burckhardt's own reference to "religious indifference," although not so far as to agree with Giuseppe Toffanin's ordination of a "great lay-priesthood of humanists." Even Lorenzo Valla's *De Voluptate* is interpreted more in the light of Christian than of Epicurean ethic. This reinterpretation is so substantially documented that there can hardly be a return to the point of view which prevailed when the "reception" theory of Northern humanism still predominated. In examining the nature of the Italian influence, therefore, the nature of that influence and not merely its reality must be borne in mind. In particular, the Florentine school of Marsilio Ficino is no longer looked upon as "Platonizing, half

Paganizing," as was once the case.[8] Today Ficino's effort to develop a constructive theology, synthetic in character, attempting to conciliate divergent philosophies in a "great peace," is at last understood in something near its true terms. The conciliatory formula in his commentary on the *Timaeus* can now be correctly appreciated in the light of Ficino's high regard for Thomas: "The peripatetics have positive reasons, the Platonists superior reasons." [9] The new evaluation of the Florentine's *religio docta* or *philosophia pia* has implications also for northern humanism which have not as yet been fully assessed. [10]

Egidio da Viterbo, who was named a cardinal in the fateful year 1517, believed that the triumph of the Platonic theology marked the return to a golden age. In his *Commentary on the Sentences* he complained: "Oh, if only Plato rather than Aristotle had come into the hands of our theologians!" He considered Plato a Christian before Christ who had discovered the secret of the Trinity through natural theology. This faith in the validity and power of the *philosophia pia* was characteristic of the verve of the Italian Platonists. The influence of the Platonic Academy in Germany was in part a direct result of conscious zeal for the propagation of the faith, as well as of their earnest, subjective, contagious enthusiasm. The most popular Italian humanists among their German counterparts, in fact, were Valla, Ficino, Pico, and Baptista Mantuanus, the pious poet who was General of the Carmelite Order. One reason for the sympathetic hearing accorded Ficino was his high regard for the ultramontanes, in contrast to the pose of superiority adopted by Poggio, Antonio Campano, or Aeneas Silvius, who infuriated some of the older generation, such as Gregor Heimburg, the half-literary jurist who was a relative of Celtis. The new appreciation of the tremendous influence of the German Cardinal Nicholas Cusanus on Italian humanism as well as on his German compatriots provides one more link between German and Italian Platonism.[11] Historians have finally caught up with Leibniz, who once remarked that Valla and Cusanus had the two best minds of the "Middle Ages."

Ficino maintained many personal contacts with German men of letters. In Florence he played host to a good many of the German savants on their *Italienische Reise*, a tradition of medieval standing. In March 1482, for example, he welcomed the learned retinue of Duke Eberhard of Württemberg, including Johannes Vergenhans (Nauclerus), Peter Jakobi von Arlun, Gabriel Biel, and Johannes Reuchlin. Ficino wrote to Vergenhans and Reuchlin,[12] and carried on an extensive correspondence with Martin Prenninger (Uranius), a noted canon lawyer of Tübingen, who founded a veritable cult to Ficino and whom Ficino considered his alter ego. Though in 1492 Ficino informed Prenninger, who had asked him for a list of his students, that properly speaking he had no students, only Socratic *confabulatores* and younger auditors, the Germans recommended to him many young men aspiring to Greek learning. In Basel, Paulus Niavus, the "German Filelfo," lectured on Ficino's writings. Konrad Pellican, the pioneer Hebraist, was inspired by both Ficino and Pico's writings. Amerbach and Froben published various works of Ficino. In Augsburg, Georg Herivart always cherished the memory of his visit with Ficino in Florence, the "happiest day of his life," as he put it. The list of Germans who knew Ficino and Pico, read their works, or were influenced at least indirectly by them might be extended to great length to include such lesser humanists as Nicolaus Gerbellius or Nicolaus Ellenbogen, the Benedictine prior who assembled an anthology of passages from Plato, Paul Middelburg, a mathematician and astronomer, Dr. Mencken, a professor of canon law at Cologne, and more illustrious figures such as Celtis, Mutian, Pirckheimer, Dürer, Beatus Rhenanus, Trithemius, Agrippa of Nettesheim, and reformers like Zwingli as well.

Ficino, an ordained priest, considered himself a "fisher of men" like Peter, using the Platonic philosophy in order to catch the intellectuals. This apologetic goal determined to a large degree the structure of his theosophy. He was interested in exploiting the Platonic and Neoplatonic philosophies in the interest of a constructive theology. In one passage he has Plato say to Plotinus, "This is my beloved son in whom I am well pleased." But Ficino read Plotinus, whose *Enneads* and other works he knew well, as translator and editor, to a degree through the eyes of Dionysius the Areopagite, as had the long medieval tradition before him. The result was not a lifeless repristination of the thought of Pletho, Dionysius, Plotinus, or Plato, but Ficino's own system tuned to the needs of his time. Certain features of his thought are particularly characteristic and worth identifying, for they reappear in the religious thought of some of the leading German humanists.

The *religio docta* presupposed an epistemology of poesy and faith. Divine poetry provides a veil for the true religion. Formally, Ficino's theory of knowledge was premised on Plato's doctrine of innate ideas. In the religious area Ficino tended to the rhapsodic and mystical. True poesy is theology encompassing more than can be included in a precise intellectual formula. "I certainly prefer to believe by divine inspiration," wrote Ficino, "than to know in human fashion." [13] It is interesting to discover that the term *sola fide* was a favorite expression of Ficino's, though with it he meant essentially merely a tool for the apprehension of trans-empirical reality, and not Luther's *fiducia*, the faith that moves mountains. True religion is identified closely with wisdom and is not coterminous with Judaeo-Christian revelation. Truth is revealed in many forms and wisdom has been transmitted through a long tradition from the ancient philosophers. All the elements of this *prisca gentilium theologia* are to be found in Plato and the Platonic tradition. The border between revealed truth and inspired wisdom was quite indistinct in the *philosophia pia*. It might even appear from the arguments that the Christian faith found authority in its wisdom rather than the reverse. There is, it seems, a tendency discernible toward a syncretistic universalism.[14]

Basic to the cosmology and anthropology of the Florentine Platonists was their conception of the hierarchy of being. The fundamental concept is that of God as the ultimate unity of all things. Plotinus, building on Philo, described the "One" as the absolute and uncontradicted original essence, prior to any specific beings which imply pluralities. The relation of the "One" embracing in itself numberless numbers to the lesser creatures is to be understood in terms of the great chain of being. There is a stepladder of bodies, qualities, souls, and heavenly intelligences to the eternal "One" which marks the way of ascent to God. Man's position in the universe is a guarantee of his dignity and moral worth. Yes, God's immanence in man should lead man to trust his own divinity. The goal of life is to enjoy God (*Deo frui*) and to make this possible for men, Christ became the intermediary (the τὸ μεταξύ) between God and man. Christ is the archetype of the perfect man serving as the example. At the same time he demonstrates God's love for man, freeing the soul for the ascent to God. Here church and sacrament, priests and saints, above all Mary, play their part in the highly spiritualized understanding of dogma and ecclesiology. Some day man will enjoy God's presence without mediation.

Certain prominent threads run through the entire texture of Florentine Platonism. The light metaphysic is exploited for literal and symbolic representation. Involved in this problem besides questions of general ontology is the notion of astral influence and Saturnine melancholy. The theory of love directing man's preferences in terms of good and evil, beautiful or displeasing, for the problem of aesthetics runs parallel to that of ethics in his thought, is intimately related to his epistemology. It is in harmony with an innate idea in man and it corresponds in quality to that unity which binds the world together, turning chaos into cosmos, and which determines man's judgment. The Platonic assumption of a substantive soul involving the issue posed by the Averroists and Alexandrists of the nature of immortality is a major concern of the Florentines. These are basic themes of Ficino and his *conphilosophi* which should reappear in the assumptions of the German humanists who came under their influence.

It is common knowledge that Neoplatonism had been a major ingredient of the medieval intellectual tradition. It was important in the thought of the Dominican mystics as well as being frozen in formalized scholastic structures. The temptation for the "revisionists," therefore, is to write off the evidence of Neoplatonic influence on the thought also of the German humanists as merely a carry-over of medieval Neoplatonism. On the surface this seems plausible enough and a measure of continuity can in the course of things be assumed, particularly among those humanists who came from the Rhenish areas where mysticism was common or who had been trained in the *via antiqua*. To isolate the distinctive influence of the Florentine *Theologia Platonica* requires a close examination of the particulars, therefore, since merely asserting arguments a priori must in the nature of the case be unrewarding.

Pico's popularity in the North was perhaps due to the appeal of that theme in his writings to which he intended to give full expression in the *De concordia Platonis et Aristotelis*, a hope never realized. Both Nicholas Cusanus and Heynlin de Stein, for example, wished to resolve the contradictions between Plato and Aristotle. Later Melanchthon wrote, " Let us love both Plato and Aristotle." Pico's humanist-scholastic synthesis was sure to find a sympathetic response wherever the *viae*, especially realism, still showed some vitality. His famous letter to Ermolao Barbaro, June 5, 1485, defending scholastic philosophy, would have found many sympathetic recipients in the North. His theses on the Cabala and the utility of Hebrew letters influenced Pellican and Reuchlin, as well as the whole development of Christian Hebraism in the sixteenth century. Pico is now seen to have been a very religious young man, who once confessed, " I believe that the world crucified Jesus for my sake." It was Savonarola who dressed him in the robe and hood of a Dominican friar shortly before his death. Though Giovanni Pico died prematurely before the full development of his thought, his nephew Francesco Giovanni Pico became an intimate friend of many leading German humanists during his years of exile, so that the influence of Pico's learning carried on also in the North. Nevertheless, no German humanist so seriously cultivated the theme of the natural and essential goodness, wisdom, and dignity of man as did Pico in his *Oration* or various theses.

If Italian humanism went through its various phases of literary and civic humanism leading up to the Platonic revival in the second half of the *quattrocento*, German humanism reflected this same sequence. Significantly, many outstanding members of the older generation of humanists, nearer in point of time and intellectual background to the main line medieval tradition, and to earlier Italian literary humanism, are practically devoid of Platonic or Neoplatonic philosophy. Even a knowledge of and a certain enthusiasm for Platonism could, of course, leave a German humanist's thought not greatly altered. But other leading humanists illustrate the positive and varied effect of Florentine Platonism on religious thought in the North. Of the various influences both North and South operative on the humanists of the high generation, Neoplatonism is apt to be the most elusive and evanescent and it is for this reason, and not in order to prejudge the issue, that its basic elements have been spelled out here.

Because much of the scholarship in the field of Renaissance history has been plagued with abstractions and the use of disembodied concepts, it seems the better part of wisdom to follow the most concrete methodology possible, the study of the men and their ideas, for particularly religious ideas cannot be understood apart from the men and circumstances from which they emerge. This case-study method, used successfully by Friedrich Meinecke, Crane Brinton, and other intellectual historians, is not to be restricted to the study of authentic types in Max Weber's sense of the term, nor will the construction of models be the social scientific end sought for. Rather, the men selected for direct and detailed examination were not merely representative of various intellectual and religious types. They were themselves in their own right the most important of the German humanists because of their personal achievements, their contributions to the movement, the extent of their personal influence, and their reputations among their contemporaries and in the eyes of historians. Conceivably another historian might have substituted others in place of some of those chosen, but it would be possible to give him a very good argument in any case. In keeping with the effort for concreteness, these humanist reformers will be given an opportunity to speak for themselves once again as often as it is suitable and possible to do so.

In Germany, Rudolf Agricola, the so-called father of German humanism, is clearly the important representative of the older generation. Schoolteacher humanists like Johannes Murmellius or Rudolf von Langen, scholastic humanists like Conrad Summenhart or Paul Scriptoris, and conservative types like Sebastian Brant or Heinrich Bebel do not compare with him in importance for humanism. Of the older generation Jacob Wimpfeling, who lived on indecently long, is plainly the best example of the priestly, conservative type of reformer. He is important for his role of leadership among the Alsatian reformers, as a moral purist, and as a strong patriot. His thought world was relatively simple and monolithic. His influence extended not only to his fellow humanists, but reached the young Luther himself.

Two of the humanists included in this study were students of Agricola, at least informally, Reuchlin and Celtis, and they moved from their point of contact with him in two different directions. Johannes Reuchlin, a jurist of solid character and serious mentality, even though serving as a legal advisor and secretary to a prince, worked hard as a pioneer in Hebrew studies and built up a constructive philosophy based on Neoplatonism and the Jewish Cabala. He became the central figure in the famous controversy which is sometimes described as the preliminary to the Reformation struggle. Conrad Celtis, on the other hand, moved on to become a lyric poet and wandering professor of poetry and rhetoric. He was made the first German poet-laureate and earned from posterity the title of "Arch-humanist." He and Agricola were the only two humanists represented in this volume who did not live into the Reformation period. Ulrich von Hutten, however, was very much a part of the Reformation struggle. But this young knight had fought many a romantic campaign even before Luther appeared on the scene. His critical assaults on the established church, the glimmers of enlightened thought, and his position in the Reformation make an examination of his life particularly rewarding.

A man with an entirely different personality was the pensive, reflective, though at times frivolous, intellectual canon at Gotha, Conrad Mutianus Rufus. Mutian was given to radical speculation, but was so torn by the conflict of ideals that he was unable to integrate his vast learning and produce a positive system of religious thought. As head of the Erfurt circle of humanists, however, Mutian had a tremendous influence upon the younger and more aggressive humanists, among them Crotus Rubeanus and Ulrich von Hutten, the authors of the *Letters of Obscure Men*, which proved to be such a powerful weapon against the scholastics. A member of the upper middle class of merchants which dominated the city councils and managed urban culture and reform before and after the start of the Reformation was Willibald Pirckheimer, patrician humanist. Superbly educated, from a family with a long tradition of Italian study, Pirckheimer was himself a first-rate Greek and Latin scholar. He is particularly interesting for his ambivalent position toward the Reformation. Condemned by the first papal bull together with Luther and Hutten, he cleared his name and maintained external conformity, but his orthodoxy remained compromised by his retention of many Lutheran ideas, ideas which he held much longer than is usually believed. His life provides an interesting look inside one of the leading imperial cities, Nuremberg, during some of its most brilliant days. Albrecht Dürer was Pirckheimer's closest friend.

Erasmus, the prince of the humanists, presided regally over the German humanists, but he himself carried the ecclesiastical and religious humanist reform program to its fullest development. The question naturally arises as to whether the religious thought of the German humanists was Erasmian in a derivative or an analogous sense. To do Erasmus justice requires digesting mountains of scholarly material on him and epitomizing briefly the results of thousands of monograph pages, in addition to analyzing his own tremendous works. His position in humanism and toward the Reformation cut across nearly all the problems in which the lesser humanists were involved. Luther was not fond of Erasmus personally. "He is as slippery as an eel," he once commented, "only Christ can catch him." But even after their famous exchange, Luther had such a high regard for the mind of Erasmus that he continued to read his works. His *philosophia Christi* is an excellent summary of some of the major ingredients of the humanists' religious thought and ecclesiastical reform programs.

The question of Luther and humanism is a microcosm of the larger question of the relation of the Reformation to the Renaissance which has agitated thinkers from Nietzsche and Troeltsch down to the present time. Luther becomes, then, the essential terminal point for this study of representative figures of the high generation of German humanism. His own association with the humanists and with their cause and conversely their identification with his involves the larger problem of the validity of Christian humanism in the light of the new evangelical insight.

It is now time to meet the leading German humanists in person. The biographical information included for each of them is in inverse proportion to the degree in which they are generally known. An effort will be made to point up the inner development of each man as well as this can be done in brief scope. The innermost thoughts of their minds, the delicate inarticulate longings, their fleeting inspirations and passing reflections, their true stance *coram Deo* must remain their own secret, for historical research has developed no method of getting at them. But it will be possible to judge them, as we judge other men, by what they said, wrote, and did, and by the possibilities and viable alternatives which we know from our knowledge of their milieu to have been open to them.

AGRICOLA
Father of Humanism

B Y an interesting literary convention, the intellectual paternity of German humanism has come to be ascribed to Rudolf Agricola, a chaste bachelor who would have been most amazed to behold his numerous and disparate cultural progeny. Of course, in history a movement as broad and complex as Renaissance humanism rarely, if ever, is absolutely dependent on one man even in a single stage of development and diffusion. But in this case there is a special justification for this pleasant aphorism, since the humanists themselves believed in Agricola's unique position as a kind of cultural hero, a symbol of their own hopes and aspirations. "It was Rudolf Agricola," wrote Erasmus, "who first brought with him from Italy some gleam of a better literature." [1] He meant for Germany what Budé was to France. Indeed, ventured the cautious prince of the humanists, "Agricola could have been the first in Italy, had he not preferred Germany." [2] Melanchthon agreed that he was the first who undertook "to improve the style of speech in Germany" and the other humanists joined in the chorus of acclaim.[3] Even the proud Italians, men like Ermolao Barbaro, Pietro Bembo, and Guicciardini paid him special tribute. He was at the time of his death the foremost humanist north of the Alps, a man whose thought world merits exploration.

Agricola's power lay in his personality, not in his pen, for he wrote little and aside from a poem or two he published nothing during his lifetime. He belonged to the generation which exhausted its energies in acquisition and transmission rather than in the creation of new knowledge. But he had a first-rate temperament and that was the key to his influence in the limited company of humanists which emphasized individual versatility and capacity for friendship. He was an artist at living and a genial dilettante who could conduct himself with ease in the Italian court society of the day. An able, though not outstanding, athlete, artist, musician, conversationalist and linguist, he was the North's modest candidate for *uomo universale e singolare*.

Agricola belonged to the tradition of literary humanism from Petrarch, through Salutati, Bruni, and Aeneas Silvius, a tradition which was given a critical scholarly direction by Valla. It is uncanny, in fact, how many sympathies and antipathies Agricola shared with Petrarch, patriarch of Italian humanism. Both loved their fatherlands, but loved as well to travel. Both were forced to study law, but turned to the *politiores litterae*. Desire for personal freedom and independence kept Petrarch from the chancellery of Avignon and prevented Agricola from serving the Burgundian court or a far worse fate, teaching school.[4] Self-conscious elitism and disdain for the masses coupled with unabashed flattery of the patron prince were superficial conceits which Agricola acquired from Petrarch and the Italian humanists.[5] Petrarch sought solitude for meditation and self-realization. Agricola was anxious to retain his quiet for studies.[6] To that end both remained single for, as Agricola explained to Reuchlin, his kind of life prevented marriage.[7] Both in their last years determined to study Sacred Scriptures with all diligence. There were differences, for Agricola was less self-centered and more capable of true friendship, and never indulged in invectives. On the other hand, in terms of literary production he remained the poor man's Petrarch.

Perhaps it was an intuitive association, a subconscious sense of affinity to a like mind, which drew Agricola to Petrarch. In Italy, at any rate, he composed a life of Petrarch to honor the "father and restorer of good arts." [8] He based his biography factually upon a *Life of Petrarch*, published in Italian in a second edition of the *Rime Sparse* (Rome, 1471), which in turn was a condensation of the *Vita* written in Italian in the middle of the *quattrocento* by either Piero Candido Decembrio or Francesco Filelfo. Agricola's treatise, more than twice the length of his Italian model, showed a deeper appreciation of Petrarch's spirit, lauded precisely those characteristics which they had in common, and displayed a respectable mastery of the language. He took the *Epistola ad Posteros* at face value and painted a pretty picture of his soulmate. "We are indebted to Petrarch," he intoned, "for the intellectual culture of our century. All ages owed him a debt of gratitude — antiquity for having rescued its treasure from oblivion, and modern times for having with his own strength founded and revived culture, which he has left as a precious legacy to future ages."

Such personal verve and humanist enthusiasm were truly a septentrional phenomenon. In fact, for over a century after Petrarch's death in 1374, not a single biography of Petrarch came from the pen of a non-Italian author. Compared with his contemporaries, flighty poets like Peter Luder, half-humanist scholastics like Conrad Summenhart, or half-literary jurists like Gregor Heimburg, Agricola possessed both substance and energy which were truly remarkable.[9] His spirit was unequaled in Germany and revealed in miniature those northern and southern influences which were shaping the minds of a new generation.

Agricola was born under cold northern skies on February 17, 1444, in Baflo, near Groningen in Frisia.[10] His father was a parish pastor, not an ordained priest, at Groningen for many years. He was elected abbot of the monastery at nearby Zelwaer, and ruled this Benedictine house for thirty-six years. Agricola's first education was in Groningen at the St. Martin's school under the influence of the Brethren of the Common Life.[11] As a bright boy of twelve, perhaps intended for the priesthood, he set out for "many-towered Erfurt" where he is said to have earned his bachelor's degree within three years.[12] He turned next to the University of Louvain, where in addition to scholastic philosophy he learned French, studied mathematics, practiced organ, and, most significant of all, developed an interest in classical literature and came to realize the importance of Greek letters. He was awarded the Master's degree there, perhaps in 1465.[13] In May 1462, he had matriculated in the arts college of Cologne and may have returned to Cologne after Louvain for the study of theology for which he maintained an interest his whole life, although he reacted negatively to the inept logical and metaphysical dogmas there propounded.[14] Then, to the discomfiture of his biographers, Agricola drops out of sight, to reappear in Italy in 1469. It is possible that in the intervening years he studied in Paris under the realist Heynlin de Stein, but there is no real evidence for assuming that he did.

The Renaissance was in full flower when Agricola came to Italy. He was quite overwhelmed by it all and stayed ten years, longer than any other leading German humanist. These were decisive years for his development from his mid-twenties to mid-thirties, interrupted only twice, in 1470–71 and 1474, for visits to his homeland. Italy offered him the very milieu which he desired — intellectual stimulation without heavy duties, learning combined with pleasure, art, and companionship. To a priest of St. Martin's in Groningen who came to see him in Pavia his first winter there he exclaimed: "Does it not seem glorious to you to see Italy, once the ruler of the nations, the home of such excellent, such famous and earnest men?" [15] At the University of Pavia which enjoyed the largesse of the Sforzas, Agricola was ostensibly studying law. But he had early developed an avid interest in those masters of eloquence Cicero and Quintilian and in time gained a reputation himself as an orator, regularly delivering the inaugural lectures for new rectors of the University, a fact especially remarkable as Melanchthon observed, for even Erasmus refused to speak publicly in Italy out of fear of Italian derision.[16] It was in Pavia in 1473 or perhaps 1474 that he wrote his *Vita Petrarchae*.

As his interest in the humanities mounted he moved on to Ferrara, "the very home of all the Muses," as he wrote in 1475, the year of his arrival. There he supported himself as the organist in the ducal chapel of the house of d'Este and drank deeply from the fountain of antiquity. Theodore Gaza's memory still lived on. Battista Guarino, son of the famous educator Guarino da Verona, continued the tradition of his father, combining interest in Greek and prose style with a passion for morality. Ludovico Carbone was Agricola's actual mentor in Greek and Titus Strozzi in poesy, neither men of much stature. Perhaps a better faculty might have stimulated Agricola to greater things. He delivered one noteworthy oration *In laudem philosophiae et reliquarum artium oratio*, but for the most part his energies went into mere translation of minor selections from Greek to Latin. He began a major work, *De inventione dialectica*, which he did not complete until his return to Germany.

A longing for home drew him northward again in 1479, but he found, like Dürer, that he "froze after the sun." From Groningen he lamented to Alexander Hegius that he was losing his capacity for thought and for ornamented style. His spirit would not respond.[17] Nevertheless, he remained for three years, frequently visiting the monastery of Adwerd whose abbot, Heinrich von Rees, there assembled the lowland friends of Christian humanism. Often he talked with deeply religious Johann Wessel until late into the night. He represented Groningen at the court of Maximilian in Brussels for half a year in 1482. An Italian education for a northerner in the *quattrocento* meant as much as a European degree in America in the nineteenth century. He was sought after by his home town, by Antwerp for the reform of the Latin School, and by the Burgundian court. Agricola shied away from the discipline and routine of regular employment. He wrote to his friend J. Barbirianus, "To take over a school is a bitter, difficult, joyless affair, viewed merely from the outside, a very hard and sad thing: for I must think of blows, tears and howling, a perpetual prison life . . . I should take over a school? Where would I find the time for progress in learning? Where would be the quiet and the cheerful frame of mind for my own research and thought?"[18] Finally Elector Philipp of the Palatinate won his services, largely by promising him absolute freedom.

At Heidelberg, he spent the last three years of his life studying, participating in disputations, and lecturing unofficially when it pleased him on logic, physics, astronomy, Aristotle's *De Animalibus*, a novelty, Pliny, but especially on eloquence, Latin, and Greek literature.[19] But even this freedom seemed too great a burden.[20] He was about to find relief. The Elector sent a delegation to Rome headed by Bishop Johannes von Dalberg to congratulate Innocent VIII upon his election to the papacy. Agricola accompanied them and wrote the oration which Dalberg delivered in July 1485, before the pope and the College of Cardinals. On the return trip Agricola became ill with an acute fever and died at Heidelberg on October 27 in the Bishop's arms. He commended his soul to God and his body was laid to rest with the Franciscans.

A master theme gave unity to this restless and seemingly unintegrated life: the desire for a renewal of learning in Germany and thereby of religious thought and life. " I have the brightest hope," he exclaimed, "that we shall one day wrest from haughty Italy the reputation for classical expression which it has nearly monopolized, so to speak, and lay claim to it ourselves, and free ourselves from the reproach of ignorance and being called unlearned and inarticulate barbarians; and that our Germany will be so cultured and literate that Latium itself will not know Latin any better." [21] By Latin, Agricola meant not just the language itself, but an idealistic reconstruction of selected cultural values from the resources of antiquity which could be exploited in remedying educational deficiencies and filling the spiritual reservoirs which had become so dry. Like Johann Wessel, Agricola was a severe critic of late scholasticism as a blight on refined culture and genuine religious thought.

Petrarch had been opposed to scholasticism to a large extent because its arid abstractions covered over the real heart of Christianity. In the case of Averroism its ratiocinations had even led to very heretical positions. For Petrarch the struggle for closeness to life and a personal reformation of culture led to a new inwardness of religious feeling. This malaise against scholasticism became a constant ingredient of literary humanism, though not always with the acerbity of a Valla. It reappeared in Agricola who privately attacked the "rude, barbarous, stinking filth of the schools in our native land." [22] The nature of his criticism conformed perfectly to the familiar pattern. "As to theology," he queried, "what is it that it is truly necessary to say? These days, if you were to take away from it metaphysics, physics, and dialectic, you would render it bare and destitute and unable to preserve its own name. Therefore, since the people must be taught and exhorted to religion, justice, and continence, some inextricable disputation is drawn out from these arts which prolongs the time and strikes the ears of the hearers with a foolish din. They teach, as the boys are accustomed, to propose in an enigma, what they then indeed may not know themselves, either those who teach or those who have learned. I have often heard these complaints from most weighty and most learned men." [23] It was not by mere chance that in citing the authors of great theological classics, he failed to mention a single scholastic.[24] Melanchthon related that Agricola struck at the false pride of the scholastics, but he appreciated the utility of the *summas*, while comparing critically the similarities and differences of recent writers with those of the ancient church.[25] This was a shrewd insight, for Agricola like the preponderant number of Renaissance humanists did not dissent from the Christian content of scholastic philosophy, but reacted against the method, the style and the by-products of their combination. Agricola was himself a moderate realist, in line with the tacit assumptions of the Brethren of the Common Life and his Thomist academic conditioning. A few notes on the problem of universals were incorporated by his editor into the first book of his major work. But there can be no thought of his humanism growing out of an association with the *via antiqua*. At the end of his discussion of universals, in fact, Agricola emphasized in words reminiscent of a passage in Cusanus' *Idiota*, that he was not interested in the defense of authorities and school traditions, but in establishing an independent truth.[26] Though there was no major clash of principles between the humanists and scholastics, the rumbling of Agricola against the schoolmen grew to a deafening roar as younger men took up the refrain.

The reform which Agricola envisioned and for which he worked in a haphazard fashion was to take place on two levels, intellectual and religious, not mutually exclusive. Characteristically, in view of his habit of nonpublication, his ideas on intellectual or educational reform are best known from a letter advising his Antwerp friend, Jacob Barbirianus, as to what kind of studies he should choose and the method by which he could achieve the best results from the subjects chosen. This letter, later often published under the title *De Formando Studio*, 1484 belonged to a genre of pedagogical writing with a long and respectable ancestry in antiquity and in Italian humanism, much as Silvius' *Adhortatio ad studia*.[27] But it, in turn, as the first in Germany, could claim a long line of descendants and served itself as a sketchy summary of humanist pedagogical theories. In this work Agricola employs the formula *philosophia Christi* for his doctrine which sought to mediate between antique wisdom and Christian faith.

Agricola begins with an attack on "the loquacious pursuits clattering with inane noises which we now commonly call the arts and spend the day in perplexing and obscure disputations or even (to put it more truly) in enigmas which for so many centuries have found no Oedipus who could solve them for which none will ever be found". The noblest study is true philosophy which embraces two major parts. The first is moral philosophy providing wisdom for a right and well-ordered way of life.[28] This wisdom is not to be gained only from professional philosophers as Aristotle, Cicero, and Seneca, but also from the historians, poets, and rhetoricians who distinguish good and evil and, what is more effective, present examples of each as in a mirror. Above all others, the Holy Scriptures are the most dependable guide in life. The second division of philosophy is a knowledge of the nature of things. If the old search for the essence of things is not really necessary, it can add luster to the spirit. It is most important, however, to make things themselves one's possession. This natural philosophy embraces the lay of the lands, seas, mountains, and rivers, the peculiarities of the peoples, their customs, borders, their nature, and their empires, the powers of trees and herbs, which Theophrastus and Aristotle explored. It is necessary to disregard all that one has learned and turn to the classic authors, especially those whose knowledge of rhetoric enabled them to put the best light on worthwhile things. It is necessary for the student to master rhetoric in turn, an essential condition of the utility of truth. The skill of the rhetorician, if combined with training in logic and knowledge in a given field, enables one to handle almost any problem presented, like the masters of style, the sophists of ancient Greece, Gorgias, Prodicus, Protagoras, and Hippias.

The most striking features of Agricola's treatise are the limitations he sets to speculative knowledge, the new value ascribed to example rather than precept as depicted by historian, poet, and rhetorician, the emphasis on eloquence and form, and the recognition of Roman orators and the sophists as the exemplars of philosophy in this new key. In all this, however, Agricola is merely echoing beyond the Alps the precepts of his honored teacher, Battista Guarino, summarized in his *De ordine docendi ac studendi* (Verona, 1459).[29] Only his special stress on *cognitio rerum* is not to be found there in equal force. But Leonardo Bruni in his *De studiis et literis* had explained that true human erudition derives from the knowledge of letters (*peritia litteratum*) and the knowledge of things (*scientia rerum*). By the knowledge of letters, Bruni meant above all a knowledge of classical texts, the philosophers, poets, rhetoricians, and historians. By a knowledge of things he meant the experience of another world revealed by the divine Word and a deeper understanding of the reality surrounding man. The extent of Agricola's dependence on these basic themes of Italian humanism seems obvious.

Agricola's own contribution to dialectic took the form of an introductory manual, primarily for teachers in the arts course, *De Inventione Dialectica*, in which he sought to demonstrate the true function of logic as an element basic to rhetoric which through straight thinking and effective style produces conviction. In seventeenth-century England the work would have been called "the compleat orator" rather than an "introduction to logic." [30] The express purpose of his work, Agricola explains in terms similar to Valla's in his *Dialecticae disputationes*, is to help those to achieve the necessary rhetorical skills who govern the republic in affairs of the state, as peace and war, those who preside in courts of justice, accuse or defend, and those who teach the people righteousness, religion, and piety.[31] This was the main dialectical work of the German humanists, eliciting praise from Erasmus and his fellows.

Like Valla, Agricola tended to direct dialectic away from Aristotle to Cicero. Cicero had distinguished the technique of discovery (*ars inveniendi*) from that of judging (*ars iudicandi*). Agricola planned a comprehensive work covering both these aspects of dialectic, but completed only the *Inventio*. In three books he presents two dozen topics (τόποι, *loci*), grounds for proof, shows how these topics are to be used, and demonstrates how rhetoric helps to achieve conviction in the hearer. The work is completely eclectic, in tune with Agricola's own mediating nature. In the selection on logic, in spite of his pyrotechnics against the sophistry of the schoolmen, Agricola is very much dependent upon the traditional sources. He retains Aristotle's definition of dialectic, supplies twenty-four improved *loci* related in genre to Aristotle's, the seventeen of Cicero, and twenty-two of Themistius, as a conceptual framework for the *quaestiones* or problematical sentences, the Scotist concept of *haecceitas* in distinguishing the individual from the universal, and the like.[32] With appropriate modesty Agricola declares that he has added nothing new himself and names the authorities on whom he is dependent, Cicero, Trebatius, Quintilian, (especially in book two), Themistius, a fourth-century Peripatetic known through Boethius, and Boethius himself. All the medieval texts, too, had reflected Boethius' mixture of Cicero and Themistius in the same way.[33] The tradition-bound character of Agricola's dialectic raises the question of his reputation as a protagonist of a "purified Aristotle." [34]

Agricola was mildly critical of Aristotle, which endeared him to Peter Ramus decades later, but his criticism was neither systematic nor even always well-founded. "I think," Agricola ventured in a statement typical of his oblique criticisms of the traditional great names, "that Aristotle was a man of the highest genius, doctrine, eloquence, knowledge of things, and prudence and (as I repeatedly say) indeed the greatest man, but I think that he was nevertheless a man; that is, something could be hidden, so that he did not first find everything, so that some things remained to be found by others." [35] He scored Aristotle's dark and unclear diction, a common complaint during the Middle Ages. Moreover, he held that the self-styled Peripatetics who claimed to have read the writings of Aristotle were far from knowing the true worth of his teachings.[36] He even occasionally corrected isolated terms or propositions in Aristotle.[37] Certainly he made no such a thorough criticism of Aristotle's dialectic as Valla who sharply attacked his dialectic as well as that of Boethius and Porphyry, preferring Quintilian by far. Agricola at times misinterpreted Aristotle, now and then accepted him in preference to other authorities, but almost invariably understood him in the light of the medieval dialectical tradition. His Aristotle can be called "purified," that is, philologically and philosophically exact, only by courtesy. But this does not at all prove that Agricola was a late scholastic or bound by an entirely traditional mentality. Rather, it means that the primary significance of his major work lies elsewhere than in its dialectical presuppositions.

Broadly speaking, the three disciplines of the trivium each had its special hour on the medieval stage. During the scholastic period dialectics superseded grammar in the major role. Now rhetoric moved front and center for a lively dialogue with a revitalized grammar. Agricola was not one merely to repeat traditional ideas for there is no difference, he held, between one who merely passes on the learning of the schools and a schoolbook.[38] The novelty, for the North, of Agricola's work on dialectic was the great emphasis he placed upon the practical use of dialectic, and the importance of rhetoric in achieving for it real social utility in the Roman manner. In many respects, Agricola was really assimilating the art of dialectic to rhetoric. Especially in the third book Agricola teaches how a speech can be made to create "effect" or produce conviction. One result of this emphasis on practical application was that the distinction between the two disciplines became less and less clear. Agricola was no philosophic systematizer, nor did he want to be.

Agricola's influence was felt strongly in the dialectic discipline of the trivium, which continued to be central in the traditional arts curiculum in spite of the humanists' efforts to give preponderance to grammar and rhetoric. Erasmus, for example, in the second book of his *De ratione concionandi* stressed grammar and rhetoric, arguing that dialectic without grammar is blind. Agricola's logic took Paris by storm, where Johann Sturm made it popular while teaching there from 1529 to 1536. Agricola's book was often republished in Paris, where at least fifteen editions appeared between 1538 and 1543. It was influential also in England where in 1535, in the Royal Injunctions to Cambridge, Henry VIII directed that the students in arts should read Agricola, together with Aristotle, Trebizond, and Melanchthon instead of the "frivolous questions and obscure glosses" of Scotus and other scholastics. Agricola's influence upon theological study developed out of the carry-over of dialectical study from the arts course to the higher faculties. It was given wide currency in Protestant education also indirectly through its impact on Melanchthon's work on dialectic. His work fit the mood and satisfied the needs of the hour.

Hegel's negative assessment of the theoretical significance of the philosophical literature of the Renaissance was only typical of the predominant attitude of modern philosophers since Descartes effected his decisive break with the humanist tradition. In Agricola two lines of influence converge which were both essentially nonspeculative in nature. The practical Christian piety of the Brethren of the Common Life which helped to form his youthful outlook coincided perfectly in this respect with the Roman popular philosophy revitalized by such Italian humanists as Valla, emphasizing living skills and moral sense over metaphysics. Agricola and his literary fellows were like mental engineers standing in awe before the great pyramids of the system builders, but quite deliberately resolving that henceforth the products of the quarries should be turned to more practical uses. This decision in no way reflected loss of faith in human reason, for Agricola shared the wholesome respect for man's rational capacity and the grandeur of the human spirit which characterized the Western Christian tradition. "For enormous, immense, incredible is the power of the human mind, and for it almost nothing is difficult except what it does not will," he exclaimed with great fervor.[39] Just as in the inanimate world a meaningful ascent in the categories of purpose can be assumed, Agricola reasoned, for God as a good housefather has set his house in order, so also in realms of human knowledge there is a meaningful ascent discernible. Without a comprehensive understanding of the master blue print of the new structure in being, Agricola was building on old foundations with stones from the classic ruins. Quintilian, too, had waxed eloquent about the glories of human reason, and moved on to the practical possibilities open to it. Agricola was his apprentice.

Rhetoric provided the new key to his philosophy. There is a hint in Agricola of the attempt to make language the philosophical basis of reality in the manner of Vico. For Aristotle rhetoric represented the application of logic to the character and feelings of the audience. Superficially, taking his own definitions at face value, Agricola considered rhetoric merely as the art of ornamented speech which adorns, whereas dialectic was the manner of speaking credibly.[40] But closer analysis shows that for him, logic is no longer just logic, but both dialectic and rhetoric serve the word, oral and written. This development may be tagged the "new rhetoric," or with reference to the receiving end of the process, the "new philology."

The Italian humanists rediscovered the ancient definition of man as ζῷον λόγον ἔχον, a living being having the power of speech.

Language was, then, the indispensable medium for the *studia humanitatis*. The classical languages were not just tools for acquiring more information, but by a kind of philological existentialism the immediate revelation of the essence of man's highest culture. This antique culture was something to be experienced and not just known. The task of philology was to arrive by a study of the text at an objective understanding of the essence of man, not merely in an intellectual or rational sense, as a phase of thought, but through direct apprehension of the whole range of human capabilities. The task of the new rhetoric was to communicate this true experience of the senses of man and make it available for the guidance of others. Though of less stature than a Bruni or a Valla, Agricola stands in this line of development.[41]

Within this broader concept of philosophy Agricola like his Italian and ancient predecessors emphasized particularly the love of wisdom in the root sense of the word philosophy, the centrality of virtue, and the mastery of an encyclopedic range of knowledge. In the *De libero arbitrio* Augustine, for whom Cicero's *Hortensius* had been so decisive, wrote: "It is one thing to be rational, another to be wise." [42] There was ample precedent in Christendom for such a distinction, but the antique apostles of eloquence, Cicero and Quintilian, with the concurrence of Stoic Seneca, had given the concept of wisdom special formulation. For Quintilian the task was not merely good speaking, but the comprehensive development of those intellectual and ethical qualities which make man *sapiens et eloquens* at one and the same time. The truly classical expression of the wisdom ideal, however, was that of Cicero, who in the *De Officiis* [43] defined it as "the knowledge of divine and human things and of their causes." Agricola repeated this definition verbally and in part came to structure his thought on it. But, as we shall see, in the final analysis he laid preponderant emphasis upon the value of things divine.

Virtue has always seemed to many men a major ingredient of wisdom; for Agricola it was the heart of the matter. He wrote to his brother Johann, in a letter accompanying his translation of Isocrates' *Parenesis*, "There is nothing . . . that I could more fittingly offer you . . . than the furthering of your erudition and a better moral life . . . I will surely not be doing something unworthy, if I gather ethical precepts for you related to the proper orientation of life . . . May it then become not only an aid to your speech but truly also improve your soul." [44] He was merely reflecting the conviction of Isocrates himself who in this very selection wrote, " I think that a multitude of precepts is preferable to many riches, for these sink swiftly away, those remain in all time. For wisdom alone of all things is immortal." [45] Agricola most certainly recognized absolute religious commands, but in locating a major source of wisdom and ethical precepts in the moral manner and historical examples of antiquity, he was following the lead of Petrarch and the literary humanists in developing the standard for ethical decisions from the human experience of the ancients. At this point, too, there was an easy coincidence of the quasi-stoical ethical teachings of the Brethren of the Common Life, among whom Seneca was a favorite author, and the moral emphasis of the literary humanists.

The knowledge of things human called for encyclopedic learning about the world of nature as well as the world of men, a learning appropriated directly by experience, or better yet, through the savants of a wiser, better age. Once again, Agricola stressed that this knowledge is to be gained primarily from orators, historians, poets, and all kinds of erudite men, not merely philosophers.[46] For Cicero and Horace, the natural was normative, since nature agrees with what is good and right. Moreover, in agreement with them and indeed with the highest level of medieval tradition, Agricola assumed a correspondence between the world of nature and that of reason which led him also to stress the value of mathematics. In spite of the intense interest of Agricola and the humanists in astronomy, geography, botany, and related subjects, nothing could be more mistaken than to overvalue their contribution to modern science. In the natural sciences they looked backward to the old authorities and then only as a study subordinate to their philological-rhetorical interests. Agricola's preoccupation with history is somewhat more impressive. Melanchthon reported that Agricola worked out an epitome of ancient history, following the Bible and Herodotus for Assyrians and Persians, Thucydides and Xenophon for the Greek states, Diodorus and Polybius for the Macedonian empire. He assembled worthy reading from the Roman historians as well, and gave many examples of the utility of church history for resolving dogmatic disputes. If Agricola's work had not been lost, he might well have become the founder of humanist historiography. Like the classic histories, his writing, too, was pragmatic in purpose, intended to warn and admonish princes and statesmen. His admonitions were woven into the thread of his history.[47]

Agricola presented his views on what knowledge is of most worth with the greatest verve and succinctness in the oration *In laudem philosophiae* delivered in 1476 before Duke Ercole in Ferrara.[48] After a preliminary encomium on the loftiness of philosophy, a gift of the Godhead which raises man above his humanity, ennobles him, and puts him above fortune, Agricola proceeds to analyze the component parts embraced by the concept. First, there is logic or rational philosophy which includes grammar, dialectic, and rhetoric. Second, there is physics or natural philosophy which includes physics proper or medicine, then mathematics in four subdivisions — geometry, arithmetic, astronomy, and music — and finally, suprisingly enough, theology. Third, there is ethics or moral philosophy. Some even declare, he says, that this moral philosophy is alone worthy to be called philosophy. The oration concludes with the expected flattery of city and prince. Once the dullness of the obvious recapitulation of the old trivium and quadrivium organization is peeled away, fresh humanist ideas are found beneath the surface. Once again, philosophy appears as "the love of wisdom, that is, the love of knowledge of divine and human things tied in with the search for a well-ordered way of life." [49]

Conveniently, the areas embraced by this grand concept turn out to be Seneca's scheme of the three parts of man, rational, natural, and moral. Once again, Agricola includes within philosophy the grand sweep of natural and human knowledge to be learned from historians, poets, and orators.[50] Theology seeks the divine will and power which directs the world mass perpetually with certain laws. Finally, there is the familiar almost Stoic call to order life according to ethical norms, thus surmounting vices, evil, and pain. Delights are sweet, he warns, and so corrupt more easily. The chief merit of Socrates was that he first brought philosophy from heaven and lay its sphere of action in the cities and in human society. Agricola's praise of philosophy turns out to be basically the praise of the *studia humanitatis* as embraced by the broad sweep of the new philology-rhetoric of humanism. For eloquence, as Cicero had witnessed, was nothing else than wisdom speaking well. So Italianesque had Agricola become that only a small step would have taken him to the side of a Manetti or Pico in his admiration for the dignity of man.

Too much of Agricola's energy went into mere Greek and Latin translations and conventional commentaries. Erasmus praised his genuine, powerful, cultured, and clear style, "among the Latinists he showed the finest command of Latin and among the Graecists, the finest of Greek." [51] But the humanists habitually lauded their devotees and the departed without due reservations. Translations are no substitute for creative original work. On the surface the materials selected for translation give the impression of being a mere potpourri of minor works. Closer examination, however, reveals that they were predominatly rhetorical in nature. The sophists were represented by Isocrates, Aphthonius, and pseudo-Hermogenes, the orators with Aessinus, Demosthenes, Cicero, and Seneca, the philosophers with a pseudo-Plato and Boethius, and, in strange company, the cynical Lucian, who came to be so popular with Hutten, Erasmus, Pirckheimer, and many of the next generation. The selections were chosen to provide material support for the tenets of his philological-rhetorical philosophy, in the translating of Guarino da Verona and his son.[52] All this preoccupation with the classics was pleasant enough, but it did not satisfy the deeper longings of Agricola.

In his *Life of Petrarch* Agricola had observed that in old age he was most interested in sacred letters. Agricola had no sooner returned to the North from Italy than he announced, as a man of thirty-five, that he would devote his old age to the study of Sacred Scriptures and as an aid to that end would seek to master Hebrew.[53] Possibly it was the influence of the earnest Johann Wessel which prompted this decision.[54] But Agricola had always been highly moral and deeply religious, placing theology at the top of the pyramid of learning. Melanchthon reports how he embraced and venerated the Christian religion with his whole heart and abhorred impiety.[55] At Heidelberg he engaged in many theological discussions and was even looked to as an authority in disputed matters. The precise nature of his views on church and dogma is of critical importance for understanding the man and the nature of his influence.

Agricola was not an overtly critical or reforming type. He makes only the mildest suggestion that there were grievous ills in Christendom. There is nowhere even a hint of anti-hierarchical or anti-curial sentiment. On the contrary, he was a most obedient and devoted son of the medieval church. This fact becomes crystal clear in the address which Bishop Dalberg invited him to deliver in August or September of 1484 to the clergy assembled at Worms, *Exhortatio ad clerum Wormatiensen*.[56] In this address Agricola's main theme is praise for the worth of the priestly calling, the meaning of the priest for human life, and the special religious quality required of the priest. He stresses the great sacerdotal power implicit in the Office of the Keys and the awesome prerogative of the priesthood in presiding over the mystery of transubstantiation in the Mass. There are a few allusions to classic culture, but otherwise the address is not intended to promote humanist learning among the clergy. Rather, it is the ideal spiritual priesthood which he depicts with pious admonitions and encouragement. He stresses the Old Testament appreciation of the priesthood, and draws heavily upon the New Testament for Christ's commission to his disciples and Paul's description of the qualities of the bishop. Similarly, in the oration congratulating Innocent VIII on his election, it is not surprising to find him propounding a papal solution for all the problems confronting Christendom.[57] All men, he demands, owe faith and obedience to the Roman church and its head. It is necessary for all Christendom and especially the princes to help the See of Peter with money, counsel, power, and progress, when it advances the welfare of the church. Rome should be the capital city of the world and under the pontificate of the new pope it will at last become a place of salvation for all Christendom. Nothing has become so lax and abused that it cannot be set right by the purity, prudence and piety of Innocent. This is unadulterated ultramontanism, which shows that there was no conciliarism to be found in Agricola, nor any sign of the anti-curial sentiment of the younger humanists and reformers.

The undisturbed serenity with which Agricola accepted the received dogmatic tradition and sacramentalism of the church is further proof of how little he had appropriated for his inner religious life the meaning of the wisdom philosophy which he had acquired intellectually and to which he paid such eloquent verbal tribute. He did not even go so far as Petrarch in the direction of a new inwardness of religious feeling. There was none of the tension in him resulting from an individualizing of the traditional dogmatic world-view on the basis of a new ideal of piety and culture. This is evident from his poetry, from a highly revealing Christmas oration, as well as from his serious, but uncomplicated correspondence.

If in poetry, as Shelley said, futurity casts gigantic shadows on the present, then Agricola's rimes were scarcely poetry. His poetry, aside from occasional verse to friends and a few epigrams, was entirely hagiographic in nature. These poems, to St. Judocus, to St. Antonius, to St. Catherine, the patroness of learning, to Mother Anne, in fashion at that time, and a song of praise *To All the Saints*, were very ordinary in form and almost devoid of real content. Pagan flourishes like "Jupiter tonans" were to be found as well in the medieval *Legenda aurea* so popular in Germany in that very century. Agricola's interest in art, so far as the evidence goes, was limited to religious art, and he saw its greatness "in depicting God with the skill of man." [58]

In the Christmas oration which he delivered in 1484, he described the marvel of the incarnation with warm Christian appreciation.[59] Christ was the true Son of the Father, begotten from Eternity, who took on mortality so that we might conform to the image of immortality. Christ came with love and salvation for man born with original sin and guilt, subject to wrath and death. The theme was taken from Psalm 118:23: This is the Lord's doing; it is marvelous in our eyes. Of special interest relating to his image of the classic period is his description of the dark underside of the Roman empire in the time of Christ. For, he pondered, just as Christ was born in the darkest, longest, night of the year, so there was no age in which a darker shadow of error and the worst vices of all kinds lay upon the world than that in which the Son of God came to help man in his misfortunes. It was an age of godlessness.

Those very men who had often maintained that one cannot lie even in the smallest matters did not venture to give honor to the truth regarding the great God. At no time were passion, greed, pretension, luxury, and debauchery more monstrous than in that age. There was knavery in public and private life, crimes and bloodshed were rampant, and into this deep darkness came Christ, bearing light. In this way the father of humanism described the Augustan age.

It is obvious that while Agricola from the humanist point of view worked for intellectual and educational reform, simplification and greater practicability in theology, and purification of clergy and church life, he remained entirely within the dogma and institutions of the old church. There is no good evidence that Italian humanism arrived at any religious universalism before the coming of the Platonists. Certainly there is no sign of it in Agricola. Moreover, by not following through to its logical consequences the implications of Cicero's dualism, he escaped the hazards implicit in his ethical teaching borrowed from the Greeks. Cicero's sharp division of the world into a natural-rational and an irrational sphere had appealed to patristic Christianity. But beneath the formal agreement lay a treacherous deception, for the natural-rational side of Cicero's dualism embraced also the highest ethical activity of man, a view quite incompatible with the idea of original sin and the supernatural in Christianity. Agricola, by not thoroughly integrating his wisdom-philosophy, so dependent on Cicero and Quintilian's rhetorical tenets, with his Christian anthropology, managed to avoid, though not resolve, the problem. There are advantages to simplicity.

By the same token there is also no sign of "reformation tendencies" evident in Agricola. Only Melanchthon reported that he once heard from a well-known and honorable man, Goswin de Halen, that in his youth he had heard Agricola and his master Johann Wessel in a conversation in which they spoke many hard words against the darkness ruling in the church, the abuse of the Mass, the celibacy of the clergy, and, with reference to St. Paul's doctrine of justification by faith, against the prevailing work-righteousness of the church.[60] For lack of other evidence, this account which is so out of character for Agricola must be assigned to faulty recollection by Goswin and to wishful thinking by Melanchthon.

Agricola, then, represents the type of Northern literary humanist with deep roots in the piety of the Brethren of the Common Life who spent many years in Italy under the influence of Italian literary humanism, and the new philological-rhetorical wisdom philosophy. He was much more a humanist than such contemporaries as Johannes Murmellius or Rudolf von Langen. He shows in his own person how the basically nonspeculative practical and stoical moralistic aspect of the *Devotio Moderna* coincided with the corresponding emphasis of his pious Italian teachers. From both sources he derived somewhat greater though tentative inwardness of religiosity and a drive toward the sources in the Scriptures and fathers. But in Italy he acquired his flaming enthusiasm for classic learning which he in turn brought back to the Brethren in the person of the more conservative Hegius, the great teacher of Erasmus at Deventer. "When a man of forty I came to young Agricola," Hegius confessed, "and from him I have learned all that I know, or rather all that others think I know." He wept when he announced Agricola's death to his students.

Agricola was untouched by Florentine Platonism and shows what German humanism might have remained, if it had not been for the impact of the Villa Careggi. He was only vaguely conscious of the deep tension between antiquity and Christianity, but this easy peace between the two, resulting from a happy failure to draw logical consequences, was a phenomemon familiar also in Italian humanists like Boccaccio, Poggio, or even Aeneas Silvius. In Agricola's case Buffon's famous dictum, "le style c'est l'homme même," would be misleading indeed.

Agricola died so young, when only forty-one, and just when his studies of sacred letters were getting under way. He was the only one of this group of humanists who did not live beyond the *quattrocento*. At the time of his death, Trithemius reports, he was making a new translation of the pseudo-Dionysius, which may provide a hint as to the direction his interests were taking. The Italian humanist Jovio lamented: "The gods or stars merely showed this richly endowed man the earth and tore him away in the midst of life ending his glorious development." His influence lived on in the leading German humanists. Reuchlin delivered his funeral oration, and Celtis wrote a lugubrious epitaph. Years later Wimpfeling reflected that Agricola's true greatness consisted in the fact that all the learning and wisdom of the world served him only to purify himself of passions and to work in faith and prayer on the great building whose architect is God himself.

III

WIMPFELING

Sacerdotal Humanist

WHEN in the year 1495 the gregarious poet Conrad Celtis invited Jakob Wimpfeling, the cathedral preacher at Speyer, to join the Rhenish Sodality of humanists in Heidelberg, Wimpfeling responded with the shy demurrer that he would only be a crow among the nightingales or an owl among the falcons. He was right, for if Rudolf Agricola belonged in spirit to this circle of younger men, Wimpfeling, who lived on for almost three decades into the sixteenth century, was in temperament and intellectuality quite too dated for them. He was the most conservative of the leading humanists, yet typical of a large segment in German humanism throughout the whole period. He was a cleric through and through, a priest's priest, the good bishop's delight, and the wicked bishop's bane. A dedicated institutionalist, he was an earnest moralist, a whip and a scourge, a furious defender in rear-guard actions. He showed practically no mental development and seemed in temperament to be an old man his whole life. His uncomplicated psychology and unsophisticated single-mindedness, coupled with a touch of the cantankerous, kept him constantly embroiled in feuds and turmoils as he struggled to hold his purist ideals without compromise, as a brave soldier in the church militant.

Wimpfeling had no patience with learning for its own sake, but felt the urgent need to get to the people. He was a publicist, not a thinker, and his writings included over a hundred titles. This literary baggage was made up largely of discourses, prefaces, brochures, poems, letters, and treatises on questions of religion, education, history, and politics, mostly polemical or apologetic in nature. The pattern was conventional, with heavy support for his contentions drawn from the testimony of the authorities who were generally cited without consideration of their time or the specific context of their testimony. The minute size and value of some of his publications lent some point to the charges of his critics that he rushed into print to satisfy his ego, although the cause was always uppermost in his mind. He was a man of few themes, which he repeated with tireless energy and tiresome recurrence, and they were the same on his last pages as on his first, just as he moved often during his life, but always returned to the same cities. His program for the *restitutio Christianismi* can therefore be analyzed to greatest advantage antithetically, as he applied his basic ideas in a variety of polemical situations.

Under attack in later years from monkish opponents, Wimpfeling penned a brief *Expurgatio contra detractores*, in which he outlined the main facts of his life and pointed to that simplicity and regularity which put him above their reproaches.[1] Wimpfeling was born on June 25 in the jubilee year, 1450, the son of a saddler in Schlettstadt, "the pearl of Alsace." He attended the Latin school of Ludwig Dringenberg, who had studied at Deventer and emphasized ethical-religious training in the best traditions of the Brethren of the Common Life. Upon the death of his father he turned to an uncle, a priest in Sulz, who sent him as a fourteen-year-old boy to study at the University of Freiburg im Breisgau. There he came under the influence of Geiler von Kaisersberg, university lecturer and famous preacher, sharp critic of vanity, splendor, and show, a puritanic sumptuary-law type, who remained his close friend for almost half a century. He received his A.B. in the *via moderna* at Freiburg after two years of study. A sickly youth who developed into a constantly ailing man, his further studies at Erfurt were interrupted by illness and he continued at Heidelberg, where he received his M.A. in 1471. After two years devoted to the study of canon law, he switched to theology, a decision which he never regretted. "In the text and glosses," he explained, "I found too little about God, his angels, the souls of men and their powers, the necessary virtues, about the life, suffering and death of the Redeemer . . . for already as a youth I had noted the saying of St. Jerome, 'He easily despises all, who always thinks of his last moment.' " Wimpfeling had come into his own.

Wimpfeling stayed on to teach at Heidelberg, compiling a book on metric which served as the basis of his lectures and composing Latin poems which show his contact with the humanists of Bishop von Dalberg's circle. In the spring of 1477 he delivered an address to the clergy at Worms in which he keynoted the themes on which he was to dwell thereafter, the need to maintain the high ethos of the priesthood, to handle the divine gifts with pure hands, and to achieve reform through the golden means of pedagogy.[2] Wimpfeling rapidly climbed the academic ladder as vice-chancellor of the arts faculty, dean, and then rector of the University. As rector, on Pentecost in 1482 he delivered an oration in the church of the Holy Ghost in which he criticized the students for not keeping the customs of the good old days and flayed monastic abuses, holding up the ideal of St. Bernard.[3] Called by the Bishop of Speyer, he became the cathedral preacher for fourteen years. From 1498 to 1501 he was back in Heidelberg, lecturing on the letters of St. Jerome and the poems of Prudentius. Wimpfeling's next move was to Strassburg to be near his friend Geiler and the poet Sebastian Brant, who had returned in 1501 to his native city to serve as syndic and later as town clerk. In Strassburg Wimpfeling supported himself by the income from a modest "living" and by tutoring the sons of wealthy patricians, traveling on occasion to Basel or Freiburg. He complained constantly about his ill fortune, poverty, and sickness, as though he believed in the healing power of lamentation. He retired at last in the summer of 1515 to his home town where he lived out his days until 1528, long past his prime and usefulness.[4]

In the *Expurgatio* Wimpfeling pointed out with a sense of relief, not to say pride, that he had never been in Italy, France, or even Swabia. He is a good example of the possibilities and limitations of a Northern humanist without benefit of the Italian experience. He was to be sure a humanist in the formal meaning of the term with a knowledge of the classics certainly superior to that of most educated men of today. He read widely over the course of many years, but never deeply, and remained in detailed knowledge and comprehension inferior to an Agricola or Reuchlin. Nevertheless, he enjoyed the respect of his less critical contemporaries as a Latinist in prose and poetry. The Abbot Trithemius, for example, in his *Catalogus illustrium virorum Germaniae* called him "the most excellent orator and poet of all." Actually, he had no feeling for formal beauty or literary artistry. Compared with the standards of a Valla or a Politian his works were quite without merit. But he had caught the major idea of the need for a return to the earliest and purest sources, a principle of the greatest utility to him in his ecclesiastical and patriotic controversies. He saw the grammarian's role in the *explication du texte* as the Italian humanists conceived it.

Two major contributions enhanced Wimpfeling's reputation as a pioneer of humanist learning. He was the author of the first drama of German humanism, a satirical comedy "in the manner of Terence," and the head of his own humanist sodality. His Heidelberg students performed *Stylpho* on March 8, 1480, to the delight and especially the edification of all.[5] The moral of the play would have taken Terence aback. *Stylpho*, a promising young student, goes to Rome seeking prebends. He lives as a prodigal, fails his examinations, and cannot become a priest. The mayor of his town in pity appoints him the official pig herder. "What a change of fortune!," concludes Wimpfeling solemnly, "Such is the lamentable end of ignorance."

Following the lead of imaginative Celtis who had called into being the Rhenish and Danubian sodalities of humanists, Wimpfeling during his Strassburg period organized the *Sodalitas literaria Argentinensis*, a loose association of local friends of the classics, like Sebastian Brant, Hieronymus Gebweiler, Jakob Sturm, Matthias Schürer, and even lesser men. In August 1514, the sodality played host to Erasmus on his way from England to Basel. Wimpfeling as spokesman hailed him as "the prince of all belles-lettres, the priest of all humanity." Erasmus responded graciously: "I congratulate our fatherland which has produced so many leading men, men who are not only distinguished in every kind of learning, but also all of whom show the same ethical purity and modesty."[6] Perceptive Erasmus struck precisely the right note, for good learning and ethical purity were Wimpfeling's chief concerns. Gratefully he paid tribute to this hero of the humanists as "the most learned among the learned."[7]

Clever Erasmus must have known very well that Wimpfeling for one was not distinguished in every kind of learning. Not only did he have a complete blind spot for fine arts, like many literary humanists, but he was indifferent to astronomy and nature study as well. Moreover, his qualified response to Italian humanism and crucial reservations in the use of the classics shed an interesting light on his conservative mind. He saw the bright renaissance through smoked glasses which filtered out everything he did not wish to see.

The paradox posed by Wimpfeling's ambivalent attitude toward the Italian humanists is rather easily resolved. On the one hand, he had a temperamental reaction against them. "I do not know by what chance," he writes in his major work, "certain very learned Italians are attracted more by pleasant fables than by histories, more by pagan practices and ceremonies than by Christian, more by the names and deeds of the gods and goddesses than those of Christ and divine Mary, more by unchastity and impure love than by holiness and charity." [8] On the other, he once expressed regret at not having seen and heard Pico, Ficino, Pomponio Laetus, Beroaldus, and others, concluding: "I praise the abilities of the Italians who, well educated from their earliest years, learn necessary and useful things." [9] It was not only that Wimpfeling absolutely distinguished good and bad humanists, but also that he saw only the side congenial to himself in those whom he accepted. He appreciated Petrarch, for example, almost exclusively for his inward ascetic side. On three occasions Wimpfeling very nearly withdrew to cenobitic solitude in the Black Forest. The primary pull in this direction, he confides in the *Expurgatio*, came from his repeated reading of Petrarch's *De vita solitaria*. Again, Wimpfeling wrote a preface to Emser's edition of Pico's works, congratulating the German youth on this event, for in Pico they had a shining example of virtue and learning.[10] To Wimpfeling, Pico was a secular theologian and in the *Expurgatio* he lists him in the company of his professor in the *via antiqua*, Pallas Spangel, with Geiler von Kaisersberg, Lefèvre d'Étaples, and others. Proof positive is Wimpfeling's selection of Baptista Mantuanus as the most outstanding poet of Italian humanism.

Baptista Mantuanus, the general of the Carmelite order whose tremendous influence on Northern humanism has not as yet been adequately assessed, seemed to Wimpfeling to be hardly inferior to Virgil, whom he assiduously imitated. Wimpfeling extolled him above all other Italians, for his "clean and pure poems could be taught to the youth by a mature teacher without poison and because love for poesy did not extinguish in him zeal for the Sacred Book and of philosophy." [11] In place of "the gods and heroes he sang the Virgin and the saints, and in place of the principles of the Stoics and Epicurus he recommended virtues, consolations, and the felicity of the Christian life." Wimpfeling urged Sebastian Murrho to write commentaries on his works, a project at which he and Brant made a brave beginning. Wimpfeling failed to persuade Amerbach in Basel to publish a complete edition of his works, so he eventually published elsewhere the seven books of the *Parthenice*, a biographical description of the Virgin Mary and other saints, the *Bucolica*, which had a "modesty and an honesty" which he considered lacking in Virgil, and finally the *Fasti*.[12]

Wimpfeling had learned how to read the texts, but he was strictly selective about which texts he read. He was limited entirely to Latin literature and did not trust himself to recommend readings in Greek letters. Whereas Alexander Hegius of the *Devotio Moderna* wrote expressly on the utility of the Greek language, Wimpfeling merely conceded that Greek must be worthwhile, since Augustine had recommended it.[13] He had none of the excited enthusiasm of a Petrarch who thought Cicero so wonderful that he had to wonder at those who did not wonder at him. Not even all of the Latin classics were to be used, but only those which after careful testing proved to have didactic value. In choosing his canon of censored classics, Wimpfeling seems to have been more concerned about the deletion of immoral and pagan passages than about the deeper and more dangerous possibility that a different thought structure might follow upon the new formal structure presented by treacherous antiquity. As for himself, he once confided to Brant that he was not in the habit of studying the poets, but preferred the sober histories of men like Sallust.[14] His own most daring gesture was indulging in a common humanist conceit, using classical names as *Jupiter Tonans* for God the Father, or *diva parens* for the Virgin. But then, Mantuanus and the Carolingians did the same.

Pagan authors had a provisional utility, for they could be

helpful in understanding Christian writers and served in the interim until they could be replaced by superior Christian men of letters. At his best, Wimpfeling defended classic authors against a one-sided condemnation and showed what a practical kernel of wisdom they presented for the students, for without them the works of Augustine and Jerome are rendered difficult, since they contain copious borrowings from heathen poets. The Apostle Paul himself cited heathen authors. On his approved list were Virgil, Lucan, Horace (except the Odes), Terence, Plautus (at least the passages not emphasizing love), Cicero, Sallust, Valerius Maximus, and Seneca. On ethical grounds he ruled out Juvenal, Ovid, Martial, Tibullus, Propertius, Catullus, Sappho, and, on grounds of incomprehensibility, Persius. The Christian authors passing muster were Ambrose, Jerome, Lactantius, Petrarch, and such contemporaries as Leonard Martinus, Platina, and Philesius, and especially his favorite, Baptista Mantuanus.[15] A priest should restrict his reading to Psalms, hymns, and works of edification like those of Gerson. Above all the priest must not read the pagan poets, nor Plato, Averroes, or Alexander Aphrodisius, whom, he says, Lefèvre d'Étaples called the three plagues of Italy.[16] Later, in an acerbic controversy with the bumptious young poet Jakob Locher, Wimpfeling heatedly declared the baseness and superfluousness of the heathen poets, pronouncing that for school lectures at the most Virgil, Mantuanus, and other Christian poets should be considered, for all else was dangerous and ruinous.[17] There is no real system or theological emphasis discernible from his selections, the only criterion apparently being the utility of the work for promoting morality.

Wimpfeling's intellectual timidity and the tentative nature of his humanism stemmed basically from his anxiety for the preservation of ecclesiastical practice and dogma as he had always known them. He understood them, moreover, in every detail precisely as an orthodox late medieval priest should. He formed his ideals early and kept them as they were. In the early 1470's he penned a poem in honor of the Bishop of Speyer. Later he did a poetic description of the magnificent cathedral of Speyer, its towers, bells, sculptures, ceremonies, and services, ending with a Paean of praise to the Virgin, its patroness.[18] He was every inch a Catholic churchman. His histories of the bishops of Mainz and the bishops of Strassburg are significant, not for their excellence, but for the characteristic materials included, such as accounts of the obtaining of relics, the foundation of monasteries, and reform efforts.[19] In dogmatic questions he stood firmly within the semi-Pelagian tradition and saw in the incarnation the purest inspiration for virtuous living.[20] In the veneration of the saints and of the Virgin Mary he was second to none. In his poem *De triplici candore beatae Virginis* (1492), on the threefold luster of Mary, he took his stand with Trithemius, Brant, and other humanists against the Dominicans in support of the idea of the immaculate conception of Mary. In this respect at least he was in step with the future. But then, had not Gabriel Biel proved this very dogma by scholastic argumentation?

An excellent test case of Wimpfeling's reaction when confronted by a choice between tradition and innovation was his defense of scholasticism against a poet younger than himself. An Ingolstadt theologian, Georg Zingel, had ventured that poetry was after all only a means to an end. A student of Celtis, the self-assured Jakob Locher, who began his lectures on poetry with the ringing of a bell, attacked Zingel. Wimpfeling could not stand criticism, to say nothing of insult, coupling complaints about the wicked world and his opponents as a matter of course. After some delay in 1510 he fired his heaviest shot, *Contra Turpem libellum Philomusi*, defending subtle dialectic and the modern scholastics against the poets, an uncomfortable position for a humanist, though for him fairly easy.[21]

It was at Heidelberg, he recalled in his *Expurgatio*, that he had discovered the narrowness and poverty of philosophy and metaphysics — whose first principles he had already acquired — and looked for more marrow.[22] At Heidelberg he had delivered an oration, *Pro concordia dialecticorum*, in which he attacked the jealous rivalries of the schools and energetically promoted the *literae humanitatis* against the entrenched prerogatives of scholastic studies.[23] In Wimpfeling's last writing on the reform of university education, *Ad doctorem Florentium de Venningen*, 1521, he returned once again to the problem of the scholastic approach to learning. Virtue, he held, can be taught better by humanist than by scholastic methods, an attitude which marked a shift from emphasis on understanding to practice. He was impatient with obscure and subtle speculation, with dissembling mere opinion under the disguise of abstract terminology. Even Agricola's dialectic was too subtle for tyros, he held, preferring Aristotle himself to Peter Hispanus. Disputations have never yet converted a Jew or a Turk, he remarked in words reminiscent of Nicholas Cusanus. Like any other literary humanist from Petrarch to Erasmus, Wimpfeling felt no call to refute scholasticism with a new system or offer a new religious principle. His real desires he expressed succinctly in a letter to Erasmus addressed "German to German, theologian to theologian, pupil to master":

Thus our Oecolampadius, agreeing with us, shrinks from those theologians who reduce theology to verbose loquacity, and (as Gerson says) to a wintry mathematics, who offer very frequently the better sentences from Aristotle, Averroes, and Avicenna, draw nothing from the law, from the prophets, from the gospel, and from the Apostles, who raise a fragile reed to defend their sayings, and keep concealed in a sheath the sword sent from heaven, never conquerable, in which they could trust.[24]

And yet, in another Heidelberg oration he had declared, "Philosophy is the only ship which carries us to God, its study makes us so truly pleasing to our Creator," and stressed the need to understand Aristotle.[25] He urged his students to devote themselves to philosophy and sacred letters.[26] When theology should be useful to the church and serve as a defense for the faith, it "needs dialectic, metaphysics, moral and natural philosophy." [27] With fine impartiality he urged the study of Thomas as well as Duns Scotus, Marsiglio, Occam, Buridan, and Gabriel Biel: "In philosophy be an Aristotle . . . imitate the highest of all the theologians, Christ, and after him especially St. Augustine." [28]

Wimpfeling's defense of scholasticism was not really out of character, but his attacks upon the poets show how tenuous was the hold of humanism on him and how easily he shook it off when he felt tradition, even the medieval scholastic tradition, threatened. He struck at Locher with a vigor like that of Bernard when he was attacking Abelard. He adduced the authority of all great men who had found scholastic theology worthwhile. He now calls for a ban on antique poets, citing Jerome to the effect that the verse of secular poets had been nurtured by demons. Poetry does not merit the name of science or of liberal art, for it does not rest on the demonstration of principles and does not serve for proofs or for drawing conclusions. If Locher did not retract what he had dared to say against "the subtle scholastic theology," Wimpfeling fumed, "he should be struck by the anathema of the bishops, banned by the princes, or put into a cage as a spectacle for the people." [29] Wimpfeling could be imaginative under pressure.

The deeper meaning of this sudden turn against the poets, aside from sheer temper, was that Wimpfeling's initial criticism of scholasticism did not stem from a basic dogmatic difference, but from a formal one feebly apprehended. To Wimpfeling the security of the tradition, including as it did both the *viae*, was more important than poetic culture. He had little love of and desire for the rebirth of classical antiquity. The "spirit of the Renaissance" scarcely shines through.

The story of Wimpfeling's youthful conversion offers a clue to his reforming drive. At Freiburg in the throes of undergraduate romantic agonies he had penned some frankly sensuous love poems. Then in Erfurt his gaze fell one day upon a motto on the church wall painted in large letters: SIN NOT, GOD SEES. These words so gripped him that from youth to old age, he recalled, he labored for the preservation of purity.[30] His feverish activity stemmed from a strong moral compunction, not a new religious mission. He commended Geiler for not placing the true essence of Christianity in ceremonies, but in the keeping of the commandments. He was a teacher of righteousness in a highly ascetic vein, revealing the quickened conscience of some prophets in this period. His standpoint throughout was that of the devoted reformer of the secular clergy, protecting his order from itself, from the monks, from secular authority, and from the Reformation, such was the pattern. He could sense any threat to the priesthood from afar and quickly came to its defense as soon as he detected danger from without.[31] In his determination he resembled Cusanus, who as Bishop of Brixen made a spirited though futile effort to reform his diocese over the brutal opposition of Duke Sigismund of the Tyrol.

Gregory Nazianzen stated the case for Christian education pointedly: "I think that all those who have sense will acknowledge that education is the first of the goods we possess." Wimpfeling echoed this sentiment with enthusiasm. Leading the clergy and church back to their earlier ethical purity must begin with the young, he believed. His educational goal, like that of Gerard Groote, was ethics and not eloquence. "The mind must be formed to virtue" was his motto. Especially during his Speyer period and later at Strassburg he preoccupied himself with the problem of how to prepare a generation more honest, learned, and worthy of church and country. As a schoolmaster Wimpfeling was a transmitter rather than a creator, for schools are generally strongholds of conservatism where the old mold the young. From the beginning, as priest and professor he had been persuaded that ignorance was the first source of the evils from which church and society suffered, and that ignorance in turn was the result of the insufficient care given to the education of the youth. With a naive Socratic view, he concluded that knowledge would remove the evil.

In the first of Wimpfeling's two major works on education, *Isidoneus*, he concerned himself basically with Latin grammar and literature, showing the teachers how they can help the youth master both in much less time. Although in Italy the youth are prepared for a calling, in Germany after years of study all they can claim to have mastered is both parts of Alexander's *Doctrinale*.[32] The binding of grammar to logic and metaphysics and the endless commentaries do not help the students to read even a little preface from Jerome. The goal of grammatical studies is to enable the students to read the ethical classical authors and Christian literature. He reiterates that the teachers must set the example in word and deed for growth in learning and morality.[33] The second work is the *Adolescentia*, containing a mass of material largely intended for ethical instruction.[34] It is an omnibus volume offering such special delights as sentences from Petrarch arranged alphabetically and an exhortation to Maximilian to lay the Turks low and recover the Holy Land. It is replete with tips for clean living and useful quotations from classical authors, Christian writers, and contemporary Italian humanists, all chosen in tune with the spirit of the *Devotio Moderna*. Wimpfeling helped to make a school discipline of humanism in the North.

Wimpfeling's plans in 1501 to establish a school in Strassburg for the liberal arts failed to materialize. The idea which he urged on the city council in his *Germania* was sound, that a three-to five-year intermediary school would allow the students to learn and mature before beginning their university studies. But it was first realized in 1538 when Johann Sturm founded the first evangelical *gymnasium* in Strassburg with its goal of *sapiens et eloquens pietas*, reflecting the program of Martin Bucer and Jakob Sturm, like Melanchthon, to make humanism fruitful for the church of the Reformation.[35] In the *Adolescentia*, Wimpfeling had reiterated that reform must begin with the youth, but there was little time left for the old church and the new generation would belong to another.

Wimpfeling's program for the reform of the clergy constituted latter-day evidence for the failure of conciliarism. The ecclesiastical abuses which he decried were the same as those which the conciliarists had denounced. "It will not be possible," he avowed, "to stand easily upon the safe ground of religion, unless the renewal in *head and members* is at last actually put into effect." [36] But now, half a century after the bull *Execrabilis*, he could envision only a papal solution. His ideal image was none other than Jean Gerson, *doctor Christianissimus*, a secular cleric and conciliarist. Not only had he, too, battled for reform, Wimpfeling declared in his defense of Gerson against a mendicant detractor, but he kept the commandments of the Lord, avoided idle speculations and subtleties, and drew strength from his *theologia mystica* for his reforming endeavors. Wimpfeling was glad to assist the Strassburg circle with an edition of Gerson's works, begun by Peter Schott and by Geiler, who made a pilgrimage to France in order to visit the cities where his hero had lived and worked.[37]

Wimpfeling fired repeated broadsides against all kinds of clerical wrongs great and small: verbosity in the pulpit, liturgical malpractice; ignorance of the Scriptures, the fathers, and the doctors; avarice, arrogance, and bad manners; promotion because of noble birth; exemptions for bishops and archbishops; and countless other ills.[38] But his two main targets were the same abuses which seemed in those centuries endemic to celibate hierarchical sacerdotalism — simony and nepotism — a concomitant of concubinage. Wimpfeling was a barometer with its needle stuck at "storm." He was sensitive to the mounting pressure of lay criticism, and in 1504 he warned that the people would rise and reform the clergy, if they did not see to it themselves.

He had personally been a victim of simony, for he was deprived of a prebend in Strassburg, for which he had received expectancies from Rome, by the dean of the chapter who gave it to a favorite and excommunicated those canons who spoke in Wimpfeling's behalf.[39] This injustice triggered yet another round of attacks upon this clerical abuse. The major assault upon simony was his *Apologia pro republica Christiana*, which he sent to his students with instructions to burn; and in fact it was left unpublished for several years.[40] It is basically a plea for theology against canon law, which is so often exploited only for acquiring and keeping benefices. In it Wimpfeling paints a picture of unrelieved gloom, for the Turks triumph, the Christians war among themselves, entire peoples rebel against Rome, the laity despises the clergy, dispensations are dishonest, discipline is relaxed, ignorant men or youths are appointed to office, parishes ruined, all is lost in decadence.[41] Striking the pose of a prophet of Israel, he sounded forth an ominous call: "How long, good God, will you tolerate this? How long, o German nation, will you remain stolid and patient in a mule-like way?" Wimpfeling lived to receive the answer.[42]

Wimpfeling dipped his pen in the bitterest gall when he wrote against concubinage — which he did at length and continuously. Attacking priests who, while conducting divine services, had their mistresses at home, he explained, "Posterity will scarcely believe it!" [43] His major work on the subject was the *De Integritate*, intended to help priests to abhor the very pernicious love of women.[44] He documented his charges of laxity with specific examples, interesting case studies for the social historian. But the major burden of this chaotic volume is to suggest remedies for lust in a time-honored vein. Elsewhere he virtually declared the bankruptcy of celibacy when he conceded that, in view of the weaknesses of human nature and the fact that men are not angels, if they lacked the power to resist temptation they should at least sin in secret to avoid giving offense.[45] Some of his smaller tracts were as incendiary as the Reformation *Fliegende Blätter*, mocking the milk penny and child tax collected by the priest, instructing concubines on how to get to the priests' money sack, recounting anecdotes worthy of the *Epistolae Obscurorum Virorum*, but bitter.[46] The priest's task, he once remarked, is to lead people to tears and not laughter. He was so strident and persistent that Erasmus ironically suggested he should turn his full armor against the Turks, since he had waged war against the concubines long enough.[47]

In the *De Integritate* (chapter 31) Wimpfeling opened another round in the battle of secular and regular clergy with his assertion that Augustine was never a monk and that wisdom did not dwell in cowls. A storm broke over his head for which even he was unprepared. He was driven from Freiburg by the Augustinians, whole cities and universities chose sides, the bishops of Basel and Strassburg supported him. In the *Apologetica* and *Soliloquium ad Divum Augustinum* he went even further, showing that the *Sermones ad Eremitas* were not written by Augustine, and charging the monks with opposition to reform, ignorance, greed, and leading the people from parish churches to monastery chapels. His citation to Rome was dropped only when he appealed to Julius II on grounds of age and ill health.[48] The Pope enjoined to silence both sides in this jurisdictional dispute. In a limited way this affair was a preliminary of the Reuchlin controversy, at least the opponents were the same. Some humanists as Zasius, Bebel, Beatus Rhenanus, and Peutinger came to Wimpfeling's defense. And yet, Wimpfeling kept entirely aloof from Reuchlin's cause. Even when Reuchlin wrote him in 1513 about the process in Mainz, he did not reply.

Wimpfeling saw the problem of abuses clearly, but the solution he envisioned had nothing really new to offer. On a personal level, he wrote literally thousands of letters encouraging individuals to the good life.[49] He advocated synods large and small in which the clergy could discuss theological topics. But basically he believed in a papal solution, in reform from the head downwards. "I have always known," he avowed, "that the salvation of the whole church depends upon the welfare of the supreme pontiff. I have, in fact, always believed, and believe so today, that the Roman church is the mother and leader of all the churches." The pope's sword reaches to the ends of earth and nothing can resist his arms.[50]

Wimpfeling passed damning judgment upon the person of Sixtus IV, which makes his appeal to Alexander VI for protection against the persecutors of the clergy all the more ironical. He believed that if Julius II only knew about conditions, he would do something about it. He favored a Lateran council under papal auspices. He still hoped, around 1514, that the new pope, Leo X, whose sanctity and zeal he celebrated, would bring a remedy for the universal ills.[51] He failed to see that the papacy, involved in personal and political concerns, was unable to act from purely spiritual or even ecclesiastical motives.

Born on the western front, Wimpfeling, like many sons of the border, was an arch-patriot. During his youth he had experienced the assaults of the Burgundians upon Alsace and later the threatening encroachments of the French. Like the other Alsatian humanists — Sebastian Brant, Thomas Wolf, Hieronymus Gebweiler, Beatus Rhenanus, and the rest — Wimpfeling's patriotism was one of his major driving forces. As defender of the Fatherland, he lauded the Emperor, feuded with Gaguin over Charles VIII's rejection of the Habsburg princess Margaret, charged the Swiss with disobedience, criticized the warring noblemen, engaged in the famous dispute with Thomas Murner over the German character of Alsace, and wrote the first history of Germany which purported to be nothing more than that — a fiery patriot indeed.[52]

But patriotism posed its problems for it involved him in a basic conflict of loyalties as he sought for a solution to the ills of church and state. As a patriot he was appalled at the sums of money sucked from Germany by the Italian courtesans and French monastic orders. He was angered all the more by the pose of cultural superiority of Italian churchmen from Aeneas Silvius down. In line with the ancient proprietary church tradition he admonished the princes, councils, and kings in cases where the bishops neglected their duty, to care for the churches, expressly advocating secular intervention against abuses such as pluralities of benefices.[53] But when the Emperor called on him to outline plans for a major realignment of imperial policy toward the church, he backed away and managed to extricate himself clumsily from a delicate situation.

Maximilian, angered by the pro-Venetian policy shift of Julius II, decided in the summer of 1510 to undertake ecclesiastical reform measures within the empire. On the suggestion of his secretary, Jakob Spiegel, Wimpfeling's nephew, he turned to Wimpfeling for a plan. On September 18, Maximilian sent Spiegel to Wimpfeling with a copy of France's Pragmatic Sanction and instructions in which he expressed his determination to follow the example of other people and set up provisions and edicts so that Germany, which for years had sent its money and resources to Rome, would at last win back its old freedom and live according to wholesome rules and ordinances. Therefore, he continued, he was turning to Wimpfeling, who had shown his respect for the empire and imperial house in writing small works and treatises, had already invited the princes to strive for the present goal, and had admonished Maximilian to establish an imperial treasury to stop the flow of monies from the empire. The advice requested of Wimpfeling should deal with three problems: the intriguing of the courtesans; the cessation of annates; and the possible establishment of a permanent legate in Germany for mediating ecclesiastical cases in Germany itself, to expedite them and prevent the payments from leaving Germany.

Here, if ever, was Wimpfeling's opportunity for decisive action on the world stage. His tentative reply was that he would oblige the Emperor but only "so far as it would be possible before God and without injury to conscience." His advice, when it came, showed a complete loss of nerve. He warned against adopting the Pragmatic Sanction arguing that the highest pontiffs had rarely violated the concordats with the princes, which were quite good enough. Instead he listed ten grievances of the German nation which agreed basically with the *gravamina* that Martin Mayr had in 1457 delivered to Aeneas Silvius and which had been common currency at diets for decades. They cited again the old complaints about the curial courtesans, abused elections, reservation of benefices for higher clergy, expectancies, annates, ignorant appointees, new indulgences following the revocation of suspension of the old, Turk money, and legal cases referred to Rome at great expense which could be settled locally. He pointed specifically to the see of Mainz as a prime example of financial exploitation, as Luther did later. His advice to Maximilian? He should approach the Pope and ask the Holy Father to "deal more kindly with his sons in the German nation" lest a persecution arise against the universal priests of Christ or many people defect from the Roman church as in Bohemia. In the *Avisamenta ad Caesaream Maiestatem* Wimpfeling turns on Maximilian with dour predictions of the outcome should he go too far. The three spiritual electors would turn against him, the mendicants would stir up the people against him, the Pope could influence adversely the election of his successor and stir up neighboring nations against him or remove the bonds of obedience from his subjects. On the plan for a permanent legate, Wimpfeling quails, "I fear, however, that the highest pontiff has prescribed against us, because a privilege is lost through lack of use." [54]

In a decisive moment, Wimpfeling was found wanting. But actually, this reaction of his was perfectly predictable, for in any real clash between the two swords there could be no doubt on which side he would stand. When a monk named Angelus in 1511 attacked the anti-papal council of Pisa, which Maximilian supported, Wimpfeling seconded him with his *Orationis angeli confirmatio*, urging the secular princes not to be anti-papal, reiterating that only the Pope can reform the church with the help of a council. In reality, probably nothing more would have come of Maximilian's plan than of most of his others. But of Wimpfeling's true loyalties when forced to choose between *papa* and *patria* there can be no question.

Some men have the good fortune to die young or at the crest of their power and influence, so that posterity can praise their promise and bewail their loss. It was Wimpfeling's fate to live indecently long, seventy-eight years and some months, for that age of low actuarial statistics, far past his best days. He was a pitiable and tragic figure toward the end, for the Reformation left him stranded, like a piece of driftwood on a shoal when the tide runs out. Events moved mercilessly beyond him during his last decade, and he complained that he was ignored and that his letters were often left unanswered. The Reformation was to be his final skirmish, in which he won a battle, but lost the war.

Wimpfeling at first saw in Luther a fresh ally in his struggle against Roman abuses. He applauded his attacks on Tetzel's sale of indulgences, as though Luther were the fulfillment of Geiler's prophecy that God would raise up a man to renew the corrupt religion. In the very month when Eck was spreading the bull of excommunication against Luther, September 1520, Wimpfeling had Schürer in Schlettstadt publish the letter of Erasmus to Albert of Mainz in which Erasmus expressed his solicitude for Luther's cause. In his accompanying letter to the Bishop of Basel, Wimpfeling demanded fair treatment for Luther: "May the German bishops as well as the German and Swiss authorities urge our most holy and pious lord Leo to mildness toward Luther, so that he does not allow Luther to be ruined, for he acts not only in his teaching but in his whole life like a Christian and evangelical man. May the representative of Christ show the mildness and gentleness of Christ! For if Luther had hallucinations in a number of things, he had not thereby denied his human nature and would let himself be taught better by those who were free from pride and hypocrisy . . . I know, too, that among the heathen fathers punish their children lightly for the greatest misdeeds. Why should that not be the practice also among Christians and above all in the case of the honorable and highest princes of the faith, the leaders in Christian piety?" [55]

Like the expert at Roman Law, Ulrich Zasius, who had once declared that whatever he heard from Luther he accepted "as from an angel," Wimpfeling, too, turned against the reformer, when he perceived that events were moving toward a schism in the old church. He was badly shaken when Lutheranism came to Schlettstadt itself. There Paul Phrygio, his friend and member of the Schlettstadt humanist sodality, preached according to the new evangelical principles. Johann Witz, Sapidus, a former pupil of his, now rector of the school in Schlettstadt, declared himself against the old ceremonies early in 1520. Bernhard Wartenbach, a reformed teacher, wrote a letter in 1523 jibing at Wimpfeling under the name Jakob Rympheling. Wolfgang Capito in a public sermon in Strassburg in 1523 attacked prayers addressed to Mary. His own favorite nephew, Jacob Spiegel, admonished Capito in writing, scorned Wartenbach, threatened Sapidus with the Inquisition, and saw the council drive Phrygio and the Reformation out of the city, following the defeat of the peasants on May 20, 1526.[56] In Schlettstadt, thanks in part to Wimpfeling and even more to the maneuvering of Aleander, the Counter Reformation scored an early and lasting victory. On May 23, 1524, Wimpfeling addressed a letter to Luther and Zwingli to accompany an edition of Emser's *Canonis missae defensio*, urging them to read this treatise carefully and convince themselves that the canon of the Mass contained nothing contrary to the teachings and usages of the ancient church and not to reject everything simply because it came from Rome.[57] The aged priest had written his last apology and it was fitting that it should be a defense of the Mass.

It was sheer irony that unctuous Aleander should force upon the ancient fighter one final humiliation — an abject submission to Rome under threat. Aleander attributed to Wimpfeling the authorship of the anonymous *Litaneia, hoc est supplicatio ad Deum . . . pro Germania*, containing aspersions against the monks, the greed of the courtesans, and concubinage, and through Jakob Spiegel demanded a justification from Wimpfeling. Spiegel informed his uncle that it was high time he had made his stand on Luther known unequivocally. Wimpfeling obliged with a letter to his nephew who could send a copy on to Rome and see to it that the Nuntius had a copy in his papers. Wimpfeling meekly explained that his health would not allow him to engage in such literary activity; he could not betray his loyalty to the papacy and respect for the present pope; he had opposed a move toward a council; he had defended scholastic theology; he had been justified before Julius II, when the Augustinians began a process against him; he had written this tract for church reform in 1510 only because Maximilian had demanded it; his feud with the Augustinians precluded any sympathy with Luther, the Augustinian. Small wonder that Aleander was fully satisfied! Nevertheless, Wimpfeling was not spared another summons to Rome in 1523, though he was finally excused from going.[58] Rome's vision was so blurred that she could scarcely distinguish too ardent friend from foe.

A pattern of continual advance and retreat is clearly discernible in Wimpfeling's career. He turned from youthful adventures to a rigidly ascetic life. He promoted humanism, but feared the consequences of unrestricted cultivation of the classics. He labored for educational reform, but within the safe outline prescribed by the *Devotio Moderna*. He criticized scholasticism sharply, but rose to its defense against its detractors. He lashed at the abuses of the clergy, but took up their cause against the monks and secular lords. He was a fiery patriot, yet sided with the papacy rather than the emperor. He greeted Luther and the Reformation, only to turn back to the medieval church. Each time Wimpfeling withdrew from the periphery of novelty and progress to the same position, the center of the traditional — conservatism revisited.

The earlier convention of viewing Wimpfeling together with Geiler and their kind as forerunners of the Reformation has been justifiably abandoned. Wimpfeling was a stern Savonarola type, though he lacked the ecstatic character and mystic fanaticism of the Florentine, and what is more, Strassburg was no Florence. If the now dated theory of the Reformation as primarily a reaction against abuse were tenable, then, to be sure, Wimpfeling could be considered a reformer before the Reformation. Whatever contribution Wimpfeling made to the historic Reformation was completely unintended. With his absolute idealism and uncompromising purism, he was a good example of the dangerous radicality implicit in a too consistent conservatism. How it must have hurt him to see his prize student and future city councilor, Jacob Sturm, turn protestant and help win Strassburg for the Reformation. He must have felt like an aged sculptor who discovers too late a flaw in the marble which he intended for his masterpiece. How it must have shocked him, when in answer to his remonstrances, Sturm replied: "If I am a heretic, you have made me one."

Was it still possible to reform the church with Wimpfeling's tactics of direct assault on abuses from a lowly station? Was reform in head and members a viable alternative to a change of heart? There was not a breath of fresh air in Wimpfeling's writings, for all his mighty blasts. His humanism scarcely contributed to a formal to say nothing of a dogmatic revolution. There was no change in the way in which Christianity was experienced. There was no new spirit, no new religious insight, no renewal of faith. He was far from the depths of evangelical Reformation theology. Wimpfeling held to the old ways and was remarkable mostly for the vigor and determination with which he clung to them, though deeper religious needs of the people required satisfaction and time was running out. Wimpfeling, Geiler, Brant, and the other conservative humanists, were essentially retrospective, longing for a past which they seemed unable to recapture and uneasy about a future which they could not control. Erasmus, who was easily moved by deaths, was deeply moved also by that of Wimpfeling. Perhaps he saw with the passing of this stalwart, the end of a respectable, though frustrated, generation. If Wimpfeling saw most clearly the need for external reform, another admirer of Agricola, Johannes Reuchlin, felt the need for reinvigorating Christian thought with strength from new sources.

IV

REUCHLIN

Pythagoras Reborn

To his contemporaries like Mutian, Johannes Reuchlin seemed the most erudite of the Germans. Hutten called Reuchlin and Erasmus the two eyes of Germany. Reuchlin was truly a consecrated scholar, the restorer of Hebrew, the hero of the humanists, and a religious philosopher of real significance. Though he is often tagged a mere philologist, he thought and spoke the language of philosophy. In the *Rudimenta hebraica* he exclaimed: "I reverence St. Jerome as an angel, I prize Nicholas de Lyra as a great master, but Truth I worship as God!"

Although Reuchlin was a lawyer engaged in the active life of a chancellery, he was a genuine academic type (figure 2). A savant to the core, he was driven by an insatiable *libido sciendi*. He grew up in a pious home environment and began his course of studies at Freiburg when only fifteen. He was educated entirely in the North; at Paris under the realist Heynlin de Stein, at Basel, Paris again, then in law at Orleans and Poitiers. It may have been at Basel that he developed his great interest in Nicholas Cusanus, who contributed to his speculative metaphysical interests. In later years he owned many of Cusanus' works and even lent some manuscripts to Lefèvre d'Étaples, who wished to edit them. Finally, after a career as a jurist, he ended his days at Ingolstadt and Tübingen, as a professor, his true calling. His official duties brought him to Italy a number of times. In March 1482, he visited Florence in the retinue of Duke Eberhard of Wuerttemberg. There he learned to know Ficino and received a letter from him later. On his second trip, in 1490, he met Pico and perhaps saw Ficino again, an event of the greatest moment for his intellectual development. The next year he entrusted Dionysius, his younger brother, to Ficino as a pupil.

Reuchlin showed his bookish inclinations early, publishing, when only twenty, a Latin dictionary, *Vocabularius breviloquus*, of no great value. He so impressed the Greek John Argyropulos with his exposition of Thucydides that Argyropulos supposedly declared that Greece had now "flown over the Alps." More than that, he was the first rightly to bear that triple linguistic tiara — Latin, Greek, and Hebrew. Celtis called him the interpreter and philosopher of three languages. Reuchlin, four years before his death, made a brief sketch of his own mental development, as every intellectual should. He described the maturing of his interests from a preoccupation with Latin style to the study of Greek and Aristotelian philosophy, his reaction against scholasticism, and, finally, his devotion to Hebrew. "Pledged to Christ," he concluded, "I devoted everything to the Christian church . . . I am led by genius and the love of piety." [1]

As early as November 9, 1482, Rudolf Agricola wrote to Reuchlin about their mutual interest in Hebrew letters.[2] Perhaps also Wessel Gansfort helped to stimulate Reuchlin's interest in Hebrew. But he was almost forty before he began seriously to study the language. Reuchlin named as his first revered teacher Jakob ben Jehiel Loans, a physician to Emperor Frederick III, whom he met at Linz in 1492. He seems, however, actually to have begun his studies briefly in 1486 with an otherwise unknown Jew named Calman. His library included thirteen Hebrew manuscripts and at least eight Hebrew books, acquired largely in Italy. Among the volumes were David Kimchi's grammar and the important work of the Spanish cabalist Joseph ben Abraham Gikatilia, the *Hortus nucis*, the major sources of Reuchlin's grammatical and cabalist learning.[3]

In the *De rudimentis hebraicis*, 1506, he offered to the world the first fairly reliable manual of Hebrew grammar by a Christian scholar, expressing the hope that Christian theologians might with great diligence learn from him. (It may comfort many a modern author to learn that even this great pioneering work did not sell and Reuchlin lost money on it.) To accompany the grammar, he published an edition of the Seven Penitential Psalms giving the Hebrew text, a Latin translation, and a grammatical explanation, as he put it. Years later, in 1518, he published still another work dedicated to God and pious learning, *De accentibus et orthographia lingvae hebraicae*. Reuchlin had predecessors in the field. The best known among them was Conrad Pellican who published a guide to Hebrew studies in 1501, *De modo legendi et intelligendi Hebraeum*, which was unfortunately replete with errors. Reuchlin, therefore, felt himself to be a pioneer. He could not restrain a victory chant: "No one before me was able to bring together the rules of the Hebrew language in a book. And should envy break his heart, nevertheless, I am the first. I have raised aloft a monument more lasting than bronze!" [4]

Reuchlin felt that Hebrew brought him closer to God than any other language. Some held it to be barbarous, for it is lacking in flourishes of speech and the grace of elegances. But Hebrew is simple, pure, uncorrupted, sacred, concise, and consistent. Through Hebrew, God conversed with men and men with angels, face to face. Hebrew is older than any other tongue, for Moses was the most ancient author. The Hebrew chronicles alone provide a record of events before the Trojan war. Homer and Hesiod first sang a century and a half later. In spite of its age, however, Hebrew is the richest of languages and all others are poor and barren in comparison. When Reuchlin read Hebrew he was both stirred by a strange terror and excited with ineffable joy. His study of Hebrew was almost as much a religious exercise as a scholarly preoccupation.[5]

Herder acclaimed Reuchlin enthusiastically. He was not only the awakener, but, what is more, he was the protector of oriental literature. He spoke the word of power: "Stand up! Arise, o dead one!" And the dead arose, as he was, bound in rabbinical shroud and his head wrapped in a napkin. The second word was and is incomparably easier: "Loose him and let him go!" And that, concludes Herder, is the praiseworthy service of Reuchlin to posterity.[6]

How ironical that in view of Reuchlin's pious purposes the stalwarts of Cologne should have plagued him as they did. The great controversy became the *cause célèbre* of the humanists who considered him their head, a cultural symbol. When he was threatened with a summons to Rome, the veterans of Celtis' sodalities, the fighters of Mutian's circle, and Pirckheimer's coteries rose to his defense with such a hue and cry that Reuchlin's own attitude toward his role at the center of the uproar has been somewhat obscured. The prudent Mutian opined that Reuchlin had been too forward, that he should have acted more modestly, refrained from injuring the monks, not offended the pious ears of the simple, and deferred to the opinion of the common crowd with proper honors. "To confute the authority of the church when you are a member of this body is both an outrage and full of impiety, even if you perceive errors." [7] Erasmus equivocated and never tired of emphasizing that the Reuchlin affair was none of his business, a sorry posture indeed for the prince of the humanists.

Reuchlin would not buy peace at any price, yet he was anything but a fighter. He was for the most part on the defensive, made many concessions (too many from a modern point of view) on which Hebrew books could be sacrificed to the fury of the zealots, desired to avoid offense and scandal, repeatedly begged for peace, and considered the whole affair an unjust persecution inflicted upon him in his old age by monks whom he had served almost three decades.[8] His posture was that of a new Athanasius defending himself, God's name, and the truth. It was the monks who did not practice true Christianity, who, like Savonarola, were guilty of pharasaical disobedience to the church. He and his defenders truly exalted the Christian religion, *orthodoxa fides nostra*. Reuchlin envisioned himself, not as a crusader for humanism, but as an injured defender of pure Christianity. As a true son of the church he was ever ready to submit his writings to her judgment. He was concerned with defending his own orthodoxy, not subverting her authority. He wished to spend his declining years quietly reading divine writings, seeking lasting salvation, tranquillity of heart, and true joy.[9]

Reuchlin, a layman, dedicated all his major works to churchmen, from his brother, a priest, to Pope Leo himself. Even his lesser works, with the exception of his dramas — *Sergius*, which satirized the abuse of relics, and *Henno*, done in the manner of Terence for the pleasure of Dalberg's Heidelberg Circle — served a wholesome and even pious purpose. His *Vocabularius*, designed to raise classical standards, included references to religious and theological works. To the *Rudimenta hebraica* he attached a genealogy of Mary which was really that of Joseph, supplied by Luke, slightly transposed. His *De arte praedicandi*, 1502, was designed as a homiletical handbook for the Dominican monks of Denckendorf who had given him refuge during a plague. It was conventional and thus very popular. There was nothing revolutionary about any of his writings.

Reuchlin felt that theology was too exalted for him. He was no theologian and did not pretend to be one. He frequently demurred with such expressions as these: "I will not speak on the meaning of the passage as a theologian, but on the words as a grammarian," or, "But follow the most noble grammarians of the Hebrews." [10] He denied having meddled in theological matters when, at the urging of Maximilian, he had prepared a brief defending the use of Hebrew writings. It was therefore quite pointless for the Dominican Kollin to sneer that it was no wonder a jurist could not grasp theological subtleties. Reuchlin had already modestly confessed that he had not learned theology in the schools, but civil law.[11] At one time, to be sure, he expressed his resolve to turn to the study of the New Law and its salvation, for a Christian must be concerned above all with the Scriptures. He cherished especially the writings of Paul, his "leader," "bright sun," and "measure of truth." But he did not persist in this determination.[12]

Yet Reuchlin's two major works were nothing if they were not theology, constructive theology. For in his negative emphasis, Reuchlin's views can be considered only typical of the common humanist criticisms. In the dedication of his *De arte cabalistica* to Leo, for example, he expressed regret that the Italian philosophy had been plagued by the barking of the Sophists and buried for so long in shadows and dense night. But through the brilliance and generosity of the Medicis the arts of eloquence and rhetoric developed by Petrarch, Filelfo, and Aretino were brought to Florence in the person of such men most learned and skilled in the ancient authors, men like Chalcondyles, Ficino, Vespucci, Landino, Valori, Politian, and Pico. The scholastics had in this age brought philosophy into disrepute with the masses. Reuchlin was more moderate in his criticism than many of his fellow humanists, more sparing than the two *viae* frequently were of each other. He was, after all, opposed to the dated form of scholastic expression, to their way of obscuring religious truth by multiplying words, to their syllogistic method, to their trifling concerns. He was not opposed to their basic Christian premises and ultimate pious purposes.[13]

It is true that Reuchlin flayed the abuses in the church and the ignorance of the monks. He frequently pointed out errors in the Vulgate and the Septuagint. He raised the question of why the evangelists writing an eloquent Greek interposed incorrect Hebrew forms.[14] But his preoccupation with the exegetical significance of each letter led him to defend all the more the verbal accuracy of the original texts.[15] Indeed, he viewed himself as a defender of Christian truth, an apologist who had discovered the best foundation yet on which to build a new support for the faith. "I have suffered innocently for many years," he wrote, "because of my immense desire to strengthen the orthodox faith and my most ardent desire to enlarge the Catholic Church, because I felt that those who were outside the faith, the Jews, Greeks, and Saracens, would not be attracted to us by insults. For I thought it was not suitable for the church that they should be driven to holy baptism by tyranny or severity." [16]

In both his attitude toward the Scriptures and in his concern for the conversion of the Jews, Reuchlin reflected many ideas of the Franciscan scholar Nicholas de Lyra (d. 1340), whom he admired intensely. In the second prologue to his monumental exegetical work *Postillae perpetuae in universam S. Scripturam*, Nicholas de Lyra complained that due to the errors of copyists and correctors the Vulgate had come to diverge seriously from the Hebrew text and should be restored to accuracy by comparison with the Hebrew codices. Nicholas learned Hebrew himself and in his exegetical work used the commentaries of such Jewish scholars as the renowned Talmudist Rashi. Although Nicholas complained that the mystical interpretations in the Christian exegetical tradition had all but choked out the literal meaning of the text, he himself used allegory extravagantly. In this respect he could not lead Reuchlin to a historico-literal interpretation or check his phantasy. In his sermons and writings Nicholas worked for the conversion of the Jews. The influence of Nicholas de Lyra on Reuchlin is quite evident, but Reuchlin received an even stronger inspiration and direction from one of his own contemporaries.

The special turn his apologetic took, Reuchlin owed to Florence and to Pico. We can date Reuchlin's interest in the Jewish Cabala at the earliest with the end of the 1480's. It was most likely Pico with his youthful zest and exaggerated enthusiasm who fired Reuchlin with an interest in the Cabala on his visit to Italy in 1490. Around 1480 in his *Epistula secretorum* the converted Jew Paulus de Heredia had undertaken to demonstrate that the fundamental Christian truths were to be found in the Cabala. Pico was convinced that it was possible to establish the grand unity of a Christian philosophical system with the Cabalist and Hellenic metaphysics. Pico agreed with the cabalists that Hebrew was the first, purest, language. In his *Conclusiones* and *Apologia*, Pico explained that the great teachers such as Moses had transmitted many of their ideas orally through the seventy wise men in unbroken tradition until they had been embodied in the Cabala. It was the surest and most trustworthy key to Christian secrets, "greatly" confirming the Christian religion. In it could be discovered such basic Christian doctrines as original sin, the Trinity, and the incarnation. In the *Apologia* he declared that nothing makes one surer of the divinity of Christ than the Cabala.[17] It was Pico who in his *Heptaplus* suggested the parallel between the ideas of the cabalists and the Pythagoreans. Pico derived from Ficino the idea that Platonism itself was based upon older Hebrew sources. Reuchlin fell heir to Pico. "I hope," wrote Mutian, "that you will shortly accomplish precisely that which Pico promised." [18]

Reuchlin took up the challenge: "Marsilio [Ficino] produced Plato for Italy. Lefèvre d'Étaples restored Aristotle to France. I shall complete the number and I, Capnion, shall show to the Germans Pythagoras reborn through me." [19] St. Augustine in the *City of God* (viii, 2) held that there were two schools of early Greek philosophy, the Ionian and the Italian. The Italian meant Pythagoras and his mysterious arithmology. What a pleasing harmony of history that this Italian philosophy should be reborn in the age of Italy's rebirth. Reuchlin required an even greater antiquity. He accepted uncritically the notion that Pythagoras derived the heart of his philosophy from the wise men of the East — *ex oriente lux*. His was the *Ur-Philosophie*. The distinctive mark of the Pythagorean ideas was that they bound together philosophy and religion more than any other pre-Socratic group. It seemed clear to Reuchlin, therefore, that the knowledge of the Hebrew cabalists was in essence the same as that of the Pythagoreans.[20] In the *De arte cabalistica* one of the disputants, Philolaus the Pythagorean, concludes significantly, if belatedly: "For now I see clearly, that whatever Simon [the cabalist] shows us corresponds exactly to the Italian philosophy, i.e., the Pythagorean, so that I have decided for this reason that everything of both the cabalists and the Pythagoreans is of the same sort. For all of our studies of both lead ultimately back to the salvation of mankind."[21]

Reuchlin considered the Cabala, not Hebrew for its own sake, his major concern. He referred to it in his grammar and in his lexicon, expressing his intention of writing on the subject in order to explain its proper nature and defend it against abuses at the hands of the ignorant. To devote one's life to it would be a pleasure. Almost a quarter of a century lay between his two major works and his amazing progress in cabalistic studies is very evident from a comparison of them. Nevertheless, the formal structure of the two is almost identical. Their purpose and general argument are the same. Each is divided into three books with three participants in the time-honored device of dialogue. Neither is a genuine discussion. Rather, brief questions interspersed provide the cues for learned discourses which develop the thought.

The preoccupation with names, also divine names, as symbols for and conveyors of the reality which they represent, Reuchlin may have derived from Cusanus, whose dialogues *De possest* and *De non aliud* were concerned with speculations about the divine names. In the third chapter of his *De mente* Cusanus argued that when one knows the full significance of a name one knows all about that which it represents, an idea that recurs again in his *De venatione sapientiae*, in the thirty-third chapter. Less immediate sources for this line of thought were perhaps Plato's own dialogue *Kratylos* or Dionysius' *De divinis nominibus* which Ficino had translated into Latin with a commentary.[22] It is clear that the *De verbo mirifico* is moving within the universe of medieval and Renaissance Neoplatonism. Cusanus had a much greater influence on Reuchlin than has heretofore been supposed.

The *De verbo mirifico* was published in 1494 preceded by a letter of Conrad Leontorius to Jakob Wimpfeling in which Reuch-

1. *St. Jerome in his cell*

2. *Johannes Reuchlin*

lin's scholarly work and especially the excellence of this work was highly praised. No philosopher, either Jew or Christian, can be preferred to Reuchlin. The dialogue takes place in Pforzheim. Sidonius leads the discussion on the first day with a discourse on an eclectic pagan philosophy which was basically Epicurean with Baruch acting as antagonist. They cover a bewildering variety of topics from the mysteries of India, the Greek nature philosophers, Lucretius and sense perception as opposed to the Spirit and revelation as a key to the secrets of nature, to the wonder-working word which unites God the infinite with finite man. On the second day Baruch expounds on the secret words and lofty doctrines of the Hebrews. Moses, using the most ancient tongues, was the wisest teacher of antiquity. There are many names for God, including that which Plato used (τὸ ὄν), who had learned Jewish theology from the Egyptians. The most sacred is the Tetragrammaton *Jhvh*. On the final day Capnion moves to the center of the stage to reveal at last the wonder-working word. The word, "Logos" to the Greeks, was both word and reason. The Logos, as John has it, is the Son of God, born of a virgin and crowned with the wisdom of God. Gabriel pronounced his name Ihsvh. That is, the great, secret, holy, honored, wonderful, wonder-working word. The fifth letter is added to make the Tetragrammaton pronounceable, the Shin (ש), signifying holy fire and holy name. In ancient times in many lands this name worked miracles. The cross is its symbol. At length Capnion asks whether Baruch and Sidonius are not convinced by his demonstration from Pythagoras and the Cabala. They both concede that his reasoning is persuasive.

The *De arte cabalistica*, 1517, reveals Reuchlin as a matured Hebraist and the leading Christian expert on the Cabala. Marranus, a Mohammedan, and Philolaus, a Christian Pythagorean from Byzantium, having dinner in the same inn, meet and agree to travel to Frankfort together to visit Simon ben Eliezer, a noted cabalist.[23] In the conversations with Simon which follow, Marranus plays a very minor role. In the first book Simon dominates with his explanations of the Cabala. In the second, Simon cannot be present because of the Sabbath, and Philolaus discusses Pythagoreanism. He claims that every cabalist proposition which Simon set forth can be found in the writings of Pythagoras. In the third book

Simon returns to reveal the deepest secrets of the Cabala which provide support for Christian truth. The discourse itself meanders baroque-like and it is difficult to follow a progressive line of argument. But closer analysis reveals an organic pattern of thought and a coherent philosophic orientation on the big questions of man, the universe, and God.

The Cabala was Reuchlin's major source. He viewed it as a symbolic reception of divine revelation, which leads to the salvation-bringing contemplation of God. The true "Cabalici," he explained, were partakers of the heavenly inspiration. They are to be distinguished from their pupils the "Cabalaei" and their imitators the "Cabalistae." [24] The true tradition was handed down orally from Adam to Moses who revealed the art of interpreting the secrets of Holy Scripture to only a select few, such as Joshua. It was transmitted then through a long line to the Cabalists, the "reception" of the Cabala. The apparent pleonasms and obscure passages in Scripture contained secrets which could be fathomed only through the key of Cabala. The Cabala was a veritable symbolic theology in which not only the letters and names but the very things themselves (*res*) are signs of still other things. The Sabbath, for example, is a mystery of the living God. It is a symbol of the higher world, of the eternal Jubilee, where all labor ceases.[25] Reuchlin was convinced that the Cabala is nothing else, speaking in the manner of the Pythagoreans, than a symbolic theology in which the letters are not only the signs and names of things, but are truly the things themselves.

Reuchlin employed all the major devices of cabalistic exegesis. The Gematria operated with the notion that the alphabetical letters represented numbers and that words thus equivalent numerically could be used interchangeably. The Notarikon was a complicated acrostic system whereby, with many variations, the initial or final letters of a series of words might be joined to form a new word. The Themurah, transposition, is actually a combination of the letter substitutions of the code and the anagrammatic interchange of the resultant letters.[26] John Colet once wrote Erasmus, after reading the *De arte cabalistica*, that, although he was really not qualified to judge, it seemed to him as he read it that "the wonders were more verbal than real." In view of the source and method, the coherence of Reuchlin's religious philosophy comes necessarily as a surprise.

What is man? In Reuchlin's cabalism man is viewed as a unique creature, situated at the center of the great chain of being, able to descend or ascend until united with the *One*, as in Neoplatonism. He was made from the dust of the earth but with the breath of life. He is clearly that extraordinary Idea, not of the brutes, not of the plants, nor of stone or wood, but born from the mouth of God and in his image. He is, as the Sephiroth has it, a "microcosm." Man alone of all the animals stands erect with head up to converse with the angels in heaven. His hands are midway between feet and head so they can reach toward the earth and work to support the body or reach upward toward heaven in contemplating eternal life.[27] But man is more than an effigy of this world. For the mind in man is called a god, the image of the highest and first Mind, either through homonymy or through participation. The rational soul which inclines its will through the mind to virtues and the best things is spoken of as a good demon or genius. That which draws the will through phantasy and depraved affections to vices and the worst things is named an evil demon. For this reason Pythagoras prayed God that He should free man from evil and show to all which demon they should employ.[28]

Man's crowning glory is his immortality. Precisely here lay the strength of the Pythagorean philosophy, for it supported the idea of resurrection and immortality where Aristotle was silent. For Aristotle believed nothing which he could not touch with his hand, see with his eyes, or apprehend with a syllogism. The followers of Lucian ridiculed Pythagoras, to be sure, but it is not for all to know the hidden mysteries, for all are not able to understand.[29] With the transmigration of the soul, the Pythagoreans really meant nothing else than the transmigration of the "spirit" of the Cabala.[30] The goal of both the Cabala and Pythagoras is to lead the souls of men back to the gods, that is, to raise them to perfect beatitude. In this life already they prepare men for the perpetual blessedness of the age to come.[31]

The road to such celestial preferment was for Reuchlin essentially ethical. On man's side there is need for moral effort. According to his rather superficial psychology human affections and passions are moved to joy or sorrow by the evidence of good or evil.[32] Moral alternatives are built into the very structure of the universe. That incorporeal heaven of the mid-world and the invisible olympus of the blessed admit nothing impure. For Pythagoras taught that if you live by right reason, sorrow over evil, and rejoice at good deeds, and if you have prayed that the gods will perfect your labor, then, having laid aside the body and ascended to heaven, you will become an immortal god.[33] "For this is the sum total of our philosophy," says Simon, "that by living well we may die well." There is then no need to fear Tartarus or the avenging furies.[34]

How do we know? The mechanism of Reuchlin's epistemology is basically the old Neoplatonic formula familiar with variations in the Christian tradition from Augustine to Hugh of St. Victor, Bonaventura, and beyond. Man is aided by an illumination from above. The exterior sense presents an object through its own medium to the interior sense. This in turn presents it to the imagination, imagination to judgment, judgment to reason, reason to intellect, intellect to mind, and mind to light, which illumines man and he takes up the illumination in himself.[35] A nobler knowledge results when the light of the mind, falling upon the intellect, moves the free will to believe. Knowledge acquired thus is far better than learning demonstrated by syllogisms. Revelation is the best source of all.[36]

Man as the mid-point of the universe acts toward things below through reason and toward things above by faith. Reason operates in the realm of *scientia*, faith in the realm of *sapientia*, a distinction as old as Augustine. The former is changeable and only knowledge which is reinforced by divine faith is certain.[37] Moreover, right faith is the door of miracles. The Neoplatonists Plotinus, Porphyry, and Iamblichus agreed that through God alone man has the power to send the good spirits against the evil. By faith the early Christians cast out devils, healed the sick, raised the dead, and performed similar miracles. The cabalists concur in this.[38]

The Cabala lifts men up from visible to invisible things, increases faith, confirms hope. This is the advantage of the Cabala over the Talmud, for the Talmudists stay in the sensible world and the cabalists raise men above creation to the world beyond.[39] In religion the faith of simplicity is better than the persuasive reason of inquisitiveness, as Athanasius put it. The twelve letters in the names for the three persons in the Trinity (אב בן ורוח הקדש), for example, are derived from the Tetragrammaton, the three in one and one in three. Oh how great is this height, how great this profundity, which is comprehended by faith alone! *Sola fide*! Faith alone — two words which were about to sound across Europe with a mighty thunder. Reuchlin used them often, but for him they meant a cognitive principle for trans-empirical reality. It was not the faith that moves mountains.[40]

Applying a modern solvent to Reuchlin's cosmology, it becomes readily apparent that it, too, was in essence the Neoplatonic great chain of being transmitted through cabalist channels. Cabalism came equipped with an elaborate cosmology. The *Opus de Breshith* (בראשית), the history of creation, was concerned with matters of natural science, just as the *Opus de Mercava* (מרכבה), the divine apparition to Ezekiel, with spiritual science or metaphysics. This was entirely to Reuchlin's taste. He referred often to the problems of nature as the problems of the origin of matter and the essence of time, distinct from those of metaphysics. He discussed them in the light of the Greek nature philosophers, Aristotle, and Pythagoras.[41] This world is but the imitator of the eternal incorporeal world which contains its first principles. These principles (ἀρχαὶ, beginnings) are ideas produced from the divine mind. Whereas the Talmudists take the terms "heaven and earth" in the creation story literally as form and matter, heaven as everything beyond the moon, the cabalists interpret them as a reference to corporeal and incorporeal, visible and invisible, sensible and mental, material and ideal, the world above and that below.[42] Beyond the lower corporeal world and the higher incorporeal world is that splendid dwelling place of the true gods in the sublime vertex of ether outside of time. The higher world flows into the whole lower world and the lowest are led back to the highest. But nothing creaturely can be led back to the third world, for nothing is by nature capable of such great sublimity except God. The third supreme world containing all the other worlds is of the Deity alone and is composed of the one divine essence. God existed before all else. He is the source of all things.[43]

The extent to which Reuchlin disengaged himself from the

magic and astrology often attached to this view of nature is laudable. Sebastian Brant had chided:

> The world is full of superstition
> Men prophesy by star's position
> And every fool deems this his mission.[44]

The Cabala, Reuchlin held, leads man to salvation, but magic to perdition. Miracles are done only in God's name and with his power and will. Like Pico, he rejected prediction by the stars, although a friend of his did do his horoscope and he had his playful moments.[45]

Reuchlin's cosmology was not simply a mechanical recapitulation of the Neoplatonist system. It was more than that. It was at least an attempt to maintain the unique Hebraic distinction between the Creator and creation, based in strong patristic tradition upon the concept of the *creatio ex nihilo* dating from the time of the Maccabees while accepting the Hellenic ontology describing nature as an emanation from an eternal source, being as the undifferentiated ground of all reality. Reuchlin made a brave, if not lucid, effort at this point to resolve the tensions between these two major components of Western culture.

Reuchlin's conception of God was a far cry from the staid scholastic premise of God as pure being. His picture was that of an ecstatic poet, transrational and enthusiastic. God, the author of light, dwells in the burning ether of eternity where there is no body, place, vacuum, time, old age, or change.[46] What God truly is we cannot know or understand, he writes in words reminiscent of Cusanus' *docta ignorantia*. God is both *Ens et nonens*. Dionysius the Areopagite in his book on mystic theology (*Celestial Hierarchy*) describes God as being neither number, nor order, nor one, nor unity. What then is He? Reuchlin has Hieronimus Simonides respond: "The more I think of it, the less I understand." If one were to ascend beyond all being, he would find nothing but an infinite sea of nothingness and the fountain of all being remaining forever in an abyss of shadows. "Oh the height! Oh the profundity! Oh our infirmity!" exclaimed Reuchlin. "What we know about Him, that which He has revealed to us about himself, ought to seem sufficient." [47]

Abscondite, beyond all comprehension, God is, nevertheless,

immanent in the world. Man moves in God and God dwells in man.[48] Nothing exists outside of God for He is the founding cause and the framer of all being.[49] God is our life principle. The Trinity can be compared with the sun, for as the sun has a globe, a ray, and a light, and all three are one sun, so the Father, Son, and Spirit are all one God.[50] Reuchlin quite naturally fitted his dynamic description of the transcendent yet immanent God into the orthodox definition.

The cabalists speculated much about the Messiah to come. Reuchlin could very easily transfer these impressive prophecies to Christ the Messiah who had already appeared. The very first Cabala confided to Adam after the fall and transmitted to the patriarchs to David, and through a long line of rabbis to Pico, was the promise that a Savior would be born who would abolish sin and win for man universal salvation. This pacific king would rule in a golden Messianic age.[51] This Messiah was the step on the cosmic ladder between the superior angelic world and that incomparable supersupreme third world where dwells the thrice-holy deity.[52] The association of this cabalist notion with the Johannine Logos came quite easily. The orthodox Christology of the eternal generation and incarnation followed then as a matter of course. Christ was the Son of God, the Word through whom all things were made, the image of the invisible God, Immanuel born of a virgin, the *virtus Dei*, the God-man, one with God himself (ὁμοούσιος).[53]

Reuchlin took special pains to refute the Nestorians, as he put it, and uphold a Pauline conception of Christ's person and work. The Talmudists, he charged, viewed the Messiah merely as a liberator from bodily captivity, warlike, conquering territories, and leading Israelite armies to victory. But the cabalists understood correctly that the Messiah would free miserable mortal humankind from the chains of sin, satisfy the merciful and forgiving God, so that through him man may live in eternity.[54] And yet the emphasis in Reuchlin is predominantly on the Christ who reveals God to man, the Word who illumines man through his mind's eye, who opens the last age of understanding.[55]

The discussion of the Messiah is without doubt the climax in both of Reuchlin's major works. All the lines of the argument converge on the revelation that "Jesus" is the wonder-working word and that the Tetractys of Pythagoras was but a symbol for the Tetragrammaton, those four letters from which the name of the Savior is composed.[56] Through this name many well attested miracles were performed in centuries past. Reuchlin's Christology remains more a matter of gnosis than atonement.

There is an unmistakable tendency in Reuchlin toward a religious universal theism. By the very nature of the evidence which he adduces to support Christian truth he lends a measure of authority to his non-Christian sources. The cabalists, Neoplatonists, Pythagoras, nature philosophers, Philo, Plato, Aristotle, and Mohammed are called upon to testify on such questions as immortality, miracles, and the nature of God. But he clearly used them to buttress the Catholic faith. He had no conscious intentions of raising them to its level, to say nothing of lowering the faith to their level. Did not Justin Martyr do the same? [57]

Reuchlin, old for those days and weary of controversy, lived on into the first five years of the Reformation. To Protestants like Flacius, Seckendorf, and D'Aubigné, he was, indeed, the bright morning star and the father of the Reformation, the "very source and fountain of the purest streams of Protestant intelligence." [58] The association of Reuchlin, whom Erasmus called "our Germany's glory," with the new movement was only natural. Luther had been sympathetic toward Reuchlin's cause. Melanchthon, the grandson of Reuchlin's sister Elisabeth, became Luther's lieutenant. On Melanchthon's urging Luther wrote a letter of encouragement to Reuchlin:

> Through your power the horns of this beast have been quite badly broken. Through you the Lord brought it about that the tyranny of the sophists has learned to attack the true friends of theology with greater caution, so that Germany could again breathe after having been not only oppressed but almost destroyed for some centuries thanks to scholastic theology. The beginning of a better knowledge could be made only through a man of great gifts. For just as God trod under into dust the greatest of all mountains, our Lord Christ (if one may use this analogy), and thereafter from this dust allowed so many mountains to arise, so you also would have brought forth little fruit, if you had not likewise been put to death and trod into the dust, from which so many defenders of the Holy Scriptures have arisen.[59]

Both Luther and Melanchthon appreciated Reuchlin's contribution to language study which was so crucial also in the reformer's drive to the sources. But Reuchlin did not reciprocate. He stayed in the home of Luther's foe Dr. Eck, while teaching at Ingolstadt. There out of love for books he prevailed on Eck not to burn Luther's works. But Reuchlin was aloof and then hostile to the Reformation. Erasmus wrote Reuchlin that he always tried to separate his affair from that of Luther. If the friends of learning, he opined, had been united things might not have come to such an uproar.[60]

Erasmus himself had never found the Cabala or Talmud pleasant, preferring the classics. Luther and Melanchthon disparaged cabalistic nonsense, though Melanchthon found some good in it. How remarkable that with the notable exception of Eck, Reuchlin's pupils became leaders in the Protestant movement, so that Germany and Switzerland became centers of Hebrew scholarship down to our day.[61] One of Reuchlin's favorite students, Johann Forster, worked with Luther as a Hebraist on the translation of the Old Testament. Hutten was furious with Reuchlin himself for turning from Luther and his true friends to kiss the feet of Leo.[62] "Oh ye immortal gods, what do I see?" exclaimed Hutten.

In answer to Hutten, it is possible to point to a number of differences between Reuchlin and Luther which make his stand seem not at all surprising. "God be praised," Reuchlin is reported to have said, "that now the monks have found someone else who will give them more to do than I." But his relief was short-lived, for the conflict soon reached a crescendo louder by far than his own controversy. Reuchlin disliked polemics and he wanted no part of it. Perhaps Reuchlin may have felt that the Reformation was damaging to the free scholarship and research which as a humanist he prized. Reuchlin had cited with approval Pythagoras' use of symbols to confuse and flaunt the common crowd, those cheapjacks and hecklers. Reuchlin's work was esoteric and elitist, intended for the educated also among Mohammedans and Jews.[63] Luther turned to the people, whom he loved. Reuchlin remained a good Catholic to the end and seems even to have become a tertiary in the Augustinian order before his death. But Luther, too, had been a most devout monk. All these explanations are merely peripheral. The main difference between them lay elsewhere.

The real obstacle which kept Reuchlin from crossing over to Luther's position was the tremendous chasm lying between their theologies. Copernicus in the preface to his *De revolutionibus orbium caelestium* relates that he was inspired by the Pythagoreans to his theory of the earth in motion about the sun. Reuchlin had missed it there. Luther was the Copernicus of theology, returning to the Christo-centrism of that religious Aristarchus, Saint Paul. Reuchlin had failed to read him aright. There was, then, a wide gulf between Reuchlin's anthropology, cosmology, theology, and Luther's Pauline christology. This was the basic difference between them.

Reuchlin's religious philosophy was more than a mere haphazard eclecticism. It is a mistake to dismiss it as merely the *diliramenta Cabalae*. He wove many threads of the Western intellectual tradition into an organic texture. His ideas were more than poetic effusions. They had a deep objective connection. As Kristeller demonstrated in the case of Ficino, Renaissance philosophy had both rhyme and reason. Goethe could rightly pay him tribute in *Zahme Xenien* (V):

> Reuchlin! Who would himself with him compare,
> In his own time a wondrous sign so rare!

Reuchlin's philosophy was predominantly a *philosophia supernaturalis*. His great emphasis on faith as the major tool for knowledge and the elixir of life eternal suggests that, far from being the pre-dawn herald of the age of reason, he was more believing than his rationalistic scholastic contemporaries. He transcended reason in the narrow sense of logic and syllogism. He soared beyond measure in the classic sense. There is a distinct parallel to the reaction of the late-thirteenth-century cabalists against the overintellectualism of Moses Maimonides and the Jewish scholastics. Since Lovejoy's appropriate strictures, one hesitates to use the word "romanticism" without due qualification. But at least in a very general sense, Reuchlin's mentality seems nearer the romantic than the rationalistic pole. The easy association of Renaissance and *Aufklärung*, so often made, needs serious restudy.[64]

Reuchlin's achievement had an independent value even when compared with that of the great Florentines Ficino and Pico. There can be no doubt that Ficino's contribution to Renaissance philosophy with his detailed exposition of the complex Neoplatonic conception of the universe was the more important in over-all terms. The revival of "Platonism" provided a congenial atmosphere for the growth among Christian scholars of interest in the Cabala, so heavily laden with Platonic mysticism. This was the major debt which Reuchlin and the cabalists owed to the sage of Careggi.

Pico, on the other hand, was an innovator precisely in his introduction of the Cabala to Christian philosophers. Others had preceded him in mentioning the Cabala and in its study, but he was the first to put it to a decisive and dramatic use. He saw the possibilities in the Cabala for the Christian thinker, the authority of antiquity in Hebrew, the value of an oral tradition, the fascination of esoteric symbolism, and the utility of a source outside revelation (*scientia*) for supporting Christian dogma. He was original in this area and Reuchlin was his debtor. Pico had new and creative ideas, but he lacked the temperament and the time to work his brilliant conceptions into a complete coherent system. His total contribution amounted to 119 theses out of 900 in the *Conclusiones*, together with the appropriate retrenchment and rubrics in his *Apologia*. There is nothing of value in his other works and correspondence. Pico aimed at fitting the cabalist philosophy into an all-embracing system and thereby lost his kingdom in a gamble on world conquest. But, then, he died at thirty-one, two years younger than Alexander. Reuchlin lived longer and had the patient scholarship to work out in detail the lines of thought which Pico had merely suggested. The dialogue form which he adopted was unfortunate, it is true, in making his argument indirect and meandering. But it served as a useful device for bringing out several points of view and objections at various levels. Moreover, it is possible with due perseverance to discover in Reuchlin an elaborate synthetic philosophy which nature and time had denied to Pico. This was Reuchlin's major achievement, whatever it was worth religiously and philosophically.

It is quite clear that, although Reuchlin's essential Christianity was rooted in Northern piety, the positive philosophical influences on his constructive theology, except for the major role of Cusanus, were essentially Italian in origin. What was novel came from the

South, from Italy and indirectly from Spain. But the nature of that influence has been misunderstod. Now that we appreciate more fully the Christian concerns of the Italian humanists, thanks to the work of the revisionists, we are in a better position to assess the goals and methods of the Northern humanists, such as Reuchlin. In the *guerre de savants* that has raged over this question, some right, as usual, must be conceded to both sides.[65] Recent research has disclosed that Reuchlin before his death was ordained into the priesthood, a practice common to some of the very pious.[66] Reuchlin's design was to use Pythagoras and Cabala for Christ. When Reuchlin's days were ended on June 30, 1522, Hutten's brave words rang out after him: "Who lives thus never dies."

V

CELTIS

The Arch-Humanist

ONRAD Celtis, the best lyric poet among the German humanists, illustrates the possibilities and the limitations in the contributions of poetic culture to the renaissance of Christendom.
Like Reuchlin he was informally a student of Agricola and both
were present at their master's death, but unlike Reuchlin, he took
a less constructive attitude toward the church and theology. He
was the first major German humanist to get his basic humanist
education in the North before his Italian journey. He became in
turn the teacher of reformers such as Vadian and Zwingli. Representative of a vanishing species, the *Wandervögel* of the early
phase of humanism, Celtis belonged to the generation of humanists
which lived on the eve of the Reformation as yet untouched by the
new religious power of the evangelical movement. This fact adds
to his value as a case study in the religious thought and lay-reform-
ing mentality of a leading intellectual during the time when the
medieval tide was running out.

Celtis was born in 1459, a peasant's son, in a village near
Würzburg in central Germany. He ran away to school, studying
at Cologne, Heidelberg, Rostock and Leipzig. Celtis then began
what he referred to as his ten years of wandering. In 1487 he
crossed the Alps for a quick tour of Italy, doing Venice, Padua,
Bologna, Florence, and Rome. But after unpleasant experiences
with the superiority complex of the Italian humanists, he hurried
back to Cracow and moved on from there to Nuremberg and Ingolstadt. After a bumptious career there as professor of rhetoric he
accepted the invitation of Maximilian to the University of Vienna
in 1497. He founded the College of Poets and Mathematicians,

wrote poems and plays, and taught until his premature death in 1508, a victim of syphilis.[1]

When Emperor Frederick III crowned the twenty-eight-year-old Celtis with laurel upon the citadel at Nuremberg on April 18, 1487, he made him the first German poet laureate of the Empire. Though at the time Celtis hardly deserved such an honor, he lived to become the best lyric poet among the German humanists, whose ambition it was to be remembered as the German Horace. "Oh sacred and mighty work of the poets," he declaimed, "you alone free all things from fate and lift up mortal ashes to the stars!" [2] The influence of Italian humanism can be most plainly seen in the poets, for the purest type of humanist *poeta* was to be found in Renaissaince Italy. But Celtis had some predecessors among the Germans, the pioneers of early humanism like Peter Luder, who moved restlessly through the land, wandering through Italy and Greece, lecturing on poetry and rhetoric in Heidelberg and other German universities where he scandalized his scholastic colleagues with his verse and way of life. Luder's Latin speeches, his poems praising the Elector, and his laudatory description of Heidelberg all reflected the influence of Italian humanism, though his traveling about was reminiscent also of the medieval traditions of wandering students and troubadours. In the sixteenth century this type became extremely rare and among the Germans one can point with a measure of justice only to Hutten's teacher Aesticampianus, Hermann von dem Busche, and Jacob Locher. Celtis opened Book Four of his *Amores* with an elegy in "praise of wandering and what is necessary for a knowledge of wisdom and philosophy." Leave the paternal herd and behold foreign stars, he urges, if you wish to travel celestial paths. If you want to learn the secret causes of nature, then visit different lands to your own profit.

Celtis was the one really genial personality among the German humanists. As a university professor he was the dean's despair, for he dismissed classes for weeks at a time while he went to visit a friend and missed many a lecture while he went off to taste the new wines. "May sweet liberty remain mine!," he exclaimed.[3] Celtis was a great though fickle lover, who lived his conviction that love is the most ingratiating, natural, and powerful of all human drives. "Nothing more beautiful has been created under the fiery sun," he penned, "than an alluring young woman who relieves one of weighty cares." [4] His own *Amores* celebrated in four books four of his loves — Hasilina, Elsula, Ursula, and Barbara Cimbrica — symbolizing the four parts of Germany. Hasilina, the young wife of an old Polish nobleman, his mistress in Cracow, once wrote chiding him for all the embarrassment his published poems describing their intimacies were causing her. A dinner guest had even read them at the table, which proved to be understandably disconcerting to her. But Celtis was merely carrying out his threat to make her known throughout the world if she spurned his love. His love poems are frank and revealing, erotic and physical, spontaneous revelations. The poet at a stage of sensitivity beyond the strictly rational arrives at a condition characteristic of mankind before the inhibitions of logic direct thought into preestablished channels. *Es denkt in ihm*, as C. G. Jung explains this phenomenon — thoughts happen in him. This process of unconscious response and irresponsible reaction is evident in the lines of Celtis' poetry. He was by nature a poet whose work could in part draw its life from the life of mankind. But he was not a great poet, for his preoccupation with his particularized self, his life, enemies, debts, diseases, and women inspired poems which were not sufficiently and generally meaningful to all men. This weakness was a limitation of the man Celtis and cannot be ascribed merely to the form or pattern of his poetry which was imitative of the classics. He did have original creative impulses and he did produce some successful passages. In the *Odes* he rises to high levels in writing of life, love, and learning. His Epigrams were often clever and cutting. His own individual self interested him the most. From Cicero and Horace he learned the sophist-rhetorical theory of the art of poetry as a passionate and rousing power, the motif of poetic madness and intoxication. He was fond of the term *vates*, restored to favor by Virgil, which meant the poet-philosopher, the prophet or sage. The true poet or *vates* has a divine genius which leads his spirit to strive heavenward.

Celtis represented the two major tendencies in German humanism, both the mounting tide of romantic cultural nationalism and the interest in religious enlightenment. Once again studying the changes which humanism underwent as it crossed the Alps proves to be instructive. The movement from the city-state nexus in Italy to the larger concept, however vague, of empire was reflected in the strongly national feeling of the German humanists. In the case of Celtis it was largely a cultural nationalism inspired by a jaundice against Italian superiority and a new love of the fatherland. Celtis' love for Germany was stronger than that of all the earlier humanists and could be rivaled only by that of Wimpfeling and Hutten. He was zealous in searching out cultural documents of her past. He was without reserve in singing her praises. On a hilltop overlooking the walls and spires of Cracow, he recalls, Apollo had appeared to him in a vision and had urged him to "rise and let his members seize their ancient vigor so that he might sing of the four corners of his fatherland." [5] In his *Ode to Apollo* he called upon the god to bring the muses like the imperium northward:

> Phoebus, who the sweet-noted lyre constructed,
> Leave fair Helicon and depart your Pindus,
> And by pleasant song designated, hasten
>   To these our borders.

His *Inaugural Address* at the University of Ingolstadt rang with a fervor not unlike that of Fichte's *Speeches to the German Nation* as Celtis summoned his Germans to a cultural rivalry with Italy. Arminius was his hero as well as Hutten's.

In 1500 Celtis published Tacitus' *Germania* as a student text. He was the first humanist to lecture on Tacitus in a German university. He ignored the earlier fantastic accounts of the Trojan descent of the Germans and accepted the dictum of Tacitus that *Germani sunt indigenae*. His interest in establishing the high level of culture among the Germans during the Middle Ages was the chief stimulus to his search for documents which produced the famous codex of Roswitha's plays dating from the Ottonian Renaissance and the epic poem of Ligurinus which in ten books praised the deeds of Frederick Barbarossa. In the preface to the Ligurinus edition of 1507 Celtis' humanist friends spoke of that *peculiaris amor patriae* which had inspired the whole undertaking.[6] The Germans were the inventors, he boasted, not only of destructive gunpowder, but of that greatest boon to learning, the printing press, a discovery which he celebrated in verse. The poem

Germania Generalis which Celtis published with the Tacitus edition was intended to be a preliminary for the *Germania Illustrata*, that poetic historico-geographical compilation which Celtis intended to be his major work. His splendid descriptive book on Nuremberg, the *Norimberga*, was to serve as an example of what the complete *Germania Illustrata* would be like. It was to weave together history, topography, and a picture of life in the cities in one grand glorification of the fatherland, an idea doubtless inspired by Biondo's *Italia Illustrata*. But Celtis' work remained in fragments, in spite of the aid of many humanist comrades, largely because of its impossibly grand design and because of Celtis' own general disorganization.

The shadow side of this patriotic drive was his antagonism toward all others, especially toward the Jews, Bohemians, and Italians. His many epigrams on Rome are for the most part satirical and hostile. When, for example, workmen discovered the well-preserved body of a Roman girl in the Via Appia in 1485, Celtis took the occasion for a jibe at Italian decadence:

> Concerning a Girl Found at Rome
> A thousand years enclosed within this tomb I lay
> Now released from this tomb to you Romans I say:
> I do not now see Roman citizens in the manner of old,
> Distinguished for justice and men of piety.
> But with sad heart I look upon such great ruins,
> Now only a monument to the men of times past.
> And if again I shall see you after a hundred years,
> Scarcely anything I think will be left of the Roman name.[7]

Celtis, in fact, was torn between his admiration for the culture of the Italian Renaissance and his hostility to the Italians, just as he was caught between his dedication to the high literary classic culture of the ancient Greeks and Romans and at the same time to the noble innocence of the primitive Germans and contemporary simple men of nature, the speechless Lapps. Celtis' antipathy toward the superior Italian humanists was very easily transferred to Italian churchmen as well. He not only reflected the anticurial sentiment of the Germans in those decades, but he added to it with his poems against the supreme pontiff and his court. Typical was his proud repugnance at having to kiss the foot of Pope Innocent VIII:

> Concerning the kiss of the Emperor and of the Pope
> When you gave the sacred crown, Frederick, my Emperor,
> You placed bland kisses on our cheeks.
> But when at Rome I saw the house of Innocent (Nocentis),
> He commanded me to kiss his foot.
> I, lying prone, gave kisses, but the lips of Caesar
>   delight me more
> Than to give kisses to a noxious foot.[8]

"Take up again, Oh German men," he exclaimed in his *Inaugural Address*, "that old spirit of yours with which you so many times were a terror and specter to the Romans!" Certainly these were themes and sentiments which were portentous for the coming Reformation struggle with Rome.

Celtis was above all the great organizer of the humanists. If in Agricola's generation the humanists were culturally isolated, Celtis' special genius as a gregarious personality with a flair for the dramatic was to bring the humanists together into sodalities and inspire them to mutual aid and comfort. He drew the humanists of the upper Rhine into a loose association known as the Rhenish Sodality. Later upon his arrival in Vienna he called into being a similar organization known as the Danubian Sodality. Other local societies of the humanists sprang up under his aegis in Linz, Ingolstadt, Augsburg, Olmütz, and perhaps Leipzig. Wimpfeling followed suit in Strassburg and the circles of Mutian and Pirckheimer were analogous. It is striking to note how many of the members were laymen, especially professional people like doctors and lawyers. With the blessing and support of Maximilian, Celtis founded the College of Poets and Mathematicians at the University of Vienna, chartered in 1501, for the express purpose of promoting humanistic and natural scientific studies. His enthusiasm was so contagious that in 1507 Nicolas Gerbellius, one of his students and a member of the Rhenish Sodality, wrote to Trithemius: "I congratulate myself often on living in this glorious century in which so many remarkable men have arisen in Germany." Celtis tried to recruit the *sodales* as contributors to his *Germania Illustrata* and engage them in other patriotic tasks. The feeling of collective strength and the consciousness of belonging to a movement opposed to conservative scholastic theology gave to the humanists a sense of cohesion and confidence which stood them in good stead during the Reuchlin controversy which shook the world of humanism and during the first years of the Reformation when many stood on Luther's side. When in 1512 Beatus Rhenanus cited the humanists who under the leadership of Erasmus were the real ornaments of Germany, almost half of those whom he named were alumni of Celtis' sodalities.

Celtis delighted in being addressed as a "doctor of the threefold philosophy." With this *triformis philosophia* he meant both the wisdom to be gained from Latin, Greek, and Hebrew literature and the traditional *philosophia spiritualis*, *moralis*, and *naturalis*. In the woodcut of "Philosophia" done for the *Amores* in the work-shop of Albrecht Dürer and based upon sketches of the great master himself, Philosophy is given these lines to speak (figure 3):

> Whatever heaven contains, what earth, the air and the water,
> Whatever can exist among all the things that are human,
> Whatever the fire-god makes in the whole circle of earth,
> All that I, Philosophy, carry within my own breast.[9]

Philosophy in the broad sense of the term meant for Celtis all the humanist knowledge to which rhetoric and divine poetry held the key. Together with his Inaugural Address, Celtis published an ode to a friend of Cracow days, Sigismund Fusilius, on what the young philosopher ought to know. In it he stresses Roman grammar first, then astronomy, geography, history, contempt of fortune, and moral philosophy. "Discover," Celtis urges, "with soaring mind the causes of individual things!" [10] The ode concludes with a bit of moral philosophy on following the path of virtue to the heavenly home:

> Scorn the favor of unstable fortune
> And learn to bear hard blows.
> All your days will thus pass for you
> In blessed time.
>
> Rise and high-minded mount up
> The straight and narrow path of virtue
> Which alone enables you
> To lead a life secure.
>
> Virtue alone promising pleasant honors
> Offers blessedness in the heavenly abode
> And removes fear of the black shadows
> In the Stygian prison.

Of the three divisions of philosophy, Celtis was least concerned with moral philosophy. In his way of life he separated the aesthetic from the ethical. In his writings he could not stand the strain of moralizing. Some of his passages have the making of a morality religion, such as his Ode to Sebaldus, for example, in which he praises the active life, suggests educational reform, urges the care of the temple, and praises the gift of a good conscience. But he concludes the Ode with the words: "But refrain, Clio, from describing the fate of wicked men with a more severe song, restore Bacchus, who is accustomed to more gentle muses!" [11] His customary advice is to banish cares with sleep, sadness with wine, and to seize the joys of a short life which flees like a shadow. "Whatever the truth is," he wrote in an epigram to Jove, "may we seize the joys of a doubtful life, since it will return to nothing, for it once was nothing." [12]

Celtis made just a few gestures in the direction of developing a moral philosophy, but they remained merely gestures for the most part. He discussed with one of his Ingolstadt students his plan of writing a little work entitled *De vera nobilitate*, on the true nobility which stems from the virtue of good deeds. [13] He also made a playful comparison of the gladiator's combat and moral philosophy. [14] Some of his admonitions have the makings of a primitive morality religion. Thus he says that the man who is fortified by virtue is worthy of the love of the gods and the scepter of Jove, so that when he has left this transient earth he will be included in the company of the divine heroes. [15] He repeatedly ties in the life of virtue with the gift of immortality and the reward of heaven. Honesty and virtue alone promise immortality in the world, together with the learned songs of which posterity approves. [16] Again, he affirms, the sacred writings teach that the Lord will place man's soul in heaven, if by imitating His sacred laws he bravely spurns the perishable joys of the false world. [17] He is satisfied with commending the quiet wisdom of the ancients as the highest goal. What he has to say about the independence of man from external influences, of virtue and self-control is typically moralistic humanism. This emphasis no doubt prompted him to publish with his domestic poem *Oeconomia* on the philosopher's household two selections from the fourth-century poet Ausonius. Perhaps Celtis was attracted to Ausonius because of his poetic descriptions of the Mosel River region of Germany. Ausonius as a reluctant convert to Christianity with great love for the classic past was spiritually a mirror-image of Celtis, who came a thousand years later in the Christian era and experienced the joys of conversion to classic letters. Celtis published Ausonius' *Ad Drepanum de ludo septem sapientum* and the accompanying explanations, *Sententiae septem sapientum septenis versibus explicate.* Ausonius has the seven sages of Greece deliver in his defective verse their wisdom for life, reflecting especially the influence of Terence and Plautus. This wisdom consists of such wholesome and wholly banal sayings such as: know thyself; judge no man happy until he is dead; never too much; nothing demands greater care than to think what must be done; water is the basic principle. Celtis clearly had not chanced upon either great poetry or great moral philosophy here.

When Celtis spoke of philosophy in the narrower sense he meant natural philosophy almost exclusively. He had a passionate interest in everything that *parens natura* creates and orders. She is the exemplar and mirror of life, the proper object of devoted study. Throughout his writings Celtis emphasizes repeatedly this one basic theme — the need to explore the basis and cause of all things in nature, to learn to know the inner essence of the universe, its principle of unity and all its parts, and to reveal the works of nature through mathematical truth. This idea lay behind the peculiar combination of poets and mathematicians in the Vienna College. Cicero's program for "learning to know the causes of things" appealed also to Virgil. This ideal of the intellectual pursuit under Lucretian influence still inspired the imperial poets whom Celtis admired. Like them he offered theories far removed from experimental foundations. What are the hidden powers of nature? he asked. How did the "wandering seeds of the earth" develop out of the lap of chaos? He really believed that he was seriously philosophizing when he treated questions of natural philosophy poetically.

Celtis derived his love of nature and interest in natural philosophy from very divergent sources. Memories of his early days among the vine-clad hills along the beautiful Main River valley stayed with him his whole life. At Cologne University he learned to know the natural scientific writings of Albertus Magnus, who remained his idol ever after. Albertus Magnus, the great Dominican scholastic, was educated primarily in Padua, where he was introduced to the writings of Aristotle. He studied theology in Bologna and Paris and taught at Cologne where he died in 1280. He had a remarkable knowledge of mechanics and chemistry and with the possible exception of Roger Bacon he was the most widely read scholar of his day in this area. The best student of Aristotle up to his time, he was influenced also by Neoplatonic thought more than was the younger Aquinas, which made his thought even more congenial to Celtis. Celtis dedicated two epigrams to Albertus celebrating him for his genius which revealed to the Germans what the earth, sea, and atmosphere contain. To learn true doctrine one must read his brilliant writings.[18] In Dürer's woodcut in the *Amores*, Philosophy pronounces these lines:

The Greeks call me Sophia, the Latins Sapientia,
The Egyptians and Chaldaeans discovered me, the Greeks wrote of me,
The Latins translated me, the Germans glorified me.[19]

The philosophers pictured to represent the contributions of each people are Ptolemy for the Egyptians and Chaldaeans, Plato for the Greeks, Cicero and Virgil for the Latins, and Albertus Magnus for the Germans. Celtis was evidently quite impressed with the *Summa de Creaturis*. Cusanus influenced his thought on the problem of the relation of God to nature. Agricola inspired his interest in direct observation of the world itself. At least the year after his contact with Agricola he wrote in his *Ars versificandi et carminum* (1486) lines which could just as well have been those of Agricola:

For the true poet's task is to present in picturesque and beautiful garment of speech and of song the customs, affairs, happenings, localities, peoples, lands, rivers, the course of the stars, the true essence of all things, and what moves the heart of man.

These interests were further reinforced by his contacts with Pomponius Laetus and Callimachus of the Roman Academy as well as by his studies in Cracow with Albert Brudzewo, a student of Peuerbach and Regiomontanus and the teacher of Copernicus.

Celtis was attracted to the cosmology of Lucius Apuleius, a Platonic philosopher and rhetorician born in Madaura in Numidia about A.D. 125, best known for his *Metamorphoses* or *Golden Ass*, which revealed the influence of the Egyptiac Isis mystery religion. Celtis lectured in Vienna on Apuleius' *De Mundo*, and shortly after his arrival there he published an edition of it for the use of his students.[20] Celtis offered this small edition as an appetizer, "a little morsel such as the merchants offer prospective customers so that they might be drawn as by an appetizing drink to the mysteries which are treated in philosophy and divine poetry." The student could learn from it, Celtis explained, the process of the creation of the world-all, how it was framed and how it exists as a whole and in all its parts, "according to the number and order of that Creator and Father of all things with the highest wisdom and wonderful beauty." Things divine and human are inseparably bound together in the universe by love, Amor, Celtis continues, so that to contemplate on it in this short life is a worthy preoccupation, for the spirit is thereby lifted up from its bonds into divine and heavenly realms and enjoys a taste of eternal salvation. It shares in the tables of the gods with the nectar and ambrosia of Jupiter.[21]

Apuleius' *De Mundo* was a loose translation and adaptation of a work of the early second century after Christ, Περὶ κόσμου, attributed to Aristotle and Theophrastus. The treatise begins with the thought that philosophy which shares in divine things is concerned with the interpretation of nature and the investigation of things invisible to the eyes. The world is made up of the heavens, the abode of the gods, and the earth. There follows then a discussion of the stars, ether, the elements, planets, seas, islands, winds, nature, and music. God, the author and governor of all things, is present in all things, an opinion held by all the *vates*. He is the ruler also of the heavenly bodies and the Divine Mind affects everything. Just as one cannot see the mind of man but only what man does, so one cannot see God, but only his working in the cosmos. He is in the world giving commands like the captain of a ship. As Plato held, God, the Divine Reason, rules through principles and sacred laws. Apuleius clearly belonged to those men whom Celtis had praised in his Inaugural Address as those "who reveal the work of nature and the wisdom of its Governor by mathematical truth and who go a little further into things than the common crowd."

The Platonic and Pseudo-Aristotelian cosmology lent itself very nicely in Celtis' philosophy to a Neoplatonic elaboration, just as it had in the intellectual experience of late antiquity. Celtis became increasingly obsessed with the Neoplatonic view of the universe as an organism tied together by sympathetic bonds. This was the highly spiritualized Renaissance view of the world exemplified by Ficino. It in turn influenced Copernicus, who was more of a Pythagorean than empiricist, Bruno, and Kepler. Ficino had described this macro-microcosm, the sympathy of the world above and that below in poetic prose, describing the influence of heavenly rays on stones, plants, animals, the bodies and the souls of men. Like Ficino, Celtis explained phenomena such as the tides as demonstrating the regular breathing of the world, a living organism. He wrote:

> Everything in the world has its own special ray, since all the stars of the heaven move under the earth. But the human spirit excels every living thing through its rays, for its own seeds rise from related stars and it is said to stand near to the etherial gods.[22]

In the dedication of the *Amores* to Emperor Maximilian, Celtis celebrated love as the principle which unites the entire universe. Through love, he explained, heaven and earth and all creatures are by nature attracted to each other and are drawn to mingle with each other through a secret agreement. Through divine love for his creatures the Creator (as one can read in Ovid's *Metamorphoses*) separated heaven, earth, and all parts of the universe which lay confused in chaos and bound them together with the firm bond of love. This is the love which the philosophers call fire, water, vapor, or air as the principle of nature, but which we call "Deus optimus maximus." The great Master-Craftsman created everything out of love, Celtis continues, and placed in man a greater portion of love, for man was to be the highest creature. "We, however," Celtis explains, "name Him the highest God who made man from a lump of earth and slime and implanted in him as in all living beings, plants and seeds, yes in inanimate things as stones and colors, the power and characteristics of love, so that they as a result of a natural relationship and a silent inner agreement seek and desire to join each other." Through love the cosmos and its glorious beauty arose and continues to exist. Through love the cities, states, and empires arise and continue to exist. So great is the communion between heaven and earth through mutual love that the poets symbolize it with the marriage of the gods and goddesses.[23] In tone this preface to the *Amores* is reminiscent of Lucretius' *Ode to Venus* as the creator of all things. Thus man and the universe are bound by the same laws best described through the Neoplatonic love and light metaphysic. This Neoplatonic nature-mysticism dazzled the poet himself, who was moved to confess: "Who can give a sure account of the causes of all natural appearances? Weak is our conjecture, shaky and uncertain our combination." [24]

Like Ficino and other humanists inspired by late antique philosophy, Celtis was a firm believer in astrology. Many of his contemporaries like the Abbot Trithemius, Lorenz Beheim, Heinrich Bebel, or Johannes Tolhopf were fascinated with the occult, with alchemy and astrology. He learned from Macrobius, a fifth-century grammarian, that the seven planets control the fate of men.[25] In an ode to Albert Brudzewo, his Cracow astronomy professor, Celtis pronounced that the stars determine the fates of men and that poet-philosophers can by astrology foretell the future.[26] In the preface to the *Amores* Celtis declares one purpose of the work to be a demonstration of the influence of the stars on human life. The major source of this whole belief was clearly the Neoplatonic light metaphysic. Through the mixture of their rays, Celtis believed, the stars determine the characteristics of things, binding and loosening body and soul.

Celtis was completely caught up by this sidereal delusion. Only once does he protest that the astrologers should cease and desist because Jove, after all, rules in the sky.[27] Usually he merely attacks their ignorance, their errors, and their greed, rather than their basic premises.[28] This combination of protest against the grotesque aspects of astrology and a basic belief in it was common among the humanists. Ficino himself, in spite of his own polemic against the errors of this dangerous science, allowed a broad range of influence to the stars. Astrology was much at home in the North among peasants, shepherds, businessmen, chancellors, and even church dignitaries. Aquinas had called astrology the devil's work but had nevertheless allowed the stars an influence on body-build, differences of sex, and other personal characteristics. Dante had limited the area of its influence without denying its validity altogether.

It would perhaps be expecting too much in an age when popes and cardinals indulged in this superstition to look for a clean break from the humanists who were sodden with the lore of late antiquity. Pico as in so many ways was quite exceptional in arguing against astrology in his *Disputationes adversus astrologiam divinatricem.* Thomas Murner in his youthful work *Invectiva contra astrologos* called astrology a madness which subverted the free will of man. Nevertheless, he believed that the signs of the heavens have much to teach about sickness, storms, and the like. In his *De verbo mirifico* Reuchlin cursed the ideas of the superstitious astrologers who erred from mathematics and astronomy. But he himself consulted horoscopes and made a few grudging concessions. Trithemius in his *Epistolae ad familiares* protested against the errors of the common crowd and the vicious deceptions of the astrologers. But it was this same Trithemius whose phantastic idea of basing a philosophy of history on an angel-planetary myth marked the high point in the triumphal procession of astrology in this century which saw its greatest successes. The contrast with some late scholastics and with the reformers is instructive. Heinrich von Langenstein, for example, in his *Tractatus physicus de habitudine causarum et influxu naturae communis respectu inferiorum* (1407) concluded that secondary causes can have only a limited influence on the lower world, for only God works through intelligence and will. Therefore, astrology contradicts philosophy and truth. Luther, in turn, appealed to Scriptural and Augustinian arguments against astrology because of the exclusiveness of God's sovereignty and on experiential grounds.

Celtis found the whole delusion too congenial to his personal penchant for phantasy and too well adapted to his nature mysticism to give it up. On the other hand, his whole personality was much too ebullient, sanguine, and choleric to allow him any brooding over the melancholy influences of Saturn.[29] Celtis was familiar with this nexus of ideas, for during his visit in Florence Ficino was working on his "dietetic of the Saturnine man," the *De vita triplici.* Dürer associated the idea of melancholy with the cold North in the woodcut of "Philosophia" in the *Amores.* But Celtis was too much the activist and too little the reflective thinker to sink into the grip of futile melancholy.

A great admirer of Reuchlin, Celtis found a certain fascination in Pythagorean number-mysticism. He toys in his poetry with numerology, with combinations of threes, fours, and sevens, but this is all more a pleasant game than a serious pursuit. Similarly he plays poetically with the idea of magic and witchcraft, but once again he heaps ridicule upon their serious practitioners.[30] Fortune-tellers boldy trifle with God's secrets. Alchemists are sunk in greed. Palmists might as well read the soles of the feet, for they know nothing of the science of astrology or horoscopes. Celtis represented a strange amalgam of superstitious and enlightened elements.

Of all the German humanists, Celtis in an irresponsible way raised some of the most searching theological questions. God is both immanent in nature and in man, he believed, and at the same time God is abscondite and unknowable, a strange paradox. Celtis, a student of Mutian, shared some of his teacher's theological conceptions as well as many of his doubts. He owned by theft from the Benedictine monastery of Tegernsee the Platonic commentary *Chalcidius super Timaeum Platonis*. He read in Ovid's *Metamorphoses* of Eros as the divine principle of unity and of the "god within us." [31] But, above all, Celtis owed his conception of God in nature to Ficino and his conception of the abscondite nature of God to Cusanus.

Ficino in his *De vita coelitus comparanda* urged men to remain in the free heaven, in high and pleasant places where the rays of the stars might work on man unhindered. Light, sunlight, and wine are particularly essential for the sunny nature of literary people. The idea of the macro-microcosm was basic in the religious thought of the Florentine Neoplatonists. God is within us. We are little gods. Celtis was neither a philosopher nor was he so religious as Ficino. He was not concerned as Ficino was with apologetic responsibilities and not interested at all in combining scholastic and Platonic philosophies into a new synthesis. He never experienced Ficino's mystical desire and thirst of the soul for communion with the divine. Ficino was a sensitive priest and Celtis was a bold poet who dared to seek God where he would.

In the *Vita* appended to the 1513 Strassburg edition of the *Odes*, Celtis' friends called him a lover of the sun, woods, and mountains. It was in nature that he loved to seek God. In an ode he exclaimed:

I would behold the flaming fire of heaven, of the sea and of the earth, and I would learn to know the causes of the wind, the fog, and the snow! I would find Thee, Father of all things, through whom the immeasurable world has been established and whose nod would send it reeling off into chaos again! Omnipresent the Spirit sweeps through the world, enlivening every single part, whom only pure minds are able to see and apprehend.[32]

At times, though not often, he even put his natural religion in antithesis to ecclesiastical religion. In a sharp ode addressed to Crispus, the buffoon of the poets, he contrasted the beauties of worship in nature with the noisy shouting of the dullard priest preaching to a crowd of ignorant people.[33] His most radical expression of the advantages of a natural over an institutional religion was his bitter ode against one of his own critics:

> To Sepulus the Superstitious
> You marvel that I never move my lips in any church
> Murmuring through my teeth in prayer.
> The reason is that the great divine Will of Heaven
> Hears the small inner voice.
> You marvel that you so seldom see me
> Dragging my feet into the temples of the gods.
> God is within us. I do not need to meditate on Him
> In painted churches.
> You marvel that I love to seek the open waters
> And the warm sun.
> It is there that the mighty image of omnipotent Jupiter appears to me.
> There are the highest temples of God.
> The woods are pleasing to the Muses, a city is hateful to poets
> And so is the evil of milling crowds.
> Go now and deride my gods with your foolish words,
> My blustering Sepulus! [34]

And yet, for all his stress upon the immanence of the divine in nature and in man, Celtis was struck by the abscondite and unknowable nature of God. Is there a God? If so, what is his nature? "Does God concern himself with the world, at work within its mass," he queried, "or has He withdrawn from His work, so that all depends upon chance and fate and God comes staggering after with an uncertain step?" [35] In his approach to the problem of the nature of God Celtis was furthest removed from the positive theology of the scholastics and most in the tradition of the negative theology, familiar in the mystic tradition from Dionysius the Areopagite to

Nicholas Cusanus. Following the doctrine of the analogous predication of the concept of being, the Aristotelian scholastics had tried to prove the epistemological value of analogy for an affirmative theology which bridges the chasm between the infinite Creator and finite creation and allows positive expressions about God. The negative theology also proceeded from the same conviction of the total otherness of God, but went one step further. The negative theology argued that God is not the cause of all that is in the ordinary sense of the word cause, for to assert that He is creates the danger of ascribing to Him things unworthy of Him. The negative theology sought rather to describe Him as the "Wholly Other," the one who can not be described as being not merely other than all created things but as not even being merely "not other" than all created things. If the positive theology spoke of God as cause in an analogous sense of the concept, the negative theology spoke of God as not being cause in the empirical sense of the word. The great master of the *theologia negativa* in the fifteenth century was the incomparable Cusanus.

Cusanus believed that analogies are really not at all the real thing. They are not actual but are actually a negation. His denial that expressions about created things can be utilized even negatively in describing God really amounts to a denial of the denial, a negation of a negation. God is not that which is "not other." Cusanus' formula is: "The not-other is nothing other than the not-other." The insight that God is no longer rationally conceivable constitutes the kernel of the *docta ignorantia*, the learned ignorance. Just two years before his death Cusanus developed his thought about God as not being the not-other in a fascinating dialogue entitled *Directio speculantis seu de non aliud* in which he, Nicholas, explains this doctrine to Ferdinand, an Aristotelian, to Abbot Johannes Andreas, a humanist, and Petrus Balbus, the translator of Proclus. Even though the early editions of Cusanus' works, including the one prepared under his own direction, did not contain the *De non aliud*, the humanists knew of its existence. Lefèvre d'Étaples while preparing his edition of Cusanus' works wrote everywhere, but failed to locate a copy. The only manuscript of it was in the possession of Hartmann Schedel of Nuremberg who had a copy of it made in 1496.

Hartmann Schedel was a close friend of Celtis and may have acquired the manuscript from yet another intimate of Celtis, the Abbot Trithemius, who in his *De scriptoribus ecclesiasticis*, published in Mainz in 1494, had listed it along with the first lines of the text. To this day Schedel's copy is still the only source of the dialogue extant. Celtis read Schedel's copy of the *De non aliud* together with the twenty propositions which Cusanus worked out as a summary and elucidation of his philosophical notion of the "non aliud." These twenty propositions really belong together with the dialogue itself, but Celtis took them to be a separate writing. In 1500 he had Johannes Winterberg in Vienna publish them under the title *Propositiones reverendissimi Domini Nicolae cardinalis de virtute ipsius non aliud*.[36] Various paths may have led Celtis to his special interest in the negative theology of Cusanus. Albertus Magnus had done a commentary upon the writings of Dionysius which Cusanus used and annotated. Cusanus greatly influenced Reuchlin's *De verbo mirifico*, and Celtis celebrated its appearance with a sapphic ode. It is interesting to note that a year after Celtis' death Agrippa von Nettesheim held lectures on Reuchlin's book in Spain in the spirit of Cusanus. Celtis published the *Propositiones* together with his *Carmen saeculare*, a sapphic ode such as Horace had composed, commemorating the end of one century and the beginning of a new one. Celtis hoped that the new century would bring new greatness to Germany and published his song together with this sample of the deepest German thinker of the century past. What did Celtis derive from the learned ignorance of Cusanus? Cusanus was explicitly Trinitarian and emphasized especially the indwelling of the Holy Spirit. But Celtis derived from his concept of the "non aliud" a kind of vague theism. The last lines of the *Carmen saeculare* are indicative of his mood:

Thou in whom the wandering stars of the heavens rest and all which is upon the earth, lend a favorable ear to our petitions. Thy name and Thy power we are not able to recognize. Whoever Thou art, be kind to Germany in whose cities many altars pour up smoke to thee.

God to Celtis was clearly not only immanent, but abscondite.

The universalist element in Celtis' religious philosophy peculiar to him is less a matter of his preoccupation with the classic pantheon than of his Teutonic nature myths. He praised the classic philosophers and poets to be sure who had achieved such a harmony in the light of nature and of grace. He regularly employed classic names for God and the saints as well as classic myths and phrases for Christian references. God the Father became Jupiter, and Mary the mother of the Thunderer.[37] Mercury became the guide to the world beyond, heaven the Elysian field, hell the nether world of the Furies guarded by Cerberus and ruled by the judge Radamanthus.[38] But the Carolingian poets had used the appellation the "Thunderer" as an acceptable literary flourish, forgetting, it seems, the admonition of Gregory the Great that the praise of Christ should not be joined with the praise of Jupiter. And Baptista Mantuanus had summoned the whole of Olympus to praise the Madonna. Since Christianity had conquered, they argued, one could use pagan names without harm. But it was this open and consistent practice which stirred up the suspicions of Celtis' colleagues. It caused the pious nun Charitas Pirckheimer to rebuke him and to call upon him to abandon the artful fables of Diana, Venus, Jupiter, and other idols. She was right, of course, for a mind preoccupied with antique letters would eventually be somewhat conditioned by ancient religious thought. This proved to be true of Celtis to a far greater extent than he himself knew.

Celtis really seemed more genuinely himself when rhapsodizing over the pure religion of the early Germans. How excellent was the religion of the forefathers who worshiped in protective groves of oak trees in the dark forest without concrete objects as in the image-loving South, devoted to the secret powers of nature, understanding the secret of departing and renewed life. In those days there were no priests and Germany was not yet subject to foreign gods. No one served the Italians or acknowledged the saints who so often plundered German lands. The *Germania generalis* breathes an entirely heathen atmosphere, describing the creation of the world according to the myth of the Demogorgon, the ancestor of the gods in whose lap rests the chaos from which the world arose. Celtis no doubt learned this distortion of the demiurge stemming from late classic paganism from Boccaccio's *Genealogia deorum gentilium*, in which pagan myths are given a neologistic interpretation designed to give them a new allegorical meaning. Celtis discovered his ideal values not in Ottonian culture of Roswitha's day nor in the Benedictine culture of Charlemagne's courtly renaissance, but in the German *Urzeit*, in the primitive age in which the Germans had not merely an unspoiled culture but a pure natural religion with uncorrupted druid priests who did not have to be bought with eggs and cheese. The crisis of the European conscience, it would seem, did not really need to await the discovery of far-off foreign places by Jesuit missionaries. Journeying back into time could be as problematical as travel through space.

Celtis' radical estrangement from orthodox other-worldliness led him to question the destiny and immortality of the soul. Though piety demands burial rather than cremation, he reflected, would the soul itself return to that nothingness from which it came? [39]

Phoebus, who directs the fate of the united world . . ., I beg you to tell me clearly whether the spirit, when it leaves the sleeping body, blessed adds a divinity to the stars, whether it is pulled down into the surging waves of the Lethean stream to return again at some given time, or whether it escapes like an extinguished spark, lifted up over the earth, like a dense vapor and finally is lost in a thin breath of air.[40]

His happiest poetic solution was that when the soul leaves the body it returns to its star.[41] This thought was familiar to Celtis, as it was to the men of the Middle Ages, from Plato's *Timaeus* (XIV) where he opines that the soul who lived well throughout his allotted time should be conveyed once more to a habitation in his kindred star and there should enjoy a blissful and congenial life. Celtis suspected that the punishments of hell for sentient shades, the hot regions of Pluto, or a severe cold were the inventions of the slothful priests with which they rule the blind hearts of the masses. One should despise their murmurings.[42] The only real assurance of immortality is fame. Celtis had a full measure of the humanists' desire for fame, which Dante called "lo gran disio dell' eccellenza" and Boccaccio "perpetuandi nominis desiderium." Only fame can rescue man from the abyss of nothingness, that is, fame and virtue. Nevertheless, Celtis could not suppress his anxiety about a divine judgment. Troublesome cares arise, he confided, lest perchance the gods do care for the pious vows of good men and condemn wicked men.[43] He could not quiet his negative conscience. "Despiser of the gods," he intoned, "beware lest Fortune with

3. *Philosophy*

EXITVS ACTA PROBAT QVI BENE FECIT HABET

APOLO   MERC

CVNCTOS VRNA SVPREMA VOCAT

QVID NON LIBITINA RESOLVIS

GER·ILLVS

AMOR.   EPIGRA   ODAR.

OPERA EOR.   SEQVVTVR ILLO

D M S

FLETE PIIVATES ET TVNDITE PECTORA PALMIS
VESTER ENIM HIC CELTIS FATA SVPREMA TVLIT
MORTVVS ILLE QVIDEM SED LONGV̄ VIVVS IN EVVM
CŌLOQVITVR DOCTOS PER SVA SCRIPTA VIROS
CHVN·CIL·PROVIENNĘ LAVREĘ CVSTOS˙E COLLATOR
HIC IN CHRIS. QVIE SCIT VIXIT AN· IXL· SAL· SESQVIMILL
SVB DIVO MAXIMIL: AVGVST: ET VII

·H·B·

4. *Celtis'* Sterbebild

wandering feet assault you. For no mortal can long safely prevail as the despiser of the gods." [44]

The specter of a capricious and unscrutable fate haunted Celtis as it did many of the Italian and German humanists. Moira, Fatum, or Tyche-Fortuna had made its debut in the high Middle Ages. Dante portrayed fortune in a twofold aspect, as a goddess of luck favoring all alike and as an incomprehensible fate, defying all human calculations. The father of Italian humanism, Petrarch, had referred to the problem only casually and without consistency. Most of the German humanists arrived at no better solution than merely identifying fate with the changeableness and transiency of all things and with the incalculableness of the powers presiding over life. His ode on fate and felicity describes the working of impenetrable fortune. Only He who sits upon Olympus, mixing joys with sorrows, knows and governs the causes in our lives, gives and denies. Our hearts cannot perceive these acts through the dark shadows. He has appointed proud fate to give his certain gifts, which come at the appointed time, even though man may close all windows tightly against it. But drunken fortune plays with a wandering step oppressing the mind with care, joyous hope, or fear. The wise man must courageously persevere with a vigor of mind equal to the challenge.[45] In a similar vein Celtis wrote: "A blind goddess spins an uncertain game and governs the wheel with a dubious countenance, which a wise man supported with his own vigor spurns and despises." [46] Like a trivial and quite undramatic Hamlet, Celtis stood before the two-faced goddess and debated between suffering her slings and arrows or taking arms against them. The activist in him usually won out.[47] His solution was not unlike that of Machiavelli who agonized over the problem in *The Prince*. But Celtis frequently returned to the idea that God, after all, holds fate in His hands.[48] He begged Jove the All-highest as the ruler of destiny to reveal the laws by which he governs, lest oppressed men assume that all things are directed by capricious steps and are governed by no established rule. Otherwise destiny will remain forever blind in a way inimical to virtue and limited by no law.[49]

It is clear that for Celtis the certainty and immutability of the Christian faith was badly shaken. Making due allowances for rote

imitation of classical themes and for poetic license, it still seems
that Celtis with his enthusiastic romantic nature-mysticism coupled
with streaks of enlightened skepticism had lost a great deal of the
substance of the revealed Christian religion, a fact which did not
escape the notice of his contemporaries. His constant carping at the
clerics had both nationalist and religious grounds. His many
attacks especially upon clerical immorality and financial exploitation were typical of both the popular satirical literature of the time
and of the humanist protest. He was usually shrill, unrestrained,
and humorless. He once smirked that guilty parties trembled before
his epigrams for fear of finding their own name there. Even when
couched in couplets his denunciations were as fierce as those of
the fiery Hutten, thirty years his junior. He had a copy of Valla's
De donatione constantiniana, like Hutten who later published an
edition of it so shocking to Luther, so that his misgivings about the
clergy reached beyond priest and monk to the See of Rome itself.[50]
    Celtis attacked various religious practices as well. He mocked
the priestly power to effect transubstantiation in the sacrament.
Thus he told of a priest who preferred a fat capon to salted herring
during a fast. He therefore invoked his power of changing bread to
body and making the sign of the cross he effected the desired
transformation.[51] Fasts and prayers are for the hooded monks, not
for the humanist comrades. God sees nothing in a fast. What does
chattering prayers in Latin mean, if no one understands what the
monk is praying for?[52] Celtis' consciousness of being a layman
appears time and again. Thus he relates how the priests attempt to
suppress the possession of religious books by the people, but in the
future all people and not merely clerics will have a knowledge of
divine wisdom. "Now there are so many printed books in Germany," he exults, "that every inn has a copy of the Holy
Scriptures." [53] Celtis expresses in these passages a hostility to abuse
and the formalization of religious life through sacramental-
sacerdotalism of poor spiritual quality which is of the same genre
as the protests of Wimpfeling, Pirckheimer, or Erasmus. But he is
inwardly less bound by the received tradition and dogma of the
church than they.
    The relation of Celtis to scholastic philosophy is more complex
than it seems to be on the surface. He is noisome and rude in de-

nouncing the scholastics who "speak from the *cathedras* brokenly and crudely and against all art and rule of speech like quacking geese and lowing oxen." Celtis had studied both at Cologne and Heidelberg and had thus been introduced to both the *viae*. He had a high regard for Albertus Magnus and Cusanus. But he was not a good student of scholastic philosophy, for he failed to distinguish between Thomism and Occamism or to show any further signs of interest in the intellectual questions at stake. The scholastics filled the chairs of all the universities throughout Germany, he complained, and forced the students to devote fifteen years to the study of logic alone. None knew what the divine books of Plato have to say or what the works of Pliny and Cicero contain.[54] This was the very complaint that Luther later made when he regretted that no one had instructed him in the poets and historians, but only in the philosophers. Luther's complaint was only incidental, however, to a more serious religious difference. For Celtis the great wrong of the scholastics was the neglect of the Roman tongue and of natural philosophy compounded by their opposition to the poets who promoted both with enthusiasm. In the Ingolstadt *Inaugural Address* he pronounced judgment:

Those who interpret the Latin poets and writers are suppressed and those who try to solve the riddles of nature and the wisdom of its governor by means of mathematical truth, who in any way go beyond the views of the circle of common men, are held up as infamous. So pitiable is the philosophy of these men, flat and watered down, that by their methods they deform the beauties of nature with incorporeal concepts, monstrous abstractions and vain chimeras.[55]

All the same Celtis was able to teach on the same faculties with the scholastics without a major intellectual encounter and with only occasional frictions and unpleasantries. He objected more to their interests and method rather than to their religious premises or basic conclusions. He even planned a work which would effect a harmony between the poets and theologians, the *Parnassus biceps*, but this work was either subsequently lost or, what is more probable, never begun.[56] This idea of harmonizing humanism and theology was a thought at home among the Heidelberg humanists. A similar attempt at pacification doubtless prompted Celtis to publish in 1500 St. Jerome's *Epistola ad Magnum, oratorem Urbis, de legendis et audiendis poetis.* Celtis through his pupil Jacob Locher may have influenced Thomas Murner's *Reformatio Poetarum.* Locher himself drew the fire of the conservative Wimpfeling, it will be recalled, who wrote a pamphlet aimed at him and the radical poets, *Contra turpem libellum Philomusi Defensio theologie scholastice et neotericorum.* But the classic controversy, at least in emotional energy expended on the relation of poetry and theology, remained that of Martin Polich and Wimpina. Nothing really intellectually significant emerged from any of these efforts.

If Celtis' attitude toward scholasticism was ambivalent, he had also a second side to his religious self. His stunted moral philosophy and deviationist natural and spiritual philosophy did not block out a large measure of very traditional religiosity in his psyche. He not infrequently spoke with concern about the welfare of "our religion." He boasted of the seven powerful archbishoprics of the Fatherland and contributed many kindly epitaphs for monks and abbots.[57] Jodokus Sturnus urged him to put his talents into the service of the church.[58] In fact, he accepted uncritically many of the cruder religious practices soon to be assaulted by the Reformation. He accepted the full hagiology of the late Middle Ages and composed poems to St. Catherine, to Anne, Martin, Sebaldus, and Leopold, the patron saint of Austria.[59] He entered the lists with the upper Rhenish humanists against the Dominicans in support of the dogma of the immaculate conception of Mary. He devoutly placed Mary's icon at his door and implored her aid in his illness.[60] Vacillating between skepticism and credulity about miracles, he rationalized the remarkable survival of a Father Nicolaus who allegedly lived for years without food, while at the same time he accepted the authenticity of the sweating breastbones of the holy Walpurgis without a single critical comment.[61] Ravaged by disease, he made hopeful pilgrimages to the shrine of Alt-Oetting in Bavaria.[62] He arranged in advance to have Masses read for his soul. When he died *pie et christianissime* a funeral procession including the entire company of Vienna University students and faculty followed his coffin to St. Stephan's Cathedral where he still lies buried under the smaller tower not far from the sarcophagus of Emperor Frederick III who had crowned him the German poet laureate (figure 4). It is a striking commentary on the synergistic theological climate on the eve of the Reformation that the Minorite monk and theological professor at Vienna, Johannes Camers, could pen an epitaph for Celtis which reads like this:

> Life ever so brief is allowed to men by law
> And hastens away destroyed by various mishaps.
> What nature denies, lofty virtue still allows
> Which does not permit life to perish.
> Jealous death has robbed Celtis of his shadowy form
> But renowned virtue returns the stars to the man.
> Mortal parents have given their child his body,
> But Jupiter has given these unperishable things to the poet.
> If you wish to live a better life after these earthly fortunes,
> Virtue alone as companion will give you what you demand.[63]

As an intellectual, Celtis does not rank with Reuchlin, Mutian, Pirckheimer, or Erasmus. Nor is there any point except by way of formal classification in comparing his work with Goethe's *Römische Elegien*, as is sometimes done in literary histories. His close friend Ulsenius gave the first palm to Agricola for service to the Latin muses and only the second to Celtis.[64] His interests were extensive rather than intensive so that in no single area did he excel. His many services to humanist learning lay in another direction. Celtis was the great propagandist for humanism. This was his main significance in the history of Western thought. "Turn, oh Germans, turn to the more gentle studies!" he cried in his *Inaugural Address*. Unlike the imperious Erasmus who worked best alone, Celtis was extremely gregarious. He was the inspiration and the life of the sodalities. He formed the first phalanxes of the humanists for offensive action. Though his own reform efforts at the university level were not successful, they were not without effect. He helped put scholasticism further on the defensive. It is true that the opposition of the humanists and scholastics has been exaggerated and its nature misunderstood. Nevertheless, there was keener opposition between the adherents of the new learning and those of the scholastic tradition in Germany than elsewhere in Europe. Celtis with his frontal attack helped to shake the confidence of the scholastics even before Reuchlin, Hutten, or Erasmus entered the lists.

If humanism is defined as an intellectual movement, primarily literary and philological in nature, rooted in a love of and a desire for the rebirth of classical antiquity with its aesthetic, philosophical, and ethical norms, then Celtis was deeply committed to it. His humanist concerns were scarcely an independent native product. They were certainly not derived from the *via antiqua* and its grammatical reform or from the late medieval mysticism of the Brethren of the Common Life, except indirectly through Agricola. Rather it was the Italian influence which became finally definitive with his studies in the South which proved to be of the greatest importance for his intellectual development. Who among the leading humanists of that generation was more devoted to this cultural ideal and way of life? Agricola maintained a more even balance between his Northern piety and humanist enthusiasms. The religious Brant and the schoolmaster of humanism Wimpfeling were both far more conservative in outlook. Mutian was torn by a conflict of ideals which hardly concerned the more callous Celtis. Reuchlin, Melanchthon, or Erasmus were far more intellectual, scholarly, and ascetic than he. The patrician Pirckheimer was bound to be less radical socially and culturally. Hutten was more his type, but younger and more preoccupied with national interests. In his spontaneous enthusiasm for classic culture and the freedom of his way of life Celtis may be said to have represented the left wing among the German humanists. In that sense he might by way of a pleasant turn be called "the arch-humanist."

Celtis was far from approaching the concern of an Erasmus for religious enlightenment. Nevertheless, the idea was there no matter how primitive or unsystematic the form. In his criticism of the church he went beyond attacking abuses and touched upon matters more central to its teachings. In a way he represented a new independence of the layman vis-à-vis the clergy and of the secular disciplines vis-à-vis theology, pointing to the possibility of autonomous culture outside of the old ecclesiastical culture. But much of his negativeness was the rancor of a patriot against exploitation by the Roman church. Of greater consequence was the suggestion in his thought of a religious universal theism.

Celtis' religious philosophy has the appearance of being a mere pastiche. That he was a poet and no philosopher bears repetition. It was, in fact, more an assembly of opinions than reasoned conclusions, but it was not just a chaos of conflicting opinions. His ideas set into context reveal the makings of a new conception in religion not unrelated generically to Erasmus' *philosophia Christi*. His religious insight, drawn largely from Neoplatonic sources,

emphasized the immanent working of God the creator and legisla-
tor. With aesthetic enthusiasm he saw much of the Good and
Beautiful in the world. The thought that the world was a reflection
of the divine was clearly of Platonic inspiration. The divinity had
been active in various religions and philosophies and was to be seen
everywhere at work in nature. Cusanus in the *Idiota* had suggested
that the layman could read God's books everywhere, but he kept
the idea of the natural knowledge of God in an acceptable relation
to the revealed knowledge. Celtis was not so reflective. If he was
far from a monistic world-view himself, he at least pointed down
one path that leads to it. It is understandable how this humanist
"theology" might be considered potentially the most dangerous
enemy of the contemporary church.

How radical was Celtis? At both Ingolstadt and Vienna his
religious views were questioned. Ironically, the theological faculty
at the University of Vienna appointed Celtis' friend Johannes
Camers, who had done his epitaph, as inquisitor to examine the
Odes for heresy.[65] Celtis' name was listed on the *Index librorum
damnatorum* by the Spanish Inquisition though it was not on the
general Roman index.[66] On the Protestant side, Flacius Illyricus in
his *Katalog der Wahrheitszeugen* considered Celtis a bad Christian
and one who denied specific fundamental doctrines. What a
change from the genial indifference of the Renaissance church
which had accorded him a cathedral burial!

For his time and in the Northern cultural milieu Celtis was most
certainly a free spirit. He was a complex bundle of conflicting
characteristics, for he was at the same time critical and credulous,
skeptical and believing, enlightened and superstitious, religious and
secular, spiritual and earthy, a natural philosopher much concerned
with the supernatural. Compared with his more conservative contemporaries he was free indeed. But it is essentially unhistorical to
associate his freedom with the liberalism, skepticism, and rationalism of a later age as did many nineteenth-century liberal historians.
Far too much historical, scientific, philosophical, and theological
change has intervened to make a simple identification of all this
possible.

Why did his work lack permanence and his fame, for all his
prominence, go into such rapid eclipse? Vadian bemoaned the fact
that Celtis was less fortunate with the written than the spoken word.

His literary efforts lacked enduring value. Latin was an unfortunate medium. There is small comfort in calling him a German poet who happened to write in Latin. To the old cliché that by purifying Latin the humanists killed it must be added the rubric that they usually buried their own works in and with it. Many of his ideas Celtis wished to restrict esoterically for the benefit of the few. "For if the common crowd could grasp certain secrets, as we philosophers comprehend them," he declared in his Inaugural Address, "it would be hard to restrain their impetuosity." Typical of German humanism, his efforts were directed more toward a change in learned culture.

Why does Erasmus with his quaint smile beckon to us across the centuries rather than Celtis? He was a more accomplished writer, but today except for the *Praise of Folly* and the *Colloquies* people read little more of Erasmus than of Celtis and his colleagues. There was rather another more fundamental difference between the two. Celtis was humanistic with his interest in classic letters. Erasmus was a humanist devoted to the great human values, *humanitas* in the full sense of the word, humaneness, urbanity, toleration, richness of mind, love of peace, and devotion to God. Erasmus, a more deeply religious man than Celtis, did not have merely two divergent sides to his religious personality. He sought as a synthesist to make classical culture available for religious purposes and apologetically useful to the Christian faith. This effort of the synthesists had much to commend it and it elevated their program to a higher plane. That is what made Erasmus a man of greater stature, the greatest of the humanists.

Celtis did not appeal to the deepest need of his time, the longing for religious certitude. No matter how one approaches the intellectual life of the Germans in that epoch, one always encounters an overwhelming drive toward a renewed religious life. The Germans pressed not toward an aesthetically refined form of life, not toward a fulfillment of earthly existence with the help of a renewed antique beauty and learning, and also actually not toward a new knowledge of the world and of man, but rather toward an inner renewal of their church and a closer relation to God. If the humanists expected to make progress, they had to address themselves above all else to this decisive tendency of the time. It never occurred to Celtis seriously to use his ideas in the religious area to help change religious life in Germany. His friend Schreyer, moved by the scourge of Turks, Tartars, and disease, called for a "restitutio et reformatio," but Celtis looked for an external enlightenment to Frederick and later to Maximilian.[67] He urged Christians to read poetry.

Celtis lacked religious depth and spirituality. Far from righteous, he had no real consciousness of sin and seemed incapable of self-examination or reprobation. His religion was synergistic and mechanical. Celtis is typical of the theological uncertainty of the intellectuals as well as of the masses at the end of the Middle Ages. His search for aid in his physical distress was on a contractual basis, a pilgrimage for relief. Nor did he, conversely, feel the need for justification before God very urgently. Filled with the *Eros* of Neoplatonism he had little room for the *Agape* of St. Paul. There is a lack of final consequences which removes Celtis far from the men of the Reformation, from men like Luther with his oaken strength, his force, sincerity, consistency, outspokenness, faith. The reformers put their whole being at the service of religion.

Humanism did much to make the Reformation possible, and Celtis added his contribution. He promoted classic learning and the drive to the sources which was important also for the Reformation. He added fuel to the fires of nationalism which were to give a certain direction to the movement later in the century. He helped to shake confidence in the old authorities. Many of his students were prominent leaders in the Reformation movement. Laurentius Corvinus led the reform in Breslau and was a close coworker of Luther and Melanchthon. Andreas Althamer, who read Celtis' odes with enthusiasm, won fame as the Lutheran reformer of the Hohenzollern Frankish lands. Aventine's histories with their antipapal and anticlerical bias were standard reading for two centuries. Zwingli became the Swiss reformer much under Erasmian influence. And Vadian, another student of Celtis in Vienna, led the reform in St. Gallen. But at the very center, in the theological concern for a renewed Christian faith, Celtis was a stranger to the basic impulses which gave birth to the Reformation. Because it answered the deepest need of man in that century, not humanism but the Reformation became the decisive event for German history.

✛VI✛

HUTTEN

Militant Critic

T HE year 1521 was tense with crisis. All eyes were turned toward the Diet at Worms where Luther made his courageous stand in what J. A. Froude described as "perhaps the finest scene in human history." Germany was alive with excitement. Above the tumult rose a persistent, strident voice, heard often before, but soon to be heard no more — the voice of Ulrich von Hutten, German knight. He had called to Luther: "Long live liberty!" Now the die was cast. Hutten would not turn back, though church and empire conspired to crush him. That year he penned these words:

> With open eyes I've dared it
> And do not feel regret.
> Though I should fail to conquer
> True faith is with me yet.

Here indeed was a romantic figure raised on the shoulders of Uhland, Herder, Wieland, and Goethe to the stature of a national hero! Freedom was all to this tempestuous, restless, daring young man — free learning, free Fatherland. The weapons he chose for battle were sword and pen. Mutian characterized him as "sharp and vehement and a great poet, but such that he can be irritated by the slightest word." [1]

Hutten was born of a noble family in the fortress of Steckelberg on the border of Franconia and Hessia, April 21, 1488. His pious family sent him at the age of eleven to the ancient monastery of Fulda to prepare for life as a religious. But at seventeen he fled from the monastery, only a few weeks before Luther entered one at Erfurt. Years later Hutten explained his reasons for leaving.

Having learned to know life a little better, he had concluded that in accord with his nature he could serve God more pleasingly and be of greater use to the world in another calling.[2] He denied that he had broken an oath in leaving. Like Celtis, he hurried first to Cologne University. From there he wandered to Erfurt, Frankfort on the Oder, where he took his baccalaureate degree in September 1506, then to Leipzig, Greifswald, and Rostock. The traveling humanist Rhagius Aesticampianus exercised the most telling influence over Hutten in these years. He became a self-conscious humanist at war with barbarism.

The first period of Hutten's brief life span was dedicated to poetics, the second to polemics. "Behold, posterity," he penned, "the songs of Hutten the poet, whom you are rightly able to call your own." [3] His early poems were conventional pieces on morals, good virtue, and the transient nature of life done according to the rules of the profession which he laid down in his *De Arte Versificandi* in 1511. He did not compose a single true love poem like Celtis. He was often an angry young man and many of his polemics poured from the depths of his choleric soul like a libation from the vial of his wrath. Such were his *Querelae*, blistering attacks upon his former hosts, the Lötze family of Greifswald, and the savage assaults against Duke Ulrich of Württemberg, the murderer of Hutten's unfortunate uncle. He went through the motions of gathering and editing several classic manuscripts, but he was no scholar at all and had to leave such labors to men of greater patience. He successfully resisted the attempts of his family to make a lawyer of him and returned from Italy a foe of Roman law, academic degrees, papal rule, and all enemies of the Emperor. His literary efforts, which were really better than is commonly conceded, earned for him the laurel wreath, when he was crowned in Augsburg on July 12, 1517, poet laureate of the Empire. In a letter to Pirckheimer the next year, Hutten cited the growing strength of the humanists, men like Oecolampadius, Budé, Erasmus, Lefèvre, Cop, and Ruellius, and exclaimed: "Oh century! Oh letters! It is a joy to be alive! It is not yet time to lapse into repose, Willibald. Studies thrive and minds flourish! Woe to you, barbarism! Accept the noose, look forward to exile!" [4]

Two major elements determined Hutten's personal outlook. As

a knight he belonged to a class which was rapidly losing status and utility. Politically he looked back to the great days of imperial glory and longed for their restoration. With intensified patriotism he leveled his lance against foes of the empire within and without — the princes, the Venetians, the courtesans, the Turks, and the papacy. As a humanist he was devoted to the growth of good learning. The chief foes of letters were the hypocritical priests and superstitious monks. Behind them stood the real *bête noire*, but it was only gradually that Hutten made the Pope his major target. In the *Trias Romana* Hutten has Ernholdus articulate what really amounted to his own program: "Truly it is a great and excellent deed to bring it about by persuading, exhorting, inciting, driving, and impelling that the fatherland come to recognize its own debasement and arm itself to win back its ancient liberty." "Even if it cannot be attained," responds Hutten in the dialogue, "there is merit in having tried."

Conditions in Germany were aggravated precisely because ecclesiastical influence and control were more effective than in France and England. For decades a meeting of the Reichstag never passed without an airing of the grievances (*gravamina*) of the German nation. As a cavalryman, Hutten believed in the attack strategy. To the explosive compound of an aggressive personality and patriotic discontent was added a bitter satirical element developed under the strong influences of Lucian, who in his own dialogues made such radical thrusts at second-century religion.[5] Hutten's strictures ran the gamut from the moral indignation worthy of a Geiler von Kaisersberg and the cunning folkish jibes reminiscent of Sebastian Brant to the clean cuts of Italianesque Renaissance wit. His catalogue of ecclesiastical ills including the usual abuses — simony, nepotism, benefice-hunting, immorality, neglect of duties — all candidly recognized already by those conciliarists who had called for a "reformation in head and members."

In a letter to Count Hermann von Newenar, Hutten decried the low spirituality of the clergy, lacking zeal for religion, preaching the gospel with no remembrance of piety, acting proudly, crudely, immoderately, and insolently. Before making war on the Turks, Germany should first find a remedy for her internal ills. It was this kind of abuse which led the Bohemian nation away from the church, he hinted darkly.[6] In the dialogue *Febris II* (Fever the Second) Hutten called for the abolition of celibacy with its unfortunate results and the reform of the numerous and wealthy clergy in the interest of sincere vocation and pure conduct. The Emperor should take the initiative in such reforms for a harder working, better educated, more ethical clergy, he wrote in words reminiscent of Wycliffe's *De dominio civili*. Above all, greater poverty was necessary. The higher clergy came in for special belaboring, those courtesans and their unsavory dealing with the Fuggers. Hutten the nobleman turns to clergy and bourgeois to cry a plague on both their houses. In *Febris Prima* (Fever the First) and the *Inspicientes* (Spectators,) breathing the spirit of Lucian, Hutten caricatured Cardinal Cajetan as a dissolute papal lackey come to cheat the Germans of their money to provide the Romans with luxuries, while pretending to be collecting for defence against the Turks. He would go home empty-handed, for the Germans would grow wise to him. Similarly, it was the financial losses involved which stirred Hutten's ire against the sale of indulgences by those pardon-merchants, not the religious principle involved.

With the exploitation and hypocrisy of the priesthood Hutten coupled the ignorance of the monks. To him the greatest monument to monkish folly was the construction of the scholastic system. In the preface of his *Nemo* [Nobody], addressed to Crotus Rubeanus, written under the immediate influence of Italian humanism, he decried the centuries of darkness under scholastic domination:

The Paris theologists have judged otherwise, to their own great shame and infamy. When I reflect on it, I realize how this theology has damaged the Christian religion for three hundred years. For when the old true theology was abandoned, then religion truly declined together with learned studies and the very worst of plagues broke out, superstition, which with its darkness so obscured the true worship of God that you could not know whether many things which you observed belonged to Christ or to some new god who will reserve for himself this last age of the world. Moreover, they have the greatest accumulation of the worst books, while they neglect those ancient and rightly learned authors.[7]

Their syllogisms illustrated the frivolity of their concerns, for example, whether St. Paul snatched up into the third heaven could see something more clearly than in his own cell. Their power was so great that Alexander VI himself declared he would prefer to make war with the most powerful king or prince than with one of the mendicant orders. Hutten objected to the way in which these preposterous disciples of Christ, who knew mercy, treated heretics. Yet they feared the Bohemians. They were ferocious where there was no work to be done, but where there was peril they withdrew and alleged that religion requires peace and quiet. "Oh customs! Oh studies!," he cried, "Oh you leaders of this age! Why do we not drive away these clouds and once again contemplate truth!" [8] In view of his assaults on scholasticism it is all the more amusing that in the *Epistolae Obscurorum Virorum* Hutten and his friends vote no-confidence in Pope Leo, because as a poet he is incapable of understanding Thomas Aquinas' *Summa Contra Gentiles*.

The ill-will between the humanists and scholastics, under control for two decades, rose suddenly to the boiling point in the dramatic Reuchlin controversy. This affair, often viewed as a dress-rehearsal for the Protestant revolt, meant to the poets a battle for culture against scholastic ignorance and monkish superstition. Hutten, of course, was in the thick of it. Through Crotus Rubeanus and Eobanus Hessus, a bright young poet whom he had known since his first visit to Erfurt in 1506, Hutten had established close contact with Mutian's circle which now rushed to the defense of Reuchlin. In 1517 Hutten published a long poem entitled *Triumphus Capnionis* proclaiming victory over the rustic, barbarous, sophistical, ignorant, envious, obscure theologists.[9] In the preface addressed to Maximilian he cited the advance in learning already achieved: Jerome reborn, the New Testament brought to light, many things produced from Hebrew and Greek.[10]

But the most telling blow was the immensely popular *Epistolae Obscurorum Virorum*. "What prevents us from speaking the truth with laughter?" asked Pirckheimer in the words of Horace. Hutten conceded that the jokes were not half bad. In the second part, for which he was largely responsible, he refers to himself as "an arrant brute" who declared that if the preaching friars insulted him as they had Reuchlin he would lop off the nose and ears of every monk he met.[11]

Hutten's opinion of the papacy progressively degenerated. He at first viewed the Pope as an enemy of the Emperor, but in the end as a foe of Christ himself. He expressed in a poem on Germany some hostility to Rome because of the bad effect of the popes and Italian churchmen on German morals, a modern echo of Tacitus. To Maximilian he wrote that the Emperor is the head of Rome and the head of the world and urged him to assume leadership. The Emperor is the true shepherd who will feed the sheep and drive the robbers out of Latium.[12] But it was on Italian soil that Hutten's antipapal animus came to full bloom. His epigrams addressed to Maximilian were for the most part written there.[13] It was precisely on account of these epigrams that Dr. Eck denounced Hutten to the Curia, and with good reason.

Hutten's attack on the papacy took two forms: general ridicule and historical argumentation. The warrior pope Julius II was his primary target. This successor to Peter, in a long line far removed, never prays for the people. He bears arms and rejoices in blood. Paul had a beard and a sword, but there the similarity ends. Julius is known for his perfidy. Unlike Christ and Peter, his work is death, his delight luxury. A merchant, seizing the whole earth by fraud, he sells the heavens, though he himself does not possess them, writes Hutten in words reflecting the views of the amusing anonymous tract *Julius Exclusus*. Julius with the Giants will drive the gods from Olympus, and when Jupiter is no longer there he will sell the stars and heaven itself. "Give us, o ye gods, another Brutus," cries Hutten, "for as long as Julius is in Rome it will perish!" At last Hutten paid him his final respects with a saucy epitaph:

> A shepherd wolf lies here concealed by this rubble.
> He used to sell bulls, but was only a bubble.[14]

In a series of epigrams addressed to Crotus Rubeanus from the city itself, Hutten mocked the rampant venality of Rome where God himself is sold for gold. Unlike other commercial cities, Rome traffics in holy things. How can it be that this city of orgies once had a Curius, a Pompey, and Metellus, he writes in the epigram *De Statv Romano* in words which parallel Celtis' poem to a Roman girl? [15]

The climax to Hutten's caustic campaign came in his *Vadiscus sive Trias Romana* (Roman Trinity), which was published in February 1520. In it he plays spokesman for the Germans who have always been the most pious and godfearing people. He catalogues in threesomes the ills of the nation. The bishop must buy his pallium in Rome; the priests prevent the conversion of unbelievers; the beautiful golden church is like the body with the real Church of Peter and the Apostles but its shadow. Three things are always under way in Rome, but never completed: the saving of souls, the rebuilding of churches, and the war against the Turks. Three things very few people in Rome believe in: the immortality of the soul, the communion of saints, and punishment in hell. One may kiss the hands, altars, and cheeks, but the feet only of the Pope. Three things are most lamentable: the wicked clique of Florentines ruling Rome, the flatterers who hold the Pope as God, and the Pope's assuming too much power in granting indulgences and pronouncing anathemas. The guile of the Italians and the inertia of the Germans prevent reform. In the *Vadiscus* Hutten even came out for the elimination of compulsory celibacy as a way to eliminate immorality, for it is better to be married than to consort with whores and handle holy things with soiled hands. "I have dared it!," concluded Hutten with a flourish.[16]

Hutten's imperial leanings determined the nature of his historical arguments against the temporal power of the papacy. The deepest cut in his surgical operation for papal health was his new edition of Valla's *De donatione Constantini*, 1517. In an unctious dedication to Leo X, the "restorer of peace," he expressed the hope that this age would move from the long darkness of tyranny to the light of liberty. The pontiffs who invented the Donation were not shepherds but devoured the sheep of Christ and dragged governments and nations under the yoke. Hutten reminds Leo, the "father of studies," that Valla was befriended by his pontifical predecessors, implicitly suggesting himself as a parallel case worthy of consideration.[17] Hutten looked to a Medici pope for progress, but with grave misgivings.

Hutten drew also on the literature of the investiture controversy which was ready-made for his purposes. In the preface (addressed to Archduke Ferdinand of Austria) to his edition of the *De unitate ecclesiae conservanda,* 1520, he states expressly that he was not fighting the papacy in blind hate, but with the intention of improving its picture. He wishes to make a true pontiff out of a tyrant, a father of a king, a shepherd of a robber.[18] He concluded a letter attacking the Pontiff, Leo X, in December 1520, with the phrase, "Let us break their chains asunder and cast their yoke from us." [19]

At last the issue was clearly joined. There was, he now believed, such an unbridgeable chasm between the teachings of the Pope and Christ as to make of him an antichrist. To prove his point he composed a dialogue between Christ and the Pope, bringing out in sixty-four exchanges the discrepancy between their teachings and practice.[20] The contrasts are mostly matters external, however, and show little basic understanding of the dogmatic development from the Gospels to the sacramentalism of the medieval period. Christ says that his kingdom is not of this world; the Pope replies that he is the lord of the empire. Christ says that he had not where to lay his head; the Pope answers that he has Rome, Sicily, Corsica, and other lands. Christ was crowned with thorns; the Pope with gold. Christ turned the other cheek; the Pope uses force. Christ says "drink ye all of it"; the Pope objects that his priests alone should drink the sacramental wine. Christ assures us that he died for man's sins; the Pope protests that indulgences must be purchased. This latter exchange is the nearest approach in the dialogue to the central issue of the evangelical controversy. The *German Requiem for the Burnt Bulls and Papal Laws* contains a prayer to God that He should let these papal instruments rest in peace lest some antichrist or antichrists reawaken them in a Pythagorean manner and allow the Germans no rest.[21] In his *Expostulatio* against Erasmus, Hutten offered himself body and soul to the devil if Erasmus did not perceive as well as he the chasm between the Roman and Apostolic churches.[22] Christ is the true head of the church, not the Pope. Then, under the spell of the Reformation, Hutten pushed to its logical conclusion the historical contrast first brought to his attention by Aesticampianus, a careful student of patristics. Aesticampianus ended his days in Wittenberg.

Could such a tempestuous and critical activist, devoid of deep religious consciousness, develop a constructive philosophy of his own? There are some suggestions of positive religious reform ideas analogous to the notions of Celtis, Mutian, and Erasmus. This clearly raises the question as to whether or not these were entirely derivative, faint reflections of pale Erasmus. Baptista Egnatius of the New Academy, who learned to know both Hutten and Erasmus in Venice, called Hutten a "disciple of Erasmus." [23] Their early contacts led to mutual adulation in the best humanist style. In 1510, in the first edition of the *Nemo*, Hutten showed evidence of an acquaintance with some of Erasmus' works and in the new preface to the piece (1518), he praised him as a godly restorer of early Christian teaching, the "old theology." [24] "What could be more Christian than the labors of Erasmus?" he asked. Their first direct contact dates from the time of Hutten's second Italian journey, when on October 24, 1515, Hutten wrote asking Erasmus to commend him to his Italian friends. Thereafter for five years they maintained friendly relations, though not without tensions. Hutten, the knight, called Erasmus "the theologian," the light of Germany, Hercules,[25] and wrote Erasmus that he showed his *Adages* to all the learned men in Rome.[26] Erasmus, in turn, in his *Annotations to I Thessalonians* of 1516 praised Hutten as a young man of illustrious ancestry.[27] Hutten seems to have received his appointment at Mainz as a protégé of Erasmus.[28] It was, in fact, on a mission in 1517 for the Elector to the French court that he broadened his associations to include such leading French humanists as Budé and Lefèvre.

Hutten and Erasmus were comrades in arms in the Reuchlin affair, Erasmus confiding to Hutten that he favored Reuchlin for the sake of learning.[29] Yet as the controversy became more violent, Erasmus increasingly withdrew, while Hutten grew all the more virulent, a sign of things to come. For, when the acid test came through Luther's final challenge, Erasmus turned back, but Hutten charged ahead. Hutten saw the difference between Erasmus and himself with a clear eye. He knew that it was a matter of issues and not merely one of personalities. He saw the estrangement in the offing and on March 6, 1518, he predicted to Erasmus that there would be a great uproar in Germany shortly and that Erasmus would chide him for his audacity rather than praise him for his fortitude.[30] In the same letter in which he denied reading Luther's works, Erasmus complained of Germany's many importunate young men.[31] Then frictions increased. Hutten, while recognizing Erasmus' legitimate concern for the *Respublica christiana*, accused him of destroying the *Epistolae Obscurorum Virorum* and opposing Luther whom he once supported.[32] Hutten charged Erasmus with greed for glory, fear, jealousy of Luther, and other outrages. "Flee from us," he urged.[33]

For Hutten's uncomplicated mentality issues were always clear, decisions were easy. He could not appreciate Erasmus' equivocation regarding the Reformation. In the *Expostulatio* he reminded Erasmus that he had himself not long before helped to resurrect piety and brought the gospel back to the light of day and now he turns away, although no pious Christian is unwilling to see the Roman church destroyed, which would be good for all Christendom. Hutten believed that the courtesans opposed Martin, not because of his teachings on free will, the sacraments, and the like, but because he had hurt their greed and exposed their rascality. He urged Erasmus not to keep silence about Christ's teachings because of the uproar and not to abandon the Word of God. Erasmus has acted against conscience and has sat down between two stools.[34] If Hutten's expostulation was uncalled for, Erasmus' *Spongia* was unworthy.[35] Melanchthon tried to dissociate Luther and himself from Hutten's mania in attacking learned Erasmus.[36] Luther regretted Erasmus' rejoinder, asking, "If this is to wipe away with a sponge, I wonder what it means to malign and revile?" [37] Erasmus replied that Luther should not have expected moderation about such a robber as Hutten and accused him of grave crimes: debauchery, prostitution, hopeless corruptions, and fatuous boastings. Hutten, Erasmus complained, was tolerant of no one, however friendly and forbearing. He was guilty of bankruptcies, of extorting money from the Carthusians, of cutting the ears off two preachers, and of robbery. He had assaulted three abbots on the public way, on account of which evil deed he was cut off by the head of his family, and had committed other crimes of which he had not even noted a word in the *Spongia*.[38] The friendship of Hutten and Erasmus was ruined beyond repair. These two humanists were so radically different in outlook that the influence of Erasmus on Hutten was necessarily more a matter of individual impressions from specific writings rather than of the impact of his total person on the younger man.[39]

Hutten's criticisms of abuse in the church were clearly of the same genre as the jibes of Erasmus. It is easy to point to similarities even in detail between the *Praise of Folly* and the *Fortuna* or *Febris Prima* and *Febris* II, the strictures against the monks, hypocrisy, repetitious prayers, and the abuses of celibacy.[40] But when Erasmus turned to the task of constructing his *philosophia Christi*, Hutten caught only an occasional glimmer of its import. Nevertheless, at the point where Hutten ceased merely attacking his opponents and pressed for reform in terms of an ethical ideal he entered the Erasmian humanist reform movement.[41] These reform impulses of Hutten fell into two broad catgeories: the desire for the advance of true religious culture against ignorance and barbarism, and the desire for the reform of the church in administration and morals.

Already in *Nemo* Hutten had outlined his attack on obscurantism. In terms paralleling Sebastian Brant's *Ship of Fools* he scored the scholastics and theologists who subverted true religion for three hundred years. He opposed pomp and circumstance, the lawyers, academic titles, and ignorant monks who tried to suppress the new philosophy. He challenged the Inquisition which interfered with developing cultures in the foreword to all free men in Germany in his *De schismate extinguendo*.[42] He called for freedom of studies in his preface to the *De unitate ecclesiae conservanda*.[43] Similarly, in the *Vadiscus* he ridiculed Leo X's suppression of a Tacitus edition with a bull forbidding its publication in other lands as an illustration of the way in which the church maintained the ignorance of the German people.[44] On July 21, 1517, Hutten wrote Erasmus that he had seen his New Testament.[45] Thereafter, he cited the Scriptures more often in the Latin translation of Erasmus than in the Vulgate, a move against the *textus receptus* of the medieval theologians.[46] But Hutten did not have the patience for a constructive program so comprehensive as Erasmus laid down in his *Enchiridion*.

Hutten called for the church to return to its basic spiritual function.[47] In a letter to Charles V, September 1520, Hutten complained because he was persecuted for opposing the fables of the Pope and fights for Christian truths. "Finally," he wrote, "where is religion, where is piety, if it is not necessary to remember what Christ has taught and we think that human traditions are to be preferred to his immortal instruction?" [48] Toward this end in the *Vadiscus* he urged the convening of a council and also republished a conciliarist tract which he had discovered written by a follower of Felix V dating from the period of the Council of Basel.[49] The election of bishops should be returned to the people. He attacked Leo for calling an appeal to a council a crime and cried out against the bulls of Pius II and Julius II, "Oh fraud! Oh violence!" [50] He hoped that as a result of effective reform the reunion of the Bohemians, Greeks, and Russians might come about, since they would no longer be offended by the Pope.[51]

There is only a faint trace of criticism of the sacramental system or inner substance of Catholic dogma which he left basically intact. How little he appreciated the evangelical issue involved in the matter of indulgences is evident from Doctor Reiss's argument in the *Epistolae Obscurorum Virorum:* "Naught can be compared with the Gospel: and whoever does well will fare well. If someone receives those indulgences a hundred times and has not lived well, he will perish and the indulgences will not help him." [52] Here was sheer moralism opposed to crass formalism.

Hutten's closest approximation to philosophical speculation was his reflection on the problem of providence and fate. He could never escape the notion that blind fortune spun the wheel of life and gave him many bad turns, a figure going back to Boethius and the classics.[53] In *Nemo* fortune posed its problems, and the theme recurs constantly in his correspondence with such friends as Pirckheimer. The idea was common enough as portrayed in Dürer's famous woodcut of Fortuna striding over the globe (figure 5). Hutten may have known Petrarch's *Fortuna*, as well as the notions of Lucian and Aeneas on the influence of Fortune on court life.[54] In his own dialogue *Fortuna* of 1519 Hutten fails to come through with a clear-cut solution. He uses the device as a vehicle for his personal grievances against life. On the matter of providence and fortune, Hutten comments noncommittally that religion teaches something quite different. He concludes that, since Fortune cannot be held responsible for her gifts, he should hold to Jupiter.

But Fortune tells that people are themselves much more to blame. He then compares human life with a ship voyage and shifts the theme to all the world's a stage and all the men and women merely players.[55] After much torment, at the end of his dialogue Hutten turns to the Christian chapel to beseech from Christ the Reedemer his desires.[56] The woodcut of Fortune on the title page of his *Dialogi*, 1520 shows the hand of God reaching from the clouds to turn the wheel of blind Fortune, with the inscription: "It is terrible for God and fate to battle." That is where Hutten left the problem — on a speculative level. As an activist the challenge that really moved him was that he should have the *virtú* with which to oppose fortune, the major concern of his Italian contemporary Machiavelli.

It is clear that Hutten had not appropriated very fully the religious ideas of Erasmus. His constructive suggestions were only faintly reminiscent of the *philosophia Christi*. He was not at all affected by the speculative ideas of Florentine spiritualized piety. For the "Pythagorians" he had only ridicule and there is no indication that he remotely understood Reuchlin's real purposes in his studies of the Cabala. But nowhere did his lack of religious depth in thought and feeling so clearly stand out as in his relation to Luther and the Reformation.

Hutten's great historical role began in earnest in 1520 when he joined Luther in his battle against the papacy. It was, in fact, for many years in vogue for historians to write of the two great reformers, Hutten and Luther. When the Wittenberg affair first came to his attention, Hutten, like Leo X, thought it was a mere monks' quarrel like that over the immaculate conception. "Devour and be devoured in turn," he chortled.[57] But he soon discovered Luther and addressed him as "You, my dear brother." He cheered Luther on: "They tell me that you have been excommunicated. How great, o Luther, how great you are, if this is true!" [58] He followed up this encouragement by announcing to Luther that he was ready to attack the priestly tyranny with letters and with arms.[59] Hutten was as good as his word and the writing in defence of Luther poured from his inkwell as from a fountain. His *Febris Prima* and *Inspicientes* seared Cardinal Cajetan, Luther's interrogator and judge. In his glosses on the *Bulla Decimi Leonis, contra errores Martini Lutheri* Hutten began by citing the New Testament on the antichrist who sits in the temple and shows himself as if he were God. He praised Luther for preaching Christ's evangel, attacked the cupidity of the Pope, the papal arrogance of forbidding any appeal to a council. He charged the papacy with associating the church with force and terror, not with love as Christ had done. Therefore, Hutten responded with Tertullian: "When we are condemned by you, we are absolved by God." [60]

Hutten followed this with a whole series of dialogues. The most dramatic among them was the *Bulla* or *Bullicida*, a conversation between the Bull, German liberty, Hutten, Franz, and other Germans. The bull called for aid from the canons, decrees, and excellent decretals.[61] His *Monitor I* and *Praedones* (Robbers) are a prize example of how Hutten could appropriate the form of Luther's ideas without really understanding their meaning. In the *Monitor* he has Luther speak of the liberty given by Christ, the ministry of brethren as opposed to the pretensions of the Petrine succession, the primitive simplicity of the church which lacked triumphal splendors. Hutten shows that he has missed the precise center of Luther's theology when he has him say: "I truly marvel at men who place the protection of salvation in gifts, which induce the cessation of good works, when they know that faith without works is dead." Again he has Luther announce that "to give to the poor: this is the true, living, and everlasting church of Christ." [62] In the *Praedones* Hutten reflected Luther's conception of the priesthood of all believers, arguing that Christ was the head of the church on earth, which had no need for a second head. But he advanced this notion as a cure for the frauds and superstition of the clergy, not as a concomitant of Luther's emphasis on personal faith which justifies.[63]

Hutten had not been without influence on Luther himself. On February 23, 1520, Luther wrote Spalatin that in reading Hutten's edition of Valla's *De Donatione*, he was angered, surprised at God's patience, and was nearly convinced that the Pope was the antichrist.[64] Now Luther repaid his debt in full. Hutten swam along with the torrent of his words. Under the impact of his popular appeal, Hutten lost his humanist inhibitions and turned to the people in their own language:

> For Latin penned I up to now,
> Which everybody did not know,
> Now cry I to the Fatherland,
> The German nation in its tongue,
> Vengeance to bring for every wrong.

His first German tract was *A Remonstrance and a Warning against the Presumptuous, Unchristian Power of the Bishop of Rome and the Unspiritual Spiritual Estate.*[65]

In the reform program which Hutten addressed to Frederick the Wise, he spoke like a Lutheran of his efforts in behalf of evangelical doctrine. But the tone quickly changed and he reverted to the old familiar themes of the curial greed for profit and the servile state of the Fatherland which of all nations loves liberty most. With an apocalyptic flourish he predicted the early fall of Babylon, the mother of whoredom and abomination, which has corrupted the earth with its prostitution. God will set things right, but through the hands of the princes, who would drive the antichrists from the land.[66] Like Luther he made an *Address to All the Estates of the German Nation.*[67] In December of that critical year Hutten composed in German some of his most telling lines in the *Gesprächbüchlein* (figure 6);

> The truth is born with a new chance;
> Deceit has lost appearance.
> Let all give God due praise and honor
> And heed the fearsome lies no longer.
> Yes, I say, truth which was suppressed
> Is hereby once again redressed.[68]

The theme of Hutten's apologetic writings is always the same. In the *Invective against Aleander*, the *Invective against the Lutherchewing Priests*, the *Exhortation to Emperor Charles V*, and the *Litany to the Germans*, Hutten's thought conforms to the same pattern. The papal tyrant and his minions are trying to suppress Luther, the most faithful preacher of true evangelical doctrine and champion of German liberty, therefore the Germans should rally around the Emperor and break the tyrannous yoke.[69] Hutten was committed emotionally to Luther's cause without ever really understanding its essence. On April 17, 1521, Hutten wrote to "the most invincible friend of the gospel" to fight strenuously for Christ, and not to give way to evils, but to go against them more daringly. Luther thanked him for the letter, and on April 20, Hutten wrote a second letter declaring his faith that Luther would remain Luther.[70] Hutten wrote to Pirckheimer describing the unfairness of the trial at Worms, where Luther was given only one choice.[71] But for all his enthusiasm for the reformer, Hutten remained vaguely aware of the difference between them.

In the first of the letters which Hutten wrote to Luther during the opening session of the Diet of Worms, he gave the classic expression to this difference: "We have, to be sure, different thoughts, for mine are human, but you, more perfect, already live entirely for things divine." [72] Hutten felt that in a certain sense he never was a Lutheran at all. In the *Expostulatio* Hutten explained that, though he considered himself an independent, free of party affiliation, he allowed himself to be called a Lutheran on the strength of the fact that he fought the Roman tyranny.[73] "I admire Luther's spirit," he wrote, "and his incomparable power in interpreting the secrets of Scripture, but Luther has been neither my teacher nor my comrade." [74] It was symbolic that Hutten rode off to join Sickingen and not Luther in his war against tyranny.

Luther appreciated Hutten's writings in his behalf and his poems which were not calculated to please Babylon.[75] But Luther could not condone Hutten's appeal to the sword as the final argument. On January 16, 1521, Luther wrote to Spalatin: "You see what Hutten wishes. But I do not desire to do battle for the gospel with violence and murder and I wrote him as much. Through the power of the Word the world is conquered, through the power of the Word the church has been created — and through the Word it will also be restored." [76] Erasmus was all too right when in his *Spongia* he sneered that some Lutherans, like Hutten, had nothing of Luther about them except that they maligned the Roman pontiff.[77] Hutten stood primarily for the outward freedom of the German man rather than like Luther for the inner liberty of the Christian man. His was the liberty for which Arminius fought, freedom from the new Roman imperium. Yet to his final days Hutten acclaimed Luther a hero of the Word, a prophet who gathers a following of the best men, a priest who is one with the Word he preaches. From his sickbed at Ebernburg not far from Worms,

Hutten had written: "Not much depends upon two men. There are many Luthers and many Huttens here. Should either of us be destroyed, a still greater hazard confronts you. For then the avengers of innocence and punishers of injustice will make common cause with the men who are fighting for freedom! . . . Do you not see that the wind of freedom is blowing?" [78]

Hutten remained essentially a medieval Catholic in the inner core of his religious life. These evidences of a medieval religious mentality are more than vestigial remains. They reveal that his understanding of sacerdotalism, sacramentalism, and popular medieval practices remained basically unchanged. Hutten denied vociferously that he was opposed to priests as such, but claimed that he had always been favorable to the true and honorable priesthood, citing his own poems to prove his point.[79] He had attacked only the abuses and the evils, not the clergy itself. Hutten maintained intact the medieval-estate system in his social thought. He held to the distinction within the church of the two estates which Christ ordained, the clergy and the laity.[80] The clergy should follow the counsels of perfection, while the laity could keep to this better way. The great offense for Hutten was the interference of the clergy in the affairs of the secular authority. He wished the return of the papacy to spiritual concerns, not its destruction. Like Cellini in his autobiography, he pictures the warring popes, Julius the bloodhound and Leo the man of force, last in a line of popes who for several hundred years had warred against the German emperors.[81] What Hutten really desired was not the abolition of the papacy, but the elimination of false practices.[82]

The very same conventional attitude is evident also with respect to the sacraments. His criticism of church practice at no point led him to strictures against medieval sacramentalism. There is no hint in Hutten of either rejection of the *ex opere operato* feature or an attempt to spiritualize the sacraments through a Neoplatonic mystique. Even though his own radical *Vadiscus* appeared at about the same time as Luther's *Babylonian Captivity*, Hutten took offence at this rejection of the traditional sacramental system.

Moreover, for all his satire in the *Letters of Obscure Men*, Hutten preserved intact many practices typical of medieval religiosity. In the last year of his life he still wrote in the *Expostulatio* of the saints, churches, and altars with all the deference of folk piety.[83] In the German translation of the dialogues he baptized many antique references replacing pagan names with Christian substitutes. He wished Michael von Sensheim well on his pilgrimage to Jerusalem in 1515.[84] What is more, if Crotus Rubeanus had not ridiculed the notion, he might at one point have gone on a pilgrimage to the Holy Land himself. His *Exhortation to the German Princes to Undertake War against the Turks*, 1518, was strictly in the medieval tradition. The princes would be called the active, brave, and pious liberators of the Christian world.[85] Here again he had occasion to complain of Leo's interference in the affairs of state, collecting a tax for war against the Turks instead of devoting himself to prayer. But the most damaging treatise of all, reflecting the very worst side of medieval superstition and prejudice, was his blast at an unfortunate Jew with the same name as Reuchlin's opponent, Johannes Pfefferkorn. He accused this miserable fellow of a whole catalogue of crimes and scandals, including desecration of the host, murder of Christian children, maligning a saint, defacing an icon, and worse.[86] He congratulated the Elector for having eliminated such a monster from the world.

D. F. Strauss in his day cheerfully depicted Hutten as the songbird of a new rosy dawn. It was even possible for one liberal writer to describe him as a rationalist in things religious.[87] Nothing could be further from the truth. Hutten was basically not at all philosophical. Like the Italians in the first phase of the humanist movement, he was essentially critical from the formal point of view without the philosophical substance to discuss the basic questions of metaphysics. Hutten's was the philosophy of the activist. "And lest you think I propose anything unreasonable, listen to this," he wrote: "all we who philosophize in the shade and do not in some way proceed to do things, what we know we do not really know!" [88] His philosophic and religious capacity was very narrowly circumscribed. Nor did his program require an intellectual effort of the first magnitude. Precisely because he was merely anticlerical and not antisacerdotal, antischolastic and not antireligious, pro-Lutheran and not anti-Catholic, he could satisfy his acerbity by surface criticisms without encountering the deeper issues at stake. This lack of a third dimension, real religious and philosophical depth, spared him the agonies of a dichotomy in his spiritual personality such as plagued so many of his fellow humanists. It has always been difficult for any man in any age to combine success-fully criticism and satire with constructive philosophy — witness Rabelais, Montaigne, Voltaire, or Nietzsche. For Hutten it was impossible.

Hutten was basically a romantic, imperialist, political propa-gandist, not a rationalistic liberal humanist. His social thinking was contained entirely with traditional concepts of the *corpus chris-tianum*, and his basic criticisms of the church stemmed from his belief that the Curia and its minions had encroached on the Emper-or's prerogatives and those of his imperial knights and had violated the ancient liberties of the empire.[89] He conceived his historical mission to be the restoration of the right order of things. Seeing Hutten in this light resolves many perplexing problems with regard to his ambiguous relation to humanism and the Reformation.

For Hutten the belles-lettres even of the classic authors were not an end in themselves. Rather they were an instrument for the cultural and political rejuvenation of the empire. But Hutten could not expose himself to the radiating brilliance of antiquity without experiencing some inner change. This is the secret of those rays of the *philosophia Christi* shining here and there from his religious thought, analogous to the ideas of Erasmus and in part derived di-rectly from him. But he was never altogether committed to this middle way with mind and heart.

As a militant critic Hutten was a pioneer and ally of the Re-formation. If the now-dated view of the Reformation as primarily an attack on ecclesiastical abuses still prevailed, Hutten would rightly be considered one of the reformers. But Hutten did not understand the basic religious impulse of Luther's movement. To him the Reformation was but an ally in a program dictated by his own class status and personal bent. This is why he did not view with alarm the overshadowing of the renaissance of learning by the revival in religion. For him both movements served the same end. A controversial figure in a polemical age, he demonstrated to per-fection that the conservative and traditionalist when he assumes the offensive may upset the world more than the self-conscious radical.

How ironic that in the end he was driven from the very empire for which he had dared all! Befriended by Zwingli, he sought refuge on the island of Ufenau in Lake Zurich. There he died in August 1523, of the same dread disease which had claimed the life of his foe, Julius II, the Aztec's revenge.[90] He was then only thirty-five and when he died his pen was his only possession. Even the sword of this brave *miles Christianus* was gone.

MUTIAN

Intellectual Canon

CROTUS Rubeanus, upon his election as rector of the University of Erfurt in the autumn of 1520, following his return from Italy, had his coat of arms displayed surrounded by those of sixteen humanist and reformer friends (figure 7). In the four corners of the design, larger than the rest were the shields of Luther, Erasmus, Reuchlin, and Mutianus Rufus, symbolizing their special place in the intellectual life of the day and suggesting a unity between them which was destined soon to be shattered. The study of the religious philosophy of Mutian holds promise for a better understanding not only of the relation of these great historical figures, but of the nature and spiritual content of Northern humanism itself. Mutian was not an activist, yet he stirred others to action. A tentative type, he nevertheless advanced far in the direction of religious enlightenment. A sharp critic, he shrank back from the frontal assaults of the reformers.

A study of the intellectual development of Mutian should be rewarding for several reasons. He himself was an important personality in the cultural life of his day. He held the undisputed leadership of the Erfurt humanist circle, not unlike the Rhenish sodality of Celtis or the Erasmian Strassburg league. As the key figure in the humanist movement of central Germany, he maintained a kind of literary censorial office which extended his influence far beyond that of his immediate personal contacts. In his own day he was highly regarded by such fellow humanists as the legist Ulrich Zasius, who, although not a member of the Erfurt circle, nevertheless considered Mutian "the most learned German,"

a second Varro. Mutian on his part with due respect for Zasius
whom he regarded highly, thought such adulation "stupid" and
said so quite plainly.[1] Posterity has given him fourth place after
Luther, Erasmus, and Reuchlin. This prominence suggests that
Mutian participated actively in the intellectual life of the period
and will serve as a useful index to the changing thought currents of
the time. He is a particularly useful subject for study because in
him the major conflicting sources of the religious thought of
Northern humanism combined or sought to combine. The product
of a home environment representative of the new rising lay culture,
he absorbed in turn the Northern piety of the *Devotio Moderna*
with its mystic tradition, piety, and biblicism, the late scholasticism
of the *via moderna* predominant especially in many university centers, and the Italian religious philosophy developing particularly
in Florence toward the end of the century. Moreover, he was only
a few miles removed from the center of Protestant activities during
the crucial initial years of the Reformation movement and was in
close contact with its principal and secondary figures.

Conrad Mutianus Rufus was born in Homburg, Hessia,
October 15, 1471, into relatively prosperous circumstances. His
father, Johann Muth, was a patrician and popular city councilor
and mayor. The family fortune was adequate to afford Mutian a
measure of financial independence during his travels and years at
Gotha, although his unstinted hospitality and costly book purchases, especially from Aldus and Froben, steadily depleted his
resources until his small stipend as canon became his sole remaining
income. When this was eliminated in 1525, he was reduced to
absolute poverty and dependence upon his friends. It is, however,
perhaps not too fanciful to see in his bourgeois background the
influence of the rising lay culture. It was perhaps this which produced in Mutian that optimistic mood which prompted him to
predict the advent of a new better world, an *aetas superior* in which
ingeniosi would grow, life and light would flourish.

Mutian's intellectual development was conditioned during three
distinct periods of formal education in Deventer, Erfurt, and Italy.
At the age of ten he entered the school of the Brethren of the
Common Life at Deventer. Estimates of the position of Deventer
in the development of Northern humanism have varied greatly.

It is clearly impossible to consider the Brethren's founder, Gerard Groote (d. 1384), the "father of Northern humanism." Rather, the trend of recent scholarship has been to stress the medieval character of the Brethren. The strong emphasis on piety was a prominent characteristic of the *Devotio Moderna*. The Westphalian Alexander Hegius was responsible for Deventer during the years of Mutian's studies there. Under Hegius, Deventer was dedicated to Thomistic realism, and Hegius, who learned Greek and made partial concessions to humanist learning, was himself concerned with problems of *post* and *ante rem*. Metaphysics was still the "praestantissima omnium scientiarum," high above grammar and rhetoric, alone deserving the name of wisdom. In his work directed against skepticism, the *De scientia et de eo quod scitur*, he argued that Aristotle was basic to a knowledge of the *res naturales* and to metaphysics as well and expressly polemicized against Plato and Platonists.[2] Such was the Hegius and Deventer that Mutian knew.

In 1486 Mutian entered Erfurt University where he received his A.B. degree in 1488 and his M.A. degree in 1492.[3] The following two years he taught at the university where he was an able and popular teacher.[4] The University of Erfurt, founded in 1392 as the fifth university in the Empire, was distinguished during the first century of its history by two characteristics, the antipapal sentiment of many of its leading figures, and the adherence in the faculties of theology and philosophy to the *via moderna*.[5] Several factors combined to accentuate the independent, antihierarchical tradition of the university. It was established during the great schism and sought authorization from several popes in succession, Clement VII, Urban VI, finally opening under Boniface IX, a fact not apt to benefit papal prestige at Erfurt.[6] Like Cologne, it was a bourgeois foundation, controlled by the city council. During the conciliar movement the university sided with the conciliarists and supported the recalcitrant Council of Basel after most of the other schools had returned to the papal fold. Two members of the faculty were especially widely known for their dissenting sentiments. Jacob of Jüterbock was a confirmed conciliarist, a close friend of the sensational popular preacher Geiler von Kaisersberg. The rector of the university in 1456, Johann of Wesel, a Marsiglian, after many years of criticizing abuse, received wide attention through his

5. *Nemesis*

6. Hutten's Gesprächbüchlein

famous tract against indulgences on the occasion of the papal Jubilee. Jacob Wimpfeling hailed him as the "Doctor saecularis." He was opposed by Heidelberg and Cologne, recanted at Mainz with the attendant burning of books. Luther stated over half a century later, "Johann Wesel and his books ruled the University of Erfurt where I received my M.A." Much antipapal feeling, however, was not overt and there was actually a great deal of external conformity on the part of the faculty as a whole. For example, on the occasions of his visitations in 1502 and 1504, Cardinal Raimund von Gunk was well received at Erfurt.[7] Nevertheless, the critical tone persisted and gained volume through the first decades of the sixteenth century.

Much Italian humanism was severe in its attacks upon church conditions and the scholastic philosophy. It was this fact in part which has deluded some scholars into a premature discovery of humanism at Erfurt and even to conclude that the "University of Erfurt was the first in Germany to decide for humanism."[8] In Erfurt the chapter school had established the *studium generale* long before Charles University or its own University had been founded. Moreover, the writings of Nicolas de Bibera around 1282 show that to a certain extent the classics were in use in the thirteenth century, for he cites freely from Juvenal, Terence, Horace, Plautus, and Virgil.[9] But the poems of Nicolas, the *Carmen satiricum*, for example, were after all essentially ecclesiastical and medieval.[10] For at this stage of development, as at Deventer under Hegius, the attitude toward classical learning was still *uti, non frui,* use, but do not enjoy for its own sake. The more purely humanist approach received new momentum with the increasing influence of the traveling poets. Humanism as a distinct cultural phenomenon had early beginnings in the Empire, particularly in the South. In 1460 Peter Luder and Jacob Publicius (Politian) of Florence taught at Erfurt. One of their most promising students was Johannes von Dalberg who later became closely associated with Rudolph Agricola in the humanist movement at Heidelberg. In 1486 Celtis taught at the University of Erfurt and proved to be an inspiration to many of the students, including Mutian, who recalled his instruction gratefully many years later.[11] Thomas Wolf of Strassburg also taught at Erfurt during Mutian's student days, as did Sömmering,

who gave popular lectures on Terence.[12] But in spite of this introduction of humanist learning and its gradual extension at Erfurt,
the *via moderna* was still the characteristic and dominant intellectual mode at Erfurt to the end of the century, that is, through and
beyond Mutian's student days.

It is true that the three leading figures at the University at the
turn of the century — Henning Goede, professor of jurisprudence,
Jodocus Trutvetter, in philosophy, and Bartolomäus Arnoldi of
Usingen, the leading theologian — made concessions to the new
learning and even promoted it in a limited way. But it is also true
that the young "humanists," including Mutian, were still formally
within the framework of the old pattern, debating *quaestiones*
with zeal. Significantly, one of the most important questions under
consideration in this late scholastic philosophy was the problem of
epistemology. The basic scholastic presuppositions were under examination and the next decades were to see a variety of answers to
this leading *quaestio*.

If the scholastic philosophy showed surprising virility and
longevity, the transition to a humanist predominance was rapid
and sensational. Henricus Aquilapolensis, a humanist of the more
tentative hesitant type, was active in reforming the old medieval
grammar. In 1494, the year of Mutian's departure from the University, Maternus Pistoris, an avowed humanist, joined the philosophy faculty. Camerarius later praised him lavishly, Eobanus Hessus
called him "the foremost devotee of the Muses," and Mutian himself corresponded with him concerning classical learning.[13] In 1501
Nicolaus Marschalk published the first Greek book in Erfurt, but
the following year he moved to the University of Wittenberg.[14]
In the year 1509 Mutian wrote to Herbord, a wealthy young protégé who was, after a long conflict between pressure for a legal
career and classical learning, becoming an important figure at the
University, "I congratulate the younger instructors, for they are
freeing themselves from barbarism." At the same time he wrote to
the rector of the University: "You may like it or not, but the
number of the cultured is increasing. I want you to know it." [15] A
city revolution took place in that year in which the townspeople
fought the council.[16] The consequent disturbance resulted in the
temporary disbanding of the humanist circle, but by 1512 most of

Mutian's friends had returned to Erfurt and in the summer of 1512 one of them, Heinrich Eberbach, was chosen rector of the University and humanism had at last gained a triumph. But Erfurt was by no means the pioneer in the establishment of a humanist program. By 1520 the new culture had made its way into all the larger universities of the Empire. In fact, the Rhenish universities of Basel and Heidelberg were at least twenty to thirty years ahead of Erfurt.[17] In the struggle for humanist learning at Erfurt Mutian was a participant, rather than a direct beneficiary, of its triumph. In its progress he and the circle of poets gathered about his pupil Eobanus Hessus played a decisive role.[18]

Up to the time of his departure for Italy, Mutian had been exposed to a variety of influences. At Deventer particularly, he was impressed with the emphasis upon inner piety that remained a component part of his religious philosophy. Classical learning was but a means to serve religious ends. He had been alternately exposed to the *via antiqua* and with equal enthusiasm to the *via moderna*. He was personally committed to neither and became increasingly hostile to scholasticism of any kind. The severe criticism of ecclesiastical practice and dogma made a lasting impression upon him. The intense concern for the problem of epistemology must have raised for Mutian the question of validity and certitude and inspired him to a further search for a satisfactory philosophy. Perhaps it was this stimulus in addition to the humanist inspiration supplied by Celtis and others which prompted him to give up his position at the University of Erfurt and journey southward. His itinerary included Bologna, Ferrara, Rome, Mantua, Venice, and Florence. He enjoyed the friendship and hospitality of the then popular poet Baptista Mantuanus and of Francesco Piccolomini, later to become Pius III. He devoted a year and a half to legal studies at Bologna. Above all, in Italy, at a still impressionable age, he learned to know the philosophy of the Florentine Platonists. After a brief term as councilor upon his return to Hessia in 1503, he entered the Chapter of Mary in Gotha as a canon where he spent the remainder of his life.

A strong scholastic and Aristotelian tradition persisted in Italy throughout the fifteenth and sixteenth centuries, particularly in the University of Padua. This was not merely a residue carried into a new period from a former one, but was an indication that the earlier humanism had not provided a substitute in the form of real philosophy. The humanists produced primarily literature, not philosophy, and while bitterly criticizing scholasticism and opposing Aristotle, they put in his place not Plato, but Cicero. It was only in the last half of the century that Manetti, Pico, and Ficino sought to construct a new metaphysical synthesis. There was some truth in Guiseppe Toffanin's attempt to describe humanism as an orthodox Catholic movement, which was designed to defend the church against unchristian individualism. But it is more accurate to understand the Florentine movement as an effort to reconstruct scholasticism not only by way of an apologetic or change of form, but as a new theological affirmation, with the special objective vis-à-vis Averroism of maintaining the dignity of the individual soul. Pico's *Conclusiones* and *Apologia* as well as his three theological works were very much in the scholastic tradition.[19] Similarly, Ficino's *Theologia Platonica* was as much a reconstruction of a positive metaphysical structure as a defence against Averroism. He believed in the harmony of Platonism and Christianity, both representing real spiritual values in identifying the highest good with the knowledge and enjoyment of God.[20] Thus humanism, which began as a nonphilosophical reaction against scholasticism, in order to supply a philosophical substance came to absorb the scholastic tradition. It has been suggested with some plausibility that the Savonarola episode tended to repress this speculative philosophy further into the older Catholic piety. In any case, the Florentine Platonism which Mutian learned to know represented an effort at a constructive theology in the service of Christian piety and in opposition to Averroism, lifeless scholasticism, and the half-stoic eudemonistic religiosity or irreligiosity characteristic of a small segment of Italian humanism.

The full and most significant impact of the Italian travels and studies upon Mutian must be measured not in terms of his increasing impatience with abuse or of his phenomenal acquisition of a broad humanist learning, but primarily in terms of the influence of Florentine Platonism upon his thought. Platonism was far from being a new phenomenon for Mutian. Neoplatonic thought, of course, had contributed much to Christian theology throughout the patristic and medieval period, so that one scholar has ventured the suggestion that what could be learned from Plato and the Neo-platonists for the purposes of a constructive distinctively Christian theology had been learned long before.[21] Moreover, some of the men at Erfurt who directly or indirectly exerted a great influence upon Mutian were not strangers to Platonic ideas. Johann Wesel, for example, prized Plato above Aristotle and studied himself under the Greek Platonists in Italy. But the consciously constructed synthesis of the Florentine Platonists with its striking Neoplatonic features made a special impact upon Mutian's thinking.[22]

Mutian wished to be considered a philosopher, not a mere philologist, rhetorician, or *literatus* in the purely humanist sense of the word. He disliked very much being compared with Cicero and preferred speaking of the "philosophus sanctus." [23] Thomas Wolf the younger called Mutian "without a doubt our greatest philosopher and orator." [24] Although his suggestion for the organization of a model university was no doubt in part a jest — especially in view of the fact that, when Erfurt was reorganized in 1519 according to humanist ideals, he participated very little — it may indicate in some measure the value he placed upon the sound philosopher. He wrote to Urban in 1513: "It would be enough in a great university, if there were one sophist, two mathematicians, three theologians, four jurists, five doctors, six orators, seven Hebraists, eight Graecists, nine grammarians, and ten right-minded philosophers as presidents and chiefs of the whole literary undertaking." [25]

It was an all but inevitable result of Mutian's previous education and experience that he should react strongly against the sacramental-sacerdotal system as it had developed in the late scholastic period. As a foil to his positive philosophy this negative emphasis merits special examination. One of the dominant notes in Mutian's writing was the protest against ceremonies, including the whole concept of sacramental efficaciousness *ex opere operato*. References to the barbarous practices, mocking the tonsure, and the like are very numerous.[26] "Only the ignorant seek salvation in fasts," is a recurring theme. Himself a canon, he reacted violently to the theory and practice of rote prayers. "When I am called by the hour bell to the pious murmuring with the canons, I am like a Cappadocian fire-worshipper [Pyraethian]," he wrote.[27] Not oracular confession and prayer, but work and virtues deserve reward.[28] Relics, benefice-seeking, usury against the peasants, all were roundly condemned. He excoriated the ethics of the clergy. Rome was the "hell of all crimes." He had seen Borgian Rome. In a Donatist fashion he doubted the efficacy of the religious acts of corrupt priests. A typical example of his jibes at current beliefs and practices is his letter to Peter Eberbach in 1512:

I always chuckle heartily, when Benedict tells me of the complaints of your mother that you go to church so seldom, do not wish to fast, and eat eggs contrary to the common usage. I then excuse this unheard-of awful transgression in this way. Peter acts correctly and shrewdly in not going to church, for the temple could collapse, the statutes might fall: there are many dangers. Moreover, the priests receive money, the laity salt and water as the goats. That is why they call the people a flock . . . The fast, however, he hates, because he knows what happened to his father . . . He fasted and died . . . That he ate eggs was due to the fact that he had no hens. If these had been there, they would never again have laid eggs. When some heard this, they wrinkled their brows and said, "Who will absolve you wicked Christians?" "Studies," I answered, "and knowledge!" [29]

A second illustration of this kind of criticism must suffice. It re-emphasizes his concern for spirit over ceremony and the institutionalization of the office of the keys. To Herbord he and Urban wrote:

We are taken under the protection of the living God and confess with the Apostle, what is beyond faith is sin . . . This is worth so much to all people that usually it is believed that the keys of heaven have been delivered to us. Who, therefore, despises our keys will feel the nail and the rod . . . We pastors and bishops (for Presbyters and bishops are used in the Holy Scriptures in many places to mean the same thing) will strike you with a great scourge, if you will not listen to the meaning of our commands. You may say in opposition: "A cleric who bears weapons should be excommunicated," or, "A good priest should be no manslayer." But do you not know what the weapons are? We have accepted from the breast of Serapis a magic character, which Jesus of Galilee did not lend to his authority. With that figure we frighten the enemies, entice money, sanctify God, shatter hell, and do miracles, heavenly or criminal. It is irrelevant that we actually are only the blessed guests of Jupiter. Farewell.[30]

This raises the problem of Mutian's own ethical standards. It is clear that his criticism of the morals of the priesthood did not stem from a Puritanical attitude of superiority. He freely admitted his share of minor vices. He concluded not a few letters with the confession, "Haec scripsi bene inebrius." [31] Moreover, he himself enjoyed the income of a prebend and played the game of benefice-seeking with gusto, actually securing "livings" for a good number of his humanist friends. There is some truth in the judgment that while ethical himself he was in expression sharp and cynical. His oft-cited letters to Urban on the occasion of his difficulties with a nun in the neighboring convent reflect a want of respect for the common morality which seems to stem from the fact that the humanist ideal was aristocratic and aesthetic, distinguishing the beautiful and the ugly, the refined and the vulgar, tending toward a relativity on matters of morality. On the other hand, these letters were written to an Urban who was very distressed and Mutian may have felt that a certain amount of bravado would supply as much comfort as any other approach.[32] Many statements could be adduced reflecting a genuine concern for the "common morality." He forbade his students to write Goliardic verse. Very significantly, he opposed the crowned poets who were jealous in opposition to theology. The youth should read only chaste poets; the priests should read none, with the exception of Baptista Mantuanus. The mysteries of theology are not to be profaned.[33]

Much of Mutian's criticism was of a conventional nature in the old tradition. General dissatisfaction with prevailing conditions was increasing during these decades.[34] The general pattern of the humanist criticism is familiar to all through the *Epistolae Obscurorum Virorum* and Brant's *Narrenschiff*. Unlike Heinrich Bebel's popular *Facetiae*, which he read and recommended in 1509, Mutian's criticism employed the resources of a remarkable classical erudition.[35] But a more fundamental factor distinguished most of his criticism from the common expressions of dissatisfaction and ridicule which were the order of the day. He stressed individuality and personal responsibility in contrast to the objectivization of religion in the institutionalized framework. He consistently protested against the externalization and vulgarization of spiritual meaning and values. That his characteristic expressions were of this nature can be explained only in the context of his positive philosophy.

The characteristic attitude of much humanism was critical and negative in its orientation. Mutian in contrast opposed the poets who attacked theology. He desired renovation rather than rejection. He reflected the concern of contemporary Florentine thinkers for a constructive theology to replace in part and revitalize in part the desiccated and vulnerable structure of late scholasticism. Dogma, he believed, had become externalized and reduced to mere mechanical formulas perpetuated by a highly institutionalized organization. The superstitious practices of the common folk had reduced Christianity almost to the *quid pro quo* basis of more primitive, less highly rationalized, religions. Acts considered to be religious were on the level of the ancient Roman formula *do, ut des*, I give in order that you may give, O God. Mutian developed his religious conceptions with a full awareness of the urgent necessity for a renewed emphasis upon spirituality.

The most significant element in Mutian's constructive religious thought was his consistent spiritualization of the Judaeo-Christian theological heritage. This tendency was related to the very heart of philosophy as it was understood by Ficino. In a letter to John Gozaltes he wrote: "Since philosophy is by all defined as love of wisdom, wisdom is in truth the contemplation of divine things, certainly the end of philosophy is a knowledge of divine things." True philosophy consists in transcending the phenomenal world to the world of ideas. "For whoever is avid for truth, turns his mind to the contemplation of divine things and places little significance upon the desires of the body." The meaning of philosophy, then, is in rising above nature through the spirit, not by despising or denying the corporeal and the natural — Ficino was a doctor — but things corporeal should be strictly limited in the totality of human existence and directed toward correct ends. This dualistic world picture and the striving of the philosopher to rise above the corporeal was a dialectical conception, Ficino warned, which was not to be understood in terms of a formal logic, but rather in terms of a method for attaining to the truth. Philosophy is thus a way for the identification of man and God. The philosopher can become on earth a mediator between God and man (*Quippe inter Deum et homines medius est Philosophus, ad Deum homo, ad homines Deus*). Such was Ficino's conception of the rational ethical and religious

value whose last and deepest meaning was in the final step the redemption of man. In the end the soul of man returns to its super-
mundane home where it contemplates the secret mysteries of the
Creator. The undogmatic and dynamic nature of this view of God,
man, and nature is reflected in Mutian's religious philosophy.

In contrast to a static Aristotelian-scholastic conception of God
as pure being to be approached only through well-defined formal
theological avenues, Mutian viewed God as dynamically and im-
manently active. His was a *deus vivus*, a Spirit in and with all life
and being.[36] God could and did inspire men immediately to charity
and friendship. The Spirit of God fills the orb of the earth. "He is
that God, pure love, who breathes where He wills and establishes
true and perfect friendship among mortals. He is, I say, that divine
inspiration who makes you religious men of unanimous and harmonious minds, through whom no love is dishonest, without whose
intervention there is no pure delight. Of this must be understood
that saying: 'Whom God hath joined together, let not man put
asunder.' " [37] This view of God had also important implications for
his christology.

The significance of Christ to Mutian lay in the spiritual qualities
which He essentially was and represented. He distinguished in that
way between the Christ and the historical Jesus. True religion
recognized the Christ who descended from heaven as righteousness,
peace, and joy. Opposition to anthropomorphic views of God was
certainly nothing new with Mutian. Dante had explained it beauti-
fully:

> Few only through the senses can it grasp
> What later it makes fit for intellect.
> Therefore the Holy Scripture condescends
> To meet your faculties, and speaks of God
> As having hands and feet, but means it not.[38]

Mutian went farther. He attacked any unusual reverence for the
humanity of Christ stemming from his divinity. Reacting against
the profane regard for relics of the human Jesus, he exclaimed to
Urban: "Janus will tell you of the beard of Christ. Oh, what a
beard! Christ detested falsehood and yet no one lies more impu-
dently than the priests of Christ. I do not revere the tunic and
beard . . . I worship the living God, who did not appear in cloak

and beard . . . The theologians err." [39] Mutian suggested that the
true Christ was not crucified at all, for the true Christ is soul and
spirit.[40] To bolster his argument he cited the incident of Apollonius
of Tyana and his remarkable disappearance at his trial before Domitian. Apollonius, whom Ficino, too, had found intriguing, was
a Pythagorean who died around 98 A.D., the author of several
books on sacrifice, astrological prediction, and letters. But his real
biography had no relation to the myth which grew about him as
the incarnation of the religious ideal of the Neopythagoreans.
Philostratus' *Life of Apollonius of Tyana*, published by Aldus in
1504 and therefore available to Mutian, was clearly analogous to
the picture of Christ in the four gospels and included the story of
his trial before Domitian in Rome. This spurious biography origin-
ated most likely in the circle gathered around Julia Domna and was
designed to discredit the gospel narrative. Mutian accepted it, or at
least used it, and thereby approximated the ancient Docetist heresy
that Christ's body was a phantasm and that His passion was a mere
appearance. He faced the question posed by Ignatius, "If, as some
godless men say, Christ suffered in mere appearance, being themselves mere appearances, why am I in bonds?" [41] In his view of the
person of Christ, Mutian was on the thin edge of historic Christianity. In much the same fashion Mutian spiritualized the sacraments. He considered sacraments and mysteries as then practiced
ridiculous.[42] The real significance of the sacrament lay not in the
corporeal transubstantiation, but in the essence of the sacrament, in
love. No host can be more holy than mutual love.[43] The true Christ
is not food and drink, he wrote to Urban, in a very explicit passage:

They are ignorant of the fruit of true religion. Oh, Urban, our
Redeemer is the lamb and the shepherd. But who is our saviour? Righteousness, peace, and joy. This is the Christ who descended from heaven.
The kingdom of God is not eating and drinking, but righteousness,
fortunate faith and untroubled tranquillity in humility. This chalice of
salvation I will receive and call upon the name of the Lord. Would that
we would consume such bread of angels worthily! "My food," says the
eternal truth, the living law, the head of the church, "is that I do the
will of Him that sent me and accomplish His work." If therefore the
will of God is to obey the divine commands, if it is the highest of
commands that we love God and our neighbour, think, my Urban,
whether those fools rightly take the food of God, who devour the host

and against the sacrament of Christian love, destroy the peace and disseminate hatreds.[44]

As the basis of ethics Mutian urged the universal applicability of the law of love in contrast to legalism. The two commandments, love of God and love of fellow-man, comprise the essence of the natural law written in the hearts of man as a kind of natural knowledge.[45] This moral law is closely associated with the peace and harmony ruling in the wider universe, the law which the nations revere with the instinct of nature. He wrote to Urban:

> Moses, Plato, Christ taught it. This is prescribed in our hearts. For who does not know that harmony and mutual love is divine, holy, and very dear to God, since God rules all things in a certain order, so that nothing opposes another. From this eternal law priests and emperors make constitutions not entirely bad, if the evil of the interpreters is absent. For you yourself feel that men are evil who for the sake of money itself turn black to white and worthless glosses, so that they defend unfair interest rates and usuries. The others imitate equity and the common good and law of nations, which by me is rightly called eternal law, which I observe and admire in the world of the heavenly spheres, and the high God in that great and most beautiful and best arranged world I laud and praise with the church.[46]

Though Christ represented and made explicit this natural law to the fullest extent, it was given at least partial expression in the laws of Draco, Solon, Lycurgus, Moses, Plato, Pythagoras, the decemvirs, and others.[47] Insofar as Mutian was not bound by traditionalism or by humanist aristocratic notions, this concept of natural law also influenced his political and social thinking, though not as immediately as it did his ethical theory. When, for example, the people's party arose in the city of Erfurt against the city council, the rich bourgeois syndics, for shielding a city official from punishment for fraud, Mutian and the young humanists sided with the commoners, while Goede and the older men sided with the council and went down to defeat and exile. Mutian cited every authority from Solon down in the people's cause. He wrote to Herbord that who entered the fray was wise, the most honest, and the most virtuous. "It is foolish to believe that princely men are just born; they come often from the lowest class; already Isocrates said there would be better rulers if they were elected. An emperor is made, not born." [48] Is it fanciful to see in this association of the idea of natural law with the political representative ideal an anticipation on the individual level of the later development of the republican system based on natural right? Different social and political conditions might have given Mutian's suggestion wide historic consequences.

There is a close relation between Mutian's theory of natural law and his whole anthropology. Man is intimately related to all other beings in the universe. For Mutian, as for Ficino, man was an intermediate being in the universe, drawn toward God, truth, and goodness, and at the same time bound by the sensual. To describe this duality, Mutian used two terms current in Christian theology from Paul to late scholasticism, but not used in the *Theologia Platonica: corpus* and *carnis.* Insofar as man is a mirror of the macrocosm, a divine reflection of God Himself, he belongs to the genus of God, he is a little god. To Urban, Mutian explained: "By discourse alone we reveal the soul and the god of this smaller world who lives in the heaven of our heart and head. Whence we are spoken of as servants of heaven, if we have lived spiritually or philosophically or in a Christian way, conforming more to the spirit than to passion." [49] The religious man especially is a divine light and majesty.[50] This view of man and his spiritual and philosophical affinity to God is clearly related to the idea of man as microcosm as developed by Pico and Ficino.[51] The *carnis,* or sensate side of man, related to the material world, does not participate in the higher life and will have no part in the resurrection. Mutian at times questioned the possibility of the soul itself being sentient in an after-life.[52] The resurrection was spiritual, as the soul rises after the remission of sins.[53] Nevertheless, Mutian did not consistently maintain an absolute identity of man with divinity. A qualitative difference remained. The ethical difference still represented the chasm between absolute and relative good. God is the judge, man the judged. All will be called before the judgment seat of God. Who then will maintain the validity of worldly wisdom and secular learning before the eternal God? [54] God and man are still extremes joined in the mediator Christ.[55] Similar conflicting modes of thought are evident in his view of nature.

A new feeling toward nature appeared during the Renaissance, a kind of mystical sentiment colored by a variety of religious ideas. This view of nature very understandably prospered among the Florentine Platonists. There is really nothing bad in nature, for all the world is much alive, Ficino maintained.[56] Mutian in a similar way viewed the cosmos in a more metaphysically mystic than in an empiric way, stressing the beauty and form of the world, referring to the peace reigning in the planets and the great mother earth, our goddess.[57] Drawing inspiration from Pliny, Lucian, and Ovid, he exclaimed, "For at the same time Sol, the father of gods and men, pours out the breath of life abundantly, the true soul of the world, the highest Godhead of nature and heaven." [58] The world reflects brilliance and soul as the sun. Nature itself is pious. The earth is most holy.[59] It is this type of expression which has earned for Mutian a reputation for pantheism.

In this respect the problem of Mutian's view of nature closely resembles that raised by Nicolas Cusanus. Cusanus held God to be the *Possest*, the absolute potentiality in actuality, including all the positive attributes of God, and in this Principle is contained all that can in any way exist. Moreover, God is the *coincidentia oppositorum*, for by being infinite He is the principle of all number by being the minimum and the consummation of all number by being the maximum. Thus God for Cusanus was demonstrably the coincidence of all opposites. The world and nature was then the *explicatio complicati* by a kind of Neoplatonic emanation from God.[60] Cusanus did not teach that the concrete world was related to God as the part to the whole. Rather, he brought God and the sensible world under the same concept of a reality having two sides. God is the invisible side of creation and creation is an apparition of the invisible God. This close identification of God and nature raised the question of pantheism from his own day to our own.[61] Interestingly, Giordano Bruno in the sixteenth century arrived by an intellectual Odyssey much like Mutian's from scholasticism to Neoplatonism, to a feeling for the infinity of the universe and, in partial dependence on Cusanus, to a pantheistic position.[62] Mutian's view of nature has essential features very similar to both men: the Neoplatonic sources of their thought, the mystic view of nature, the close identification of God and nature. Several basic differences, however, must be noted.

Even in his exalted feeling about man and nature, Mutian was forced to qualify his expressions by the sheer facts of life. "Being born, we die, and the end hangs already from the beginning." Furthermore, Mutian's statements on the relation of God to the world usually occur as a result of rhetorical or literary inspiration and are buttressed by citation from classical authors. Unlike the case of either Cusanus or Bruno, he did not arrive at this extremism as a logical necessity following from a closely argued metaphysical system. Finally, his thought on the whole reflects the Hebraic-Christian historical view of the distinction between creature and Creator. He wrote, for example, "We read Aristotle and Plato and this suffices. Turned to Christ, we picture Christ to ourselves. We leave behind the entelechy of Aristotle and the ideas of Plato. God created all things from nothing. He spoke and they were done . . . We know that nature is nothing, if not, as Empedocles said, a mixture of elements. In the same tenor Anaxagoras said nature was condensation and diffusion, that is a rising and a falling." [63] Mutian agreed with Paul that God was *ultramundanus*." [64] For Mutian, therefore, time and eternity, the finite material and the infinite immaterial stood in a paradoxical rather than an analogical relation. He was intellectually clear of pantheism and even of panentheism, to borrow Dilthey's terminology.

The second major aspect of Mutian's constructive theology was the universalism implicit and expressed in his religious thinking. His spiritualization of the Hebraic-Christian inheritance with its stress upon the moral influence rather than the doctrine of vicarious atonement, militated against the uniqueness of Christianity in relation to other religions. Mutian implied such a tendency by using classic and Christian terminology interchangeably. He called Benedict "Pythagoras," heaven was the realm of Jupiter (Christ), Hell was Tartarus, Mary, the mother of the great thunderer. [65] His statements on this universalist thesis are so explicit as to merit direct quotation. In agreement with the Koran which he often cited, he stressed virtue as the essence of true religion:

New clothes, new ceremonies are introduced, as though God were honored by clothes and garments. In the Alcoran one reads, "Who prays to the eternal God and lives virtuously, he may be a Jew, Christian, or a Saracen, he receives the grace of God and salvation." There-

fore through right living and not through new garment is God satisfied: for the only true honoring of God consists in not doing evil. He
is religious, right living, pious, who has a pure heart. All else is smoke.[66]

Just as no faith has a monopoly on the essence of true religion,
so the physical accoutrements of one religion have no special significance not common to all:

I do not agree with those who hold only the churchyard for holy.
Every place belongs to the holy Tellus, which the learned call also
Ceres, Rhea, Ops, Cybele, Proserpina, and the great Mother. He is
therefore in the lap of mother, whether the credulous brother wishes
it or not.[67]

Mutian argued that the spiritual nativity of Christ occurred
before all ages, so that Christ, much as Justin Martyr had conceived
of the spermatic logos, the true wisdom of God, was present with
the Jews in Syria, with the Greeks, Italians, and even the Germans,
though their religions were observed by different rituals and
priesthoods.[68]

This religious universalism was certainly not a legacy of the
Devotio Moderna as Mutian came to know it at Deventer under
Hegius. There one brother was sharply reprimanded for writing
"thus God is spoken of in Ovid just as in Augustine." [69] Rather it
was clearly derived from the Florentine Platonists, the probable
source for Zwingli of a very similar idea. Ficino held the Alexandrine historical myth that all philosophical and religious knowledge
both before and after Christ was derived from the Hebraic-
Christian special revelation. Plato was a pupil of Moses. His
Neoplatonic commentators were imitators of St. John, St. Paul,
Hierotheus, and Dionysius the Areopagite.[70] Similarly, Pico's unity
of truth presupposed a syncretism of philosophical and religious
truths. Mutian concurred in this universalist view, but deduced it
metaphysically from his belief in the immanent activity of God's
spirit inspiring men to truth and virtue, rather than from the historical myth of transfer or borrowing from Palestinian sources.

The third major component of Mutian's positive philosophy
was the moral interpretation of Paulinism. Ficino following
Dionysius and Plotinus had stressed the idea of the free spirit and
the fatherhood of God, the overcoming of the flesh, and beauty,
purity, and form in ethics.[71] Mutian's inclination toward this type

of piety may have been partly temperamental, well suited to the *Beata Tranquillitas*, his home. "If only my life finds rest in piety and the leisure of teachings! Our study concerns God and holy men and a knowledge of all antiquity; if to delight in this itself is possible, I am delighted, and I rejoice," he confided to Urban shortly after his arrival in Gotha.[72] The return to original sources was in a sense the heart of Renaissance humanism. The stress on the return to Christian sources was the heart of the new humanism of the Florentine Platonists. Particularly Pico and Ficino were interested in a *renascens pietas*, the *restitutio Christianismi*, and in *Christum ex fontibus praedicare*. The drive to the sources led them to a renewed appreciation of the writings of the Fathers, and most significant of all, to a renewed study of the New Testament, and especially of the epistles of Paul. In urging the study of the Scriptures and Fathers, Mutian held up Pico himself as an example of respect and devotion to this type of study.[73] Ficino directed much of his study to Paul's epistles. He tried by referring to the Greek text of the New Testament to grasp the meaning of the epistle to the Romans, for example, in terms of its own historical setting and its specific concepts. It remained more noteworthy as an attempt than as an achievement, for his interpretation was so full of Plato that he failed to overcome either his own philosophical preconceptions or the dogmatic tradition by a discovery of the true historical context or of the unique religious insight of Paul. An interesting study in contrast would be the comparison of Ficino and Luther's exegesis of the Epistles of Paul. The key passages of *Romans* so significant for Luther's fidistic insight (chapter 5, for example) receive an entirely different treatment from Ficino. Faith is that which justifies by love. The accent throughout is on love and charity rather than on the anterior reconciliation with God through faith.[74] This emphasis was beyond a doubt a carry-over from his overwhelming emphasis on divine love as Plato defined it, the desire to contemplate anew the divine beauty, an emphasis fully developed in the *De religione Christiana* and the *Theologia Platonica*, both of which Mutian knew well.[75] Mutian's Paulinism was unmistakably of the Florentine type. He was less concerned with problems of grace and justification than Colet or Lefèvre, more in the synergistic morality position of Erasmus.

Mutian read and valued many of Lefèvre's writings on Aristotle, the Commentary on Paul's Epistles, the Psalms, and the like. Bossus (Florentine preacher), Zenobius (Vatican librarian and translator of Eusebius), Baptista Mantuanus, Erasmus, and Reuchlin he considered "true theologians." [76] Although he does not seem to have read Colet, Mutian knew Erasmus well, corresponded and exchanged gifts with him, and developed a striking intellectual affinity with him.[77] Mutian knew Biblical literature and the Fathers, having read all of Augustine, Ambrose, Leo, and especially Jerome.[78] He cherished Erasmus' edition of Jerome and of the New Testament. He called Erasmus the restorer of theology upon whose shoulders Oecolampadius, Melanchthon, and Luther stood.[79] This first aspect of Mutian's ethical Paulinism, the return to the original norms of Christian behavior and primitive sources of inspiration in the early church had the result of minimizing the importance of the sacramental-sacerdotal system.

The second aspect of Mutian's ethical Paulinism, also parallel to Erasmus' *philosophia Christi*, was his emphasis on piety, the *lex Christi*. "We are pursuing a narrow and deep, arduous and difficult path . . . We aim at righteousness, temperance, patience, concord, truth and friendship." [80] "The highest God must be revered with the greatest piety." [81] His appreciation for Benedict, Bernard, and other monastic leaders stemmed not from their ascetic lives or foundations (he hated Francis, Dominic, and the mendicant friars especially), but from their examples of Christian virtues. He praised Bernard for his humility on the one hand, and the humanist Eitelwolf von Stein for his learning on the other, with perfect consistency.[82]

This trust in piety and ability to lead the good life presupposed a confidence in human freedom and moral capability. Mutian himself lacked a deep sense of sin, the meaning and implications of the ethical and qualitative difference between God and man which he himself acknowledged formally. At one time he said that he himself had lived innocently for twenty-two years and had lived without offending anyone. He could say with full conviction that piety is the guide to life. Tranquillity of conscience and the security of innocence removes all doubt as to sinless self-sufficiency.[83] The essence of the *lex Christi*, then, was not a sin-grace antithesis, but was the teaching of Christ as the new and highest revealer of true ethical principles. The essence of the new dogma lay in the good examples, holy morals, Christian rules. "The Christian religion teaches me that it prohibits the evil which I would prefer to enter into," he wrote to Urban.[84] This was "the heavenly and pious philosophy," he wrote in Erasmian terms.[85] Through his higher morality and keener insight, Christ gave man decrees and laws by which men can bring their lives to a richer fulfilment. He wrote, "I therefore rest quietly in the simple gospel, having turned myself wholly to the decrees of Christ and cast off all cares." [86] This piety, while possibly related to the self-assurance of the rising lay bourgeoisie, was nevertheless not a secular morality divorced of ecclesiastical implications. In 1510 Mutian wrote:

I have decided to direct my studies and my learning to piety and to take from the poets, philosophers, and legists only that which serves a pious life. It is godless to try and be wiser than the church. Should I offend God and men through frivolousness? Certainly I must not offend. We carry on our forehead the seal of the cross, the standard of our King. We do not wish to be transgressors. No one can serve Christ and Baal. Holy is the army of our general. Nothing shameful shall be with us in our camp.[87]

This last statement in particular raises the question of Mutian's conformity to institutional standards of life and dogma and of his mysterious desire to restrict his ostensibly considered religious ideas to the knowledge of a few intimate friends. This attitude of Mutian's has puzzled many students of Northern humanism. Ludwig Geiger asked whether this Mutian who asked Urban and Herbord to burn his letters was the Mutian who boldly condemned the Cologners for burning the *Augenspiegel*. Did he wish to forbid the unlearned entrance to the sacred halls? Was he a hypocrite, offering one hand to the learned and another to his unlearned friends? Was it fear of joining in the cry "woe to the vanquished"? Who can solve this riddle, the solution of which would be important with respect to the individual man, but becomes of the highest importance, since in a sense it characterizes a generation? [88] A variety of possible reasons might be suggested for his reluctance to publish his views. He himself described how he had resolved never to publish any of his work or seek the laurel wreath. He felt he had good precedent for his habit of nonpublication, for Galba, Socrates, and Christ had written nothing.[89] Scholars know of only one sizable work by Mutian, a book on rhetoric which Melanchthon planned to publish in 1538 but never actually did. But Mutian sought to restrict the circulation of his own letters in an age when the common code allowed the printing of personal letters. Mysteries must not be popularized, he wrote to Urban.[90] To Herbord he wrote: "If you love me, you will tear up my letter. If you fail to do so I shall not dare cavil as I do." [91] He even refused to lend his reading notes to Herbord for fear they might be made public.

One possible explanation for this esoteric restriction of his views to his philosophic friends may be that of personal timidity. He frequently pleaded, after expressing some unconventional religious viewpoint, that he was merely jesting, just playing. Another possible factor was the aristocratic tradition of humanism. Perhaps, though this seems unlikely at least in any immediate and direct sense, he may have absorbed the Averroist view of the three levels of truth, the philosophical, theological, and popular truth, similar to Comte's three levels of knowledge, which may have prompted his restriction of certain philosophic religious views to "top-level" men. Even the Occamist tradition of the division of rational and revealed or willed (voluntarist) truth, may have influenced his distinction between restricted and common knowledge. Certainly the problem was not unique with him. Possibly all these factors were of importance in the formulation of his attitude. The most likely explanation, however, lies elsewhere.

The basic reason for Mutian's reluctance to express his positive philosophy openly was the fact that he himself was not completely certain of its validity in relation to the old norms and he feared the consequences of its popularization. This did not mean mere timidity out of fear for his own quiet and reputation, but a genuine concern for the good of Mother Church. In March of 1514, even while supporting Reuchlin with Crotus and the Erfurt men, he wrote in a letter to Urban:

Leave to us the paternal religion, most learned Reuchlin, and harm the Christians not, while you defend the Hebrews. You actually harm them, however, when you introduce two Nazarenes with the name of Jesus and oppose to us testimony of Celsus, Julian, Porphyry. For what else is it than that you create a new dogma and darken the truth with old deceptions? [92]

Was this expression of concern for the paternal religion the result of a sudden return to religion, an answer to a call received while reciting the breviary? During and after 1514 expressions of regard for the church and its religion are more numerous. In that year, after a lapse of a decade, he returned to the celebration of the Mass. To Urban he wrote: "I shall sing to the Lord a song mystic and divine. I cannot save piety and still stay away longer from the altar and sacrifice. Up to now I have been more an observer than a participant . . . Now I wish with God's grace to sacrifice the Lord's supper and remembering pay for the living and the dead." [93] In that year he accepted Urban's poem *Carmen de doctrina domini nostri Jesu Christi pendentis in cruce per modum dialogismi Christi et Christiani*, which he had written at Mutian's suggestion in a manner reminiscent of the believing mystic of earlier centuries. Nor was this religious manifestation the familiar phenomenon of an old age conversion. By 1524, says David Friedrich Strauss, Mutian had exchanged Virgil for the Psalms.[94] Baptista died in 1518 as the general of the Carmelite order, Wesel's last request was that he be buried on monastic grounds, and Pico was laid to rest in a Dominican monastery. But Mutian was not old. Both before and after 1514 he expressed both sides of his religious thinking, the novel and the conventional, varying only in frequency and emphasis. Perhaps the shift in emphasis was a matter of temperament, so that after the storms of the Reuchlinist controversy, he retired to the quiet and rest of conformity. But he had always been fond of the Psalms and had written poems on them. He urged Baptista to honor Benedict in verse in the early radical years.[95] In August 1513 he wrote:

To reject the authority of the church, with whose body you wish to be a member, is damaging and full of impiety, even if you perceive errors. We know that many things are lies to the wisest men and we are not ignorant of how to lead life successfully, as men who are beguiled by religion. In one way the simple reader, in another the erudite understands it. That one is content with bare history, this one, however, is inspired by mysteries, searches the anagogic, allegoric, and tropologies.[96]

In 1509 Mutian wrote to Herbord, "Who should not submit himself to the authority of the church?" [97] At no time, therefore, in spite of abuse or the impulse toward his own constructive theology did Mutian entertain the idea of harming or leaving the church. He desired reformation and not rejection.

In this fundamental viewpoint lay the crux of Mutian's differences with the Reformation. He had taken a more consistently conservative turn long before 1517. At Erfurt with a student body of around two thousand, Luther had known some of the larger circle of Mutian's poets. In 1516 Luther and Mutian became friends through Lang and Spalatin, but the friendship was not close or of long duration.[98] In 1521 Mutian still admired Luther, but vacillated wildly and finally as disorders increased and the Reformation became a matter of obviously serious consequences, Mutian turned against it.[99] One reason for the division between Mutian and Luther was simple misunderstanding. For example, Luther repeated the report which came to him that Mutian denied God's omnipotence.[100] Mutian's timidity and a certain amount of self-interest was undeniably a factor. In June 1521, Mutian wrote to Lang, "I am a good friend of the Lutherans. But I must consider my circumstances and position. Doors are broken, windows smashed, and one lives in barbarity. I would be a fool to acknowledge the boisterous Lutherans openly. The holy fathers would murder me. If you good people were in my position, what would you do." [101] Two months before, Luther had faced the Diet of the Empire. In the same year Eoban wrote that Erasmus pointed out what pruning was needed in God's vineyard and that Luther, a greater man for that reason, took the axe and did the pruning.[102] Why did Mutian and Eoban differ at this point? The really fundamental reason for Mutian's opposition to the Reformation lay in the fact that his universal religious ideas, ethical Paulinism, his conformity to the church tradition and institutionalism were simply not compatible with the intensive personal religious ideal of the Reformation. Mutian was not in accord with the *sola gratia, sola fide,* or *sola scriptura,* the three cardinal elements of Luther's movement. In the conflict of reason and faith, an almost perpetual metaphysical problem and specifically the legacy of the Augustinian and Occamist tradition, Mutian never overcame the bifurcation, the conflict of ideals. Unlike many of his circle of Erfurt humanists, he did not decide for the Reformation.

In brief, Mutian was assuredly not a Renaissance man in the Burckhardtian sense. Aeneas Silvius in the preceding century was perhaps a better example of this type of churchman. Mutian was not only a pantheist by intention, but was intellectually clear of this position. He was a theist. While he stood in a long tradition of criticism of the church, he made an effort to supplant the intellectually sterile scholasticism with a positive philosophy. His constructive theology might be described in terms of Erasmus' *Philosophia Christi*, but it was clearly analogous and not derivative. It comprised three main elements: the spiritualizing of dogmatic and ecclesiastical conceptions, the promotion of universalistic ideas, and the moral interpretation of Paulinism. Neoplatonic sources, specifically the Florentine school, had the decisive influence upon his thought. Plato was to him the *summus Philosophus*. Finally, in the course of his intellectual development, in statements derived from various sources, and even in single letters, there is revealed a conflict of ideals which he never fully resolved.

His last written words were: "The peasant knows many things which the philosopher does not know. Christ, our life, died for us. This I do believe as most certain." And so in his last days he turned to a thought which he had learned at Deventer from the *Imitatio Christi* of Thomas à Kempis. He had never ventured very far beyond the shelter of that faith.

✦VIII✦

PIRCKHEIMER
Speculative Patrician

IN June of that historic year 1517 Johannes Cochlaeus, newly created doctor of theology (Ferrara), wrote to Pirckheimer from Italy, "Erasmus, Reuchlin, and Willibald, bound together by the same spiritual interests as by their close friendship, shall one not hope for and expect a better and greater future for all Christendom from these three stars?"[1] It seems truly surprising to find the name of Willibald Pirckheimer, a wealthy man of practical affairs, placed in a heady intellectual constellation such as this. But, as shrewd Erasmus perceived, Pirckheimer differed from the rest of Nuremberg's upper bourgeoisie. "You are," he wrote, "absolutely the rarest bird of this century, for you join extraordinary erudition with such a brilliant fortune, again, with such great friendliness and humanity."[2]

Albrecht Dürer caught the strength and vitality of his most intimate friend in his copper engraved portrait of 1524, when Pirckheimer was in his fifty-third year (figure 8). With an insight into his subject gained from years of close association and a community of intellectual interests, Dürer knew Pirckheimer's true self. The massive bull-like shaggy head rests heavily upon his powerful frame. The eyes dominate the countenance, large, expressive, sensitive, intelligent, manly. The nose is flattened, as though to allow greater prominence to the mouth. The lips are pressed firmly together, but the corner lines betray a touch of Lucian scampishness. The garment with its fur collar marks the dress of a gentleman. The inscription reads: "He lives by his creative spirit, the rest will belong to death."

Nuremberg, feted by Aeneas Silvius as the center of Germany

and of Europe, was the jewel box of the Empire and the queen of the South German cities. Celtis celebrated the busy commercial center in his *Norimberga*. Luther called it the eye and ear of Germany, and Melanchthon, another Athens. Nevertheless, Nuremberg was not, as Hutten once wrote Pirckheimer, the first of the major German cities to open its doors to humanism. If Pirckheimer was not typical of Nuremberg's aristocracy, he at least had soul-mates, if not equals, in other German cities. In Nuremberg itself Pirckheimer did not get along well with most of his social peers and there was almost constant friction. As Celtis observed, the burghers were characterized socially and politically by their conservative mentality. Their attitudes were marked by reserve and a certain negative quality so that they quite naturally were critical of Pirckheimer's novel intellectual interests and of much of what he said and did. Outwardly they allowed him to win honors but, as one of his friends once wrote, when he was not present they predicted that he would come to a bad end.[3] Only Lazarus Spengler and a few other members of the intellectual elite could appreciate Pirckheimer's cultural interests.

Right on the market place, opposite the "Schöner Brunnen," in the heart of the city stood his magnificent patrician house. It was, as Celtis put it, a hospice for erudite men. At his table dined many leading figures of the day — Luther, Melanchthon, Celtis, Hutten, Regiomontanus, Galeazzo di San Severino, Leonardo da Vinci's sponsor in Milan, and others. The list of his correspondents reads like a dictionary of Renaissance scholars, or like the index of Trithemius' *De viris illustribus*, and includes such names as Erasmus, Spalatin, Beatus Rhenanus, David de Marchello, Giovanni Francesco Pico della Mirandola, and Zwingli. Pirckheimer stalked books like a hunter and had as his game room one of the best libraries of the time, partly inherited, collected from churches and monasteries, gifts and inheritances from friends, and purchases from the book fairs. It included especially many Aldine Greek editions,[4] so that in 1504 Pirckheimer could with some plausibility boast of owning all the Greek books printed in Italy. Pirckheimer was a literary arbiter, indefatigible translator, and a patron par excellence.[5]

Pirckheimer was the last to bear the name of an illustrious

family having long-standing ties with Italy. In the mid-fourteenth century the Pirckheimers were among the German merchants of Venice.[6] Willibald's grandfather, Hans, studied in Perugia, Bologna, and Padua. His grand-uncle, Thomas, studied in Bologna, Pavia, and Padua. Both were close to the circle of Aeneas Silvius and had friends who were near to Nicholas Cusanus. His own father, Johann, continued the tradition and received his degree as doctor of both laws at Padua in 1465. In Italy he belonged to the circle of the wandering poet, Peter Luder, and learned to know such renowned compatriots as Hermann and Hartmann Schedel, of chronicle fame, and Georg Pfintzing. Johann was caught up by the interests of Italian humanism. He copied or had copies made of a whole series of classical moral tracts and of Lactantius. He owned the treatises of contemporary humanists, such as Vergerio's *De ingenuis moribus*. He read Ficino and purchased many "newly printed books in theology." With such a family background Pirckheimer's star was sure to lead him to the homeland of the Renaissance.

Pirckheimer was born on December 5, 1470, in Eichstätt, where his father was legal counselor to the learned bishop. His father later served the Duke of Bavaria and the Duke of Tyrol and took young Willibald along on his diplomatic missions to Italy, to Switzerland, and to the Netherlands. Willibald began a courtier's training in chivalry at the court of Wilhelm II von Reichenau, Bishop of Eichstätt, and his father had to dissuade him from a military career with arguments for the utility of learning. At eighteen Pirckheimer left for study in Italy, where he remained seven years. Only Agricola and Mutian had an "Italian experience" comparable in length. He followed the familiar family route to the University of Padua, which since 1403 had been the university for Venice, one of the most vigorous intellectual centers of Italy. There, from 1488 to 1491, he nominally studied law, but he was attracted strongly to the *humaniora* and slightly to philosophy as well. One major achievement was the mastery of Greek, which he studied with L. Camers (Creticus). Both the Thomists and the Scotists were represented in theology at Padua, where the "prince of the Scotists," Antonius Trombetta, lectured during those years. In philosophy the university was in a turmoil, for it was not, as has sometimes been asserted, merely a stronghold of Averroism. Alexander Achillinus, an averroistic Aristotelian, was a prominent figure. About the time of Pirckheimer's arrival, Pomponazzi began his public lectures, though his publications and real fame came two decades later. Nicoletto Vernias, who sought a mediating position on the question of the unity and immortality of the intellect, and Alexander Niphus attempted to harmonize Averroistic and Platonic ideas. Giovanni di Rosellis and Gabriel Zerbus lectured on Plato.[7] Pirckheimer made friends with Giovanni Francesco Pico della Mirandola and through him had a personal tie to the Florentine school. It is only indirectly possible to infer the nature of the impact on Pirckheimer's mentality during this formative stage of his development. His reaction to Averroism was negative. In later years he had only words of condemnation for their impieties. Scotism may have quickened his interest in theological speculation, but it did not win him for scholastic methodology, which he consistently ridiculed. Platonism was more congenial to him, though he was not metaphysically inclined. At this point his father intervened with a stern reminder that, although the humanists were a good ornament, the study of law was useful for life. At his insistence Pirckheimer transferred to Pavia in the summer of 1491 to continue in law. Ludovico il Moro had restored Pavia to good academic standing. Pirckheimer developed lasting friendships with members of the Sforza court in Milan. He also visited Rome where he collected classical manuscripts. In the summer of 1495, his studies still not finished, he was called back to Nuremberg to begin adult life.

In October he was married by family arrangement to Crescentia Rieter, of a prominent patrician line, an alliance rewarded the following spring with his election to the City Council which he served with a brief interruption until 1523. He was senatorial in his bearing, but not in his deportment. Impetuous and cantankerous, he on occasion had to defend himself against charges of poor conduct during council meetings. "The labors of the republic weigh me down too much," he complained, "and distract me from letters with which I am singularly pleased." In 1502 he even contemplated returning to Italy to complete his doctorate.[8] The abbot Trithemius ungraciously reminded him that one cannot be equally devoted to study and riches.[9] One moment of glory alone was his, when three years after his election to the council he was chosen to lead the Nuremberg troops in the war of the Emperor Maximilian and the Swabian League against the Swiss in 1499. His expedition earned for him the title of the "German Xenophon," a sobriquet not without irony, for he had led his troops up the Alps and down again with no decisive result. His account of the Swiss war, however, had much merit as a historical narrative and revealed his sharp eye for observation and a certain literary talent. He was honored in due course when Charles V made him an inperial councilor.[10]

Pirckheimer has been applauded as the German humanist who more than any other incorporated the Italian Renaissance into his way of life. The Roman stoa and its manly feeling for life has been said to constitute the kernel of his personality.[11] Chelidonius and Irenicus, fellow humanists, praised his universality as a statesman and man of learning. His sense of duty and willingness to serve the state might be considered a kind of civic humanism. And yet, this man whose individualism and aestheticism is hailed as so unique belonged to a family renowned for its piety and devotion to the received religion. His uncle Georg was prior of a Carthusian monastery. Seven of his sisters were nuns, including the saintly Charitas, of whom four became abbesses and one a prioress. Three of his five daughters took the veil with his blessing. Erasmus in the *Colloquies* compared the Pirckheimer sisters with the daughters of More for their learning and sanctity. As the last male scion of an ancient family tree surrounded by ladies, Willibald was unhappily nursed into a willful and self-indulgent manhood. His psychology was quite complicated, a factor which affected his attitudes toward religion and reform as well.

A contemporary would have had to pronounce Pirckheimer more choleric than sanguine. He had the vices and some virtues of the patricians in an aristocratic city-state. In addition, he had some personality traits fortunately not shared by all his social equals. Pirckheimer was engaged in the defense of his honor against detractors during most of his public career.[12] He had many acquaintances but few close friends and occasionally fell out even with his family. He was self-assured, quarrelsome, distrustful, vain, and at times overbearing. He was hot-tempered and passionate, easy to arouse but difficult to pacify. He was quickly offended and harbored grudges inordinately long. His patrician appetites ran counter to conventional ethics and he indulged, unduly, it was rumored, in the joys of table and of bed.

Crescentia died in 1504 while giving birth to their sixth child in seven and a half years of married life. Pirckheimer never remarried but took comfort in a gay widowerhood. Dürer in his letters from Venice twitted him about his many affairs, observing that the role of lover suited him like the play of a large shaggy dog with a kitten. From the correspondence it appears that one of his mistresses was the sister of the canon Lorenz Beheim, wife of Nicolaus Porst. At his death, precipitated, it seems, by the *morbus gallicus*, Pirckheimer left behind a seven-year-old son, Sebastian, by his maid.[13] In his *Dialogus charitatis et veritatis* [14] Pirckheimer disguised very thinly his indignation over the fact that his sister Charitas had reprimanded him for philandering. Truth, he protested, denies women's idle gossip.

On the other hand, Pirckheimer had many excellent qualities. He was generally truthful, generous as a host, and genuinely interested in promoting good causes.[15] His good sense of humor is reflected in his clever *Laus Podagrae, Apology or Praise of Gout*, inspired by Lucian's comical little *Tragopodagra*. In the *Apology* gout, the disease which kept Pirckheimer miserable most of the time, defends herself in court against the complaints of her subjects that she is a tyrannous and unmerciful queen. He did not live simply according to the "naturalistic theories of life derived from the ancients." Nor is the line to be drawn between professed ethical ideals and hypocritical bad conduct. Rather, Pirckheimer was genuinely idealistic but, because of his lack of self-discipline and his sensuality, he managed only partially to realize his own better intentions. Ironically the touchstone by which he judged all others was *Facta, non verba*, deeds, not words.

In his famous engraving, the so-called "Dream of the Doctor" or "Temptation of the Idler" (1497–98), Dürer shows a learned gentleman dozing beside an elaborate porcelain stove (figure 9). Frightening demons whisper into his ear while in the foreground a voluptuous female figure stands with outstretched beckoning hand. The image of the scholar is strangely like Pirckheimer. In reality, Pirckheimer did have a highly revealing dream in which, however, there appeared not a seductive damsel but his deceased father-in-law, Hans Rieter. The dream, which for Petrarch, Aeneas Silvius, and Ficino was a favorite literary device, was in Pirckheimer's case most certainly no fiction. His account of the experience, which occurred after midnight on August 25, 1501, betrays his basically traditional religious mentality. Too often Pirckheimer's religious position is assessed in terms of his role during the Reformation, without adequate consideration of his matured views prior to that great historical event. In the dream both Pirckheimer's questions and Rieter's answers are of interest. Rieter explained that he was being punished in purgatory, a narrow confine next to hell. He could see demons flying to hell with the souls of men. Those in purgatory suffered alternately with blasts of fire, pitch, and sulphur and streams of cold air coming out of hell. Asked whether by charities or other good work he could be freed, he was silent, but with a gesture indicated that he wished it. Men, including the Augustinians, are condemned for the smallest fault. He had read in the book of fate that Pirckheimer would become one of the greatest and most powerful of men. He should fear God, who provides punishment for evil and reward for good deeds, and always mindful of his last days he would not sin. "I asked him," the account concludes, "that he should pray God to protect me, which he promised me swearing by the All-highest and he was immediately carried away from my eyes." [16]

To speak of a certain ambivalence in Pirckheimer's religious attitudes would be too severe a judgment, although occasional passages in his correspondence have a detectably insincere ring, as when Lorenz Beheim commends him for tending to his prayers after the fun of Fasching.[17] Pirckheimer's religious sentiments were largely conventional and in his writings he seldom made any intimate confessions of personal religious feelings. He certainly did not encounter the demands of religion existentially. He was interested intellectually in the theological problems of the day and showed a respectable knowledge of the fathers, scholastics, and the Scriptures. As a young man, for example, he tackled the hexameral problem of the creation of light on the first day and of the heavenly bodies on the fourth, citing as authorities Augustine, Aquinas, and possibly Peter Lombard and some Greek fathers.[18] Although the growing religiosity marked by new pilgrimages, saint cultus, and religious charities was evident also in Nuremberg during the decades before the Reformation, Pirckheimer did not experience a noticeable deepening of fervor or concern. Like other humanists he contributed a poem to the rising chorus of adulation for Mary, "the splendor of the stars, unique hope of the world, refuge of the miserable, sure salvation of men." But he was sufficiently outer-directed to temper the tone of his letters to the character of the correspondent. Like the poet Celtis, he became very pious in addressing his sister Charitas, as upon the occasion of her election as abbess, when he admonished her to imitate the Savior especially in the virtue of service and of obedience.[19] He was through the years solicitous of the welfare of the Nuremberg convents, representing their interests to the council, arranging financial matters, and receiving, in turn, the sympathy and prayers of the nuns in times of illness.[20] In one of his later literary creations there was a near perfect fusion of poetic art and true religious spirit, in the elegy on the death of his "best and dearest friend," Dürer.[21] Deeply moved by intense grief he excelled this once the lines of Celtis, Hutten, or any of the professional poets among the humanists.

Pirckheimer was so fascinated with the occult, with palmistry and astrology that the cultural analyst might be tempted to speak of the Gothic element in his makeup, if it were not for the fact that the humanists, drawing on late antiquity, actually were themselves responsible for the new momentum of this obsession. Largely under the tutelage of Lorenz Beheim, Pirckheimer became an avid practicioner of astrology. He owned various expensive astronomical instruments which had formerly belonged to Regiomontanus. He left behind in his papers a large number of astrological diagrams and charts. He boasted of having predicted the international military developments of the 1520's on the basis of precise astrological principles. He worked out the horoscopes of his children and even ascribed his gout to an astrological jinx. In an unpublished *Defense of Astrology* he defended the art against the attacks of the elder Pico Della Mirandola's *Disputationum adversus astrologos libri XII* and his nephew, Giovanni Francesco's

De rerum praenotione libri XII, who were following those ancient critics, Lucian and Sextus Empiricus.[22] Beheim had showed Pirckheimer a "very ancient book" from which Pico had taken his arguments, for what he added of his own was worth nothing. The refutation of the specific propositions follows. Later [1515?] Pirckheimer seems to have had a temporary change of heart, when he declared to Bernhard Adelmann that he no longer wanted anything to do with astrology or other "fortune telling" and would completely abstain from these arts.[23] But he was soon at it again, although during the Reformation years he inclined to a view which was acceptable also to such theologians as Melanchthon that in reality God produced the effects through the stars, which are only secondary causes.[24] He was intrigued also by palmistry, dream interpretation, magical medicinal recipes, and demonology.[25] He believed that all miracles among pagan nations were done by demons. He asked the mysterious Abbot Trithemius, whose name is woven darkly into the Faust legend, for his book on the art of magic to use against certain heretics imprisoned in Nuremberg who were invoking demons.[26] After all, Pirckheimer had been born in a house opposite the shrine of St. Walpurga, from whose sarcophagus oozed a miraculous stream of oil.

Pirckheimer was a veritable polymath in the range of his intellectual interests, presaging the omnicompetents of the age of erudition in the century to follow. In 1517 he wrote to his friend Bernhard Adelmann of Augsburg: "The doctors maintain that my excessive studying is the cause of my sickness, and this year I have really devoted myself to scholarly pursuits above the usual measure. But why should a man live, if he cannot study?" Like the Latin transmitters of late classic culture, Boethius and Isidore of Seville, Pirckheimer cited the Ciceronian program *causas rerum cognoscere*, to know the causes of things. He adopted the classical pragmatic presuppositions about the utility of history as the "witness of the times, light of truth, preservation of memory, teacher of life, and messenger of antiquity." [27] Religiously he heard in history the same "voice of God" that reverberates through the Scriptures. He translated Lucian's work on the writing of history as *De conscribenda historia* (Nuremberg, 1515) as an aid to the patriot who would write a proper history of the Germans for Maximilian.

Like Celtis he attacked the Germans for their inertia in writing their own history. He encouraged Irenicus, Beatus Rhenanus, and younger historians to publish. In his own work he was concerned always to relate antiquity to the contemporary condition of his fatherland. His geographical interests were related to his historical program. Clearly the most important of his translations was his Latin edition of the eight books of Ptolemy's geography inspired by Regiomontanus. Among his own efforts, his *Germaniae explicatio* most obviously revealed his patriotic interests. The first historical geography of Germany, it attempted to identify classic references to places, mountains, and rivers.[28] He was keenly interested in the new ocean voyages and in America. Like Nicholas Oresme, Gabriel Biel, Guillaume Budé, Alciatus, Melanchthon, Conrad Peutinger, and many other scholastics and humanists, Pirckheimer related his numismatic interests to broader classical learning and did not indulge in mere antiquarianism. Late in life he wrote a description of his personal collection of ancient coins attempting to show the historical connection between antiquity and modernity.[29]

In Italy, Pirckheimer had developed his exceptional linguistic skills, literary style, and feeling for form. There he had encountered the tradition of translation from the Roman court of Nicholas V and from the Florence of Leonardo Bruni, and had learned to know the Greek Demetrius Chalcondylas personally in Pavia. It was through his translations from Greek to Latin and from both to German that Pirckheimer made his greatest contribution to the world of learning, although ironically the very success of the Greek revival and the spread of Greek learning soon made his own work superfluous. He takes a place with Agricola, Reuchlin, Celtis, Regiomontanus, Melanchthon, Luther, and preeminently Erasmus as an initiator of the Greek renaissance in Germany. In a letter to Anton Kresz, July 19, 1501, acknowledging information about Greek books available in Pavia, Pirckheimer declared that he was moved with joy when he saw "good letters daily grow and increase." On December 19 of the same year he inquired whether Kresz could find a Greek in Pavia to translate some comedies of Aristophanes for a suitable price. When Pirckheimer resolved to undertake the Herculean labors of translation himself, he was con-

7. *Crotus Rubeanus' coat of arms*

BILIBALDI·PIRKEYMHERI·EFFIGIES
AETATIS·SVAE·ANNO·L·III·
VIVITVR·INGENIO·CAETERA·MORTIS·
·ERVNT·
M·D·XX·IV·

8. *Willibald Pirckheimer*

scious of his distinguished predecessors, as in the preface to his
Axiochus, a pseudo-Platonic writing, where he acknowledged the
previous efforts of Ficino and Agricola. In his understanding of
the translator's task, especially the necessity of conveying the full
meaning rather than a cramped literal rendition, he approached
Luther's grand conception in his *Vom Dolmetschen* and he appreciated fully the greatness of Luther's own translation of the
New Testament in 1522. Pirckheimer's interests were in part
purely philological and humanistic in the limited literary sense. A
few translations were done in the context of some specific controversy. But a survey of the scores of translations that he did and
the interpretation which he placed upon them reveals that they
were not only in the main ethical and religious in nature, but that
many were specifically designed to enlarge the available Christian
literature. He was much nearer to the program of Cardinal Bessarion of putting the Greek classics into the service of religion than
to the purely antique revival for which Gemisthos Pletho
labored.[30]

Pirckheimer's editions and translations represent but a sample
of his vast acquaintance with ancient literature. A single master
theme guided his selection and united most of the classic and
patristic writings which he chose to do, religious philosophy as
the *studium virtutis*, to use Pico's phrase. In the dedication to
Charitas of the first translation which he actually published,
Plutarch's theodicy, *De his qui tarde a numine corripiuntur* (Nuremberg, 1513), he wrote:

Therefore the Stoics assert that it is a gift of God that we live, but
of philosophy that we live well. Nor is it astonishing since nothing
greater or more excellent has been given by God to men. I do not
speak of that sophistical and caviling philosophy which is not at all able
to lead to good and blessed living, but of that philosophy which (as
Cicero says) heals the mind, removes useless cares, frees from desires,
drives out all fears. Instructed and armed with this philosophy, most
worthy sister, we bravely bear all misfortunes, sorrows, calamities and
labors. We especially magnanimously bear the injuries of wicked men
(for you rightly hold and understand what I say), since criminals living
or dead are not able to escape the judgment of God. For Jupiter (as
the poets put it) at last arises and compensates the tardiness of the
punishment with the gravity of the punishment.[31]

Pirckheimer goes on to explain his reasons for translating Plutarch, a most serious and learned man, because his writing fosters the rule of the spirit, not of the flesh, and illustrates that it is impossible for wicked men to obtain a stable fortune, for the slow vengeance of the divine will overtakes them. He quotes Horace on the universality of sin, Tertullian on the patience of God in suffering the deeds of wicked mortals, and St. Paul on the future glory to be revealed in man. He cites the classics, the fathers, the Scriptures, and church practices to demonstrate the value of adversities and the sure judgment of God. This introduction to Plutarch is typical of Pirckheimer's intent with the majority of his translations. Superficially it is possible to speak of his Stoic ethic, but only within the larger theological context which he personally retained.

Besides the various treatises on moral problems and ethical questions of daily living by the wholesome Plutarch, Pirckheimer did a large number by the satirical Lucian, a favorite with the Northern as with the Italian humanists. Something in Lucian's skeptical and epicurean make-up undoubtedly appealed to Pirckheimer's lighter side, but beyond that Lucian provided an arsenal of weapons for attacking fraud, superstition, hypocrisy, false pride, and such human weaknesses. Similarly in the Aristotelian and Platonic writings that he chose to translate, it was the specifically ethical and not the metaphysical treatises that he selected. For Dürer, whom he provided with a whole storehouse of classical knowledge for his Renaissance artistry, he did the *Characteres ethici* of the Aristotelian Theophrastus on irony, flattery, garrulity, rusticity, impudence, impetuousness, and similar qualities. The Platonic and Pseudo-Platonic dialogues which he translated were to provide Christendom with a stronger moral philosophy rather than with a new speculative system, as a glance at the titles suggests, *Achiochus, Clitiphon, De Justo, Eryxias, Num virtus doceri possit, Demodocus, Sisyphus,* and *Definitiones.* In doing the *Achioxus* Pirckheimer knew he was following the precedent set by Ficino and Agricola. Proclus' *Sphaera,* which remained unpublished, was in a class by itself. Aside from chance discoveries the same leitmotiv governed his choice of most of his other pieces, whether they be from Sallust, Cebes, Galenus, or Cicero. For example, Pirckheimer wrote to Kilian Leib of Isocrates' oration *ad*

Demonicum that it contains "the most salutory admonitions and most sacred precepts and agrees very much with the Christian religion. From which you will readily understand that Isocrates was not only the most eloquent rhetorician, but was also most zealous for honesty and virtue." [32] Pirckheimer once observed that Plutarch and Plato had not strayed far from the path of truth. Christian ethic and philosophy remained for him the standard by which the ancients were judged.

Luther's humanist friend Bernhard Adelmann drew Pirckheimer's attention to the Greek church fathers, urged him to translate them, and remarked that he would not find eloquence wanting in them, least of all in Gregory Nazianzen and Chrysostom. Pirckheimer followed up the lead and remarked that he would not occupy himself with Lucian if he could have a supply of those ancient Greek theologians.[33] The same concern for practical individual and social ethics guided his translation of the patristics as of the classical writings. Gregory Nazianzen's words might well have served as his motto: "Faith and practice are the preliminary steps to knowledge and theory. For it is impossible that one who does not live wisely can think wisely and share in wisdom." Gregory was, in fact, Pirckheimer's favorite father for reasons of eloquence and of piety. Reuchlin had declared that in the loveliness of song and brilliance of truth Homer had to yield to Gregory. In 1521 he dedicated a translation of six sermons of Gregory on the chief feast days of the church, *Sex Orationes Gregorii Nazianzeni*, to Wenzeslaus Link, Luther's friend and reformer in Nuremberg. "Some people," he commented to Link, "do not take it well when laymen, as they call them, turn their hands to sacred things, as though that were committing a crime, if a Christian dares to busy himself with Christian matters." [34] In his last years he translated thirty sermons of Gregory and entrusted them to Erasmus for editing with the express wish that he should dedicate them to Duke George of Saxony, Luther's foe.[35] In 1531, Erasmus discharged his obligation and in the preface to Duke George he cited Pirckheimer for the ardor of his piety in doing those ancient doctors of the church. Erasmus coupled these sermons of Gregory, "that excellent preacher of Christian philosophy," with Ptolemy's *Cosmography* as Pirckheimer's two most important translations.

He also did Gregory's oration to his sister Gorgonia, but it remained unpublished.

The lesser works of early Christian writers, Latin as well as Greek, obviously served the same moralistic purpose, John of Damascus, "How one can overcome evil inclinations of the heart," Maximus Confessor, "On the five chief virtues," and the "Logos asketikos" done together with Erasmus' "Wholesome admonition of the child Jesus to the sinner." His publication of the books of Fulgentius of Ruspe (d. A.D. 533) in 1519 was the result of a chance inheritance from the library of Abbot Trithemius.[36] His Athanasius "On the Psalms" remained unpublished. It is true that in the familar humanist fashion Pirckheimer was attracted by good style, but the religious concern remained preeminent. This is evident from the preface to the "Ethical Sayings" of Nilus, an ascetic monk (d. A.D. 426), who was neither a bishop nor a martyr, as Pirckheimer believed. In the preface (1515), addressed to his Sister Clara, who could use this work in instructing young nuns, he explained that he undertook this task of translation over the Christmas holidays as a God-pleasing work and presented it as a gift derived from true theological and divine wisdom.[37] The sum of the sayings, as Nilus explained, was that the soul must not neglect to do that which is right, for the judgment is not far off.[38] His translations clearly associate Pirckheimer with the Italian traditions of lay theologians.

Pirckheimer ventured beyond the Hellenic to oriental antiquity. Reuchlin, Celtis, Peutinger, Erasmus, Melanchthon, and other Northerners were intrigued by the mysterious East. Chelidonius even mistakenly credited Pirckheimer with a knowledge of Assyrian. At the express command of Maximilian, Pirckheimer translated from the Greek the *Hieroglyphica*, a composite work ascribed to the Egyptian Horapollon (Horus Niliacus) dating from the second half of the fifth century. The Aldine press produced the first Greek edition of the *Hieroglyphica* in 1505, printed with Aesop's fables. It was based upon the textual work of scholars in the Aldine academy under the leadership of Brother Urbano. During the next century the *Hieroglyphica* was republished at least thirty times in Greek or in translation. The *Hieroglyphica*, a strange mixture of phantastic and some accurate interpretations of

Egyptian hieroglyphs, had intrigued the members of Ficino's Florentine circle. Ficino himself commented on the idea of Plotinus that the hieroglyphs were Platonic ideas made visible. Applying the doctrine of revelation through visual symbols to the Egyptian hieroglyphs, Ficino wrote:

The Egyptian Priests did not use individual letters to signify mysteries but whole images of plants, trees or animals; because God has knowledge of things not through a multiplicity of thought processes but rather as a simple and firm form of the thing.[39]

Pico della Mirandola found in them a point of departure for theosophical speculation, for it was Pico who gave the most coherent expression to the conception of revelation through symbolism. Piero Valeriano in his commentary on the *Hieroglyphica* argued that Christ himself, the prophets, and apostles had utilized hieroglyphic expression and that Plato, Pythagoras, and "other very great men" were indebted to the Egyptians in laying open the nature of things — divine and human.[40] Pirckheimer's work with the *Hieroglyphica*, then, it would seem, was not merely a task forced upon him by the whim of the Emperor, but was related to a genuine intellectual interest of his own derived from Neoplatonic assumptions about symbol and reality. Pirckheimer's translation, completed in the spring of 1514, was widely recognized as a difficult philological achievement through which he transmitted a new symbolism to German art and letters.[41]

Dürer's illustrations for the *Hieroglyphica* commissioned by Maximilian, were drawn on the back of Pirckheimer's translation. He ignored the phonetic principle of hieroglyphic writing and shared the common Neoplatonic notion that the Egyptiac pictographs had allegorical meanings reflecting the mysteries of nature and the supernatural. That Pirckheimer's influence on Dürer's symbolism was basically conventional, however, is suggested by the schematic arrangement of the virtues on the Triumphal Chariot of Maximilian. There the cardinal virtues of faith, hope, and charity are depicted as growing out of humility, a time-honored theme.

In a letter (August 30, 1517) addressed to Lorenz Beheim preceding his edition of Lucian's *Piscator seu Reviviscentes*, Pirckheimer portrayed the ideal theologian. He allowed a proper place for scholastic training, as long as speculation is not substituted for pure religion. Besides grammar the true theologian must know Latin, Greek, and Hebrew, dialectic, properly delimited, and rhetoric. Moreover,

he must know thoroughly natural philosophy and metaphysics, but not only the Aristotelian, but that loftier philosophy in which Plato is the undisputed master. Tullius [Cicero] already calls him the god among the philosophers and St. Augustine confesses that he chooses him as his guide for this reason, that he produced better ideas on the final goal of man and the divine nature than any other philosopher. I will now keep silence about the rest of the Latin and Greek philosophers who acknowledge as with one voice that the platonic theology agrees the most with the Christian religion.

Pirckheimer inherited an avid interest in Plato and Neoplatonism from his father who instructed him to search for Ficino's works in Italy. On May 29, 1517, Adelmann wrote to Pirckheimer: "That your father ascribed great significance to Marsilius you perhaps know best of all." In 1491 he sent his father from Padua the *De triplici vita*, a work which was to have a strong influence on Dürer's *Melancholia I*. He once described Ficino as "a man who was most meritorious because of his work on Plato and one worthy of eternal memory." [42] He heard lectures on Platonism at Padua and in December 1502, he began corresponding with Giovanni Francesco Pico, a contemporary of his at Padua, who edited his uncle's work. A Vienna manuscript which Pirckheimer himself wrote in Italy contains a letter of Ficino, 1472, and his *Commentarium in conviviam Platonis de Amore* [43] and in his personal library he had various Platonic writings such as the *Dialogus de immortalitate* of Xenocrates, a successor in Plato's academy (d. B.C. 315) and the *Sermones* of Maximus Tyrius, an eclectic Platonist under the Antonines who wrote discourses [διαλέξεις] on ethical questions. [44] In referring to the many "modern philosophers" whose works Pirckheimer knew, Cochlaeus singled out John Argyropulos, Leonardo Bruni, Giovanni Pico, Ermolao Barbaro, and Marsilio Ficino. [45]

Pirckheimer certainly had the resources for the development of a Platonic philosophy, but one looks in vain for a distinctly Neoplatonic structure in his religious philosophy. There are, to be sure, various vignettes among his papers patently Neoplatonic. [46]

In reacting against Averroism to which he had been exposed in Padua his appeal was to Plato, in the manner of Ficino. He stressed that one must know for sure whether Aristotle allowed the validity of the soul's essence and on what grounds Plato proved it. With Ficino he affirmed divine foreknowledge, creation of the world, miracles, and the immortality of the individual soul. But these ideas together with the assertion that Plato stood nearest to Christianity were commonplaces since the patristic period. In religious philosophy Pirckheimer was no innovator or even a serious *conphilosophus* of the Florentine Platonists. He toyed with the term Pythagorean, as when he called Beatus Rhenanus his Pythagorean friend [μία ψυχή], but he never ventured like Reuchlin to do anything serious with it.

In an idle moment Pirckheimer once penned some lines for his own amusement which reveal his inquiring spirit:

> He who desires to turn his mind to various teachings
> Surely should seek that which shows him the true way.[47]

The element of classic philosophy which proved to be the most congenial to Pirckheimer's psychology and religiosity was a strong measure of Stoic moralism. Like Seneca he was interested in the application of its principles to the correct way of life. It appealed to his manly ideals and was perfectly compatible with his semi-Pelagian religious bent. Duns Scotus had given to religion a strong political ethical character in contrast to the speculative concerns of natural reason. Pirckheimer's greatest enthusiasm was for the Christian ethic. He was most fond of citing the Epistle of James and the Sermon on the Mount, especially the saying, "By their fruits ye shall know them."

It is a mistake to contrast his "Stoic" moralism to medieval asceticism and declare Pirckheimer a new creature. He could in one thought sequence laud wisdom which leads to a quiet heart guarded against unrest and the divine love which overcomes fleshly strife.[48] His writings are studded with references to the "nobility of virtue which endures to all eternity" or the "glory of virtue which remains firm," but the context is almost always Christian, as in the epigram for Dürer (1528), where he adds that his soul will live on Olympus. Nor does it serve a useful purpose to label his religious philosophy "Erasmian moralism." Pirckheimer and Erasmus never saw each other and it was not until January 1515, that Pirckheimer made the contact from which developed a lively correspondence. On January 24, 1515, Erasmus returned a cordial answer: "Though we are far apart, nothing prevents us from binding ourselves together in an intimate friendship." There is little evidence that Erasmus' writings had a formative influence on Pirckheimer's early development. They shared some basic religious attitudes and their reaction to the Reformation was in some respects similar, but the relation was one of partially analogous views rather than a matter of derivation the one from the other.

Pirckheimer demonstrated a critical scholarly spirit reminiscent of Valla in his *Dissertatio de Maria Magdalena* in which he argued against the traditional association of Mary Magdalene with the adulteress of Luke 7: 36ff. and Mary of Bethany, the sister of Martha.[49] He considered this association an injustice to Mary Magdalene and preferred an opinion more pious. The composition of the treatise dates from the period of the Fifth Lateran Council, 1512–1517. Lefèvre d'Étaples did a similar critical essay on the three Marys about the same time during that phase of his development when he was most strongly under the influence of Erasmian rationalism. After the initial sally against those who blindly embrace the ideas of their forebears without questioning in the interest of truth, Pirckheimer grandly announces that he shall attempt to explode a received error. He is careful to demand complete subordination to the teachings of the church. "Everyone of Christ's faithful is bound and obligated to observe the decrees of mother church and firmly to believe them," he wrote, "especially those which have to do with the mysteries of the faith." [50] In that thought sequence, however, he makes a bold assertion of the priority truth must take over tradition. "I would not venture to derogate anything from Holy Mother Church (far be it from me!), but I will not let myself be restrained from seeking the truth, which finally comes to light anyway, though it has not been searched for. For it is, as that good man Plato says, before God and men the most powerful of all things." [51] Is it necessary to read from this and similar, though less pointed expressions his acceptance of a *duplex veritas*, a double truth?

There is no real evidence that he was led to this position by Paduan Averroism. In his first tract on the Lord's Supper he denounced Averroës as godless. The suggestion that the influence of Duns Scotus with his distinction of the *theologia naturalis* and *theologia revelata* is here in evidence is a good deal more plausible. The question of the three Marys was not a matter of great dogmatic import nor comparable in gravity to such controverted matters as the Donation of Constantine. Pirckheimer's appeal was to authoritative evidence from the church fathers. Like St. Bernard, he distinguished matters of opinion, understanding, and faith, so that the incarnation, redemption, and the sacraments lay in a realm inaccessible to reason alone. In the *Defensio Reuchlini* he explained his position as follows:

It is not my opinion that the teaching of Christ is deficient without pagan literature, far from it. For divine wisdom does not need human invention. Therefore, I know very well that the way to the highest level of theology is open without Plato and Aristotle. Church fathers like Jerome, Augustine, Ambrose, Hilary in the West, Origen, Basil, Gregory Nazianzen, Athanasius, and Cyril in the East have taken it.

In his Sacramentarian controversy with Oecolampadius he repeatedly expressed the subordination of philosophy to theology, the incomprehensibility of the mystery of the Sacrament, a "miracle transcending every spirit and the order of nature." "Meanwhile," he wrote, "we admire the height and wisdom of God no less in the most holy sacrament than in the divine generation, procession, predestination, incarnation, resurrection, perpetual virginity of the Most Holy Mother Mary and in other things not at all capable of being investigated by human reasons." He was anxious to establish the patristic precedent for his views in arguing, "that the true body of Christ and his true blood are on the altar, almost all the ancient doctors affirm, who held that divine power is not measured by human reasons."

For Pirckheimer the lines dividing matters of opinion, of understanding, and of faith ran parallel to each other on different levels and philosophy and theology were not self-contained and sometimes contradictory categories divided by a verticle partition into a double truth. In the area of lesser matters of opinion or the area of understanding, embracing the natural knowledge of God, free will, personal immortality, and similar questions Pirckheimer feared no loss through free inquiry, believing Platonism to be the best metaphysical guide to truth. In the area of faith, confidence in the promises of the divine Word alone avails. At this point Pirckheimer revealed that his views were not only conditioned by medieval voluntaristic mysticism, but that he was under the spell of Reformation theology as well.

In his attitude toward the scholastics Pirckheimer was thoroughly humanistic, as he revealed in a letter to Vincent Lang (Eleutherius), poet laureate, intimate friend and colleague of Celtis in Vienna. He urged Lang to carry on with poetry and not let his spirit grow cold for, with the large number of learned men emerging, barbarism will at last be destroyed and a more cultured literature will return. He then turned to a vicious attack on the scholastics who offer the youth straw for better food. They should be called "philopompi" rather than true philosophers, adulterers rather than husbands of philosophy. They deceive the youth and unlearned, even abuse most eloquent Aristotle, lead despicable lives, are babblers and enemies of good letters, who strangle themselves with sophistical arguments and cavils.[52] When Cochlaeus attacked the curriculum of scholastic studies for detaining the students on the arts level six or eight years with Alexander Gallus and Peter Hispanus and denying that eloquence is compatible with philosophy, he knew that Pirckheimer would agree with him. Pirckheimer did agree and went on to assault those scholastics who pressed their positivistic inclination to the point of saying that the Holy Scriptures could have dispensed with the ornament of speech, for the scholastics corrupt the mysteries of the faith and heaven itself.[53]

Pirckheimer asked the younger Pico for an oration against the ignorant clergy.[54] To Erasmus he wrote in a temper:

Moreover, by immortal God, what else have they accomplished by so many sycophancies, infamies, and shames than that they have made themselves ridiculous and rendered themselves equally hateful to God and men. By their guilt it has come to this that not only is the excellent name of theology held in derision by the common crowd, but the theologians themselves (I speak of the counterfeits) are judged to be more shameful than buffoons and good for nothings.[55]

His humanist drive *ad fontes* prepared him for the Reformation's return to the Scriptures. "The Hebrews and Mohammedans," he wrote, "daily study the law, but our theologians believe that there are far more excellent, subtle, and lofty things than the teachings of the gospel." [56] Many of his attitudes toward the scholastics are summed up in the letter prefacing his translation of *Piscator seu Reviviscentes*, the fisherman or the resurrected philosophers, one of Lucian's ingenious and eloquent dramatic compositions. Much of Lucian's ironic criticism, Pirckheimer seemed to feel, applied directly to the scholastics. In the preface Pirckheimer first of all attacked the moral faults of the sophists and then presented his positive picture of the ideal theologian. It is here that he praised Plato as standing nearest Christianity. He approved the study of the great scholastic theologians. But above all, he emphasized, the basis of all theological studies must be the Holy Scriptures. This preface served also as his defense of Reuchlin, the "German Hercules" who conquered innumerable monsters, for he entered the lists, as was perfectly predictable, on his side of the great controversy.

The humanist desire for calm and leisure prompted Pirckheimer to remain detached from the Reuchlin controversy for several years. He counseled Reuchlin in 1512 not to dignify Pfefferkorn by mentioning his name, just as the Ephesians had consigned to oblivion the criminals who burned the temple of Diana by forbidding the use of their names.[57] In 1516 he still saw the ideal posture as that of Christian sentiment "requite not again" coupled with the disdain of the pagan philosopher for his opponent, but already he acknowledged the name "Reuchlinist" and "head of the Reuchlinists" as an honor.[58] His temperament, however, was really unsuited to withdrawal as hostility mounted. Through Hutten's cajoling he possibly was tempted to contribute to the *Epistolae Obscurorum Virorum*. He felt his gorge rise when the Cologne scholastics referred to him as "a certain unknown Willibald." In August 1517, he published the *Piscator* prefaced by the *epistola apologetica* or *defensio Reuchlini*, as the letter against the Cologne scholastics is variously known. It constitutes Pirckheimer's chief claim to be counted among the humanist reformers.

In this *Apology* Pirckheimer acknowledges the name Erasmian as well as Reuchlinist to be most honorable. He declares the attacks on renowned men like Peutinger, Cuspinian, Vadian, Lazius, and Hutten, the sure hope of Germany, to be criminal. He asks why the obscurantists have not excelled Erasmus in publishing or gained fame by writing something more weighty, significant, and definitive than Reuchlin's *De verbo mirifico* or *De arte cabalistica.* "But you have called the most zealous defender of theology and of the Christian faith a half-Jew," he thunders, adding that he hears Christ's name, but sees nothing of the fulfillment of his commandments. He calls for more virtue and less speculation, for the true theologian must be free of all vices and rich in virtues. Those men are most deserving of respect who prefer the evangelical teaching of our Lord Christ to dialectic, the Old Testament to physics, the doctrines of the apostles to metaphysics, the writings of the old theologians to logic. There one learns humility, equanimity, love, and all the virtues.

The defense of Reuchlin was acclaimed by the humanists. Hutten responded with passion and warmth. Erasmus was pleased but, like Bernhard Adelmann and others, puzzled at Pirckheimer's list of "true theologians," including Johann Eck with Johannes von Dalberg, Giovanni Pico, Giovanni Francesco Pico, Johann von Kaisersberg, Hermann von Newenar, Johann Hessus, Johann Staupitz, Kilian Leib, Erasmus, Oecolampadius, Cochlaeus, Murner, Link, Martin Luther, Jakob Wimpfeling, and Hieronymus Emser. Pirckheimer explained to Erasmus that he had not named all the men in his catalogue to honor them. He knew very well that the names of learned and unlearned, good and bad, friend and foe stood side by side. The learned and good men were worthy of honor, but the good and powerful, though not so learned, must serve as a bulwark against the bad. The learned but less good or the doubtful comrades had to be confirmed, while the enemies had to be made suspicious of the enemies. This scheme, Pirckheimer ventured, had not proved to be a disappointment, for he had created more confusion than he had anticipated, and those who had been vacillating had been confirmed and a majority had been won to support Reuchlin's cause with word and pen.[59] Reuchlin was grateful and hailed Pirckheimer as "the anchor of my storms and my marvelous hope" [60] As late as 1522 Pirckheimer wrote to Hutten that it was not so much his friendship with Luther as with Reuchlin that damaged him.

Pirckheimer thought of Luther as a Reuchlinist in view of his Erfurt background. In 1514 Luther had publicly criticized a Cologne scholastic who had published a scurrilous poem against Reuchlin. He had previously thought him an ass, said Luther, but now realizing that while parading the majesty of the lion he had betrayed himself to be a dog, wolf, and crocodile. Another time Luther declared that God would be true and accomplish his work in spite of the opposition and vain sweat of thousands upon thousands of Cologners. Christoph Scheurl, a former Wittenberg professor and colleague of Luther, was in Nuremberg. He believed that, with Luther working so energetically a revolution in theological studies lay ahead. Staupitz preached against work righteousness in Nuremberg's Augustinian church in Advent of 1516 and in the spring of 1517. He referred to Luther as a scholar who with wonderful talent commented on "the letters of the man of Tarsus." [61] Pirckheimer therefore was fully convinced when he cited Luther as a great theologian. They both urged a return to the Scriptures, but Pirckheimer, the moralist, read them as a law book for the Christian life. Luther, too, once read the Scriptures in that way. But on November 1, less than three months after Pirckheimer published his *Apology*, Luther posted his Ninety-five Theses, demonstrating that he had learned to read the Scriptures with a large open eye. Here was the theological reformer Pirckheimer had called for. Did he give the answer Pirckheimer expected?

Pirckheimer was shocked and angered when the papal bull *Exsurge Domine* fell also on him entirely without warning. The bull accused him of having exalted and spread abroad Luther's doctrine and demanded recantation within sixty days on the threat of excommunication. The Bull aimed primarily at Luther was the handiwork of the scholastic Dr. John Eck of Ingolstadt who had gone to Rome armed with the reports of the Leipzig debate and secured the bull on June 15, 1520. The whole proceeding was a prize example of bureaucratic bungling. That Eck used the good offices of the Curia to vent his spleen on his personal foes is evident from the names of those cited in the document: four theologians besides Luther — Carlstadt, Dölsch, Sylvius Egranus (Wildenauer), Bernhard Adelmann, and two laymen — Lazarus Spengler, the city secretary, and Pirckheimer. Adelmann had referred to Eck as a greedy, drunken, immoral, and contentious monster.

Spengler had in a German *Apology* declared his inner conviction of the truth of Luther's teaching. Pirckheimer had expressed satisfaction with Luther's assaults on Roman exploitation and his criticism of the gross work righteousness in religious practice. Pirckheimer had difficulty keeping things on an impersonal basis.

As early as 1514 Pirckheimer objected to Eck's "freshness." He criticized Eck's rationalization of interest rates up to 5 percent which had naturally proved to be so gratifying to the Fugger bankers of Augsburg. He translated Plutarch's treatise on avoiding lending money on interest, an odd choice for a Nuremberg capitalist like himself. Finally, the publication, probably in February 1520, of the sharp satire *Eckius dedolatus*, the "corner planed off," brought Eck's unrelenting hatred down upon Pirckheimer, whom he assumed to be the author.[62] The satirical dialogue had the same cutting edge as the *Epistolae Obscurorum Virorum*. Eck is ill with a fever brought on by the heat of the Leipzig debate and fails to relieve the pains with constant drink. A witch is dispatched on a goat (of Emser's family) to bring by air a physician and a surgeon from Leipzig. Before the major operation begins, the confessor censures Eck's many sins, especially his opposition to Luther. Eck concedes that only envy and avarice led him to it in the hope of becoming a papal favorite and winning a cardinal's hat. The operation begins with a trimming by seven stout men with cudgels until the rough edges are smoothed off and the patient becomes easier to handle. Next the barber-surgeon shaves off his hair which is crawling with sophistries, syllogisms, and scholastic propositions and corollaries. A piece of his saucy tongue is removed and a horrible canine tooth extracted. An emetic produces his dialectical commentaries, a "negative theology," a red doctor's hat, a letter of indulgence, and his bribe money. Then he is skinned, which reveals an enormous mass of vices, all of which must be cut out and cauterized. At last, after a further unmentionable operation even more painful than the rest, Eck is restored to health. But the old scholastic proves to be incorrigible, for he confides to his trusted Leipzig friends that he stands firm and intends to go to Rome.

This satire was done in Pirckheimer's inner circle. Luther thought it amusing and believed that it smacked of Pirckheimer himself. Pirckheimer did leave among his papers a first draft of a dialogue on bibulous John Eck, which reads like a sequel to the *Eckius dedolatus*.[63] The satire was republished at least three times and its wide popularity must have aggravated Dr. Eck even more. In his unfinished *Apology* to Pope Adrian, 1522, Pirckheimer attributed the bull to an ignoble combination of hostile forces led by Cajetan, Prierias, the theologians of Cologne and Louvain, and the Fuggers, all of whom commissioned Eck to go to Rome and secure the ruinous document. Spengler was inclined to resist but his position with the council made it necessary for him to yield. Together they sought vindication from the Bishop of Bamberg and approached Eck's temporal lord, Duke Wilhelm of Bavaria, for mediation, but Eck declared their action inadequate. In an appellation to Leo X they protested their belief in the one holy, Catholic, apostolic, orthodox church. They denied ever agreeing to heretical, schismatic ideas, or the errors of Luther, for they were always obedient sons of the church.[64] Finally, on the prompting of the council they made a humiliating confession of guilt and acknowledged forty-one alleged heresies. Eck possibly deliberately held back the report of their absolution, for it reached Rome too late, so that both Pirckheimer and Spengler were named with Hutten and Luther in the actual bull of excommunication, *Decet Romanum Pontificum*, January 2, 1521. Pirckheimer and Spengler had to seek out the Cardinal legate Aleander at Worms in August to be restored to the church. Spengler was temporizing, for when in the spring of 1525 the city council "gave the Pope a vacation," Spengler became a link between Wittenberg and Nuremberg, one of the first cities to decide for the Reformation. Pirckheimer's dilemma was not resolved with such finality.

In April 1521, about the time that Luther appeared before the Diet at Worms, Pirckheimer declared: "The disorders among us will not be remedied by order, but must be remedied by disorder." In October 1518, Luther rested in Pirckheimer's house when he returned exhausted from his confrontation of Cajetan in Augsburg. Pirckheimer greeted the Reformation with enthusiasm and recognized its theological nature somewhat more clearly than did many Reuchlinists. In his library, which was predominantly theological, he had one hundred and fifty separate writings of Luther, including two copies of the first edition of the Ninety-five Theses.[65]

Luther corresponded with Pirckheimer from the beginning, although only one letter of the early years has survived; he personally wrote him an account of the Leipzig debate which Pirckheimer for some reason did not receive. In a letter to Erasmus dated April 30, 1520, Pirckheimer classed Luther with Reuchlin, Hutten, the Count of Newenar, himself, and other friends of learning who were in danger of being charged with heresy. But Luther gradually came to mean more to him than merely a *vir bonus et doctus* and critic of scholasticism. Pirckheimer always spoke of him as "our Martin" and even referred to the Lutherans as "the evangelical church." Yet, in the crisis years of the Reformation, Pirckheimer remained cool and detached, disavowed any pro-Lutheran partisanship, and assumed a mildly mediating rather than an activist's role. Hutten's call to him to defend freedom, freedom being threatened in Luther's case, almost has an ironic ring: "Stir up your courage for I still have some hope in the cities for their love of freedom, which is especially characteristic of you."

Pirckheimer early assumed the role of conciliator between Luther and his opponents which reflected not only the humanist stand above party, but also the fact that Pirckheimer felt the validity of some things that Luther stood for. When Emser broke with Luther after the Leipzig debates, for example, Pirckheimer urged them both to refrain from invective (*Maledici regnum dei non possidebunt*).[66] Pirckheimer in his correspondence with Erasmus attempted to mollify him, when his intention to write against Luther became increasingly evident. Thus, in a letter of February 17, 1523, he countered Erasmus' comment that various Lutherans should manage the evangelical cause more intelligently, with the wish that the other party would act more prudently and be led more by reason than by passion. He believed that the whole affair could still be led down more peaceful paths, if it were managed with greater discretion, decency, and politeness, and without the threats, terrors, and tyrannical punishments which only spread the conflagration. He related to Erasmus how the offensive behavior of the papal legate Chierigati, who demanded the arrest and Roman trial of upright men, had aroused the hostility of his townsmen. In defense of the Nurembergers who were maligned as being Lutherans, Pirckheimer commented that the Romanists should have shown the same modesty and ethical purity that was still in evidence in Nuremberg. On September 1, 1524, Pirckheimer wrote another letter attempting to conciliate Erasmus who had complained about Luther's offer to overlook his timidity as long as he did not overtly attack his writings. Pirckheimer reassured sensitive Erasmus that Luther did not at all wish him ill, though he was occasionally too sharp in his writings. He was convinced that Luther would keep the peace if Erasmus did not sound his war trumpet. Nothing would please the foes of Erasmus, of learning, and of truth more than a controversy between him and Luther. But God and his friends will prevent such a misfortune! Pirckheimer continues to explain that he really did not look for a reconciliation of the two parties, for the Romanists are ready to make no concessions in matters of importance. But it will be difficult for them to satisfy the people with words now that their eyes have been opened so that they recognize the truth. Pirckheimer is sure that Luther does not approve of all that is done under the cloak of the gospel. Even the apostles had to suffer from such brothers; there are always tares among the wheat. Luther himself concedes that the reform should have proceeded with greater moderation, but how could one handle discreetly such immoderate and stubborn people who have respect neither for God nor for men? At the close of this remarkable letter Pirckheimer says he is awaiting Erasmus' book on free will and would be surprised if it did not cause quite a stir. Pirckheimer was clearly still personally attached to Luther and was trying at least obliquely to fend off a frontal assault on his position.

During the year 1523 Pirckheimer resolved to send an open letter to the new pope Adrian VI on the causes of the Reformation movement in Germany. The dispatch, which was never sent because of the death of the pontiff, revealed Pirckheimer's superficial humanist reading of contemporary history.[67] An apology for Reuchlin and Luther, the letter laid the blame for the disturbances and unrest squarely on the Dominicans and Eck. They had earned the hatred of all good, upright, and learned men through their abuse of Reuchlin so that these afterward stood on Luther's side in the indulgence tragedy. They poured such venomous gall upon that good and learned man that he was driven to bolder attempts. Failing to combat Luther successfully, because of his superior learning and

culture, they resorted as usual to stirring up the envious and ambitious against him. Cajetan came to quell the blaze but he merely
stirred it up so that it was already flaming through the roof. What
Prierias and his comrades wrote served to show how much they
were lacking in sincerity and faithfulness, in love of truth and
wholesome learning. Eck was dispatched to Rome because he was
known to be the great master of mischief and because they had
noticed in the Leipzig debates that he was their equal in shameless-
ness and insolence. He completed his mission in Rome with lies,
clamor, and empty promises and returned to Germany loaded with
bulls with which he struck not only at the Lutherans but at everyone against whom he harbored a grudge because of their integrity
or learning. He used the bulls to give his private hatred the weight
of public authority. On the surface this open letter to Pope Adrian
reads as though Pirckheimer appreciated Luther as the man of
learning assaulted by the forces of ignorance and malice, another
Reuchlin. There is certainly no indication that Pirckheimer understood the theological issues at stake. And yet, if Pirckheimer had
appropriated any deviationist opinions in matters of doctrine, a
letter to the Pope was hardly the place to expose them, if his intent
was to win a sympathetic hearing for the cause.

Angered by the maneuvers of Campeggio and the papal poli-
ticians at the Diet of Nuremberg in 1524, Pirckheimer seized his
pen and dashed off a little tract which was revealing, though it
remained unpublished, "On the Persecutors of Evangelical Truth,
their Counsels and Machinations." [68] In it he compared the Romanists with the Jews who, after deceit failed, used force against Christ.
Now the German princes, scholars, and priests, though they could
no longer crucify Christ, still strove to root out the Word of God
by force. A mischievous combination of princes and bishops undertook to persecute Luther and evangelical truth. The representatives
of Elector Frederick of Saxony fortunately arose to denounce their
resolutions, and received support from the counts, barons, and
delegations of the imperial cities. The papal party then planned to
hold the Diet in a small town, Eszlingen, where they could better
control the proceedings, and, after the majority of the delegates
had left Nuremberg, they proceeded as a rump to issue impossible
edicts. These deceits should be publicly exposed in order to protect
the inexperienced. Should anyone consider these words too sharp

and vehement, he should bear in mind that this is not a human or secular affair, but has to do with the honor of God and the heavenly king, for which every Christian is duty bound to act at the cost of blood. Here the welfare of the soul is endangered which Christ won through his suffering and death. This concerns the truth, the Word of God, and the Christian liberty for which Christ made men free. Though Pirckheimer concluded with the flourish that those who blasphemed God should hear their own heroic deeds celebrated in song, he neither completed the exposé nor did he venture to share his views with the public. Pirckheimer had acquired a Reformation vocabulary and a tenuous hold on some key Reformation principles. This piece was the product of his flare up of temper against the maneuvers of the Romanists. In that same year he composed a poem addressed to his Nurembergers expressing his pique at the steps taken by Osiander, Spengler and the Council to promote the Reformation in his own city. He was clearly no liberal in matters of innovation in his own city-state. After his resignation from the Council in 1522, Pirckheimer increasingly sought the leisure (*otium*) for humanist studies which had been denied him throughout most of his career, but the solace of complete detachment from the atonal realities was denied him as it had been to most of the Italian humanists who longed for the contemplative life.

In his last years Pirckheimer was thrown headlong into three major controversies each revealing the inner contradiction which plagued him. He was personally inclined toward the central evangelical affirmation, but he was constitutionally unable as a social conservative to accept all the innovations in ecclesiastical tradition which followed logically from the new position. He became involved in turn in the defense of the convents, the Sacramental controversy, and the debate over the second marriage of the clergy. Pirckheimer looked with growing misgivings and increasing alarm at the restiveness of the populace and the startling rapid advance of the Reformation in Nuremberg. The patrician and Gothic humanist in him shrank from the mass appeal of those religious egalitarians, the reformers. The lofty principle of inward faith and spirituality could clearly not be communicated to the mob without disastrous social effects, as the discrepancy of faith and action, the civic disturbances and revolutionary developments (1525) seemed to prove. In Nuremberg the patrician council and Spengler, the city secretary, introduced in quick succession the entire gamut of reform measures. The canon of the Mass was dropped, communion in both kinds introduced. Vigils and Masses for the dead were suspended. Osiander and the clergy of St. Lorenz and St. Sebaldus churches changed the order of service to a Protestant form. A mass exodus from the monasteries followed. The people, who became articulate through the voice of Hans Sachs, supported their leaders, who continued to appeal for a "free, safe, Christian, and God-blessed council." "The whole city is full of heretics," wrote Charitas to the orthodox Emser.[69] She herself was treated roughly by the Nuremberg mobs. Pirckheimer looked on with increasing alarm, lashing out at Osiander as "a priest without any experience" and at Spengler as "a proud secretary without any honor." "The common man," growled the old patrician, "is so instructed by the gospel that he thinks of nothing else than how a common division [of property] might take place."[70] The months-long sieges of ill health which plagued him from 1524 on added further to his gloom.

Under the proprietary church arrangement the Nuremberg council for decades had virtually controlled the affairs of the monasteries. It had favored the Observantine Franciscans. It had appealed to the general of the Augustinians, Egidio da Viterbo, for reform of the order and eventually assumed complete control themselves. After 1524 and 1525 it either closed the monasteries in the city or prevented the admission of new members. Charitas Pirckheimer, abbess of the convent of St. Clara, resisted the moves to close her house next and turned to her brother for counsel and aid. Pirckheimer urged the nuns to steadfastness and offered them shelter in his house should they be driven from the convent. He resolved to appeal to Melanchthon for his intervention. This fraternal gesture did not mean that Pirckheimer still adhered to the ascetic ideal. In the letter to Melanchthon "On the oppression of the nuns," Pirckheimer explained that he had two sisters and two daughters in St. Clara, and that the latter had entered on their aunt's prompting and with his permission, for at that time, he had erred — like the great majority of people — in believing that daughters were best provided for, if they entered a convent.[71] In November 1525, Melanchthon came to Nuremberg to organize a Protestant academy with a classical curriculum. He visited the convent of St. Clara to assure himself that the abbess and nuns were acting according to their genuine religious convictions. He then with Melanchthonian moderation urged the council to permit the nuns to remain but to prevent the reception of new members.

Pirckheimer's own advice to the nuns reveals the extent to which he had accepted the reformed attitude on the futility of the ascetic way for the religious life. In a 1524 "address to all monasteries and especially to the convents on how they could by God's grace be brought into a Christian condition," a certain Noricus Philadelphus volunteered amazing advice for his "dear sisters in Christ." [72] The general tone and internal evidence points to Pirckheimer's authorship. The tract begins with the explanation that, since God in these last times graciously and fatherly entreats with his saving Gospel and Word of grace, therefore he undertakes this Christian service out of Christian and brotherly love even though he knows that it will not be acceptable or pleasing. He appeals to the abbesses, prioresses, and rulers of the orders diligently to direct their virgins to the pure and simple Word of God and to bring them to the only way to eternal salvation. They should build their lives on Christ, the mighty, living rock, not on human deeds, law, and rule, and should hold with all their might to the one Christian rule, that is, to keep the true faith and Christian love. The steps recommended for convent reform follow:

1. The abbess or prioress and all the nuns should call upon God for grace and a strong correct faith. They should have a Christian preacher to set forth the Word of God daily.

2. God did not command his disciples Mass, vigils, observation of Friday, etc., but only the gospel, that is, the joyous, comforting word of divine grace, goodness, and mercy.

3. The abbesses themselves should diligently read both testaments of the Scriptures, as should the nuns when not preoccupied.

4. We can become righteous before God or be saved only through the Word of God. Provide the books of Dr. Martin Luther, of Philipp Melanchthon, and Johannes Bugenhagen for, in the first Psalm, David calls them blessed who give themselves day and night to the law of God, not to the deeds of men, not in the decrees of councils or popes, not in the rules and glosses of the fathers.

5. One should read, learn, and believe particularly Dr. Martin Luther's little book against human teachings.

6. The abbesses or prioresses should prescribe for Mass three psalms, three responses, and three readings from both testaments, all in German, for when people gather together for improvement, what improvement can follow from the unknown babbling of Latin.

7. The poor nuns shall have the Mass in German and it should be held with several communicants at least, since Dr. Martin urged the abolition of private Mass. God keep all from the idolatrous abomination that the Mass is a sacrifice.

8. God give all convent persons grace so that the sacrament is celebrated whole and not under one kind, for Christ established it under both kinds and thus it was celebrated for four hundred years after his resurrection. Jesus did not say, "I am tradition," but "I am the truth." [There follows a list of suggested readings, including all Luther and Melanchthon's writings on the whole Christian life, on *The Babylonian Captivity*, Melanchthon on Romans, Corinthians, and so forth.]

9. They should not be tyrannical.

10. They should free the nuns from the obligation to keep papal fasts, since there is nothing in the Scriptures on them.

11. They should leave veils, foods, and clothes up to the free choice of the nuns, for St. Paul says Col. 2, "Let no man therefore judge you . . ."

12. Observance of Friday should not be made obligatory, Col. 2, "nor in respect to an holy day . . ."

13. No one should be duty-bound to a profession.

14. No nun should be held against her will.

15. All true Christians are brides of Christ, not just the nuns.

16. The whole Christian life consists of faith, love, confession, and the cross. The right Christian faith is that we wish Him to do with us as He wills, whether He allows us to die or recover, and that I believe on Christ, that Christ died for my eternal salvation and arose again, and that I consequently love my neighbor as myself.

17. The correct worship is to believe and trust in God and love one's neighbor.

18. Abbesses and priors should rule in a godly way.

19. Above all, consciences should be instructed and strengthened with God's Word.

20. Comfort should be given against human ban, despising, and persecution.

21. Finally, that Christian schools be made of the convents so that young children may there be brought up in Christian education, teaching, and honor. One must patiently suffer, tolerate, keep, and nourish the old nuns who do not wish to leave or are unfit, and the young who out of their understanding of Holy Scriptures aspire to it should be allowed to come out with all friendship, free and unhindered.

That Pirckheimer was caught squarely between his personal acceptance of the principle of salvation by grace alone and the involvement of his whole family in the traditional religious conceptions upon which conventual asceticism was based is very evident from his correspondence with his two sisters Sabina and Euphemia. Between the years 1524 and 1528 Pirckheimer repeatedly wrote to Sabina, Abbess of Bergen, that before God works are of no avail and that man's salvation rests alone on faith in Christ's mercy. Again and again he censured her conventual works as spiritual pride, as blasphemy, which God will fearfully avenge. So severe was Pirckheimer's criticism that they became estranged; upon her death in 1529, he wrote to his sister Euphemia who succeeded her as abbess: "I had wished something better for you than to be elected to our sister's position, for the situation is everywhere such that also those who are not Lutheran suppress the convents and it is a matter of anxiety lest yours, too, become a dog kennel, for which it is not badly suited. God's will be done, whose name be blessed in all eternity." [73]

From these expressions it is obvious that Pirckheimer's 1530 *Apology* for the nuns of St. Clara as a public document produced out of a sense of fraternal obligation was not the most representative expression of his point of view. But it provides evidence of the ambivalence of his attitude toward medieval asceticism.[74] Its major theme is that those who have the true Christian faith and on the basis of that faith lead a true Christian life are able to do so as well inside as outside the convent. Pirckheimer is fighting a delaying action intended to win for the nuns the privilege of living out their days in peace, certainly not a typical traditionalist's point of view. Writing for the nuns, in the *Apology* he defends them against three basic charges:

1. That they despise the holy gospel of God and depend upon and trust more in their own works than on faith.

2. That they give too much authority to the Roman Pope and his decrees and depend too much on human traditions.

3. That they do not want to leave their convents and make light of their oaths, in order to return to secular life and marry.

The Lutheran sentiments in the *Apology* are unmistakable. Pirckheimer pays an initial tribute to the Protestant Scriptural principle by decrying anyone who would despise a single letter of the Holy Scriptures, for the gospel should be in one's hand daily and serve as a guideline for life. Man's salvation rests entirely upon the gospel, and he must trust entirely in God's grace. The problem, however, is that each fool interprets the Scriptures according to his own advantage instead of accepting the old interpreters. Pure Christian freedom is thus turned into occasion for lust of the flesh and indulgence. Contrary to the charges that the nuns depend on dead works rather than faith, they know that the justified man lives by faith and that they are not made righteous by the works of the law but freely by God's grace and redemption which is in Christ Jesus, through whom we have forgiveness of sins. A man is justified by faith without the deeds of the law. Whatever is not of faith is sin and the works of unbelievers are of no avail for salvation. Justified by faith and reconciled with God by the death of his Son, grafted like a wild olive onto a good tree, it is necessary for good works to follow in due course. All must show by their works that faith is alive in them.

At this point in the *Apology* Pirckheimer shifts ground from theological considerations to arguments for the convents based on expediency and tradition. It is preferable to adhere to the Pope as authority, whether he is a most holy or a most godless vicar of Christ, or the Antichrist, for it is better patiently to bear his power, even oppressive tyranny, as long as it is not dangerous to the soul's salvation, than impatiently to depart miserably from ancient usage. The common man, stirred up to reject the Pope and the bishops goes so far as to despise his own lords and government and holds all power and authority to be nothing, as the many plagues and much shedding of Christian blood testifies. The nuns do not substitute human laws for divine, for they know that the kingdom of God does not consist of eating and drinking. Rules of this nature are necessary for the common life; thus the discipline of silence is particularly apt for women. With all due respect for the marriage estate, the celibate life is preferable for serving and winning God's kingdom. Works are necessary, for grace is not sufficient without the discipline of the will and moderation of desires. Freedom of the will has been weakened but not destroyed by sin and can easily be reawakened by divine grace. In the matter of election, God's foreknowledge derives from his omnipotence, but is not therefore the cause of man's sin. Foreknowledge and election are two different things, the one belonging to power, the other to righteousness. What kind of righteousness would that be which would elect a man before he is born? It would be completely prejudicial to righteousness, if the lazy were crowned and the workers were condemned. The incarnation would have been without purpose if a part of mankind had been predestined to damnation and another part elected and ordained for life. With a final description of the plight of the nuns, a plea for mercy, and expression of hope for deliverance the tract ends.

The *Apology* illustrates Pirckheimer's untenable position in making concessions to the evangelical position on grace while defending the institution which more than any other represented the concrete realization of semi-Pelagian presuppositions. Moreover, it exposes Pirckheimer's inability to sustain a high order of cogency and consistency in theological exposition. His remarks on the problem of predestination are not precise and do not meet the main Protestant arguments on the matter of election. Nor does Pirckheimer really come to grips with the main Protestant objections to celibacy, and he accomplished little more than his modest goal of establishing that the convents are not harmful in themselves. Luther in treatises like the *Theses Concerning Faith and Law* (1535) or *Disputation Concerning Justification* (1536) stressed the necessity of good works and agreed with Pirckheimer's pronouncement that faith without works is dead. There is some reason to see this document as marking a return to the old religion, although in its first paragraphs it parallels Pirckheimer's earlier expressions on faith and works. A similar pattern is evident in the progression of his views during the sacramental controversy. Melanchthon, who was a frequent visitor in Pirckheimer's house in 1525 and 1526, reported on the discussion of the Lord's Supper in which Albrecht Dürer also participated.

Pirckheimer felt at home in the company of Melanchthon and the conservative reformers, but like his friend Dürer, who felt his artistic existence threatened, political stability and the moral order endangered, by the radicals, he took up the offensive not against the Reformation itself, but against those whom he considered ex-

tremists. In three major polemical tracts he retrenched his position
always more deeply in traditional territory. At the end of 1525
Pirckheimer precipitously entered the sacramental controversy
with an assault on his erstwhile friend, the Basel reformer Johannes
Oecolampadius, for his Zwinglian interpretation of the Lord's
Supper. Oecolampadius had supported the mystical Anabaptist
Johann Denk, who was deposed as rector of the school of St.
Sebald in Nuremberg. Pirckheimer came to associate him with
religious and social radicals like Thomas Münzer and Andreas
Carlstadt. In the summer of 1525 Oecolampadius published a treatise opposing the real bodily presence of Christ in the Sacrament
and interpreting the words of institution tropologically. Pirckheimer replied with his first treatise published early in 1526.[75] In it
he adopted Luther's position on the real presence in opposition to
the symbolic interpretation on the one hand or transubstantiation
with its specious distinction of essence and accidents on the other.
Like Luther he appeals directly to the words of Scripture as the
primary basis of proof. Pirckheimer borrows from Duns Scotus the
argument of the ubiquity of Christ to establish the real presence.
To deny the mystery of the Sacrament on sophistical scholastic or
natural rationalistic grounds, Pirckheimer argues, is to render all
the other mysteries of the faith uncertain. Oecolampadius should
not side with that "atheist" Averroes in mocking the Christian
sacrament. Only faith and not carnal sense is able to penetrate to
an understanding of such profundity. Throughout the work, whether the question is that of the sacrificial nature of the Eucharist
or an answer to Carlstadt, Pirckheimer defers to the authority of
Luther with expressions like these, "If Luther's answer is not
sufficient, my writings will satisfy less," or "Since Luther treated
these subjects, it would be superfluous to dispute about them again."

In spite of this constant appeal to Luther, however, consistent
emphasis on the Word of promise and the meaning of the Eucharist for the personal life of faith is missing from the treatise. Pirckheimer was not a great lay theologian and his exposition was
marked with lack of clarity and even contradictions, where, for
example, he defends the adoration of the host while maintaining
the spiritual nature of the Sacrament. His discourse aroused a public
response far out of proportion to its true merit.

Luther was pleasantly surprised by it and commented that he had not believed Pirckheimer possessed the earnestness in religious matters that he here showed. In Nuremberg itself the evangelical clergy and patricians felt gratified. The Augsburg preacher Urbanus Rhegius thanked him for his effort. Ulrich Zasius, Roman legist, exhausted hyperbole in his praise. Thomas Venatorius declared him Luther's equal as a theologian. The Catholic stalwart Cochlaeus, of course, was aghast at Pirckheimer's position. Both he and Erasmus began extensive correspondence designed to lead him to a more Catholic position. Erasmus sought refuge in the sanctuary: "Oecolampadius' opinion would not displease me, if the concensus of the church were not opposed to it . . . I do not know what the authority of the church means to others, but it means so much to me that I could agree with the Arians and Pelagians, if the church sanctioned what they taught." [76] The Zwinglians were naturally embittered. Oecolampadius, surprised and hurt, wrote to Pirckheimer on April 13, 1526, and received a sharp retort, dated June 20, warning him against clinging to his dreams and receiving the punishment of Münzer and Carlstadt. A tractarian duel followed in the best polemical tradition of the day.

To Oecolampadius' moderate reply published in Zurich in 1526, Pirckheimer in January of the following year issued a second response much sharper than his first. [77] His position on the central question remains the same, that the true body and blood of Christ are contained in, with, and under the bread and wine in the Sacrament of the Altar. He still dissociates himself from Catholic dogma, asserting that he has nothing in common with the schools and monasteries, but wants as an ally only him who seeks truth. He is offended by such gross abuses as the sale of indulgences. Though he disclaims a direct dependence on Luther and asserts that for seven years he has not associated with him, he is still friendly to the evangelical movement and charges the disturbances of the time to the extremists who under Christ's cloak seek their own riches, honor, and pleasures. Once again he tries to establish Oecolampadius' guilt by association with Münzer and Carlstadt. Erasmus' quick inoculation begins to take effect, for Pirckheimer now defers to the authority of the church, arguing that it is frivolous, dangerous, godless, and detestable to fall away from the universal church. He appeals to the apostolic tradition and to the authority of both Greek and Latin church fathers. All human conjectures fail, but the words of the Savior remain into eternity.

In March 1527, Oecolampadius replied and drew from Pirckheimer a scurrilous and unworthy blast "against the insults of that monk who in Graeco-Latin is called Caecolampadius (a dark light)."[78] On the title page he addressed his opponent as Judas Iscariot and in a temper added, "May God seize you, Satan." Out of the welter of scandalous personal assaults emerge enough arguments to indicate that Pirckheimer was veering further toward the Romanist position, for he refers to the manifest institution of eternal truth and the universal concensus of the Catholic church. The doctrine of the universal church remains firm and unshaken. The hearts of Christian princes should move them to set things in order in the *Respublica Christiana*. Pirckheimer again labels his Swiss adversary the third man in the radical triumvirate, those princes of the darkness of this century. In denying that he is a mere papist, Pirckheimer nevertheless declares that in a holy, righteous, and true cause, he would be reprehensible if he did not stand more on the papal side than on that of the false prophets. In many respects, though not in all, he prefers papistic coercion to that wild and petulant liberty which most men commend with too little thought under the pretext of the gospel. It is clear that, although Pirckheimer would have preferred to stand above parties, when forced to a choice his sentiments were on the side of the old church.

No sooner did the controversy end with his third and final blast than Pirckheimer was involved in another, this time with the Nuremberg Lutherans and with Luther himself. Pirckheimer did not endorse clerical celibacy and spoke out for the marriage of the priests, but he interpreted 1 Timothy 3:2 to mean that the clergy should marry only once. He was accordingly offended when the Nuremberg preacher at St. Sebaldus, Dominikus Schleupner, a widower, married for the second time on December 11, 1527. Pirckheimer composed and circulated anonymously twenty-eight propositions against the second marriage of the clergy.[79] Wenceslaus Link and Andreas Osiander wrote a refutation and Pirckheimer suspected them of calling on Luther for help.

Luther replied in 1528 with one hundred and thirty-nine counter-theses and published Pirckheimer's propositions along with them, letting it be known that he knew the identity of their author. Pirckheimer sent Cochlaeus a manuscript on the celibacy of the priesthood to be published in Leipzig. He also prepared five hundred theses on the question of the second marriage of the clergy. He was also, it seems, preparing a dialogue lampoon against "that monk" Luther, which might have matched in virulence his letter against "that monk" Osiander. At the time of his death he left behind three unfinished manuscripts on the question directed against Luther, Osiander, and Linck, breathing fire and threatening with all of the Grand Inquisitor's tortures.[80] His appeal also in this controversy was to the Scriptures and the universal concensus of the church, a phrase impressed on him by Erasmus. One must in the final analysis bow before the church, the depository of divine truth.

Pirckheimer was unable during his last years to decide without reservation for either the Reformation or the old church. His humanist posture of standing above party combined with his lack of religious depth to render him incapable of final decision and so he vacillated to and fro until the end came. Ethical, social, and intellectual norms, his basic criteria for judging, were inadequate guides in a stormy sea where religious currents ran much deeper and angry billows welled much higher than Pirckheimer could see. Toward Luther he waxed alternately hot and cold, speaking of him with trust and respect at times and with spiteful venom at others. Melanchthon, who was Pirckheimer's guest on his way to the Diet of Augsburg in 1530, shortly before Pirckheimer died, wrote to Luther that Pirckheimer had spoken with high praise of Luther and his teaching.[81] Cochlaeus, who perceived that Pirckheimer's criticism of the old church had been largely directed against abuses, played on his vanity and appealed to him to lead in the ethical reform of the whole church. Turning his critical eyes on the evangelicals he discovered that their works did indeed not match their profession. In the preface addressed to Ulrich Zasius before his translation of Gregory Nazianzen's oration on the duty of a bishop (1529), Pirckheimer applied the same standards of conduct to the evangelical preachers as he had to the priests, the kingdom of God is not in words but in virtue. Pirck-heimer reveals in the preface that he had not the slightest appreciation of the Reformation emphasis on the priesthood of all believers or the closing of the gap between cleric and layman.[82] His missiles skipped along the surface. Sick and suffering, mourning the death of friends and family, disillusioned, Pirckheimer, who had once pronounced disorders a necessary catharsis no longer had any stomach for continued disturbances. He expressed his disappointment with both sides in a long letter to the Vienna architect Tschertte in which he explained the defection of some Protestant militiamen during the Turks' siege of Vienna as an obvious discrepancy between faith and good works.

It is, therefore, perhaps good that one can detect how far the Lutheran word and work are from each other. Without doubt there are many pious honorable people around about you whom you hear speak sweetly about faith and the holy gospel; deem it to be pure gold that glitters, but it is hardly brass. I confess that I, too, was at first a good Lutheran, like our sainted Albrecht [Dürer]. Then we hoped that the Roman rascality, likewise the roguery of the monks and priests would be corrected. But as one observes, the situation has grown worse, so that the evangelical knaves make them pious. I can well imagine that this sounds strange to you, but if you were here with us and would see the shameful, wicked, and criminal manner in which the priests and apostate monks conduct themselves, you would be very amazed. The former ones betrayed us with hypocrisy and cunning, but these want to lead a scandalous and criminal life openly, and blind the perceptive people by saying that one can not judge them by their works, although Christ taught us differently . . . The common man therefore taught by this gospel that he thinks only of how a common division [of property] might be made and truly if it were not for the greatest watchfulness and punishment, a general plundering would soon arise, such as has already taken place in many localities . . . Luther would gladly reverse and make moderate much of his cause, which is handled so crudely that it cannot be disguised. Thus Oecolampadius, Zwingli, and others came up against Luther with their utmost, because of the Sacrament which they regarded as a mere symbol, and if Luther had not intervened so far and given resistance to Dr. Carlstadt, he would have become the head of the whole damned error . . . But I write all this not because I can or wish to praise the condition of the Pope, his monks, and priests; for I know that it would be nothing and in many ways it is criminal, and also probably needs improvement, irrespective of the imperial mandate which now stiffens the Pope in all his undertaking . . . The papists are at least unified among themselves, whereas those who call themselves evangelical are altogether disunified and divided into sects, which must run their course, like the fanatical peasants, until they at last go mad. God preserve all pious men, lands, and people from such doctrine that where it enters there is no peace, quiet, or unity.[83]

In such a jaundiced mood Pirckheimer could readily wish a plague on both their houses, though he leaned perceptibly toward the old church. His bitterness was doubtless in part the by-product of external historical events. But in a deeper sense his dark melancholy resulted from his lack of inner spiritual strength. The absence of strong conviction made it impossible for him to identify with either cause and rendered his inward citadel vulnerable to his personal vices, fears, and hostilities. Even his last days appeared problematical to his contemporaries, as they have to his biographer. There is the story of his dramatic return to the old church, which, however, he had never left. There is the theory that he rejected the dogmatism of the Reformation while maintaining a personal evangelical faith, and yet it was the Lutheran position on the Sacrament he thought he was defending. Nor is there any evidence that he reentered the confines of the Catholic doctrinal reservation, for a mind and spirit expanded by new ideas can never assume precisely its original dimensions. He did not share the urge of Agricola, Reuchlin, Erasmus, or Beatus Rhenanus to devote his last years entirely to the study of theology. To the end he occupied himself with translating both pagan and the Christian classics. The rumor arose that he was endeavoring to live without the church, so that it is still whispered that he lived and died a mere aesthete.

Times had changed since his father, Johann, like Reuchlin, had himself ordained a priest, and, like Agricola, was buried with the Franciscans. Luther had worked the change in denouncing these last minute ordinations into a holier order than that of other Christians and the burials in monkish cowls as superstition, for a Christian's baptism suffices also in death, Pirckheimer died on December 22, 1530, a Christian layman. Like Erasmus, he died without benefit of clergy. This did not mean, in his case any more than in that of Erasmus, that he was indifferent to the final ministration of the church. An entry in the family archive of the Nuremberg Catholic Christoph Scheurl, who disliked Pirckheimer, recounts his death: "He had abstained for a long time, had eaten nothing in the evening except bread with caraway. He left behind a seven-year-old boy, who looked just like him, by Barby, the Grätzen girl. He departed without confession or sacrament, *sine crux et lux* [without cross and light]." This account does not prove, as it is often interpreted, that Pirckheimer despised the Sacrament, at least not in the evangelical form as it was exclusively celebrated in Nuremberg. Death took him by surprise, for Thomas Venatorius, the evangelical preacher at the Holy Ghost Hospital, who spent a great deal of time with Pirckheimer during his last days relates that his end came suddenly, even while he was planning to rearrange his own works.[84] Erasmus at Pirckheimer's request edited his translation of thirty sermons of Gregory Nazianzen the year after his death. In the preface addressed, as Pirckheimer had directed, to Duke George of Saxony, Erasmus paid an elaborate tribute to Pirckheimer "whose last words breathed nothing but love of the fatherland and the most fervent love of the Christian religion." His last clearly audible words were: "Would that after my death all may be well with my fatherland! Would that the church may find peace!" [85]

Pirckheimer most certainly possessed a larger measure of faith than Celtis and greater certainty than Mutian, but he was not a great religious soul like Reuchlin, not to say Luther. He possessed throughout his life a certain basic piety which he extended also to his secular studies. The *Ex Libris* which Dürer prepared for Pirckheimer's volumes read: "The fear of the Lord is the beginning of wisdom" [Ps. 111:10]. Pirckheimer could be considered neither a good evangelical nor a good Catholic from their points of view. Yet he was basically a Christian exploiting the ancient classics in the interest of reform and the Christian ethic. A Christian humanist long before he came under the intimate influence of Erasmus, he tried to overcome the tension between classic and Christian antiquity, between natural and the supernatural, between the kingdom of power and the kingdom of grace, between human achievement and divine fulfillment. His virtue was that of the Stoa entirely reset into a Christian context.

In that sense the final phrase of the bronze epitaph on his grave in St. John's cemetery, Nuremberg, must be understood: *Virtvs interire nescit*, virtue can not perish.

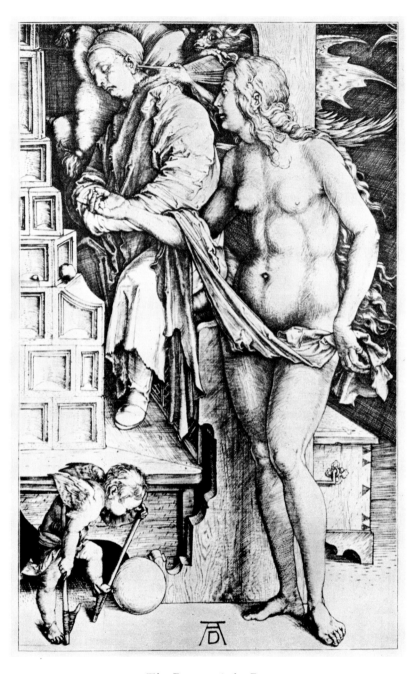

9. The Dream of the Doctor

10. Erasmus of Rotterdam

ERASMUS

Philosopher of Christi

ERASMUS as the prince of the Northern humanists was titular head also of German humanism. He did not wish to be identified with any national group, for, he wrote to Zwingli, "I desire to be a citizen of the world, common to all, or rather, a stranger to all."[1] To a Brabant countryman he once repeated Cicero's words: "Where you fare well, there is your fatherland." In 1520 he replied to Peter Manius, who had urged him to declare openly that he was a German and not a Frenchman so that Germany might not be deprived of this great glory, that it seemed to him to make little difference where a man is born. It is a vain sort of glorification, he felt, when a city or nation boasts of producing a man who has become great through his own exertions and not by the help of his fatherland. For the country which has made him great has a better right to boast than that which brought him forth.[2] His *patria* was Rotterdam and the Netherlands were still counted among the Germanies by virtue of imperial, Habsburg, linguistic, and cultural ties. Like Hegius and Agricola, Erasmus spoke of *Germania nostra* and referred to "us" and "our people" in connection with the low Germans in general.[3] In a letter to Wimpfeling, Erasmus himself said that the year 1514 brought him into really close contact with the humanist movement in Germany. His fourteen years in Basel and Freiburg meant for him even closer relations with the Rhenish humanist circle.[4] The important fact for the study of German humanism, however, is that in spite of Erasmus' cosmopolitanism the German humanists considered him their head. One of Froben's scholars referred to his "native Germany," Reuchlin and Beatus

Rhenanus called him a German, the pride of the fatherland, and with his customary aplomb Erasmus himself declared in his apology against Martin van Dorp of Louvain that many called him the "ornament of Germany." [5] Erasmus did not always reciprocate with equal extravagance, but on the whole he belonged to all nations, including the Germans, rather than to none.

Erasmus denied that his controversial motto *concedo nulli*, I yield to none, represented his own voice and was therefore an arrogant statement. But it most certainly applied to his position with respect to all the German humanists. In many ways he personified their movement, if not in cultural nationalism, then in their drive toward religious enlightenment. His stature alone would make a discussion of his ideas essential if only to identify the similarities and differences between him and his fellow humanists. Santayana once remarked that no sermon is complete without a quotation from St. Augustine. In the same way no book on Northern humanism can pass Erasmus by.

The story of Erasmus is so common that, to turn a phrase from Chaucer, every wit that hath discretion knows all or part of it. And yet Erasmus remains elusive, a proteus, a man of a hundred faces.[6] Immortalized by Holbein, Quentin Metsys, and Dürer, he looks out from the canvas with an enigmatic half-smile, an expression suggesting the complications of his personality (figure 10). Small wonder that straightforward Frederick of Saxony commented that this was an amazing little man, for one never knows where one stands with him. He was gifted with a quick and ready wit, with unusual charm and brilliance. For all his correspondence and superficial gregariousness, he was a lonely monarch who gave of himself without reservations to no one. He was no confessor, no fighter, no great man. He abhorred disturbances to the point of appearing to many contemporaries to be a timorous neuter. He was a valetudinarian, loving good living and creature comforts, petulant, querulous, flattering, deceptive, and vindictive. He saw his own weakness and feared that in case of a conflict he would like Peter deny his friends. He could speak almost distinterestedly of the tragic deaths of his friends Fisher and More. "Not all have sufficient strength for martyrdom," he confided. In a call for world missions in 1535 he expressed the wish that God would have given to him the spirit of martyrdom. But such dedication and courage were never granted to him.

Erasmus justified his lack of a heroic spirit with the comment that there have been many martyrs in Christendom but only a few scholars. Erasmus was primarily precisely that, a scholar. He was not a historian, a philosopher, a scientist, a painter, or a musician. He was not a discoverer, one of those Renaissance men like Columbus, Copernicus, or Vesalius who achieved a break-through to a new world, but he was a scholar in temperament and calling, editing and writing with a phenomenal ascetic capacity for long, hard work. He frequently worked hurriedly, standing on one foot, as he once put it. In the *Colloquies* he referred to himself as one of those prolific writers who never ceased to make war with the pen. He successfully evaded all practical responsibility in church and state in order to be free for his books. He lived in his study and died in his bed.[7]

As with most intellectuals, the development of Erasmus' mind is far more interesting than his mere biography. In his case, more than in that of most intellectuals, the end was present in the beginning so that his development was marked by gradualism and a high degree of consistency. His mental evolution was not marked off into five easily identifiable stages such as *Devotio Moderna*, monasticism, mysticism, scholasticism, and humanism. Nor can his experiences be tagged as two negative, Augustinian monasticism and Parisian scholasticism, and two positive, the stay in England and trip to Italy. Rather the two major influences of classical and Christian antiquity together with a basic view of their relation to each other were operative in Erasmus' early period as they were throughout his career.

Under the influence of the Brethren of the Common Life at Deventer and at 'S Hertogenbosch from 1475 to 1486, the formative years, Erasmus (b. 1469) absorbed both the religious views of the *Devotio Moderna* and the classical interests of Hegius and his colleagues. Religiously this meant an emphasis on the simplicity of truth, the spirituality and inwardness of the religious life, and the imitation of Christ. In terms of classical culture it meant a formal acquaintance with a selected number of Latin authors and the opportunity through self-study to range through and somewhat beyond the prescribed readings in moral philosophy. Especially at Deventer, Erasmus developed an early enthusiasm for the classics as well as for St. Paul, Jerome, Augustine, and Lorenzo Valla, who exercised the strongest influence over him. Valla taught him the elegances of Latinity, the elements of literary criticism, the importance of ecclesiastical antiquity, and even the critical use of the Vulgate.[8]

His six years in the monastery at Steyn near Gouda, which he entered in 1486 or 1487 to become an Augustinian canon regular, instead of turning him completely to other-worldly concerns actually provided the leisure for the further development of his proficiency in the classics. He seems to have been quite content the first two or three years, but then became increasingly impatient until he left never to return, finally in 1517 receiving a dispensation by Leo X from his monastic vows altogether. Like Innocent III, whose treatise he knew, and Petrarch, whose treatise he did not know, he wrote a *De contemptu mundi* (1488) filled with warnings against the "jugglings of the lewd smiling show of this world," so vain, foolish, and unstable. Though the world is miserable and defiled, in the religious life there is far greater liberty, tranquillity, and pleasure. He cites Hegius on the benefit of the solitary life, for to be a servant to many is a state of great misery. He quotes Agricola on the finality of death for all but virtue and good works which alone remain. Jesus by withdrawing into the wilderness provided the example to be followed. Epicurus is the authority for pleasure as the rejection of fleshly lusts. He refers also to Bernard and Paul as proper authorities.[9] The treatise is conventional and does not breathe a deep religious spirit. The arguments adduced point more to advantages for self than to love of God or service to neighbor. When years later he published this little work he added a preface and a debilitating final chapter (XII) calling this piece a trifle written to exercise his style, pretending to have done it for another man, who wished to talk a youth into entering a cloister, and assaulting monastic corruption, thus almost completely reversing the argument of the book and revealing his own inner ambivalence, not to say duplicity.

Another similar treatise was his *Declamatio de morte*, which in the preface to Henricus Glareanus he referred to as a youthful exercise found among his papers. In it he combined classic with Christian comforts for a father upon the death of his son. Man should be content with death, since, even if it completely extinguished the person, it would end his calamities or griefs, but the Christian comfort beyond that is that it releases the soul for ethereal joy.[10]

When Erasmus left the monastery for the summer residence of his patron Bishop Henry he took with him a rough draft of his *Antibarbari* or book against the Philistine foes of humanist learning. He argued that classical knowledge aids spiritual growth and minimized the importance of elaborate dogma. He worked on the book during his last two or three years at Steyn and finished it in the spring of 1494, though he did not publish the enlarged version until 1520. In the preface to Sapidus of the printed edition Erasmus spoke of an innate drive or impulse which drove him to the Muses as though inspired. He became an intense partisan of all who followed the humanist pursuits. Perhaps Erasmus who was as yet nothing in his own right experienced an identity crisis not unusual for his years, a crisis resolved when he first got his name into print in his early days in Paris by contributing a letter of compliment to the end pages of ailing Gaguin's *History of France* and thus finding a place in a cause bigger than himself. His career coincided with the increasing spread and power of the press and Erasmus was quick to see its advantages. The humanist printers became his natural partners.

In Paris at the College de Montagu he rebelled against the scholastic instruction, though he was possibly somewhat affected by the reform efforts of the monkish Jean Standonck.[11] A subtle change which had been many years in the making became increasingly evident during the Paris years. He found self-denial and the the ascetic way of life increasingly repugnant, but self-assertion and a mundane way of life always more attractive. The earthly joys of Gaguin's dinners, literary conversations, and the company of Faustus Andrelini and his wealthy tutees satisfied his innate craving for the pleasures of this world. The interpenetration of a subtle and pervasive secularism, which both drew strength from classic letters and in turn, heightened his inclination to respond to their terrestrial spirit, pressed him toward a closer synthesis of Christianity and a naturalistic ethic.[12] That he got on with the world very

well for a monk he showed in England in 1499, when he took to
the hunt and made conquests among the ladies, for all his hood and
tonsure. Nevertheless, he was attracted to the austere Colet who
brought out his religious concern explicitly once again.

It would be very dramatic to record that "the famouse clarke"
enjoyed a conversion in England, but there is no evidence of a
severe crisis of conscience. The six months in England, nevertheless, produced a change in Erasmus through the influence primarily of Colet. It was Colet who first inspired him to dedicate himself
to theology, that is, to Biblical studies and patristics.[13] Colet increased his impatience with those theologians who grew old with
mere arguments and sophistical caviling. On the positive side, Colet
drew Erasmus' attention to the Scriptures. He tried to interest him
in interpreting Moses and Isaiah the way he was doing Paul's
epistles, but Erasmus felt too poorly prepared.[14] "How shall I
teach what I have never learned?," he asked. Upon his return to the
continent, however, Erasmus did busy himself with the exposition
of *Romans*, reflecting Colet's influence in his choice of a theme. In
1504 he already had four bundles of manuscripts.[15] Two episodes
illustrate the serious nature of Colet's concerns which affected
Erasmus. At a dinner in Oxford where Colet played host the discussion centered on why Cain's sacrifice should have been less
pleasing to God than Abel's. On another afternoon they debated
the meaning of Christ's agony in the garden, Erasmus maintaining
that Christ's human nature was subject to human fear. Colet disagreed with Erasmus on the very principle of Biblical interpretation which Luther was to raise against him years later. Against
Erasmus, who argued that the Word of God is multiple and that
"manna does not taste the same to all mouths," Colet asserted that
the Scriptures cannot have many senses or meanings.[16] Colet's
inspirational power over Erasmus showed itself in the years to
come in Erasmus' solicitousness for Colet's school at St. Paul's.[17]
Colet's influence is still to be found in the *Enchiridion* composed
two years later. At that time he had gotten to know also Antoine
de Berg and Jean Vitrier in Paris and the lively impression they
made on Erasmus reinforced the basic tendencies which Erasmus
owed to Colet.

At forty, on the way to Italy, Erasmus wrote a poetic farewell to levity, dedicating his remaining years to Christ alone. He was not an admirer of fashionable classic culture, for ancient Rome offended him both by its paganism and by its imperialism. Nevertheless, he devoted his time to humanistic studies and turned down Cardinal Grimani's invitation to serve the church in Rome. For the last three decades of his life he was considered the greatest classical scholar. His antiquity was still more Latin than Hellenic showing a special predilection for the best period, for Cicero and Horace. The Aldine press in Venice produced the magisterial edition of the *Chiliades Adagiorum* with 3260 proverbs, as compared with 818 adages in 1500, a statistical index of Erasmus' growth as a classical scholar. In the preface to the *Chiliades* he discourses on the value of proverbs and the leading thought is that the *Adages* are intended to aid in the inculcation of philosophical or religious truths, moral and ethical precepts. The didactic, sententious content of the proverbs is frequently applied in various ways in the commentaries.[18] The same goal, beyond pleasant usage, of promoting moral philosophy was reflected in another of Erasmus' books of this genre, the *Apophthegmata*, apophthemes or brief sayings, drawing heavily on Plutarch.[19]

With the Italian journey Erasmus had definitely come of age and he returned to England in high spirits, composing his *Folly* mentally as he rode northward. A look backward reveals a strange quality of uninterruptedness in his development. The same two major influences were operative at all times though in varying degree, the Christian and classical antiquities, with a measure of subsurface erosion due to the secular interests seeping in from the world about him. The roots of his ecclesiastical reform program and religious philosophy were demonstrably imbedded in the soil of his *patria.*

Although Erasmus spoke of the rebirth of letters (*renascentes litterae*), he never referred to a Christian Renaissance, but rather to a restoration of Christianity (*restitutio Christianismi*). He looked back to the pristine sources of Christianity for the criteria of its restoration, rather than forward to a day when it would be something new and different. In the preface to Leo X of his edition of the New Testament he wrote that the leading hope and anchor for "restoring and repairing the Christian religion" was for all

Christians to learn the commandments of the Founder from evangelical and apostolic sources. It would be best if this *philosophia Christiana*, this *doctrina coelestis*, which Christ himself calls a rebirth (*renascentia*) or restoration of fallen nature, were brought to men by the pontiff. During his years of reasonably good relations with the Protestants he frequently used a term for his positive theology acceptable even to Oecolampadius, *philosophia evangelica*. He explained that his Jerome edition should serve the purpose of an *instauratio pietatis*. The reform which he envisioned was a reform in the sense of a union of the Scriptures, the Church Fathers, *humanitas* and the *bonae litterae* within the Church. The name which best suited such an amalgam was the *philosophia Christi*, a term used already by his humanist predecessor Agricola and long before him by the scholastic Abelard. Traversari had in the preceding century used the term philosophers of Christ (*philosophi Christi*) in referring to the ancient Greek fathers.[20] But Erasmus in all likelihood derived the term directly from Augustine, from the Cappadocians, the Alexandrians, or from the Apologists themselves. He echoed Justin Martyr's words: "This is the only philosophy which I have found certain and adequate."

One of the great ironies of Erasmus' career was that two of his casual writings given more to satire and criticism than to constructive statement, the *Praise of Folly* and the *Colloquies*, should have had the greatest staying power in the popular mind. But Erasmus impressed also his contemporaries with being more a critic than a constructive thinker. He believed that he was living in the final age of the world foreseen by St. John and St. Paul in which Christian love would grow cold and the spirit decline. His attacks were designed to stimulate new life and spirituality, though his laugh was at times dry and corrosive. Nevertheless, his writings which mercilessly attacked abuses cannot be artificially distinguished from his constructive works for they contained positive elements and belonged to a single reform program. From an immense field, it is necessary to select three targets which were the most prominent in Erasmus' writings: the estate of the clergy, secular and regular, various religious practices, and scholasticism. In each case Erasmus responds with a qualified approval and a modified disapproval.

Clerical abuses were the most offensive to Erasmus for they represented a double felony, moral wrong and a betrayal of a high trust. He attacked the formalism, hypocrisy and superstition of the churchmen. His dislike of monasticism was transformed into a general hostility toward the monks, and after about 1506 he joined the humanist chorus of ridicule. He continued to hold that living by the *regula* was good and proper for some people and that the orders at their best served a useful function. In 1524 he even compared the glories of nuns with those of the martyrs.[21] Though he was ready for concessions on the marriage of the clergy, he was shocked when the reformers actually took the step and he delighted in mocking them.[22] Luther's reply to Erasmus, it so happened, was his first treatise written as a bridegroom.

Erasmus' attitude toward the papacy provides a clear-cut example of his consistency within ambivalence. For Erasmus the papacy incorporated the essence of the church, and yet he reserved some of his most savage thrusts for the popes. As spiritual shepherd the pope was above all mortals, possessing heavenly authority.[23] His attacks on the papacy were consistently leveled against individual popes, usually in their secular, political, or military capacity, their theatrical splendor and wastefulness. At the same time he stressed obedience to the pope as ecclesiastical head and as capstone of the hierarchy.[24] The church was for him itself the communion of believers who agree in faith in the gospel, who honor the one Father, who found their whole trust in his Son, and who are led by the Holy Spirit himself.[25] Since the church is embodied in the papacy, whoever does not recognize the pope stands outside the church.[26] Erasmus complained most bitterly against the pope for stirring up war between the Christian princes instead of acting as peacemaker.[27] But worst of all were the popes who themselves made war and in this none compared with Julius II. "The highest pontiff Julius wages war," Erasmus once reported in words reminiscent of Hutten, having seen his triumphal entry into Bologna, "he conquers, triumphs, and acts entirely like Julius [Caesar]." [28] Erasmus held that terms like Apostle, shepherd, bishop, abbot, pope, were concepts of a holy office, not of secular overlordship, the title for an office of Christian faith and love, not for earthly power and might.[29]

Erasmus often seemed to form his opinion of various religious practices on the basis of irreligious or irrelevant personal considerations. At best his judgment frequently was made after mere reflection rather than through a struggle of faith and conscience. He criticized the abuses of indulgences, forms, superstitions, lip service, self-righteousness, and mechanical observances. He consistently scorned fish and fasts, neither of which agreed with his delicate constitution. He heaped pitiless ridicule upon the countless pilgrimages multiplying without end during those decades. At the same time he personally wrote a liturgy for a pilgrimage in 1523. He was both critical and credulous regarding the invocation of the saints. He was deadly serious in ascribing his recovery from illness to the help of St. Genevieve.

Unlike some of the early German humanists, he had personally nothing in common with the scholastics. He made sport of "Gryllard lecturing from his lofty pulpit." He contrasted the simple and agreeable evangelical precepts with the ostentatious erudition and wasteful picayune questions and precious arguments of the scholastics.[30] Like Valla, who praised Pythagoras, but attacked the Occamists and Aristotelians, Erasmus assaulted the Occamists and Scotists. Averroes was to him, as to Petrarch, a man blasphemous to Christ.[31] The competitive drive of the humanists versus scholastics appeared also in Erasmus. In a letter to Melanchthon, Erasmus asserted that the quarrels were all due to a grand conspiracy against the new learning. To Everard, Stadtholder in Holland, he confided in 1520 that theology was flourishing in Paris and Cambridge as nowhere else because they were "adapting themselves to the tendencies of the age" so that the new studies, which were ready if need be to storm an entrance, were received as welcome guests.[32]

On the other hand, Erasmus allowed a certain province even to scholasticism. He did not condemn it completely, but rather reserved it for specialists. Like Petrarch, he believed that students should not be forced to spend long years at dialectic and later in theologizing. His attack was on syllogistic demonstration and disputation. But he even approved of scholastic disputations, if moderately done.[33] He most certainly did not question any more than did Pico or other humanists the Christian content of scholastic theology. He was especially indulgent of Thomas, whom he characterized as *diligentissimus* and very circumspect. He admired his spirit and sanctity and the fact that he read the Scriptures and ancient authors. But he believed that he had contaminated the doctrine of Christ with a profane spirit. Moreover, he asked, who can carry the *Secunda Secundae* around with him for instruction. The philosophical synthesis of the summas did not interest him.

The two most popular among Erasmus' writings, *The Praise of Folly* (over six hundred editions) and the *Colloquies* (over three hundred editions) illustrate both his critical and his positive programs.[34] "As nothing" he wrote in the dedication of the *Folly* to Thomas More, "is more trifling than to treat serious questions frivolously, so nothing is more amusing than to treat trifles in such a way as to show yourself anything but a trifler. We have praised folly not quite foolishly." Erasmus intended the *Folly* to be far more than a quiver of satirical poisoned darts in the style of Hutten's Lucianic dialogues. He patiently explained to Martin van Dorp, who, as the first of many critics to miss the point, had decried the damage *Folly* had done in alienating his "learned" friends, that it really represented his whole program, since all his writings served the same constructive end. Laughter, he felt, makes unpalatable truths digestible and the criticisms were so impersonal and general that no one should be offended.

Erasmus' *Folly* was no doubt related to that fleet of medieval humor whose flagship was Sebastian Brant's *Ship of Fools*. *Folly's* subjects look like Brant's passenger list — princes, courtiers, scholars, theologians, philosophers, bishops, cardinals, popes, all ages and both sexes. Yet for Brant folly is a burden whereas for Erasmus folly is a dominant principle in a fallen world. Using many of Lucian's instruments Erasmus probes the fetid areas of human society. His surgical cuts on the churchmen are made precisely in those places where the spiritual kingdom has conformed to this world. This is the church's carnal folly while its spiritual folly, the foolishness of the cross, remains for Erasmus its true glory. The final test of Erasmus' aim in the *Folly* is the question of whether man by returning to nature's norm can be restored to the life of ethical wisdom. At times the *Folly* sounds like Ovid speaking for simplicity and for the Golden Age in which men lived by instinct under the guidance of nature or like Cicero who believed that the perfection of learning and ethical conduct was very much in line with nature. But in the *Folly* the true wisdom is the *sapientia* which comes from above and which can best be learned from the Wisdom incarnate. Erasmus does not stand on naturalistic ground, antique or modern.

The *Colloquies* are not only the liveliest expression of Erasmus' ideas but, due to his constant revisions and additions, they are also a most informative pictograph of his changing moods throughout the years. Thus with reference to criticism of abuse the *Colloquies* reached the highest point in the edition of 1526 with the addition of four colloquies belaboring the most lucrative abuses and most popular superstitions of the day. Luther and Zwingli are mentioned with approval, even after the controversy on free will, and false practices are held up to derision. From that edition to the last they drop off again in a diminuendo.[35] The *Colloquies*, begun quite innocently like the *De duplica copia* as a practice as an aid to Latin style and fluency, gradually grew into a comprehensive commentary on the whole culture of the times. Erasmus relates that as he revised he so tempered the subject matter that "besides the pleasure of reading and their use in polishing style, they might also contain that which would conduce to the formation of character."[36] Behind the negative critique, sometimes almost obscured by it, lay the positive goal of Erasmus.

The panorama of popular church life that the *Colloquies* depict was anything but edifying. There were, of course, colloquies concerned with more general social problems such as superstition, necromancy, and alchemism.[37] But Erasmus was most merciless where his religious sensitivity was affected, in the area of ecclesiastical life. He gave vent to a special peeve of his in the colloquy on "Fish-Eating" and in "The Profane Feast." Erasmus, who in 1525 received permission from Campeggio to eat meat on fast-days, claimed that fish made him ill and were not a wholesome food.[38] These dietary restrictions as popish ceremonial laws were on a level with Jewish legalism. Protesting in the "Religious Banquet" that he found no fault with the sacraments and rites of the church, but rather highly approved them, Erasmus had his protagonist blame those who teach unlearned people to trust in ceremonies from Baptism to Supreme Unction, while neglecting the internal impressions which have the power to fortify men against death, filling men's hearts with joy and Christian assurance.[39] Some of Erasmus' sharpest thrusts were against pilgrimages, absurd devotion to relics, and the veneration and invocation of the saints. The most famous colloquy of all, "The Shipwreck," recounts the invocation of Mary and the saints by the passengers when the ship founders, but the forgetfulness of the survivors. Erasmus borrowed one incident in it from Poggio's *Facetiae*, the candle promised the Virgin with the intention of forgetting about it once dry land is reached.[40] Erasmus cited St. Jerome that it is no great matter to have been to Jerusalem, but a great thing to have lived well.[41]

Through the years Erasmus directed his strongest barrages against monasticism and celibacy. At least two of his dialogues were almost certainly written under the influence of Luther's treatise *Concerning Monastic Vows.*[42] In "The Virgin Averse to Matrimony" and "The Penitent Virgin," Erasmus depicted the unscrupulous recruiting for cloisters by crafty monks.[43] There many fine minds are buried alive.[44] He blasted the pretensions of the Franciscans that to wear their habit is more efficacious than baptism, faith, and holiness of life.[45] He compared the ignorance of monks and abbots to the learning of pious women given to the study of Scriptures.[46] He borrowed the plot for "The Young Man and the Harlot" from Roswitha's play, discovered by Celtis, and took the occasion to comment that many who traveled to Rome returned worse than they went.[47] In later *Colloquies* the discrepancy between theory and reality was scored with fine impartiality.[48]

One of the most revealing of the *Colloquies* was "The Epicurean," added to the final edition of March 1533.[49] The author's posture is much the same as in his youthful *De contemptu mundi.* He obviously borrowed the theme from Valla's *De Voluptate* and his arguments are much the same, except that his Christian conclusion is more explicit, less ambivalent. "The Epicurean," predictably, argues that happiness is to be found where there is true pleasure and the least sorrow. Truly pious Christians are true Epicureans in having a clear conscience and peace with God, for the greatest pleasures proceed from the mind. Vices involved more pain than pleasure. Sin is the stone of Tantalus removed by God's mercy toward repentant sinners. In this dialogue terrestial and otherworldly motivations are fused very smoothly. The pious man enjoys the best things of this life. To that extent Christ was the greatest philosopher of Christendom and the leading Epicurean. In that way Erasmus late in life still attempted to harmonize ethics and happiness according to classical precedent. And yet his Christian piety was related to the transcendent God and reunion with Him through release from natural limitations remained the highest end of the religious man.

In the *Colloquies* Erasmus' counterpoint to each major theme was that abuse does not obviate the proper spiritual use. Beyond the negative emphasis, the essential elements of his positive theology are to be found also in this popular work. While the *Colloquies* were by no means so innocuous as Erasmus in retrospect tried to make them appear, for he frequently wrote with both verve and indiscretion, nevertheless, his apology for them was essentially sincere and accurate. "May that Spirit, which is the Pacifier of all," he concluded, "who uses His instruments in various ways make us all agree and consent in sound doctrine and holy manners, that we may all come to the fellowship of the new Jerusalem, that knows no discords. Amen." [50]

The German humanist Urbanus Rhegius praised Erasmus as the "first author of the renaissance of theology." But Erasmus, who in a letter to Colet had called theology the queen of all the disciplines, emphatically refused the name of theologian for himself.[51] His program for the restoration of Christianity called not for a theologian in the technical sense, with all the scholastic connotations of the term, but for a scholar capable of establishing the philosophy of Christ upon its ancient foundations. For Erasmus these foundations were basically Christian antiquity, but he constantly spoke of the bond between theology in that sense and good letters, *bonae literae*, and of the opposition of the scholastic theologians to the study of good letters.

The purview of even the prince of the humanists did not take in all of antiquity, for his work as editorial "galley slave" on the classics was only incidental to his theological labors. He put out various editions of treatises by Cicero, Seneca, Lucian, Quintus Curtius, Suetonius, Pliny the Elder, Livy, Terence, and translations from Galen, Xenophon, and Plutarch. In addition he did Greek editions of Demosthenes and Aristotle. Erasmus was attracted less to Cicero's political works than to the spiritual and ethical concerns of the *Disputationes Tusculanes, De Officiis, De Legibus*, or fragments of the *Republica*. Seneca appealed to him for his humaneness. Lucian suited his taste for satire and irony, for he was, as Erasmus wrote Archbishop William of Canterbury, always good for a laugh. The gentle wisdom of Horace and the high sense of morality in Plutarch made them favorites. On the other hand, he never developed much enthusiasm for the political concerns of the Roman historians, Virgil's heroics, Homer's epics, Sophocles' dramas, Aristotle's prosaic constructions, and Plato's metaphysics, which except for minor borrowings, largely of myths and symbols, seems to have left him puzzled.[52]

Like Petrarch and the Italian humanists Erasmus derived from his study of the classics a conception of *humanitas* as virtue, morality, and integrity in the Roman sense.[53] He believed that this *humanitas* was compatible with Christianity, for the church fathers in rethinking the universe in Christian terms had worked out a systematic and historical synthesis of the divine and human wisdom represented by the two traditions. Erasmus conceived of his calling in much the same way as the fathers had. Confronted with the classical revival, he labored to reconcile and combine human and sacred letters as a foundation for a renewed Christian piety and faith, the highest level of *humanitas*. Although not beyond justifying his preoccupation with the classics, as he did in the *Enchiridion*, in the time-honored fashion, arguing that classical learning may be used to decorate the temple of God just as the Israelites took gold and silver vessels from their Egyptian oppressors, for the most part Erasmus carried out his program with the good conscience of the sweet and innocent.

The cultivation of good letters or study of the sources pointed up the importance of grammar among the disciplines of the trivium, leaving Erasmus hostile to dialectic and wary of rhetoric. This emphasis reflected more than a temperamental impatience of the philologist with the scholastic and orator. Grammar was for Erasmus the preferred instrument, a tool for criticism and a pool of figurative usages.[54] In the *De Ratione Concionandi* he warned that rhetoric should provide understanding and not be reduced to the art of dissimulating, as is often the case. The precepts of the rhetoricians will offer nothing useful to the ecclesiast, who should be a good man, erudite in divinity and rich in evangelical understanding. For the same reason the ecclesiast should not learn dialectic as allied to rhetoric, since it is nearly the same thing, for Zeno signified the difference with a hand contracted and extended. The schools twist young minds and inflate them with ostentation, although rightly done dialectic can be of some use. Grammar is the basis of all disciplines, for it is more than mere rules, providing reasons for speaking which can be acquired by much reading of the ancients. Grammar embraces many things, history, poetry, knowledge of antiquity, and skill in all three languages. This century, Erasmus concludes, is to be congratulated on the recovery of that kind of letters.[55]

The issue is much more than just a matter of method, for it involves the question as to whether *humanitas* drawn from classic literature by grammarians is in the final analysis compatible with Christian *humilitas* and divine *gratia*. There can be no doubt that in Erasmus *Christianitas* suffered a loss which Luther, in turn, was not willing to concede. This is obvious especially in those instances in which Erasmus verges upon religious universalism. The colloquy "The Religious Banquet" is the best known example. In it he has Eusebius say:

> Whatever is pious and conduces to good manners should not be called profane. First place must indeed be given to the authority of the Scriptures, but, nevertheless, I sometimes find some things said or written by the ancients; yes, even by the heathen; yes, by the poets themselves, so chastely, holy, and divinely that I cannot persuade myself but that when they wrote them, they were divinely inspired; and perhaps the Spirit of Christ diffuses itself farther than we imagine; and that there are more saints than we have in our catalogue.[56]

After a discussion of the wisdom of Cicero, Cato, and Plato, Nephalius responds:

> Indeed, it was a wonderful elevation of the mind in a man, who did not know Christ nor the Holy Scriptures: and therefore I can scarce forbear, when I read such things of such men, but cry out, *Sancte Socrates, ora pro nobis.*

Chrysoglottus adds: "And I have much to do sometimes to keep myself from entertaining good hopes for the souls of Virgil and

Horace." Another extreme statement was Erasmus' urging that man in transcending his humanity and straining to be like God should imitate Prometheus.[57] In the foreword to the *Tusculanea* (1523) Erasmus said that when he read this kind of writing by Cicero he did not doubt that ideas came from the heart of that ancient pagan which were moved by a divine spirit. Without knowing Mosaic law his own thought brought him near to divine law, so that he must have had a natural knowledge of God.[58] Erasmus learned this high regard for Cicero from Ambrose, Augustine, and, above all, Jerome. He saw divine inspiration also in Plato's religious dialogues. He had anticipated St. Paul's distinction between flesh and spirit. Many of the ancients believed in God as judge, whether they named him Zeus, Cosmos, *mundus* or *natura*. Erasmus found many instances of parallel ethical conduct in the Old Testament and in the classics. He has shifted ground from Thomas Aquinas' *fides implicite* as the precondition of the salvation of the gentiles. The elements which Erasmus held to be essential for the *gentiles salvati* are faith in one God, belief in the immortality of the soul, judgment after death, and the answer of a clear conscience. He was in this formulation influenced by late medieval nondogmatic spiritualism rather than by Florentine Neoplatonic universalism. The Florentines, tying in with scholastic tradition, accepted also many Thomistic solutions to problems such as this. In this instance they stressed the Christological and Trinitarian anticipations in Plato and late classic philosophers. But Erasmus does not show evidence of dependence on them nor does he utilize their mythologies. Under the influence of the spiritualism of the late Middle Ages and of patristic thought Erasmus moved beyond the narrow medieval interpretation of Cyprian's formula "There is no salvation outside the Church." In this way he related Christianity to the best in antiquity, but still assigned it preeminence on the grounds of special revelation. He is clearly writing in the spirit of the Alexandrine fathers such as Clement and of the apologists like Justin Martyr, who wrote: "Whatever has been well said belongs to us Christians."

Perhaps the most important difference between Erasmus and Petrarch was the former's vastly superior knowledge of patrology. He personally edited Cyprian, Arnobius, Hilary, Irenaeus, Ambrose, Augustine (ten folio volumes), Lactantius, Chrysostom

(Latin), Basil (Latin), Origen, and above all Jerome (nine folio volumes). While editing Jerome he once exclaimed, "My mind is in such a glow over Jerome that I imagine myself to be actually inspired!" Erasmus accorded to the church fathers the authority reserved by some Italian literary humanists for the classical ancient dead. There can be no doubt that he inherited his appreciation for the church fathers, preeminently Jerome, from the Brethren of the Common Life who were sometimes referred to as "Jeromians." To him the patristic writings were a golden stream of sacred learning. He recognized that the fathers could err and contradict each other, and that they were not merely *diversi sed adversi*. He recognized also that in a polemical situation the fathers tended to overstate their arguments and to write primarily on controverted issues. Nevertheless, he accorded them an authority second only to that of the Scriptures. In exegesis he felt that no one was equal to Origen, followed in order by Basil, Gregory Nazianzen, Athanasius, Cyril, and Chrysostom, who excelled as a moralistic commentator. Among the Latin fathers he placed Jerome first, then Ambrose, Hilary, and Augustine, the latter being impeded by his lack of Hebrew and Greek.[59] As a labor of love and filial piety, Erasmus wrote a life of Jerome, *Hieronymi stridonensis vita*, which was a scholarly attempt to base his biography upon original sources and to free it from hagiographic myths and legends.

One example taken from *De Ratione Concionandi* must suffice to illustrate the strength of the patristic influence on Erasmus' thought. From the fathers Erasmus received a renewed sympathy for Logos theology. In this treatise he cites Hesiod's conception, known to the fathers, of the word not differing essentially from the mind from which it proceeds. The mind is the fountain, the word (*sermo*) is the image proceeding out of the fountain.[60] The term *sermo* is significant, for he substituted it for *verbum* in the Gospel of John in the *Novum Instrumentum* raising a storm of censure. He countered the criticism by demonstrating that Cyprian, Tertullian, Ambrose, Augustine, Prudentius, and Lactantius as well as other fathers also used *sermo*.[61] Justin Martyr's theory of the spermatic Logos inspiring the ancient Greek philosophers was obviously in evidence here.

When Erasmus at the age of forty was preparing for his Italian journey he did a poem expressing his resolve, like Agricola, to devote his old age to Scriptural studies. Although he had no way of knowing, Erasmus had a long time to go, years filled with work in the Greek text and Latin translation of the New Testament, his paraphrases and notes, plus commentaries on ten of the Psalms. His first work with Greek was to make a new translation of the New Testament while staying in Colet's London house, using manuscripts from the St. Paul's Cathedral library. But the masterpiece, for all its slapdash make-up and scholarly blunders, was his *Novum Testamentum* of 1516, or, as he entitled the Froben edition of 1519, the *Novum Instrumentum*.[62] It represented pioneer scholarship, preceding Cardinal Ximenes' *Complutensian Polyglot* in publication date, if not excelling it in the number and critical use of texts. It became Luther's instrument in New Testament studies and in the preparation of his German testament which Erasmus had called for in the foreword.

In the *Paraclesis* or preface to his New Testament, Erasmus expressed his desire that all women should read the gospels and epistles and that they should be translated into the tongues of all men, so that they might be known not only to the Scots and Irishmen but also to the Turks and Saracens. He continued:

> I would to God that the plowman would sing a text of the Scripture at his plow and that the weaver would hum them to the tune of his shuttle, and that this would drive away the tediousness of time. I wish that the traveler would expel the weariness of his journey with this pastime. And, to be brief, I wish that all the communication of the Christian would be of the Scriptures.

In his exhortation preceding his *Paraphrase* of Matthew, Erasmus once again pressed his drive to popularize the Scriptures. He takes issue with those who argue that it is shameful for a woman or a tanner to speak of Holy Letters. As a child, Jesus disputed with the doctors, therefore even children should not be kept from reading the Gospel. One must not dispute or reason out the mysteries, for it is sufficient to believe, he counseled, and to live according to the rule of the Gospel. The temptation is there to point to Lollard or other heretical influences on Erasmus in order to explain his insistence upon making the Scripture available to all in the vernacular. But in reality this idea is only a corollary to his whole emphasis on the practical and nontheoretical nature of theology and of religion. Nor does the fact that he limited himself to work with the Greek and Latin negate his program for the spread of the Scriptures, for he even commented once that with the money spent on wars all could be taught to read the Scriptures in the original. In his response to Erasmus' dedication of the Greek New Testament, Pope Leo X remarked that it would be useful for students of sacred theology and for the orthodox faith.[63]

Erasmus was following the precedent of Valla and Lefèvre in annotating the New Testament, a fact which draws attention to a much neglected aspect of his work, namely, the precise nature of his exegetical method. In general, in his critical method Erasmus followed Valla and in 1505 he had edited an edition of Valla's *Annotationes ad Novum Testamentum*. All too often Erasmus is depicted as a pioneer of the historico-philological method without all due reservations.

Erasmus established a certain hierarchy in the canonical books of the Bible, but it was a hierarchy of religious utility, not of authority or chronology. He held the opinion that Isaiah is more worthy than Esther (which does not mention God) or Judith (apocryphal), the Gospel of Matthew than the Apocalypse attributed to John. It is necessary to prefer the epistles of Paul to the Romans and to the Corinthians, he held, to the epistle to the Hebrews.[64] He was less interested in Genesis, the historical or legal books, and Canticles. The Apocalypse puzzled him and he did not do a paraphrase on it, fearing perhaps, that in popularizing it he would only contribute to the charismatic and radical millenarian fringe of Christendom, although he did annotate it.[65] Erasmus held that all of the canonical Scriptures were free from errors, for they were produced by the inspiration of the Holy Spirit himself, as he explained in one of his commentaries on an Old Testament Psalm.[66]

An understanding of Erasmus' Biblical exegesis provides the very best clue to his whole theology. Just as Augustine's mature theology cannot be derived from his early Neoplatonic writings nor Calvin's exclusively on the basis of the *Institutes*, so the complete Erasmus is not to be seen in the few treatises most commonly cited. The humanists are commonly credited with developing the historico-critical method of exegesis in contrast with the medieval

Quadriga [67] and with transmitting this method to Luther and the reformers. Erasmus' touchstone also in Scriptural interpretation was the passage "the letter killeth, but the spirit maketh alive." Erasmus did assert that the historic sense was basic and that it alone is the foundation of the hidden and mysterious meanings.[68] He was more conscious of the historical setting of the books and better equipped philologically for textual work than the medieval exegetes like Nicholas de Lyra. He had an eye like Valla's for textual emendations and lower criticism, pointing out, for example, that the word "poets" was added by a later hand to Paul's sermon on Mars hill, since neither Irenaeus nor Augustine used it in citing the passage.[69] Nevertheless, he was concerned with the spiritual rather than the literal meaning of the text. A literal reading of the text leads to anthropomorphisms in passages about God or to chiliasm in passages of the Apocalypse. And those who exclude other than the literal interpretation, he argued, verge on Judaism.[70]

He counseled theologians to choose those interpreters of Scripture who go the farthest from the letter, especially, after St. Paul himself, Origen, Ambrose, Jerome, and Augustine. He saw a regression through the centuries with the "divines of later time sticking very much in the letter, and with good will giving more study to subtle and deceitful arguments than to searching out the mysteries, as though Paul had not said truly that our law is spiritual." [71] He went on to attack his contemporaries who followed fantastic traditions, the imaginations and inventions of man, and despised the interpretations of the old doctors who were close to Christ and his apostles both in time and way of life. In the preface to *Annotations on the New Testament* he called patristic commentaries old wine far superior to the recent theology. Erasmus preferred the tradition of the early centuries of the church to the exegesis of the medieval period. Tradition did not establish the authority of the Scriptures but in the early centuries was in agreement with it.

The problem of authority and tradition becomes more complicated when the question of obscurities and difficulties arises due to contradictions, vanities, or absurdities.[72] Erasmus was not convinced of the *unus simplex sensus* of the Scriptures, but that their "inexhaustible riches were hidden in mysteries" so that it is not a shame for a doctor to say, "I do not understand," for some things the Holy Spirit does not wish to be fully understood. When the fathers disagree, as Origen and Ambrose disagreed with Jerome and Augustine on the *semper virgo*, the interpreter should do what is in accord with Christian modesty and Catholic dogmas.[73] This latter phrase separated Erasmus from the Reformation.

The *Quadriga* was probably developed among the Greek theologians of the fourth century, antedating Eucherius of Lyons (d. ca. 449) and John Cassian, who both used it. Erasmus' favorite Greek father, Origen, introduced allegory on a large scale, so that "to write a history of Origenist influence on the West would be tantamount to writing a history of Western exegesis." [74] Erasmus had a certain historical feeling for the stages in the development of the *Quadriga*. He appreciated the fact that every multiple method of exegesis depends ultimately upon the distinction between the letter and the spirit, a distinction which justifies the use of allegory. He explained that the ancient doctors knew only two senses of the Scriptures, the grammatical or literal, or, if one prefers, the historical and the spiritual. They called the spiritual by various names, tropological, allegorical, or anagogical, but with no distinction. Erasmus went on to explain the specialized usage of Origen, Jerome, Augustine, and the other fathers.[75] The use of allegory in the early church, he saw, was much more limited.[76]

To be acceptable, allegory must agree with the grammatical and historical sense and with Christian piety. Erasmus held that the exegete must be ready to hear with pious and Christian ears, but with his intellectual approach he was far from the posture of Lefèvre d'Étaples, who before undertaking the interpretation of a revealed text prayed for illumination. Erasmus once cited examples of legitimate and illegitimate allegories used by the patristic writers. He disapproved the application of the Song of Songs to Christ and the Church, as was the practice of the early fathers.[77] For Erasmus all types and allegories explained by the Scriptures were beyond doubt. Allegories should not be used to prove the dogmas of Catholic faith and those men sin who concoct allegories impiously.[78]

A few examples taken from his commentaries on the Psalms will illustrate Erasmus' exegesis in action. In his commentary on

Psalm I he discusses the question as to whether this Psalm applies to Christ, the Father, or Christ according to His human nature. After considering the views of Hilary he announces that he will follow the tropological interpretation. The aim of the Psalm is to stimulate all mortals by the rewards of blessedness to desist from vices. True blessedness consists of innocence, piety of life, and recognition that God is the highest good. Christ was sent from heaven to earth so that we might be led to this newness of life. What was planted in Adam has been faithfully transplanted into Christ.[79] In his sermon on Psalm IV, Erasmus accommodates the meaning to Christ as the head of the body, the church. He adds to the soteriological sense a moral interpretation applicable to daily living.[80] In a similar way he applies Psalm XIV to the purity of the tabernacle, that is, the Christian church.[81] In his exegesis of Psalm XXII, he explains that the full mystery of the Psalm is that it applies also to "our David," the true head of the church, who delivered his people from Goliath, the tyranny of Satan. Again Erasmus records which of the fathers commented on this psalm, Jerome and Arnobius, but not Augustine. He observes explicitly at which point he is consciously shifting from the historical or grammatical to the interpretation of the fourfold mysteries.[82] In his commentary on Psalm XXXIII, Erasmus attacked the demythologizers who, "swelled up with Aristotelian, Averroist, or Platonic philosophy, are accustomed to condemn the mystical allegories in the sacred volumes." He here has reference to the Old Testament incidents interpreted typologically in the New Testament, the brass serpent, Jonah, manna, the temple as a symbol for Christ.[83] He consistently applies the Messianic prophecies to Christ in the accepted way.

While nothing further is to be gained by multiplying instances, a brief examination of his exegesis of two passages of critical importance in the history of the church will be profitable: Romans 1:17 and Romans 3:21–24. His reading is virtually the same in both the *Paraphrases* and the *Annotations*. On the crucial Reformation passage Rom. 1:17 in the *Paraphrases* he explained:

Whereas before this time sundry men thought righteousness to stand in sundry points, now by preaching of Christ's gospel all men know righteousness, not of Moses, but of God himself, which standeth not in superstitious worshiping of idols, nor in Jewish ceremonies, but is won by faith, while men acknowledge and consent, that God now performs that which he long since by the mouth of his prophets promised to do. Even as Habakkuk also prophesied, saying: My righteous shall live by faith.[84]

In the *Annotations* Erasmus explains, with reference to the phrase *ex fide in fidem*, that *fides* means both *credulitas*, belief, and *fiducia*, trust, and that both meanings are intended here. He continues to explain that with "shall live by faith," Chrysostom understood the future life, but Paul is citing from Habakkuk II, which the Septuagint interprets: *Justus autem ex fide mea vivet*. This means that life has its beginning from this origin that subduing the human sense we believe the divine words. This was spoken against the philosophers.[85]

In both the *Paraphrases* and the *Annotations* Erasmus explained with reference to Rom. 3:21ff. that the righteousness which is preached by the Gospel, though needing no help from Moses' law, nevertheless was foretold by the law and prophecies. This justice,

not of the law, but the justice of *God* is to be obtained neither by circumcision nor Jewish ceremonies, but through faith and a sure trust in Jesus Christ, who alone gives true and perfect justice, not only to the Jews or to any other special nation, but without partiality to all and every man, who has a sure trust and confidence in him.[86]

As in his exegetical interpretation of Galatians, where Erasmus contrasts the moral and the Jewish ceremonial law, he is here obviously concerned with the meaning of the spirit rather than the letter. He does not read righteousness and faith in the light of a soteriological approach. His message is that it is still the "letter of the law which killeth but the spirit which maketh alive."

Erasmian spiritualism did not go beyond an almost Platonic and moralistic interpretation of St. Paul. Christ is the victor of the spirit over nature, of the heavenly over earthly, of freedom over law. Faith takes up this victory so that, though reason is spoiled by sin and needs catharsis, faith effects its healing. The true philosophy is therefore dependent on faith. Faith brings true knowledge first of all and love brings a purified will. Faith produces an inner change in man when he is moved by the spirit of God. The real world of ideas outside the cave of this world is the spiritual kingdom of Christ. Henceforth Christ rules in the heart. Although in his conception of faith Erasmus was close to St. Paul's spiritual trust and confidence in Christ, he did not understand his teaching on justification by faith in Christ the Savior's merits alone. He did not go beyond the traditional view of faith joined with love as the way to salvation.

The greatest document of Erasmian spiritualism was his *Enchiridion Militis Christiani*, "The Handsome Weapon of a Christian Knight," as an early translation had it. Written in 1501 and published two years later, it became after its reprinting in 1518, nine months after the Ninety-five Theses, one of the most popular books in Europe with a strong influence upon Zwingli, Bucer, the Spiritualists and Anabaptists, the Spanish mystics of the two centuries following, and the savants of the Enlightenment. He composed it, he wrote to Colet, not "for the mere display of genious or eloquence, but only for the purpose of correcting the common error of those who make religion consist of ceremonies and in almost more than Jewish observances, while they are singularly careless of the things that belong to piety." [87]

It is a handbook of Christian piety, as Erasmus called it, designed to make clear the difference between true or spiritual piety and false or carnal piety. Prayer and knowledge are the two chief weapons of the spirit. Erasmus urges the reading of Cyprian because he garnished the temple of God with the spoils of the Egyptians, but adds, echoing the warnings of the Brethren, "in no case would I wish that with the gentile's learning you should also suck the gentile's vices and conversation." His recommendation of Plato, coming as it does so recently after contact with Colet, merits citation: "Of the philosophers my mind is that you should follow those that were of Plato's sect, because both in very many sentences and much more in their style and manner of speaking they come very near to the figure and property of speech used by the prophets and in the gospels." [88] In the fourth chapter on the outward and inner man he depicts man as a compound beast in the Platonic fashion familiar from the *Timaeus*, from Dionysius the Areopagite, one of his favorite authors, and from Augustine. "If thy body had not been added to you, you would have been a celestial or godly thing," he writes. The excellent workman, God, had coupled body and soul together, but that serpent, the enemy of peace, put them asunder again. Chapter VI returns to the theme of the inner and outer man. What the philosophers call reason, St. Paul calls the spirit, the inner man, or the law of the mind. Plato put two souls in one man. Paul in one man makes two men so coupled together that neither can be either in heaven or hell without the other.[89] After a further discussion of man's complex nature, described by St. Paul and Origen as body, soul, and spirit, Erasmus lays down rules for true piety, to oppose the evil of ignorance with a true faith in Christ, to live with a firm purpose, to despise fearful things with courage, to keep Christ always in sight, and to rise to things invisible.

This thirteenth chapter, expanding on the theme "the letter killeth but the spirit maketh alive," is clearly the high point of the *Enchiridion* pleading for the realization of the inwardness of true spiritual life. Erasmus uses the Platonic light analogy that, what the sun is to the visible world, God the divine mind is to the intelligible world and to the spirit. Without allegory or the spiritual interpretation, the Scriptures are barren. He approves the rules for allegorizing authorized by Dionysius, *De divinis nominibus*, Augustine, *De Doctrina Christiana*, St. Paul, and Origen, thus revealing his probable sources for the Platonic sympathies which follow. He opposes those who, "content with Aristotle only expel from the schools the sect of Plato and Pythagoras, and yet St. Augustine prefers these latter, not only because they have many sentences very agreeable to our religion, but also because the very manner of open and clear speech, which they use . . . full of allegories, is very close to that of Holy Scripture." After another excursus on "the spirit maketh alive," Erasmus spells out in succeeding chapters the logical application of his spiritualist theme for the nature of the sacraments, the Mass, holy water, pilgrimages, the invocation of saints, the mystery of the cross, the spirit of Christ making an end of the law, Christ as teacher, as example, as goal (σκοπός was Gregory of Nazianzen's term), as head of redeemed men, coupled with warnings against temptations, pride, the devil, avarice, ambition, wrath, and vengeance. Erasmus' piety was Christocentric.

The letter to Paul Volz, the abbot of Hughes Court in Schlettstadt who later became a Calvinist, which Erasmus prefaced to the 1518 edition of the *Enchiridion* was itself a classic document epitomizing the most salient features of the *philosophia Christi*. The first part defines the spiritual orientation of Christian philosophy in contrast to the contemporary condition of teaching and dogma. The pseudo-doctors with their scholastic quackery have lost sight of the gospel as the alpha and omega of the Christian religion. The enfeebled church must use force, being unable to convince infidels by teaching. Souls should rather be steeped in love. Perfect Christianity must conform to the precepts of the Founder. Erasmus then gives a Dante-like picture of all Christendom organized in concentric circles with Christ as a glowing fire of love at the center. On the first sphere are the pontiffs and bishops, on the second the princes and lay lords who hold a special position in the *corpus christianum*, and on the third are the ordinary laymen. Perfection in holiness could be expected in the circles nearer the center but, since the reverse is really true, there is a need for a general reform.[90]

If scholarship has neglected the letter to Volz with its excellent statement of the *philosophia Christi*, it has more than redressed the grievance with the literature towering high above the *Paraclesis*, the brief preface to the first edition of the New Testament. Erasmus wrote it hurriedly and without much reflection which increases its value as evidence of his spontaneous expression. A summary paragraph will indicate that it contains, though in a poorly organized fashion, the now familiar ideas which made up Erasmus' religious views. Only He who is Eternal wisdom can teach with certainty, therefore, it is far worse for a Christian to be ignorant of Christ's teachings than for Aristotelians not to know Aristotle's philosophy. The *philosophia Christi* is best learned from the gospels and Apostolic epistles, and the Christian must learn what Christ taught and not scholastic subtleties. Although the Stoics and Epicureans, Socrates and Aristotle have all taught truths which are part of Christ's teaching, he taught them best and was himself the archetype and exemplar of his own precepts. All the monastic orders treasure their own rules, so all Christians should treasure that of Christ. His image visible in the gospels is more precious than all the relics.[91]

In the *Paraclesis* the emphasis is again placed on Christ as teacher and example, with an optimistic view of even the common man's ability to learn. Secondly, there is the predictable emphasis on life and action coupled with a distrust of subtle scholastic rationalism and speculation. Thirdly, there is the familiar stress on the spirit over the letter in religious observance.

Erasmus expanded the ideas in the *Paraclesis* into a work on the Method of Theology, the *Ratio seu methodus compendio perveniendi ad veram theologiam*, which was published separately in 1519.[92] This statement is as systematic as the *Paraclesis* is casual and it is justly famous together with the *Enchiridion* as the best statement of Erasmus' constructive theology. Once again Erasmus draws directly and heavily from the Scriptures and the church fathers, from the theological orations of Gregory Nazianzen, from Augustine's *De doctrina christiana*, *Civitas dei*, *Enarratio in psalmos*, *Contra Faustum*, and others, from Hilary, Jerome, Origen, Tertullian, Ambrosiaster, Basil, and Chrysostom, from their exegetical as well as their systematic works.

Theology, Erasmus argues in the *Ratio*, is properly a prophetic work which is a sacred discipline, not only because of its object but because of its uses and by virtue of the subjective disposition of pure mind and love of peace which it demands ($\theta\epsilon o\delta\iota\delta\alpha\kappa\tau os$). The three sacred languages are essential, for some authorities could and did err. Dialectic is not sufficient for the theologian who requires grammar for expediting allegorical interpretation and rhetoric in order to embellish and to achieve conviction. The Muses, especially poetry, should be enlisted in the service of theology. He recommends Origen's homily on Abraham and the sacrifice of Isaac as an example of how to affect the emotions and once again contrasts the skill of the fathers and the moderns on this, the difference between rivers and rivulets. The fathers are oracles of eternal truth compared with the little scholastic comments of men. There the solid fundamentals of the Scriptures are elevated, here the futile arguments of men. There one is lured by rich gardens, here one is torn by briars. There one finds many things of majesty, here all is sordid. The fathers, following St. Paul, used the poets rather than the Aristotle of impious Averroes. Augustine preferred Plato because he believed him to be closer to Christianity.

After a discussion of his hermeneutical method for arriving at the meaning of the Scriptures, Erasmus reaches the heart of his theology, an exhortation to follow Christ the celestial teacher, to live after his example, and to learn to despise Satan and death. The elegant passages on the person of Christ are clearly the high point of the treatise recounting his virgin birth, his two natures, his life of love. His sentences on Christ are reminiscent of Gregory Nazianzen. He urges Christians to read the New Testament and Isaiah to learn to know Christ better. The order of priority which Erasmus now gives to the Biblical commentators is intriguing. Origen takes first place followed by Basil, Gregory Nazianzen, Athanasius, Cyril, Chrysostom, Jerome, Ambrose, Hilary, and Augustine. But, he warns, they are all only men, subject to error. Nevertheless, Jerome, he remarks whimsically, is better when he errs than a great many others when they write what is true. Finally, he concludes, the true theologian must return to the ancient theology (*prisca illa theologia*). He must surrender to no wrong desires nor give in to contentious disputations. The *Ratio's* emphasis is upon the central features of Erasmus' positive theology, and the fact that in this short essay he does not develop his views on all phases of Christian doctrine does not mean that he considered them unimportant or irrelevant to the total Christian life. It is necessary to range well beyond the *Enchiridion* and *Ratio* for the full picture of Erasmus' Christology and dogmatic positions.

The Christ of Erasmus was the Christ of Chalcedon not only in credal statement but in the reality of his faith.[93] For Erasmus the Jesus of the gospels was enveloped in mystery. His person was characterized by the hypostatic union of the divine and human nature. Christ is one with the *corpus mysticum*, the church.[94] Nothing is more Christian than to abide with Christ, to live in Christ, as one body, and to be of one mind with Christ.[95] True to his *Devotio Moderna* background, Erasmus constantly stressed the imitation of Christ, the exemplar of virtue and wisdom, an imitation which involved the mystic and spiritual indwelling of Christ in the human heart, not merely the outward mimicking of his actions — as one would copy the charity of a saint, for example.[96] Christ is more than a human figure, for he is God's wisdom incarnate, as Erasmus expressed it, echoing a patristic phrase. The very conception of Erasmus and the fathers of the influence of the Spirit of the preexistent Logos on the ancient philosophers points to a high Christology.[97] Like the fathers he stressed Christ as the elixir of immortality. "What else is the whole life, death, and resurrection of

Christ," he concluded, "than the brightest mirror of the Evangelical philosophy?" [98]

The myth of an Erasmian undogmatic Christianity akin to a Ritschlian moral influence theory vanishes before the high theology of such writings as his sermon "On the Boundless Mercy of God." [99] Erasmus' subject, he says, is that eternal salvation is prepared for all men through the mercy of God. The two most sinister evils, among many which bring the human race to perdition, are self-confidence and despair, one brought about by a mind uplifted against God and blinded by self-love, the other born of the greatness of sins committed and the severity of God's judgment. "For," warns Erasmus, "if God spared not the angels that sinned, but cast them down to hell, and delivered them into chains of darkness, to be reserved unto judgment at the last day, what will be the deserts of man, a mere worm, who has crept forth from the earth, soon to be turned to earth again, if he lifts up his head against God?" [100] There are to be found among Christians those who make a treaty with the enemy, Satan. But God is infinite in power, wisdom, and goodness. "But although power is wont to be ascribed to the Father as his peculiar property," Erasmus explains with reference to the Trinity, "wisdom to the Son, and goodness to the Holy Spirit, yet there is none of these properties which is not equally common to all the persons." [101] The sermon continues with a rhapsody on the wonder of redemption, the incarnation, Christ's life, teaching, miracles, passion, cross, resurrection, appearance, ascension, and the sending of the Holy Spirit. "Is not this whole plan, I say, everywhere full of miracles, which even the angelic spirits could not fathom?" he asks.[102] Erasmus continues with an oration on the meaning of grace, repentance, and faith almost in an evangelical manner, but then he lapses into his habitual synergism by recommending love to neighbor as the chief manifestation of man's worthiness to receive God's forgiveness. In this work, too, he borrows heavily from the fathers in opposing astrology. From Lactantius he takes a complete passage on the marvelous structure of the human body.

Erasmus was perfectly orthodox and "correct" on all matters of dogma. His long apologies are replete with assertions that he had wished only to spread the true faith and that he had always been true to the ecclesiastical teaching office in all submissiveness and obedience. He found that the Creed contained the "whole philosophy of living well and virtuously." [103] His test was whether a doctrine had been approved by the church, not merely whether it was to be found in the Scriptures or was validated by early tradition. A simple example is his acceptance of the *Semper Virgo* because, although it is not expressed in the Scriptures, it is implied; moreover, that it should be otherwise is repugnant to the dignity of Son and mother; and, finally, because "the Catholic Church with such great consent has believed, taught, and fastly affirmed it from the beginning of the gospel . . . so that it ought to be not a bit less believed than if it were expressed in the Holy Scriptures." [104] He accepted the immaculate conception on the same grounds.

While he pressed for a spiritual understanding and use of the sacraments he never deviated like Pirckheimer, Dürer, or other humanists in his orthodox views. The priest, he wrote, administers divine grace through the sacraments. It is all the more a striking commentary on his personal religious life that for long periods of time he neither celebrated the sacrament nor partook of it. Through baptism, Erasmus explained, the priest makes heirs of heaven out of sons of hell, through supreme unction he adds strength against the powers of the demons, through the sacred Eucharist he binds men to each other and makes them cleave with harmony to God, and through penance he makes living men out of the dead, free men out of slaves.[105] On the highly controverted question of the confession he conceded that the practice did not go back in its later form to the authority of Christ and the Scriptures, but urged that its authority was as great as though it were instituted by Christ, "especially since the authority of the Roman pontiff accedes to it and the consensus of Christian people." He argued on the ground of its many utilities that it should be retained even though it were to be conceded that it had been instituted by men.[106]

From the lofty vantage point of his *philosophia Christi* Erasmus surveyed the world of individual and social ethics, church and state, and passed judgment. He felt almost a compulsion to educate the young in morals and piety.[107] His social program tended to be highly idealistic without any very great appreciation of practical realities. "The essentials of our religion," he wrote in the Preface to St. Hilary (1523) "are peace and unanimity." This thought

served as the guiding principle in his preference for certain forms
of government and his conception of ideal international relations.
Erasmus of Rotterdam at times favored the republican form of government on the city-state level. But he was no friend of the masses
and once even spoke of that enormous and powerful animal which
one calls the people. It is perfectly understandable that he occasionally abandoned his usual preference for a "mixed" government for a
constitutional monarchy. In the *Institutio principis Christiani*, written for Prince Charles, he stressed peace and tolerance through
Christian universalism, assuming that the prince can actually
achieve his goals, assuming that he is without limitations, a most
unrealistic view. Christ should be his exemplar in virtue and
wisdom.[108]

Erasmus, who saw in his heavenly King the Prince of Peace,
wrote passionate appeals for peace to the Christian princes. He was
no pacifist for he theoretically condoned war in defense of Christendom against barbarian invaders, although he was very much of
a defeatist so far as the Turkish threat was concerned. But he considered wars between the Christian nations treason to the unity of
Christendom. He wrote colloquies, letters to the kings and emperor,
and above all the *Querela Pacis* (Complaint of Peace), published in
December 1517. The device he used was the same as in the *Praise
of Folly*. Peace delivers a moving lament about men's coldness
toward her and discusses the causes of war, the utter barbarity and
loss of moral sense which accompany it, urging arbitration for
all disputes. Wars between Christian princes weaken Europe for
the assaults of the Turk. They give offense to the infidels, because
the conversion of unbelievers is made difficult if those who profess
to be Christian never exercize charity, explained the mission-minded
Erasmus. That the rulers of this world have felt Erasmus' needle is
clear, for through the years in times of war the *Complaint of Peace*
has been systematically censored and banned.[109] *Dulce bellum inex-
pertis*, was Erasmus' constant refrain, war is sweet to those who do
not know it. The example of Christ should mean more than the
teaching of St. Francis and St. Bernard on such a question. Erasmus
was personally no political activist and, in fact, successfully avoided
practical responsibility in church and state.

Loyalty to the *philosophia Christi* also determined Erasmus'

11. St. Jerome

12. *Luther as St. Jerome*

relation to the Italian Renaissance. He was critical of certain aspects of Italian humanism: the religious indifference he detected, the lack of deep conviction, the acquiescence in religious formalism, and the worldly, not to say pagan, spirit which some men displayed, including some high churchmen. His lack of Italian closed to him the extensive vernacular literature. But his stay in Italy (1506–1509) helped fix certain negative impressions in his mind which in controversy rose to the surface. Thus, in writing against his critic Alberto Pio he asserted that in Italy it is easier to find those of rank who laugh at sacred things than in the North. The work which best defined his own position was the *Ciceronianus*, published by Froben in March 1528. In the preface he gives the clue to his grand purpose. He suspects that, sheltered by the philosopher's name, many a Ciceronian forgets Christ and leads men back to paganism, whereas no task is more necessary than to consecrate good letters to the glory of Christ, our Lord and master. Christ is the goal of all erudition and eloquence. In denouncing the dangers of an unquestioning worship of the classics and the frivolity of the Ciceronians, Erasmus both pointed back to the more serious concerns of earlier humanists but also upward toward the *philosophia Christi*.[110]

Italian literary and civic humanism seemed to build up to the Neoplatonic revival in the second half of the *quattrocento*. Erasmus, through his contacts with Northern humanists like Lefèvre and Colet as well as through his own Italian experience, had ample opportunity to learn about Florentine Neoplatonism.[111] The influence of Plato, his favorite philosopher, can be detected on many of his ideas. In the *Enchiridion* he opposed those who preferred Aristotle to Plato and Pythagoras, who were Augustine's choices. He even cited Dionysius the Areopagite's ideas of hierarchy with approval. But Erasmus was suspicious of attempts to introduce Platonic metaphysics into theology. As guides in religion Plato and Aristotle are vastly inferior to the Scriptures, and Plato had "many mad opinions."[112] Erasmus, while allowing a carefully circumscribed mysticism, refrained from all metaphysical speculation. He once stated flatly that the Platonic Philosophy was the occasion for Origen's ruin.[113] In the *Ciceronianus*, he turned Ovid's *Est deus in nobis* to a pious use, unlike Celtis who blew it up into a poetic theosophy. But speculation on even that level was rare for Erasmus.

In the *Ciceronianus*, Erasmus referred to the erudite and pious German humanists as though to demonstrate to the Italians that the North had developed a better approach to the classics. He cited specifically Hegius, Reuchlin, Wimpfeling, Spiegel, Melanchthon, Hutten, and Pirckheimer.[114] Erasmus had been only a boy when he learned to know Agricola through his teacher Hegius. He had a high regard for Wimpfeling's moral crusade against concubinage and appreciated his adulation. He had to respect Reuchlin's learning and sympathized with him during the controversy with the Dominicans, although he refused to become personally involved, making the detached comment, "I am no Reuchlinist and I do not tolerate any Erasmians." He even chided Reuchlin for his polemical tone.[115] But upon Reuchlin's death he added "The Apotheosis of Reuchlin" to the *Colloquies*, describing the soul of Reuchlin led by Jerome ascending to heaven in spite of the cloud of blackbirds (Dominicans) which like harpies try to keep him out.[116] Erasmus seems not to have reciprocated Mutian's extravagant praise. His relations with the Nuremberg humanists like Pirckheimer were very close and in his *De pronunciatione* he even commented intelligently on Albrecht Dürer's theoretical writings. The aspects of German humanism which Erasmus himself best climaxed and summarized were the literary and religious concerns represented by Agricola. Because of his aversion to speculation and revulsion against metaphysics he was in no position to fulfill the promise of a philosophical revival suggested by Mutian, Celtis, Pirckheimer and Reuchlin.

The Reformation was an intense personal tragedy for Erasmus. At the height of his fame when Luther appeared on the scene, Erasmus suddenly found himself caught in the middle like the man, he said, who in trying to separate two gladiators met his death. "I am a heretic to both sides," he lamented. He would sooner have remained a spectator. The combat and general disturbance of the conflict pained him, although had he lived to see the evangelicals build an orderly and well-regulated church life in the decades after the decisive battles, he might have felt differently.[117] Erasmus had contributed much to the Reformation, as both friend and foe knew very well. His criticisms of abuse, his stress on going to the sources, his Biblical and patristic scholarship, and his spiritualism as opposed to formalism were all positive contributions. Even after Erasmus took his stand against Luther, he refused to condemn him on all counts and continued to duel as fiercely with such Catholic foes as Zuñiga, Aleander, Alberto Pio, Lee, Latomus, and Bedda as with the reformers. Luther, in turn, continued to buy and read Erasmus' books long after their formal break.

Zwingli once shrewdly compared Luther with Heroic Ajax and Erasmus with the wily Odysseus. But the difference between them was far more than one of personality or temperament, it was a matter of basic religious conviction. Luther perceived the difference first, as early as 1516, commenting that he detected too little concern for Christ in Erasmus. "The human," Luther wrote in March 1517, "avails more with Erasmus than the divine." Luther's emphasis was on the redemptive and atoning character of Christ's work in effecting the new relation of man to God.

Erasmus understood the faith which saves as the spiritual tool of man for believing and trusting in God. In his explanation of the Creed he described it as a very low door or gate under which one must stoop to enter, in contrast to the subtle pride of man's natural reason. Man has two principal powers of soul, understanding and will. Faith is like a light shining before us in the dark and driving away error especially in those things pertaining to health and salvation. Charity puts aside all wrong affections and desires. Faith judges and teaches what is to be done. Charity carries it out in works, as the minister and servant of faith. The eye of faith is set upon God, but charity has two eyes, one set on God and the other on the neighbor. "Faith, therefore," Erasmus concludes, "whereof we do speak, is a gift infused and put into man's mind by God through which man without doubting believes all those things to be most true which God has taught and promised to us in the books of both testaments. . . All these things we do through the gift of faith far more certainly believe than we do those things which we do gather by argumentation and reasoning or which we perceive and know by our outward senses." [118] It is clear that faith for Erasmus was first of all a cognitive principle for spiritual truths. Knowledge (*notitia*) takes as true especially the promises (*promissa*) of God and trusts (*fiducia*) in the goodness of God. It is not simply a clinging to Christ the Savior and trust in the mercies of

God. It was not for him an existential experience. He could not cry *de profundis*, out of the depths.

For Luther the way into God's presence was solely through God's grace and forgiveness. For Erasmus the way was a compound of grace and good works whereby man climbed "from the body to the spirit, from the visible to the invisible, from the letter to the mystery, from the sensible to the intelligible, from the compounded to the simple, up as on the rungs of Jacob's ladder." [119] This basic difference lay at the heart of their controversy over free will. Actually Erasmus in the *De libero arbitrio* (1524) did not advocate complete free will, but a compound of human will and divine grace varying almost from page to page in the proper proportions involved in the formula. The passages on God's grace and Christ working in man predominate and some of the expressions sound genuinely Pauline. Grace should exclude false pride; conversely man should attribute his good works to God. Nevertheless, since the deeds are the man's, their meritorious character help him to obtain salvation. Only deeds of a conscious ethical character can be meritorious. The will is not unconditionally free, he concedes, because of the wounds inflicted upon it by sin. He vacillates as to the measure of freedom that can be ascribed to the will, from much to very little, as when he says that man can do less for himself than a child whose father is teaching it to walk, so that man is incapable of gaining eternal life by himself. For Luther justification by grace came first and the godly life as a consequence; for Erasmus justification stands at the end and the Christian works upward with the help of grace and achieves salvation. In the *De servo arbitrio* Luther very forcefully made the point that grace is a benignity, itself the divine act of forgiveness which justifies man, not a factor in a compound to be infused and combined with free will. The passages which Erasmus cited, taken at face value, imply complete freedom to choose, Luther argued, but the command to act does not prove the ability to act. Erasmus was no theologian and even the *Hyperaspistes I* and *II* did not make his case look stronger. Ironically, it seemed to many of Erasmus' Catholic contemporaries that primarily he was defending himself rather than the church, and that in his *Diatribe* he did not fully represent Catholic revelatory and redemptive theology.

In the *Protagoras* Socrates is reported to have said: "Or would you not rather agree that knowledge is a thing of beauty and power, invincible, that once a man knows good from evil, nothing on earth can compel him to act against that knowledge — wisdom being sufficient to his aid?" Socrates seems to have felt that intuition must continually be associated with analysis, and both with life.[120] By substitutuing a modicum of grace for intuition in this formula, Erasmus can be seen as the ultimate example of the "Socratic fallacy." He was at any rate relatively optimistic about the educability of man.

The younger generation of "Erasmians," in a very general use of the term, turned toward the Reformation — Zwingli, Vadian, Capito, Calvin, Tyndale, Melanchthon, Hamilton, and many lesser men. On the other hand, many stalwarts of the Catholic Church attacked him, so that he might not have been surprised to see himself branded at the Council of Trent as a Pelagian and impious heretic and to see many of his writings officially prohibited by the church. The Spanish Inquisition proscribed many of his writings, and in 1559 Paul IV put him in the first class of forbidden authors. In 1532 Erasmus prayed fervently to Christ for the peace of the church. The next year he wrote on restoring concord in the church. Running through the whole gamut of controverted doctrines — free will, prayers for the dead, invocation of the saints, images, relics, confession, the Mass, holy-days, and fasting — Erasmus' answer to the question as to how agreement could be reached is simply this: learn to tolerate. This elemental wisdom was a last legacy of the *philosophia Christi*, but it failed to keep the conservatives from the intractability which made the Catholic Reformation what it was. History had moved far from the year of the *Letters of Obscure Men* when the humanists still looked to Erasmus as the reformer and hero.

While all posterity has been agreed on the quality of Erasmus' brilliant mind, there is less unanimity on his character and achievement. Beatus Rhenanus recalled Erasmus as "friendly and cordial in manner, without any trace of pride, actually in every respect 'erasmian,' that is, translated from the Greek, lovable." If this description is debatable, certainly the meaning of his life's work is equally problematical.

Two extreme interpretations of Erasmus' place in church history have received the widest currency and in this case the truth lies not somewhere in between but well beyond each. The one emphasizes Erasmus' modernism and the other his conformity to medieval orthodoxy.[121] The first interpretation stresses his optimistic moralism, his spiritual Paulinism, his critical method applied to the sacred texts, to the institutions, laws, usages, and traditions of the temporal and spiritual order, his hope of a renewal of the Christian world by the gospel and by reason. Some scholars have found Erasmus hostile to dogma, a relativist, and therefore the most dangerous enemy of the contemporary church.[122] In his own day Aleander held this opinion of Erasmus. The term "modernism" as applied to the *Philosophia Christi* unfortunately beclouds the issue because of its nineteenth-century European connotations and its twentieth-century American religious context.

To ask, as often is done in the case of Thomas More, whether Erasmus was medieval or modern is to ask the wrong question in a way which is sure to elicit a simple and mistaken answer. Rather, the problem is to what extent was Erasmus faithful to Christian *traditio*, which runs from antiquity through the Middle Ages down to modern times. The answer to this question is more complex, but more accurate and revealing. Historians have known very well that Erasmus' great life's work was as an editor of the New Testament and the writings of the Greek and Latin church fathers. But they have not fully appreciated the extent to which his *philosophia Christi* was derived directly from the patristic writers, for through the long years in his study his mind was completely saturated with the theology of Christian antiquity. The authority of *traditio* in the patristic period lay in its agreement with the Scriptures. From the fathers Erasmus derived his high regard for both Testaments. From the Apologists and Alexandrines he took the phrase "philosophy of Christ." From them he took the "universalist" element, the notion of the Logos or Christ's Spirit influencing also the noble pagans. As with them, however, Christian revelation remained the touchstone by which such inspiration could be detected, so that he was no more than they a relativist in the present-day comparative religions sense of the word. From them he derived his exegetical method, even going beyond the *Quadriga* to the distinction of literal and spiritual interpretation. In them he found his much de-cried moralism and the spiritual rather than a vicarious atonement reading of St. Paul. In them he found the spiritual meaning of the sacramental life, in contrast to the *ex opere operato* usage so com-mon in his day. There, among the Greek fathers especially, he found a living church not subject to the juridical supremacy of the Roman bishop, so that he came to stress the spiritual office of the pontiff and decry the temporal aspect and power basis of the papacy. These examples of the consanguinity of the *philosophia Christi* and the *traditio* of Christian antiquity must suffice, although they could be multiplied and documented in great detail.

Erasmus was very loyal to Christian *traditio* and many of his ideas which have been tagged "modern" really belong to Chris-tian antiquity. In emphasizing the Scriptures and early *traditio*, Erasmus was anticipating and corroborating the Protestant appeal to Biblical authority and the witnesses to the truth prior to the decline in the late Middle Ages. Conversely, it is easy to under-stand and to sympathize with the anguish of contemporary Catho-lic scholars who feel that he subverted the end by his minimizing of the means represented in later *traditio*, in the medieval church. Erasmus remained formally orthodox in the medieval Catholic sense of the term, but in essence and emphasis it was early *traditio* that weighed most heavily with him. In the light of this insight other things fall into place. Was Erasmus modern? Yes, for through Christian humanism and Protestantism early *traditio* was transmitted to the modern world. Was Erasmus modern? No, for his *philosophia Christi* was derived from Christian antiquity and can be duplicated there in all its parts. Was Erasmus medieval? Yes, for he remained formally orthodox and subservient to the dogmatic authority of the Catholic church. No, for the effect of his *phil-osophia Christi* was to subvert the sacramental religious founda-tions of the medieval church.[123] How Erasmian that the answer to a question put too simply should be ambivalent! The Protestants could appreciate his appeal to early *traditio* and the Scriptures, but regretted his formal conformity and recognition of the dogmatic authority of the Pope. The Catholics were grateful for his con-tinued affiliation and recognition of the old Church, but resented his *philosophia Christi* and his deviationism. Both Protestants and

Catholics then and now sensed in him the lack of deep and fervent religious feeling and naturally thought less of him for it.

History was leaving Erasmus behind as events moved rapidly beyond him. When Luther was taken away to the Wartburg in 1521 and all the world thought he was gone forever, Albrecht Dürer called on Erasmus to pick up the lance and continue the fight. "Oh God!," he wrote in his diary, "is Luther dead; who will henceforth so clearly set forth the Gospel to us? . . . Oh! Erasmus of Rotterdam, where art thou? Behold what the unjust tyranny of earthly power, the might of darkness, can do. Hear, thou champion of Christ! Ride forth by the side of the Lord Christ; defend the truth; gain the martyr's crown! As it is, thou art but a frail old man." But Erasmus did not have the temperament for martyrdom and he was indeed aging rapidly though he lived another decade and a half. His correspondence from Freiburg reveals his very conservative convictions during the closing years of his life. His personal piety shines all through one of his last writings "On Preparation for Death" where he concluded:

> Last of all we must with our Lord all naked ascend upon the cross, far from all earthly affections, lifted up to the love of the heavenly life, so that with St. Paul we may say "The world is crucified unto me and I to the world." And there nailed with three nails, faith, hope, and charity, we must constantly persevere, fighting valiantly with our enemy the devil until at last, after we have vanquished him, we may pass into eternal rest, through the aid and grace of our Lord Jesus Christ, to whom with the Father and the Holy Ghost be praise and glory in all eternity. Amen.[124]

To the very end Erasmus worked on his edition of Origen. How touching that, according to Beatus Rhenanus who was at his bedside, the Prince of the humanists should revert to the vernacular to breathe his last words: "Lieve Got." In the end his was at heart the devout modernism of the *Devotio Moderna*.

✦X✦

LUTHER

The Reformer

WHEN Luther entered Erfurt on his way to the Diet at Worms in 1521, Eobanus Hessus, young Neo-Latin poet and humanist, called out: "Rejoice, exalted Erfurt, crown thyself . . . for behold, he comes who will free you from disgrace." At the head of a delegation of forty or more members of the University, Luther's old Erfurt friend Crotus Rubeanus, the rector, met him at the gates of the city. Luther was to him the "judge of evil to see whose features is like a divine appearance." After some vacillation Eobanus became a staunch Lutheran and an evangelical professor at Marburg. Following a period of uncertainty during which Crotus supported Luther as the restorer of "correct piety," he made his decision to stay with the old church. If the reaction of the humanists to Luther's reformation was not uniform, subsequent opinion on the relation of Luther to the humanists and of the Reformation to the Renaissance has been equally divided.[1] To some the Reformation marks the decisive breakthrough of the modern world led by Luther, the emancipator of personal religion from Roman priestly rule. To others it was in its most significant aspects more medieval than modern. To all it was a movement, and Luther a leader, worthy of careful study, so that more has been written about Luther than about any other person with the exception of Christ.

Once again Tertullian's ancient question, which he raised in his *Prescriptions Against Heretics*, came into focus: "What has Athens to do with Jerusalem, the Church with the Academy, the Christian with the heretic?" Luther's answer was neither an unreserved affirmation of secular culture nor an absolute rejection.

Nor was it a qualified acceptance in the sense of a halfhearted or reluctant permissiveness. Rather, Luther gave enthusiastic support to humanist culture in its sphere, but sharply rebuffed its encroachments in the domain of theology where God's Word and not human letters reign supreme. The question of Luther's humanism is sometimes made a matter of his personal relations with the humanists. What was the nature of the Brethren's influence? Did he know the "right people" at Erfurt? How extensive was his knowledge of the classics? Did his trip to Rome provide an Italian experience analogous to that of Agricola, Mutian, Celtis, Hutten, Reuchlin, or the rest? These questions, while important and deserving at least a summary answer, are secondary to the inner relation of the substance of Luther's thought to the reform programs and religious thought of the German humanists.

Revolutions usually start within and are led by men who are genuinely a part of the rejected system. The Protestant revolution began with theological declarations composed by a churchman and not with the publication of the loose poems of Celtis or the radical opinions of Mutian. Luther owed much to the humanists, both to their progressive criticisms of the abuses in the church and to their cultural reform program. When he first entered the arena they hailed him as Hercules and the German Cicero. Luther reciprocated in little ways which showed that he was affected also by the identification of his cause with theirs. From November 1517, on he often signed his name as Eleutherius, the liberator. In his explanation of the Ninety-five Theses he came close to the religious expressions of a Pico or Reuchlin. During this period he was building up an ever stronger aversion to abstract conceptualizations in theology. In the twelve theses "ex philosophia" (theses 29–40) which Luther presumably prepared to accompany the theological theses for the Heidelberg disputation in April 1518, he expressed his Augustinian preference for Pythagoras and, above all, Plato to Aristotle.[2] He preferred to scholasticism the *Theologia Deutsch,* an excellent example of voluntaristic mysticism penned by a member of the Teutonic Knights in Sachsenhausen near Frankfurt. From Dionysius, Gerson, Lefèvre, Wessel Gansfort, and other sources he learned to know the Christianized Neoplatonism of tradition. From the start Luther's works were popular with the reading public so that, even though Erasmus tried to keep Froben from printing his books, Luther's works were, as Beatus Rhenanus wrote to Zwingli, "less sold than torn out of the hands of the book-sellers." But, except for incidental contacts and peripheral influences, Luther was not in 1521 a humanist in the sense that he emphasized the dignity of man in the manner of Pico, which was after all the core of humanism, or that he put the restoration of antique culture first in importance, nor did he ever become one. When, as in his commentary on Romans 13, Luther criticized churchmen for their worldliness and theologians for forgetting the Scriptures, he was following a long-standing tradition of constantly recurring monastic protest and not merely siding with the humanists.

After conventional training at Mansfeld, Luther was sent to school at Magdeburg where he made his first contact with the Brethren of the Common Life who were in charge of one of the schools there.[3] He read and continued to use the writings of such Brethren as Mombaer, Ludolf of Saxony, and Gerard Zerbolt of Zutphen, as well as the works of Wessel Gansfort, Johann Pupper von Goch, and Gabriel Biel, rector of the Brethren at Buzbach. In later years, like Erasmus, Luther recalled the constructive work of the Brethren and even more than Erasmus came to their defense when their houses were threatened in the antimonastic movement. Only once did he turn against a house of the Brethren, and that once for a special reason.[4] At Erfurt, Logic was second only to Latin in importance in the curriculum. There the *Summulae logicales* of Petrus Hispanus was still the main text. He was introduced also to Aristotle's new logic, the *Analytics* and to Aristotle's *Physics* as a guide to natural philosophy. Besides these he learned also from Aristotle's *Politics, Nicomachean Ethics, Economics*, and *Metaphysics*. Even though, under humanist influence, he later at Wittenberg University dropped the disputations from the theological course of study for many years, he always retained a deep respect for the training which dialectic gives to the mind, and after 1532 restored the disputations. Two of Luther's Erfurt professors had a particularly great influence over him, Jodocus Trutvetter and Bartholemaus Arnold von Usingen. Both belonged to the *via moderna* school of scholasticism as represented by William of

Occam and Gabriel Biel.[5] In their teaching they marked a sharp cleavage between reason and revelation and knowledge and faith. Since true knowledge is derived from inner experience and it is impossible to have such an experience of God, revelation and faith must intervene to provide a knowledge of God. Luther developed a negative reaction, a repugnance for philosophical speculation. Under the influence of Augustine, of the German mystic John Tauler, whom he supposed to be the author of the *Theologia Deutsch*, and of the humanists, Luther moved away from scholastic philosophy.

The extent to which Luther came under the influence of the humanists at Erfurt has been the center of a scholarly tempest which has not as yet completely died down.[6] When he entered the monastery he carried with him a copy of Plautus and Virgil, but this did not mean, as the old legend had it, that he tore himself away from a humanist or poet circle at the University. The influence of the only humanist professor at Erfurt during Luther's days, Nikolaus Marschalk, should not be overrated. His student, Crotus Rubeanus, was a friend of his there and he raised a loud lament over Luther's decision to become a monk. Mutian's circle of young humanists, however, did not coalesce until after 1505 when Luther was already in the monastery. At Erfurt, Luther heard Emser, who was to become his archfoe, deliver a lecture on Reuchlin's comedy, the *Sergius*. Luther read and was very moved by Wimpfeling's *De Integritate*, his strong attack on clerical abuses. Of the Italian humanists, Luther read with great pleasure the *Eclogues* of Baptista Mantuanus, the reforming General of the Carmelite Order, who had composed a great many pieces of a very pious nature using humanist flourishes like the antique names for the gods. His pastoral poems were republished in Erfurt in 1501 and were available to Luther. His combination of the themes of pastoral quietude and monastic withdrawal possibly appealed to Luther in particular.[7] But all of these peripheral influences combined did not serve to make Luther a humanist. His main course of study had been the Aristotelian curriculum combined with Occamist scholasticism. His struggle for religious certainty which became the determinative influence on his life had nothing fundamental to do with humanism. His new insight, when it came, was that of a prophet and not that of a scholar resolving a fine point in philology.

Luther retained many humanist forms and was himself not immediately clear that the substance of his message had no common center with the philosophy of even the most religious humanists like Erasmus. In 1516, when he was already beginning to feel the basic differences, he still referred to Mutian as the most erudite and humane man and contrasted his own poverty with his excellence and humanity. In 1517 he spoke of "our Erasmus" and in March 1519, began a correspondence with him.[8] His sympathies in the great humanist-scholastic controversy were with Reuchlin. Conversely, the humanists at first identified his cause with theirs, making a proper differentiation all the more difficult. Luther's earnestness, his religious feeling, his theological substance separated him from the humanist idea. Luther's battle had to be fought for goals greater than anything that the humanists were dreaming of. Jerome, Luther reflected, who knew five languages, did not equal Augustine, who knew but one.[9] In his preface to the *Theologia Deutsch* (1518) which he was the first to edit in its entirety, he remarked, "I thank God that I hear and find my God in the German language in a way in which I have not found him up to now in the Latin, Greek, or Hebrew tongues."[10] Luther respected humanist learning, but only when it was founded upon an anterior deep and simple faith in Christ. In his *Commentary on Romans* (VII, 6: *Corollarium*) Luther expressed this idea in a way which is faintly reminiscent of the Enlightenment-weary Rousseau:

It is not the most learned, who read much and many books, who are the best Christians. For all of their books and all of their knowledge is "letter" and death for the soul. No, they are the best Christians who really with complete free will translate into action what the others read in books and teach to others. But they cannot act in that complete freedom, if they do not through the Holy Spirit possess love. Therefore, one must fear for our times when thanks to the multiplicity of books men become very learned to be sure, but completely unlearned for Christ.

The tools of philology, therefore, are put to best use when applied to the study of the Scriptures, and without Christ the Scriptures are nothing.

Luther customarily deferred to humanists of Erasmus' stature, as in the *De Servo Arbitrio*, where he referred to himself as a *rusticus*, or elsewhere where he says he is writing from an obscure corner of the world. He once wrote on the table with a piece of chalk. "Res et verba [faith and culture]: Philippus [Melanchthon], verba sine re: Erasmus, res sine verbis: Lutherus, nec res nec verba: Carolstadius." [11] He felt that he had the spiritual substance without the humanist form. Although he once expressed regret that he had lost so much time on scholastic studies that he had not read enough of the classic historians and poets at the University, he did have a very extensive knowledge of classical literature and his prodigious memory allowed him to stud a great many pages with classical references.[12] What he learned from the Italian humanists, he acquired only indirectly, for the most part, through his tenuous connections with the German humanists. Lorenzo Valla was a notable exception. Luther was impressed by his exposé of the *Donation of Constantine*, which Hutten had republished, but even more so, on the theological level, by his position on the freedom of the will. "Indeed," Luther declared in part one of his *De Servo Arbitrio*, "for my part, one, Wyclif, and another, Lorenzo Valla, as well as Augustine, whom you (Erasmus) pass by, is my entire authority." Valla identified himself with Latin patristic thought, broke with the endeavors to create a synthesis of pagan philosophy and Christianity, characteristic of Ficino in the second half of the Quattrocento, and stressed theology.[13] Luther also in Valla's case was more interested in substance than in elegances. The *Annotationes in latinum Novum Testamentum* meant more to him than the *Elegantiae*. Luther, even as a theological professor, was never a scholar who was forced to excel at scholarship for its own sake. But he was a great scholar in the sense that his scholarship was directed toward a higher end and a loftier objective.[14] He personally led the fight against the artistic iconoclasts, cultural nihilists, and atavists among the sectaries. He heaped ridicule upon Carlstadt, for example, who argued against academic degrees because of Christ's words, "Let no man call you master" [Matt. 23:8], which obviously simply meant that He alone had final authority.

Side by side with Melanchthon and the other magisterial reformers Luther fought to stem the tide of obscurantism rising on all sides. Melanchthon in his *Encomium Eloquentiae* decried the spreading depreciation of classical culture. "Good God," he wrote to Eobanus Hessus in April 1523, "how preposterously do those theologize who wish to show their wisdom solely by their contempt of these good things! What is this error but a new species of sophistry?"[15] In answer to the complaints of Eobanus and others, Luther had a few weeks before, on March 23, 1529, written:

> Do not give way to your apprehension lest we Germans become more barbarous than ever we were by reason of the decline of letters through our theology. I am persuaded that, without a skilled training in literary studies, no true theology can establish and maintain itself, seeing that in times past it has invariably fallen miserably and lain prostrate with the decline of learning. On the other hand it is indubitable that there never has been a signal revelation of divine truth unless first the way has been prepared for it, as by a John the Baptist, by the revival and pursuit of the study of languages and literature. Assuredly there is nothing I should less wish to happen than that our youth should neglect poetry and rhetoric. My ardent vow is that there should be as many poets and rhetoricians as possible, because I see clearly that by no other methods is it possible to train men for the apt understanding, the right and felicitous treatment of sacred things. Wherefore I beg that you may incite the youth of Erfurt to give themselves strenuously to this study. I am often impatient that in this age of enlightenment time will not permit me to devote myself to poetry and rhetoric, though I formerly bought a Homer in order that I might become a Greek.[16]

Through many of Luther's exclamations in which he calls for a renewal of learning rings the tone of cultural nationalism familiar from Wimpfeling, Celtis, Hutten, and Pirckheimer.

> We have unfortunately rotted and spoiled long enough in darkness. We have been German brutes far too long. Let us for once use our reason so that God notices our thankfulness for his good gifts and so that other countries see that we are also human beings and people who can either learn something from them or can teach them, so that the world is improved also through us![17]

Luther believed that human culture of the highest literary and artistic quality existed by its own right as part of the order of creation. Just as secular government under the control of non-Christians is justified on the basis of natural law, so human culture in which the works are temporal and the reward temporal is justified in terms of creation. Original sin has not destroyed reason, though it has damaged it, nor does faith make irrelevant the educational and cultural goals of man's natural free will and reason, although faith puts these temporal goals into proper perspective. When Luther declared that the sphere of faith's works is worldly society and its order, he included also the educational and cultural achievement as part of the worldly order. Wilhelm Dilthey has correctly commented that "with this sentence there enters into history one of the greatest organizing thoughts that a man has ever had."[18] With Luther's understanding of faith the world and human culture is both set free to be itself and also established as the place where man's maturing responsibility has free play. The world becomes truly the place of man's responsible care and man becomes truly the heir who has come of age and whose care it is to make history and to build the highest culture of which he is capable.[19] For the Christian also the adiaphoristic realm of culture is *negotium cum Deo*.

Nevertheless, the highest achievements of the social and cultural order are temporal and transient. History demonstrates how short-lived some cultures have been and how mortal all are. Even achievements of the greatest human value contribute to a merely temporary order which remains at best but a picture, a shadow, a figure of God's kingdom.[20] Cultural achievements of the highest level do not serve as a substitute for that justice and righteousness which avails before God. Natural man's reason must necessarily act in the spiritual dark unless enlightened by the Holy Spirit.[21] In his 1535 commentary on Galatians, Luther conceded that natural reason could perceive that the creation of the world was a divine act; later he came to doubt that even this could be known and restricted natural knowledge to a general sense of the governance of the world by God. In his lectures on Genesis (1535–1545) Luther asserted that Cicero, the darling of the humanists, was invincibly ignorant about God. To be sure he knew everything that natural reason and human powers could assemble, but he was ignorant of what God wills and of his feelings toward us men. Reason is ignorant of this unless enlightened by the Holy Spirit through the Word.[22] Human culture does not make men true man as Christ was true man, without sin and spiritually alive to God. As a matter of value judgment Luther gave priority to the work of the *Spiritus Sanctus* over human *ingenium*, to stammering religious truth over shining human eloquence, to Christian faith over antique learning.[23]

The question is whether this order of priority would subvert the realm of the human or of humanist culture. Historically this had undeniably happened many times and in many places during the "Dark Ages" preceding and the anti-intellectual undertow was pulling downward in the rough waters of the religious revolution. Luther set himself against this trend of the day in order that men given Christian liberty anew might be free also for this world. Once more he took his watchword from St. Paul: "Finally, brethren, whatever is true, whatever is honorable, whatever is just, whatever is pure, whatever is lovely, whatever is gracious, if there is any excellence, if there is anything worthy of praise, think about these things." [24] Christian culture for Luther meant a full affirmation of all that is good in this realm, without limitations, with no less freedom, and with even greater responsibility. It is interesting that Luther's favorite term for the cultural sphere was the realm of *Geist*, the spirit, which is contained in the contemporary German word for intellectual-cultural history, *Geistesgeschichte*, connoting more than the usual English equivalent, intellectual history.

Luther had a teleological view of the historical role of humanism in relation to the Reformation. He believed that the culture of classical antiquity bloomed under benign Providence in order to prepare the way for the New Testament Revelation and the success of the Christian mission. In the same way, he commented, "No one knew why God allowed the study of the languages to come forth until it was finally realized that it happened for the sake of the Gospel which he wished to reveal thereafter." [25] Far from consigning these linguistic studies to neglect, this role of John the Baptist gave them a position of critical importance in the rapid developments of this new day of grace. The very nature of the eschatological situation made it urgent that these treasures be gathered in quickly while time remained.[26] Luther's program was in the tradition of that good Roman, one of the last and finest flowers of antique culture, St. Augustine. Under the leadership of

Luther at Wittenberg University linguistics, the triple tiara of Latin, Greek, and Hebrew, Biblical philology, history, moral philosophy, science, university and school reform found a sure and lasting place in Protestant culture. In March 1518, Luther personally, together with Carlstadt, proposed reforms "for the total expulsion of all barbarism." On March 21 he wrote to his friend Johannes Lang: "Our university is making progress. We may shortly expect to have lectures in two, yes, in three languages, and beyond that to receive lectures on Pliny, mathematics, Quintilian, and other outstanding lectures. But we shall throw overboard those on Petrus Hispanus, Tartaretus, and Aristotle." The young humanists who joined the evangelical movement did so, not only because the young are more inclined to break with tradition, but because they found in Protestant culture what they had felt lacking, a religious and ecclesiastical community which gave their work a new meaning in the service of the kingdom of God. If Luther saw the threat of an Erasmian culture-religion and spotted the dangerous symptoms even in the naive fusion of culture and religion in the Brethren of the Common Life, he nevertheless appreciated the great value of culture as culture, and of culture put into the service of the church. Although culture cannot lead a man to faith, the man of faith can lead culture to a higher plane. That idea is the key cultural contribution of the Reformation and the basis for that humanistic education and culture which was typical of Protestant lands until this present post-modern age.

Central to the problem of religion and culture, reformation and humanism, is the relation of faith (*fides*) and reason (*ratio*) in Luther's thought. Much confusion still exists on the question of Luther's attitude toward human reason, because of a failure to understand that Luther, like St. Bernard and Thomas Aquinas, distinguished the areas in which reason and faith are operative by a carefully drawn though at times undulating horizontal line, and he drew it clearly between the realms of nature and of grace. In the domain of the kingdom of nature, in things of this world, and in matters of human culture, reason reigns supreme as God's highest gift to man. One of Luther's clearest statements on this point, constantly reiterated elsewhere, is in *The Disputation Concerning Man* (1536), characterized by its tribute to the reason of man and the majestic position which he occupies on earth. So specific is that statement of Luther's anthropology that at least the first few of the forty theses merit direct citation:

1. Philosophy or human wisdom defines man as an animal having reason, sensation, and body.
2. It is not necessary at this time to debate whether man is properly or improperly called an animal.
3. But this must be known, that this definition describes man only as a mortal and in relation to this life.
4. And it is certainly true that reason is the most important and the highest in rank among all things and, in comparison with other things of this life, the best and something divine.
5. It is the inventor and mentor of all the arts, medicines, laws, and of whatever wisdom, power, virtue, and glory men possess in this life.
6. By virtue of this fact it ought to be named the essential difference by which man is distinguished from the animals and other things.
7. Holy Scripture also makes it lord over the earth, birds, fish, and cattle, saying, "Have dominion."
8. That is, that it is a sun and a kind of god appointed to administer these things in this life.
9. Nor did God after the fall of Adam take away this majesty of reason, but rather confirmed it.
10. In spite of the fact that it is of such majesty, it does not know itself a priori, but only a posteriori.[27]

This disputation also brings to light the definite limitations of reason, arguing that, whether it is employed in philosophy or theology or both, reason is unable to give a definitive answer to the question, "What is man?" The final answer to such a big question takes one into the area of faith and here reason arrogantly intervenes and trespasses on forbidden territory. Luther is not thinking in this connection so much of the natural limitations of finite man in grappling with problems of ultimates and infinity as he is of that arrogance of natural reason which refuses to accept God's Word and the terms of salvation as He provides it, but insists that man may approach God on the basis of his own righteousness or in view of the Gospel concludes that the law has lost its cogency and demanding force. A third concept of Luther's is that of the regenerate reason of the man of faith. This is that *ratio evidens*, natural reason obedient to God's Word and thus restored to its genuineness, to which Luther appealed in his reply at Worms: "Unless I

am overcome with testimonies from Scripture or with evident reason . . . I cannot and will not recant." When man comes to faith
and is freed of self-will, he experiences a change in his reason
which is thereby enlightened and rendered capable of a new understanding. This new understanding in turn is placed into the
service of faith. It is human reason enlightened by the Spirit and
rooted in the Word of God that should also become the beacon
light and driving force for a new and higher human culture.[28]

Because Luther's religious concern drove him to battle against
the synergism and legalism of scholastic theology, his assault on
"arrogant" reason in the second sense of the term has attracted the
most attention. Actually, Luther had no objection whatsoever
either to Aristotelian philosophy or to dialectic in their proper
spheres, but struggled mightily to keep philosophy and "arrogant"
reason out of the proper domain of theology and faith. The practical cultural effect of his position was to reinforce the humanist
tendency away from scholastic philosophy and toward grammar
and the dependence on the sources rather than on abstract reason.
He was not opposed to dialectic, but wanted it kept out of theology.
Thus, in answer to Spalatin's question as to where logic is necessary
to theology, Luther replied:

You ask how far I think dialectic is useful to the theologian. I absolutely do not see how dialectic can be other than a poison to a true
theologian. Grant that it may be useful as a game or an exercise for
youthful minds, still in sacred letters, where pure faith and divine illumination are expected, the whole matter of the syllogism must be
left without, just as Abraham, when about to sacrifice, left the boys
with the asses. This, Johannes Reuchlin in the second book of his *Cabala*
affirms sufficiently. For if any dialectic is necessary, that natural inborn
dialectic is sufficient, by which a man is led to compare beliefs with
other beliefs and so conclude the truth. I have often discussed with
friends what utility seemed to us to be gained from this so sedulous
study of philosophy and dialectic, and truly with one consent, having
marveled at, or rather bewailed, the calamity of our minds, we found
no utility, but rather a whole sea of hindrance.[29]

Regenerate reason of the man of faith has a wide range of cultural activity in which to express itself. In the area of the intellect
as well as in the areas of morality and society, faith is active in
love.[30] For Professor Luther reform began at home with the Uni-

versity of Wittenberg so that under his leadership the University became the first to adopt a curriculum designed to promote Biblical humanism. It was the first university in Germany where all three languages were taught, for the arts faculty very quickly adapted its offerings to the new program of theological studies. From 1516 to 1533 the University was in transition from its Roman Catholic scholastic period under Trutvetter, Staupitz, and Mellerstadt to its Protestant status. Fundamental changes were reflected in the *Urkundenbuch* and the *Liber Decanorum* between the years 1516 and 1518. The philosophical lectures left the *viae* for new directions and the range of humanist activity was enlarged to include the study of Pliny, Priscian, and significantly also Quintilian, as Luther had predicted. Luther himself reported with satisfaction that his New Testament theology and St. Augustine were continuing to prosper and reign in the University through the hand of God, so that in theology Aristotle was declining daily and heading toward a final fall.[31] From the very beginning Luther was gratified to find supporters in all three faculties then in being. When in the late summer of 1518 the twenty-one-year-old humanist Melanchthon arrived in Wittenberg, he was excited by the progress that had been made. In his proud inaugural address on the improvement of education for the youth, he congratulated Wittenberg and the student body, because they could already work with the pure sources, beyond the glosses and commentaries to the original texts. Most of his further demands were met in the great university reform at the end of 1521. The University became a seedbed of the Reformation for a large part of Europe. It was, the Sorbonne wailed, a whole nest of vipers in one. But Luther's interest in the humanist studies and educational ideals were reflected also in his educational reform program, in his high regard for the classical languages, in his adoption of new exegetical techniques of Biblical interpretation, in his new appreciation for history and moral philosophy, and in his beneficent attitude toward the fine arts, poetry, art, and especially music.

Luther admired tremendously the humanist learning of Erasmus, Camerarius, Brenz, and above all young Melanchthon. In addressing Erasmus he called himself *fraterculus in Christo*, little brother in Christ. Because of his modesty he was reluctant to assume the presiding role in educational reform. "I know very well," he wrote, "that others could have carried it out more effectively, but since they are silent, I shall do it as well as I can." [32] To a follower named Strauss in Eisenach he wrote on April 25, 1524: "I beg you to do your utmost in the cause of training the youth. For I am convinced that the neglect of education will bring the greatest ruin to the Gospel. This matter is the most important of all." [33] Luther won young Melanchthon for and confirmed him in the evangelical faith. "I must look there where Christ calls me," declared Luther's quiet foreman, "not where my desire draws me." Melanchthon reciprocated through the years by contributing to Luther's continually deepening appreciation of humanist learning. Melanchthon had begun his own career with an inaugural lecture in August 1518, on the *Improvement of the Studies of Youth*, an address reminiscent of St. Basil's *Admonition to the Youth* on the use of pagan learning. Six years later Luther published his justly famous *Appeal to the Municipalities of Germany*, urging a full-scale effort to reform and expand the schools.

Many phrases in the *Appeal* reflect the spirit of Quintilian as he urges more and better education for children. Luther refers to the Hellenic ideal of Paideia, languages, literature, music, mathematics — education for the whole man — whereby wonderfully skilled and well qualified people are developed.[34] The lack of sound education is a worse enemy of the commonwealth than the Turk, so that if men give a single gulden for the defense of the empire they should give a hundred to educate even one boy to become a good Christian man. If people once gave so readily for indulgences, Masses, pilgrimages, and such rubbish, they should now be ready to provide learning for the rising generation. In giving the Gospel to the present age, God has provided a multitude of men educated in the new learning and gifted with the necessary knowledge and skill to impart such education. This age, Luther continued, is the year of jubilee for Germany. If in former years students spent years of drudgery in the schools and learned neither Latin nor German properly, now Germany has been blessed with better learning and with the pure Gospel. There is no greater danger to the common good than an uneducated and ill-disciplined youth, and since the parents as a rule are too busy or too unqualified to

educate their children, the schoolteacher is indispensable. The public authority, therefore, has the imperative duty to provide schools
and teachers in the common interest. These schools should not be
content merely to provide elementary instruction in German and
the Bible. In the interest of both church and state they should fos-
ter the study of the classical languages as the best instruments of
higher education, for because of a lack of these languages the
Germans are decried in foreign lands as barbarians. By neglecting
these studies the Germans merit those supercilious gibes only too
well.

In the first place, Luther argued in the *Appeal*, the study of
Latin, Greek, Hebrew, and the other liberal arts are necessary for
the understanding of the Bible. The Gospel was revealed in these
languages and was spread through Greek and Latin in the ancient
world. In this modern age God has in almost the same way provided for their revival just before the rediscovery of the Gospel
so that it might be better understood and the reign of Antichrist
discovered and cast down. For this reason God allowed the Turks
to conquer Greece so that through the Greek refugees the knowledge of the language of the New Testament would be dissemin-
ated more widely. A knowledge of these languages is necessary if
Germany is to retain the Gospel. They are the scabbard in which
the sword of the Spirit is sheathed, the shrine in which this treasure
is laid. Without them Germany will fall back into the terrible old
barbarous educational system. Without them there can be no real
knowledge of the Word and no higher education worthy of the
name. With their decline in the ancient world true Christianity
began to fall and all came under the power of the Pope. Their revival brought about such an enlightenment and accomplished such
great things that all the world must acknowledge that men now
possess the Gospel in as pure a form as the Apostles had it, and
much more purely than in the days of Jerome and Augustine. St.
Bernard (whom Luther admired above the other doctors as a spiritual teacher though not as a religious metaphysician) because of
his lack of languages often failed to get the true meaning of the
Scriptural text. Though many fathers taught Christian truth and
attained high positions of honor in the church without these languages, many errors disfigured the exegetical writings of Augus-

tine, Hilary, and others who were ignorant of the original languages. Though a preacher can preach edifying sermons without these tools, he cannot expound or maintain his teaching against critical heretics. As the sun is to the shadow, so is a knowledge of the originals to all the commentaries of the fathers. It is folly to neglect or depreciate the study of these languages and for this reason, Luther added, he cannot approve the Waldensians (Hussites) who despise this study.

In the second place, this study serves the interest of the state as well as the church, for the state needs educated men and women for better government of land and people and the proper rearing of children in the home. The old cruel system which included so much rote memorization and drill should be abandoned in favor of a more practical education so that learning can be a joy and recreation for the pupils. Recalling his own personal experience, Luther lamented with some hyperbole that the "schools were no better than hell and purgatory, in which we were martyred with the grinding tenses and cases and nevertheless learned nothing at all, in spite of the blows, trembling, terror, and misery we suffered at the hands of our brutal schoolmasters. . . How much I regret that we did not read more of the poets and the historians, and that nobody thought of teaching us these. Instead of such study, I was compelled to read the devil's rubbish — the scholastic philosophers and sophists with such cost, labor, and detriment, from which I have had trouble enough to rid myself." By God's grace a more rational, practical, and humane method promises to introduce a new era into education through the religious transformation of the day.[35]

Luther promoted the establishment of coeducational schools and of town libraries filled with useful books, the Bible in the original languages and in good translations, the best ancient commentaries, classic authors both pagan and Christian, approved books in law, medicine, and all the arts and sciences, histories of all kinds, but especially of Germany, for histories are indispensable for understanding the past and the ways of God as revealed in the acts of man. The *Appeal* really laid down the program for that extensive educational reform including the establishment of classical secondary schools put into actual practice by Melanchthon,

Bugenhagen, and other reformers in Germany, Scandinavia, and indirectly in other parts of Protestant Europe. Small wonder that Leopold von Ranke judged it as important in its sphere as the *Address to the Christian Nobility* of 1520.[36] Melanchthon recommended it warmly to the academic youth of Germany. The magisterial reformers made an all-out effort to combat the obscurantism of the extremists and succeeded in transmitting the heritage of Christian humanism to the children of the Reformation. It was not until after 1520 that the methods and aims of the new movement in education began effectively to transform the German schools, and this eventual triumph was due as much to the support of Luther as to any pronounced success on the part of the general humanist propaganda.[37] It is interesting to note that Luther's concern was with education for the promotion of the evangelical cause and for the welfare of the nation, just as the humanists had worked for religious enlightenment and cultural nationalism. Both church and state needed poets and rhetoricians for their prosperity in the new age.

When Felix Rayther of Wittenberg announced the publication of Luther's *Appeal* to a friend of his in Constance he praised it enthusiastically with the words: "Almost the whole little book is a eulogy of languages." Luther shared with the humanists a high regard for and even a fascination with languages. Medieval man had held language to be a special divine gift and the humanists had been enthusiastic over the power of the classical languages to unlock arcane meanings of the texts. For Luther the utility of languages was functional and not substantive. He expressed his views on this subject in one of his Table Talks in this way:

Are the instruments of the arts and of nature useful to the theologian? One knife cuts better than another. Thus good tools, such as languages and the arts, can teach more clearly. Now many, like Erasmus, have the arts and languages, and, nevertheless, err most perniciously . . . But the thing must be distinguished from its abuse . . . It is the same tongue before faith and after faith, and language insofar as it is language does not help faith, but nevertheless it serves it when the heart is enlightened. Thus reason also serves faith in that it reflects on a thing, how it has been illuminated.[38]

For Luther the loftiest function of language was its service as a vehicle for the Word of God. It played a role analogous to that of reason (*ratio*) itself. Luther's emphasis on the spoken word, *verbum evangelii vocale*, his demonstration of the power of the preached Word, and his self-conscious awareness of his own skill as a "sharp orator," as he was called as early as 1515, was directly related to the humanist stress upon rhetoric and the power of speech, even though its deeper source was the theological concept of the gospel as good news proclaimed from faith to faith.

The relation of his exegesis to that of the humanist is a fascinating subject, one which is coming increasingly into focus as the significance of exegetical studies for the history of Christian thought and of the church is coming to be more fully appreciated. In the year 1512 Luther received the degree of *Doctor in Biblia*, a title of which he was justly proud and from which he drew a great deal of comfort through his years of battling for Scriptural truth. Like Valla and Erasmus, Luther was highly critical of the medieval *Quadriga*, but like Erasmus he allowed and particularly with reference to the Old Testament extensively used allegory and tropology in order to elucidate the spiritual rather than the literal meaning of the text. Reuchlin's favorite authority on exegesis, Nicholas de Lyra, whose works Luther knew extraordinarily well, popularized a mnemonic device perhaps used by others before him to explain the fourfold interpretation of the text:

> Litera gesta docet, quid credas allegoria,
> Moralis quid agas, quo tendas anagogia.[39]

In English the verse reads:

> The letter shows us what God and our fathers did;
> The allegory shows us where our faith is hid;
> The moral meaning gives us rules of daily life;
> The anagogy shows us where we end our strife.[40]

Although multiple interpretation could and often did carry out of sight the literal meaning of the text with fanciful flights of allegory, Karl Holl was certainly correct in warning against a too hasty dismissal of the Quadriga as sleight-of-hand exegesis, for it contributed to the salutary drive to exhaust the meaning of the text from every side. Medieval exegesis had made progress in isolating and elevating the literal sense. In scientific debate and formal disputations only the literal sense was customarily accepted as evidence.[41]

Luther the expositor had a good eye for what was useful in medieval exegesis, but he was quick to adopt the best that humanism had to offer. Like Erasmus he preferred the older authorities to the late medieval commentators, for the fathers represented *traditio* in its purer, though not inerrant, form. Luther made use of the humanists' philological techniques, their textual discoveries, and their linguistic and grammatical works. One finds in his New Testament commentaries phrases like, "as Erasmus correctly translates." It is well known that he used Lefèvre d'Étaples' glosses on the Psalms and Epistles, that he changed in the middle of his lectures on Romans to Erasmus' *Novum Testamentum* for a Greek text, and that as a man of almost supreme linguistic ability he mastered Greek and became a respectable student of Hebrew in order to facilitate his translations and exegesis. His knowledge of Hebrew, made possible by the pioneer work of Pellican, Reuchlin, and Jewish scholars such as David Kimchi and Moses Kimhi, enabled him to work effectively with the Old Testament and also to recognize the Hebraisms in the New.[42] Like the humanists he heaped scorn on the Quadriga, as a typical passage from his second commentary on Galatians (1535) illustrates:

> The idle and unlearned monks and the school doctors dreamed . . . that the Scripture has four senses: the literal sense, the moral sense, the allegorical sense, and the mystical sense [Literalem, Tropologicum, Allegoricum, et Anagogicum]; and according to these senses they have foolishly interpreted almost all the words of the Scriptures — as: this word "Jerusalem" literally signified that city which was so named: morally a pure conscience: allegorically the church militant: mystically the celestial city or the Church triumphant. With these trifling and foolish fables they rent the Scriptures into so many and diverse senses, that silly poor consciences could receive no doctrine at all.[43]

Like Erasmus and the medieval tradition Luther held that a doctrine or a controverted point cannot be proved by allegory. But it goes without saying that those Old Testament passages given an allegorical interpretation in the New Testament were to be understood in both the literal and the allegorical sense. The following commentary on Galatians 4:24, "Now this is an allegory," represents his usual attitude:

> Allegories do not strongly persuade in theology, but as certain pictures they beautify and illustrate the matter. For if Paul had not

proved the righteousness of faith against the righteousness of works by strong and pithy arguments, he should have little prevailed in this allegory. But because he had fortified his cause before with invincible arguments, taken of experience, of the example of Abraham, of the testimonies of Scripture, and similitudes: now in the end of his disputations he adds an allegory, to give beauty to all the rest. For it is a seemly thing sometimes to add an allegory when the foundation is well-laid and the matter thoroughly proved. For as painting is an ornament to set forth and garnish an house already builded, so is an allegory the light of a matter which is already otherwise proved and confirmed.[44]

In his *Lectures on Deuteronomy* Luther expressed very bluntly his feeling about "mystic interpretations" and allegories:

I have taken pains, however, first to treat everything in the simplest manner. I have not allowed myself to be snatched away into so-called "mystic" interpretations if at times laws came up that appear absurd or foolish to some . . .

Later, however, I have added brief allegories, almost for every chapter. This is not because I attach great importance to them, but I want to forestall the silly attempts at allegorical interpretation that some make. We see that Jerome, Origen, and other ancient writers did not employ a sufficiently felicitous and helpful method of devising allegories, since they direct everything to manners and works, whereas everything should rather be applied to the Word and to faith. Indeed, they exercised themselves in pure allegories, namely, in the talk of crazy persons. Lest readers be deceived by a false idea in allegories, I reckoned it worth the effort to show them that it is proper allegory when, so far as possible, they discover in every allegory the ministry of the Word or the progress of the Gospel and of faith. For this is the purpose of whatever figures or meanings there are in the Law and the people of Moses.[45]

Luther spotted the concatenation of theological error transmitted historically together with exegetical interpretations. He traced, for example, the idea that Paul in Galatians is speaking only of the ceremonial law from Origen and Jerome through the scholastic doctors to Erasmus, who "doth approve and confirm their error." [46]

Luther was both a preacher and a professor who wrote for the pulpit and the classroom, not just for library shelves. His sermons were heavily loaded with exegesis and his exegesis was weighted with practical application.[47] His primary concern was with the application of justification by faith to the religious life of himself and of his readers. This application gives his exegesis the appearance of a tropological method. He even referred to the tropological meaning as the *sensus primarius scripturae* in his first lectures on the Psalms.[48] But even if Luther's personal application of the text had its prototype in the tropological sense of the Quadriga, his religious insight completely transformed it. If the older method had been a springboard for moralizing, Luther's constant search was for Christ the Redeemer and for the Pauline evangel, without which the Scriptures were to him a hollow shell. The literal sense of the Old Testament was not merely factual and historical, which like Erasmus he rejected as literalism and Jewish legalism, but was the *sensus literalis propheticus*, Messianic in nature. In finding the prophetic sense to be the only literal sense, Luther stood with Lefèvre against Thomas Aquinas and Nicholas de Lyra for whom the actual historical sense was the actual literal sense. His one goal was to find Christ as the essential content of the Scriptures and to make him real and available for judgment and grace.[49] Erasmus, too, has given a Christological interpretation to the Old Testament. Luther differed from him in emphasizing soteriology infinitely more strongly. To him the simple, clear, literal meaning of the text, the historical sense, meant the significance of the text for Christ, the Lord of Scriptures, and for all his works.[50] For Luther, as for Erasmus, the spirit and the letter, the *res* and the *verba*, are distinguishable but inseparable. The words cannot be discarded or neglected without damage to the essence. The Scripture is a queen ruling with authority, "and all ought to obey and be subject unto her. They ought not to be masters, judges, or arbiters, but only witnesses, disciples, and confessors of the Scripture, whether it be the Pope, Luther, Augustine, Paul, or an angel from heaven." [51] Because he was a full-time and professional exegete with vastly greater influence in this field than any of the German humanists and because he pressed for the historical and literal interpretation as a basis for theological exegesis, Luther more than Wimpfeling, Reuchlin, or even Erasmus deserves the title "father of modern exegesis."

In spite of Augustine, Orosius, and Otto of Freising, the Middle Ages had been singularly unhistorical in their orientation. With the coming of the Renaissance, humanists like Petrarch developed a new historical consciousness which had really lain implicit in the Christian view of life, the sense of movement from the midpoint in history, Christ, toward the end of time. Petrarch himself illustrated perfectly in his *Letters to the Ancient Dead* and in his *Letters to Posterity* his sense of distance from the past and the movement from the present to the future. The Renaissance saw progress also from the innocent chronicle to the pragmatic and analytic history of early modern times. The German humanists, through the rediscovery of Tacitus and as a by-product of the rising tide of cultural nationalism which antedated the Reformation by at least a century and a half, developed a keen interest in history and particularly in the history of their own people.[52] Luther shared with the German humanists this lively interest in history.

Luther's concern with history is sometimes depicted as an easy and natural extension of his interest in Biblical history. He felt that an understanding of the Bible required a knowledge of its historical setting. The Protestants sought to discover the hand of God in history and this sharpened their critical faculties concerning the details. They saw the necessity of abandoning the view of history as merely a series of successive events. If the Protestant church was to justify itself historically, it must do so by examining the broad sweep of historical circumstances and the return to historical as well as Biblical sources. Leopold von Ranke is billed as the heir of this tradition which "moves from Luther to neohumanism and on to the romantics."[53] But to see Luther's passionate interest in history only on that level is not to see its full depth in its relation both to humanism and to theology. Luther's writings were full of historical reflections and judgments of particular events and of the entire sweep of history. He shared with the humanists the conviction that history should not be "cold and dead," but should serve a pragmatic purpose.[54] The humanists urged the utility of history as a source of moral examples and vicarious experience. They gave it an important place in the curriculum together with rhetoric and moral philosophy. Luther shared this basically classical pragmatic view of history. For him reason defined the conditions of a moral act, although the inspiration for the truly moral act of regenerate man comes from faith, because the motivating love comes from faith. But in real depth of historical thought Luther went well beyond the humanists, for he sought the inner meaning of history at a much deeper level.

Luther understood the shallowness of much "God in history" thinking, for the desecration of historical existence meant for him precisely that God can not be seen in historical events. In his famous defense of Luther in 1521, Erasmus stated that Luther had taken his whole teaching from Augustine, Bernard, Gerson, and Cardinal Nicholas Cusanus. The fact of Luther's acquaintance with Cusanus, particularly through Lefèvre, could easily lead to a misunderstanding of his concept of God hidden and revealed in history. The *Deus absconditus* of Luther's *theologia crucis* is not the subject of a speculative *theologia negativa* as in the case of Dionysius or of Cusanus. Rather, the God of history is abscondite because he works behind many masks (*larvae*) and he works deviously and by contradictions or antitheses (*a contrario*), not in a straight line and in a detectable manner. There is a hidden aspect and difficult quality precisely in the revelation through incarnation. Just as Christ's humiliation and exaltation, cross and resurrection, are mysterious contrarieties, so God's action in all history is dialectical and profound. It is possible for man to live out his historical life unconscious of or indifferent to the existence of God and without Christ. Life thus lived and history thus understood is secular and desecrated. Secular history must for this reason be distinguished from church history, not from church history in the institutional sense, but from church history as a sacred history, as the history of God's people and as the history of salvation (*Heilsgeschichte*). A knowledge of history is arrived at a posteriori in two ways. A knowledge of historical events, which to the unspiritual man appears to be secular history taking place without God, is arrived at through the historical evidence as studied and interpreted by the best historian, one who is as objective and impartial as possible. A knowledge of sacred history is acquired from Revelation which can be properly understood only by the man whose eyes have been spiritually opened. God's Word reveals the true meaning and content of history. The historian with eyes of faith will see God at work behind history, but this cannot be seen from the historical evidences and in the events themselves. Historical existence has an individual character. It is always new and unique, not cyclical. Man as a cooperator with God and under His will is permitted to make history. Luther's eschatological emphasis gave to historical movement a sense of urgency which is lacking in the humanist historians. But this element in Luther's thought must not be exaggerated to the point of distorting his sense of the development and total sweep of history. Man makes his history under God within the orders of creation subject to natural law as well as to the laws of nature.

Luther, a keen observer, has real insight into the paradoxes of man's historical existence, the discord, the demonic forces arrayed against the constructive contributions of nations, laws, and the great men of history, the "miracle men or sound heroes." In his commentary on Psalm 101 (1534–1535), he wrote:

> Now the world is a sick thing and just the kind of pelt on which neither fur nor skin is good. The healthy heroes are rare, and God provides them at a high price . . . Thus we must continue to be disciples of those speechless masters which we call books. Yet we never do it as well as it is written there; we crawl after it and cling to it as to a bench or to a cane. In addition, we also follow the advice of the best people who live in our midst, until the time comes in which God again provides a healthy hero or a wondrous man in whose hand all things improve or at least fare better than is written in any book.[55]

This emphasis on the individual and personal forces and on the outsized man in history is clearly the same romantic generic type of historical thought common to most humanists. Unlike that retrospective sociologist Machiavelli, the historian Guicciardini emphasized the unique in history, and both pointed to the achievements of the great men, men as well as nations with special *virtú*. Celtis, Wimpfeling, Murner, Hutten, Cuspinian, Peutinger, and the humanist historians as a group shared this view of history with Luther.

As early as Luther's Leipzig debate in 1519 his polemic had taken a historical turn. He was thereafter constantly engaged in the re-examination of church history. Especially in his later years he enjoyed increasingly the study of history and he personally contributed prefaces to a variety of historical works. One of the most interesting of these, because it reflects most of those features of his historical outlook which he shared with the humanists was his *Preface to Galeatius Capella's History* (1538). Capella, state secretary to Charles V, wrote this history of the reign of Francesco II Sforza, Duke of Milan, who played an important role in the wars of Charles V and Francis I. In the *Preface* Luther spelled out many of his characteristic views on history. He informs the reader that historians are most useful people and the best teachers, so that one can never honor, praise, and thank them enough; rulers should support them well. He bewails in tones worthy of Wimpfeling or Celtis that the Germans do not know their own history and do not have the example of their ancestors beyond a thousand years. "We . . . know scarcely anything about our origin," he writes, "except what we must use from histories of other nations, which perhaps must make mention of us out of necessity rather than to their honor." God is everywhere at work in history so that at every point in time there are noteworthy deeds. Heroes are important in the scheme of things. Historians are duty-bound to speak the truth without flattery or prejudice. "But that," Luther concedes, "requires a first-rate man who has a lion's heart, unafraid to write the truth." "Since histories describe nothing else than God's work, that is, grace and wrath," he concludes, "they should . . . be written with the greatest diligence, honesty, and truthfulness." [56]

Luther shared the humanists' patriotism, their classical view of the pragmatic purpose of history, their criticality and theoretical appreciation of objectivity and impartiality. But his strong sense of God's immanence gave to him a deeper sense of the mysterious, inexplicable, unique, and unpredictable nature of history. He was far from the relativity of modern historicism, for if historical relativism can be overcome only by the historian's act of faith in the system of values to which he adheres consciously or unconsciously, then Luther as a man of faith transcended relativism, which added strength if not flexibility to his historical interpretations. Just as he urged the study of history as "philosophy teaching by examples," so he also promoted the study of moral philosophy, giving those classics which were best suited for that purpose a prominent place in the curricula, precisely as Agricola, Wimpfeling, and Erasmus had done.

In his attitude toward literature and the arts Luther shared some of the weaknesses and strengths of the German humanists. His admiration for classical languages was very great and carried over also to Neo-Latin literature. Although in later years he had a low opinion of humanists like Mutian, whom he felt to be lukewarm or indifferent to true religion, he encouraged the younger generation who "must soon stand up and speak out after us." Neo-Latin literature flourished throughout the sixteenth century which produced some of the greatest names in this field. But through his German Bible Luther gave new impetus to the rising ascendancy of the middle and north German vocabulary and accent which created the language of modern German literature. Friedrich Nietzsche in *Beyond Good and Evil* acknowledges that "Luther's Bible was the best German book up to then." It was an achievement of unparalleled importance in German literary history. Reformation letters in the vernacular lacked that form and style so precious to the humanists, but supplied instead the warmth and substance of work contributing to a great cause.

Painting and sculpturing were adversely affected by the Reformation, since the incentive to erect sacred statues and the employment of artists for scenes from the lives of the saints disappeared. The literary humanists from Erasmus on down had showed a peculiar indifference to the great glories of Renaissance art. Luther fits into this general pattern, but more because of his preoccupation with theology than with classical or early Christian literary remains, as was true in the case of the humanists. Luther supported the move characteristic of painting from Giotto on away from the Byzantine etherealization of the Virgin Mary, commenting that to portray the Virgin as completely noble detracted from the reality of the contrast between the glory which Christ left and the lowly unworthiness to which he came. He was opposed to elaborateness and gaudiness for "in human weakness and nothingness God's power is particularly revealed." he once remarked that he wished he could paint on all the houses in Wittenberg "pictures from the Word of God which would help men realize what God has done for us in Christ." He believed that religious paintings are not a kind of fetish or superstition, but rather symbols and a means of proclamation, praise, and thanks through which the church communicates its message to the viewer. Luther appreciated the work of the two Cranachs, of Hans Baldung Grien, and especially of Dürer.[57] He chose Lucas Cranach, one of Dürer's better students, to do the illustrations for his translation of the Bible.

What Luther's gospel meant to Dürer, in turn, can be seen

reflected in his art.[58] "At last I have found certainty!", exclaimed
Dürer when the evangelical message reached him. In 1519 he sank
into a deep spiritual distress, from which the glad tidings of Dr.
Luther rescued him. "If God helps me to see Dr. Martinus Luther,"
he wrote in January or February of 1520, to Spalatin, "I will diligently make his portrait and engrave it as a lasting memory of the
Christian man who has helped me out of great anxieties." From
then on he lived and, as Pirckheimer attested, in 1528 died a "good
Lutheran." Dürer's art reflected this conversion both in subject
matter and in style. An interesting contrast from the point of view
of humanism and the Reformation results from a comparison of his
St. Jerome of 1514 and his St. Jerome of 1521. In the earlier, St.
Jerome in his Cell, the patron saint of the Brethren of the Common
Life and the favorite of Erasmus is sitting surrounded by books and
all the symbols of learning. This was not the ascetic Jerome whom
Lucas Cranach d. Ä. painted in 1502 beating his breast penitently
with a stone. In Dürer's St. Jerome of 1521, done in a Flemish
style, the saint is seated at a table with an open volume on top, three
smaller books underneath the reading desk, an inkpot, and a skull.
A crucifix is the most prominent feature of the background. (See
figure 1 and figure 11) Dürer, even though on the Sacramental
question he leaned toward a Zwinglian position, always appreciated
Luther's defense of religious art against the iconoclasts and radical
reformers.

But the form of artistic expression which has proved to be the
most adequate for the evangelical genius is music. The church of
the Reformation has been a singing church, psalms for some, but
chorales for the Lutherans. The hymnal was one of the earliest and
most original creations of the evangelical church. The hymns in
turn became the predecessors of such musical forms as the cantata,
the oratorio, and the passions. Both the great hymnodist Paul
Gerhardt and the incomparable Bach were inspired by the religious
fervor of the Reformation. The great body of German Protestant
church music owes its being to Luther's love of music and his re-
markably high standards. In a letter to the musician Ludwig Senfl,
written from the Coburg, October 4, 1530, he said that without
any doubt there were many seed-grains of virtue in the human
heart which can be stirred up by music.[59] He was not ashamed to

confess publicly that after theology there was no art for him the equal of music, for music alone, after theology, can do what otherwise only theology can accomplish, namely, quiet and cheer the soul of man. Man reconciled to God through the gospel can best express his new-found joy in life through music.

Luther spoke about music on numerous occasions and had a logical, sincere, and enthusiastic musical philosophy for both daily living and for church purposes. In contrast to Zwingli, whose early humanist love of music was inhibited and restricted after his "evangelical experience" in 1516, Luther appreciated the importance of music for the Christian and for the Christian church. In his *Praefatio in Harmonias de Passione Christi* of 1538, he expressed his wish that music should be praised before all people, since next to God's Word only music deserves to be extolled as the mistress and governess of the human heart. In his famous foreword (*Encomium musices*) to the Wittenberg composer Georg Rhau's *Symphoniae iucundae* . . . (1538) Luther expressed his desire that all Christians should love the gift of music, which is a precious, worthy, and costly treasure given by God to man. He called music the greatest treasure of this world and praised its natural essence as a gift of God's creation, citing the wind, the birds, and the human voice as evidence of God's wisdom and the goodness of nature. He believed congregational singing to be one of the best expressions of the universal priesthood of all believers.

Luther composed some, though he was certainly not a great composer. He encouraged the Protestant princes to support musicians. He enjoyed good secular music, but he disliked the carnal and corrupt songs of his day. Like the humanists Celtis or Johannes Cochläus, Luther associated music and speech very closely. Like them he brought music together with grammar and rhetoric, thus preserving its place in the *trivium*. "The notes bring the text to life," he observed. Although in actual practice he himself was bound to the traditional late Gothic mode, Luther's favorite contemporary composers, Senfl and Josquin, especially the latter, were *avant garde* in promoting the close correspondence of music and the text. Luther stood at the center of the new musical movement which accompanied the Reformation.[60] For him music was not an isolated talent, a special gift or instrument, but a part of that total human culture which was subject to natural man's free will and dominion, and which the regenerate man can embrace and cultivate with the verve and joy of those who can answer with a free conscience before God.

Although Luther in his life and writings gave a historical and theological justification for the aesthetic-literary secular culture of humanism, his own concern was so predominantly theological that he cannot justly be called a humanist. He was, after all, a professor of theology and not a teacher of rhetoric or a city secretary in the technical sense of the word humanist. Beyond that, he was not a Christian humanist in the Erasmian sense, for his evangelical message with its Pauline soteriology reached a deeper level of the Christian faith than did the humanists' program for religious enlightenment. To term Luther a "biblical humanist," while justifiable in a restricted sense, is more apt to mislead than to reveal, for it calls attention to Luther's formal principle but by the same token tends to obscure the essential difference between his religious anthropology and soteriology and that of the humanists. In a phrase reminiscent of the humanists' picture of the rebirth of letters after the "Dark Ages," Melanchthon once remarked that Luther brought Christ and the Apostle from their dark prison into the light again.[61] Luther's program was not merely the imitation of Christ as *homo vere humanus*, the archetype of *humanitas* at its best. Luther's message was one of the boundless love and mercy of God, the forgiveness of sin which He offers to all men, and the reconciliation of all men to Himself through Christ. For him Christianity was no synthesis of learning and revelation, but man's actual life with God. His answer to the decline in the church was to recall the church to its central saving message, Gospel as Gospel, ethic as Christian ethic, truth as redemption. Christianity meant the concrete revelations of God in the historical Christ, the Christ of the Cross, not merely the Christ of the Mount. His religious beliefs had a concrete reality, dynamism, and urgency which the cultural approach of the humanists lacked. He was incomparably more earnest and more effective than they, for he had gotten to the heart of the matter, to the antithesis of law and gospel, sin and grace. Erasmus' *philosophia Christi* owed very much to the patristic writers. In his early theological lectures Luther, too, drew heavily upon patristic exegesis. But later he wrote of the church fathers: "As many as there were, all of them failed either to observe or thoroughly and correctly to understand the kingdom of grace through Christ." [62]

In his great play *Agamemnon*, Aeschylus wrote this classic line, "Suffering is the road to learning; learning comes only through suffering; if you want to learn you have to suffer in order to do your learning." Luther experienced the bitter truth of those words in the course of his soul struggle, but the religious lesson that he learned was to let God be God, and that His mercy endures forever. He learned a lesson regarding man which he once expressed with epigrammatic force in a letter to Spalatin, June 30, 1530: "We should be men and not God. That is the sum of it." For those contemporary German humanists who lacked what Kierkegaard was later to call "a certain strenuousness of mental and moral effort," he had only disdain. The nation, and particularly the men of the younger generation, followed Luther, for he sounded a more certain trumpet. The words which Bugenhagen, a man of no mean classical learning, spoke over Luther's dead body reflected his conviction that there lay not just a professor, a scholar, or humanist, but a prophet: "He was without doubt that angel of God of which the Apocalypse speaks in chapter fourteen — flying in midheaven with an eternal gospel to proclaim to those who dwell on earth . . . This angel said 'Fear God and give him glory!' Those are the two parts of Dr. Martin Luther's teaching, the law and the gospel, through which all of Scriptures are opened up and Christ is known as our righteousness and eternal life."

✦XI✦

CONCLUSION

"A MAN will," Dr. Johnson remarked, "turn over half a library to make one book." The publications, personal correspondence, and private papers of the humanists have provided some insight into their religious mentality and reform programs. It remains now to step back and to ask the right general questions about the meaning of all this. The once heatedly debated issue of the Renaissance as Christian or pagan, never really relevant to the Northern scene, obviously has no meaning at all for German humanism. The humanists were all Christians, in their way, pious, and all had Christian deaths and burials. The two who died without benefit of clergy, Pirckheimer and Erasmus, did not do so by choice but of necessity. The most important questions for religious history are much more difficult to pose. This is necessarily so, for these men lived in a time of tremendous intellectual and spiritual as well as economic and social change. Theirs was a land alive with movements of religious protest and reform. Theirs was a day which first brought to light the tensions between the classical and Christian components of their culture. Theirs was a generation brimming with vitality and creativity, yet tormented and tentative.

The German historian Georg von Below remarked that he believed more had been written on the causes of the Reformation than on the Reformation itself. The question of the origins of the so-called Northern Renaissance has also intrigued historians and has provoked an extensive literature. This study of the leading German humanists sheds additional light upon the more limited problem of the origins of German humanism. The result has been to underline the great importance of the Italian influence upon this generation of humanists, so that the question of origins, so far as formal as well as normative humanism and the classical studies are concerned, is resolved on balance more decidedly in favor of the Southern theory than of the Northern autochthonous development theory. The solution to the North-South debate does not lie at the mid-point between the extremes. The two influences fuse so subtly that a separation necessitates a careful operation, but, as Oliver Wendell Holmes once observed, the difficulty of drawing a line does not absolve us of the responsibility for doing so.

There are many strange parallels in substance between the religious developments in the North, specifically among the Brethren of the Common Life and Reforming Augustinians, and in the South, specifically in the religious tendencies of both the literary and the metaphysical humanists. In Italian humanism there was a tendency toward an increasing inwardness and individualism in religion resulting in a lessening of regard for the church as a hierarchical institution and the spiritualization of the sacraments and of all basically institutional aspects of religion. This personalized religion involved also a stress upon the virtuous life informed by Stoic moralism. This same tendency was evident in the *Devotio Moderna* as well as among the lowland mystics. Thomas à Kempis' *Imitatio Christi*, itself a compound work containing the contributions of a number of religious mystics among the Brethren, was typical of this personalized and spiritualized religiosity and even the final book on the Sacrament stressed a subjectivity foreign to church practice. A reference to the *Theologia Deutsch* or to the Neoplatonic spiritualizing of Wessel Gansfort, whom Luther, however mistakenly, acclaimed in 1522 as a forerunner, should suffice to illustrate this point. Once again, this personalized religion, partly as a reaction to high speculative mysticism as well as to scholasticism underlined the necessity for practical good works and the virtuous life. Secondly, there was a drive back to the pristine sources also of Christian antiquity in evidence in Italy. In theology this meant a return to the church fathers, the Scriptures, including the critical study of the text such as Valla made, and to Christ the Founder. This return was in evidence also in the *Devotio Moderna* where there was the same drive toward the use of the church fathers, a spiritual interpretation of St. Paul, and direct Bible study. Among the German mystics, to cite an example or two, Wessel Gansfort opposed the Scriptures and early fathers, especially

Jerome and Augustine, against the papal decretals. Johann von Wesel declared: "I despise the Pope, the church, and councils; my love belongs to Christ: Christ's Word dwells among us richly!" In these two tendencies toward increased inwardness of religion and the return to the ancient fountains there was a decided parallel between the two sources of religious thought in the South and North. Certainly the one source was not derivative from the other, but was their similarity coincidental?

Both Italian humanism and Lowland mysticism were reactions against the unwholesome condition of religion and the lowly estate of the church in the fourteenth and fifteenth centuries. But both Christian humanism and mysticism were certainly more than mere reactions to the aridity of scholastic theology, the formalism of the sacramental apparatus, or to the power structure of the hierarchical church. They were positive manifestations of that upsurge of religious feeling and seeking which was characteristic of great masses of people during the fourteenth, fifteenth, and sixteenth centuries.[1] Everywhere among the Germans in those decades there was evident an intensified religious fervor and devotion. Whatever explanations the cultural or intellectual historians may give for the phenomenon, it is quite obvious that the devotion of the Brethren and the religious thought of the humanists had their positive as well as their negative motivation.

On one point it is necessary to insist upon a basic difference between the *Devotio Moderna* and Italian humanism and that is in the extent to which they worked for the revival of classical culture as the norm and in their closeness to antique philosophy. The case studies which were presented in the preceding chapters document the far greater importance of the Italian influence. The Brethren favored the use of the safe classics exclusively for edification, and in providing for the early education of a large number of the humanists they may be credited with bringing them this far. But there is a high degree of correlation evident between the extent and intensity of the German humanists' Italian experience, direct or vicarious, and of their enthusiasm for the classics as well as of the ease of their psychic and spiritual adjustment to classical norms and metaphysical notions.[2]

Ernst Cassirer's observation that the philosophy of the *quattro-*

cento was basically theology applies unconditionally to the German humanists of the decades following.[3] The interests of these leading humanists, who were for the most part contemporaries belonging to the high tide of humanism, were very strongly ecclesiastical and religious. Ludwig Geiger's venerable formula must, therefore, be considerably modified, since he divided German humanism into three Comteanesque periods, the first being theological, the second being the scholarly or learned, and the third being a polemical period in which humanism was on the offensive.[4] One is impressed upon studying the humanists individually both with the great variety of cultural and religious types among them and with the many similarities in their cultural postures and religious thought. The present spectral analysis reveals the differences at first glance, but to see correspondences requires a closer look.

No easy clue to the individual differences can be found in the varying social backgrounds of the humanists. Agricola and Erasmus were sons of clergymen, Celtis the son of a peasant, Wimpfeling of an artisan, Hutten of the nobility. Reuchlin and Mutian, Pirckheimer and Luther were either of the old or of the rising bourgeoisie. No doubt the urban middle classes and the town councilors were socially indispensable both to the humanist educational reforms and to the management of the Reformation in the cities, but this fact by itself provides no clue as to why the individual humanists here examined developed as they did in their particular religious and cultural direction.[5] The human spirit is far more sovereign and creative, far more capable of evocative effort, far more open to new intellectual stimuli, and far less bound by social conditioning than most retrospective sociologists can know. The causal nexus in the case of each humanist is so complex, personal, religious, cultural, that no pat formula derived from family background or social milieu will cover the whole range of humanist reform ideas and religious thought. But one very striking sociological factor is the number of laymen like Reuchlin and Pirckheimer who play the theologian. It is as though they wished to say, if the professionals will not address themselves to the pressing issues of the day, then we amateurs must do so. As parties to the rise of lay culture, they had the courage to do so.

It is easy to find broad categories within which to place any

and all of the humanists. One can differentiate the literary humanists from the speculative humanists, the Stoic moralists from the
Neoplatonists, the critics from the systematizers. But within these
broad categories it is possible to isloate distinctive individual types
and in so doing to understand German humanism more concretely
and historically. Thus Agricola has proved to be the exemplar of
those literary humanists with a long Italian experience, but under
no Neoplatonic influence of the Florentine type. Wimpfeling
emerged as the conservative, sumptuary-law, moralistic type. As
such he had critical and reformatory characteristics which could
be found in varying degrees in such conservative humanists as
Heinrich Bebel, Sebastian Brant, the pulpiteer Geiler von Kaisersberg, and even his own foe Thomas Murner. There were variations on this type. Abbot Trithemius was socially so conservative
that he wrote a heated defense of manuscript production over
printing on the grounds that parchment was more durable. He
reverted to the old monastic game of falsifying historical chronicles
and adding oaths to protect the deception. But he played Maecenas
to many humanists and his name is not without justice woven into
the Faust legend.

Reuchlin's religious philosophy was clearly a thing apart, not
to be subsumed under the usual easy general terms like "Erasmian."
It may be argued that he damaged Biblical studies more than he
aided them with the esoteric paraphernalia which he borrowed
from the Cabalists. Nevertheless, his was an independent and manly
effort to cut new cloth and revivify Christianity from new springs
of learning. As a constructive philosopher or theologist he stood
almost alone among the German humanists. Celtis lacked the stern
stuff of which philosophers are made. He is a good example of the
limitations of poetic culture as a resource for religious revival.
Other Neo-Latin poets like Jacob Locher or Eobanus Hessus may
very well be measured against him, not only to determine their
stature as poets but to see what formula they arrived at in relating
poetic culture to the Christian religion. Here the influence of
Baptista Mantuanus needs to be further explored.

Hutten, the Christian knight in armor, was for the most part
negative with respect to the institution and practices of the old
church. As such he was spokesman for a large body of the disaffect-

ed among the classes which were losing their social utility and among the humanists, where a host of lesser figures discovered that it is easier to tear down than to build. Actually, with respect to any positive contribution which German humanism might have made to religious enlightenment, the victory which Hutten and Crotus Rubeanus scored with their *Letters of Obscure Men* was a pyrrhic victory. They won the battle, but lost the war, for their laughter made their enemies irreconcilable and convinced their potential friends that their program was to be taken lightly rather than in great earnest. Luther's comment regarding humanist sallies, that some things are more an occasion for tears than for laughter, represented the feeling of many serious men. His negative reaction to Hutten's militarism and threat of arms was shared by many millions who turned rather to Luther's evangelical way.

As an intellectual patrician Pirckheimer symbolized the contribution of the progressive element in the free imperial cities strung across the empire, as well as the Swiss burgher type which was decisive in the progress and triumph of the Reformation there. It is indicative more of Pirckheimer's personality than typical of all urban councilors that, although he was well ahead in humanist learning, was influenced by German mysticism, actually adopted many important Protestant doctrines and held to them longer than is generally supposed, he finally refused to break with the old church and even defended monastic institutions. The Nuremberg Council, at any rate, passed him by in deciding for the Reformation. Perhaps it was precisely because they were more in earnest about their new evangelical convictions than he was about his humanistic religious speculations.

Finally, if Mutian was almost schizophrenic in his inability to reconcile the antithetical propositions of his philosophy and theology so that he was reduced to inaction, Erasmus all too successfully managed to bridge the gap between Christian and pagan antiquity. His own flexibility and theological superficiality enabled him to transcend the difficulties and, personally well integrated, to become productive, virtually another Petrarch in making a full-scale rediscovery of Christian antiquity.[6] Beatus Rhenanus was only the most important of a whole school of Erasmians who leaned upon the master. Conrad Peutinger, for example, of great importance as a humanist but less interesting in terms of his religious thought, advocated reform measures which might be labeled Erasmian. Peutinger was Augsburg's humanist city secretary and a syndic. A favorite of Maximilian, he became famous as a historian, but seemed to be bound by history and tradition. He was a Reuchlinist, played host to Luther in 1518, corresponded with Oecolampadius, and was an ardent student of patristics. Yet he held back from the Reformation, as did Zasius and many jurists concerned with the preservation of law and order, refused to break with the papal church, and urged all to await the calling of a church council. The humanist authors of the *Eccius dedolatus* dubbed him as changeable as a chameleon.

There were many lesser humanists, the *epigoni*, who might be characterized as Erasmians, but that the Erasmian literary humanist was not the only or even the major type should now be evident. Agrippa of Nettesheim made the *verbum Dei* and not *humana sapientia* the touchstone. He wrote of the vanity of the arts and sciences, but the excellence of the word of God, rejecting the Erasmian *philosophia Christi* and adopted as his motto: *Divina enim humanis viribus non tanguntur*, things divine are not touched by human powers. Agrippa's skepticism was similar to Mutian's conflict of ideals, however, for he was constantly torn between a Faustian drive for knowledge and concern for his soul.[7] Like Hans Denck, Sebastian Franck was distinctively different, fusing Lutheran theology, humanism, and mysticism into a unique amalgam. In Aventine, a student of Celtis, an inner contradiction of romantic and enlightenment tendencies is evident, both a spirit of resignation and of biting reform-directed criticism. German humanism offers a colorful array of individual types, but returning to the leading humanists examined in detail, it is important to inquire as to the common denominators in their religious thought. Was there a distinctively humanist reform movement and did they develop an original constructive theology?

To a man the humanists were sharp critics of ecclesiastical abuses and participated in every reform effort in the decades prior to the Reformation. From Erasmus the priest to Celtis the poet they decried clerical immoralities and concubinage, the decadence and ignorance of the monks and mendicants, avarice and exploitation by the priests and prelates. From Wimpfeling the priest to Hutten the noble they protested in the name of Germania against the tyrannical hierarchy, the spoliation of the land by the Italian courtesans, and even against Rome itself as the hell of all crimes. The satirical writings of Erasmus, his criticisms of celibacy, monasticism, idle ceremonies, and hypocrisy, appealed to the reading public most. Sometimes the humanists' assaults were as exaggerated as they were shrill and humorless.

But did their protests differ from the general late medieval chorus of disaffection? The pulpiteers and pamphleteers had for decades been attacking abuses on all levels. The conciliarists, using a formula created by William Durand, had demanded a "reform in head and in members." The echoes of their outcries against simony, nepotism, and other abuses had reverberated through the century. Each session of the imperial diet issued statements of the *gravamina* or grievances of the German nation against the Curia. The resistance to papal tyranny had ancient precedents. A document at the time of Otto III, around the year one thousand, already referred to the Donation of Constantine as a "great web of lies." Jacopone da Todi and Dante had complained of the earthly tyranny of the popes. Cusanus and Valla had exposed the forged decretals, so that Hutten merely needed to reprint Valla's tract in his paper war against the papal kingdom of this world. During the great schism the epithet "antichrist" had been hurled against the pretenders by partisans of the other candidates so that Hutten did not need to invent it. The humanists were really carried along by the general late medieval stream of protest and reform. Even their romantic cultural nationalism was merely the intensified expression of a tendency developing over the preceding century and a half. What they added differed more in degree than in kind. Their humanist learning assured them of their own cultural superiority and provided an arsenal of new moral ammunition. Lucian in the hands of Erasmus, for example, proved to be a formidable weapon indeed. Thanks to Celtis' sodalities and the cohesion developed during the Reuchlin controversy, the humanists had a sense of solidarity and strength denied to individual reformers of the medieval type. During the final decade before and at the outset of the Reformation the humanists took the initiative and offensive, but their protest and reform program represented no real innovation.

On the other hand, in their quarrel with scholasticism, the humanists did have something new to offer. Positivist historians attracted to laws and patterns in history may find pleasure in the suggestion that the humanist reaction to scholasticism was intellectual history repeating itself. Just as the first period of scholastic theology from the middle of the eleventh to the middle of the twelfth century, which had challenged the Neoplatonic tradition of the early Middle Ages, was followed by Victorine mysticism and twelfth century humanism, so the second period of high scholasticism from the middle of the thirteenth to the middle of the fourteenth century was superseded by Northern mysticism and Renaissance humanism. Similar phenomena may be observed in the case of the Arabic tradition or in Jewish philosophy, where Cabalism was in an antithetical position toward both the Talmudic tradition and Maimonidean Aristotelianism. Perhaps there is something in the human psyche which, after a period of time in which mind and system rule, drives man to the occult, to ecstasy and mystic wonder, to poetry as veiled truth. Wessel Gansfort, as spokesman for the mystics, charged the scholastics with covering over the vibrant heart of Christianity with arid abstractions and dialectical verbiage.

The humanists from Agricola to Erasmus and Luther opposed overdone dialectical training and scholastic theology on many grounds. They criticized scholasticism as harmful to culture, injurious to Latin style, hostile to poetry and the *bonae litterae*, neglectful of natural and moral philosophy, as being precious rather than practical, logical rather than grammatical and rhetorical. To the dialectic of scholasticism, far removed from an experimental foundation, the humanists opposed a religious approach based upon practical moral philosophy, drawing upon the experience and wisdom of men in ancient times, designed to persuade through feeling rather than subdue through logic, relevant to the individual and his needs rather than to universal or generic mankind. It was primarily an inner spirituality which Luther and most of the Northern mystics and humanists had in common. They could all have recited as a chorus Dryden's lines: "Faith is not built on disquisition vain." The humanists did not oppose the *viae* with a metaphysical system of their own. Many representatives of the older generation had been educated in the *via antiqua* and many more of the younger generation in the *via moderna*. But neither did their realist training make the older humanists what they became nor did their nominalist training, with its emphasis on the individual and personality, make the younger humanists what they became. Most of them, including Erasmus neither knew nor respected medieval theology. Reuchlin, like Ficino, gained a great deal from his scholastic studies. But the humanists as a whole, like the reformers, reacted negatively to scholasticism and substituted for its technical speculative theology a kind of lay experiential, revelatory theology, a new approach to the old religion.

The major contribution of the humanists to theology — and here the Northern humanists played a major role — was the rediscovery of Christian antiquity, especially the Greek fathers and the Greek New Testament. There they found *illa prisca theologia*, that ancient theology, which they could oppose to the arid systems of the scholastics. In the *Devotio Moderna* they found the initial modest move in this direction, but they went much further. Agricola preferred the early Christian writers to those of the last dark centuries. Pirckheimer not only favored Bessarion's program for putting the classics into the service of religion but cultivated patristic studies as well. Aquinas drew nine-tenths of his data from Augustine, but Erasmus could exclaim, "One page of Origen teaches me more than ten of Augustine." Luther caught the spirit of the drive to the sources. On May 18, 1517, he wrote with relish to his friend Lang that no students wished to hear lectures on Lombard's *Sentences*, but that if a professor wished to have an audience he must lecture on the Bible, Augustine, or some other church father. At the time of the Leipzig debate he wrote, "It is my custom, on the example of Augustine, of blessed memory, to follow the rivulets all the way to the fountain." [8] Melanchthon called the Leipzig debate a battle of original Christianity with Aristotle. Christianity in the sixteenth century, involved in endless difficulties of its own and confronted with a rediscovered pagan antiquity, was caught in a crisis not unlike that of the third century. The humanists, preeminently Erasmus, turned to the strategists of that first victory for winning counsel. Luther in a desperate personal crisis as well learned to cling to the Author and Fin-

isher of the faith himself. His biblical experience was the rediscovery in Romans that God's righteousness is imparted to man by
grace alone. The Word was for him the proclamation of that ancient theology, the good news of salvation, not a pure source for
religion in general.

The humanists from Agricola to Erasmus, for all their individual differences, shared certain common assumptions about man,
the world, and God drawn from tradition, the classics, and patristics. Boethius was still the ideal philosopher of the early humanists
such as Nicholas von Wyle and Johannes Murmellius.[9] He remained on the scene, but in the background, as Cicero and in his
turn Plato entered to say their piece. Probably no definition of the
highest wisdom, *sapientia*, occurs more often in the works of the
major humanists than that which Cicero gave in his *De Officiis*,
"the knowledge of divine and human things and of their causes."
When the humanists speak of philosophy they mean in the first
instance moral philosophy, best transmitted and instilled through
rhetoric. Rhetoric is a richly formed insight, as Cicero put it,
copiose loquens sapientia. Agricola defined the two parts of philosophy, it will be recalled, as moral and natural. Moral philosophy
is that wisdom gained from philosophers, historians, poets, rhetoricians, and the Holy Scriptures. Wimpfeling was essentially a
moralist. For Reuchlin the road to celestial preferment was primarily ethical. For Celtis philosophy was all of humanist learning.
Hutten's crass moralism was that he who does well fares well. For
Mutian virtue was the essence of true religion. Pirckheimer's
ethical treatises reflected Stoic moralism. Erasmus defined *humanitas* as virtue, morality, and integrity. Whether in the literary
Stoic moralist or in the metaphysical Platonic tradition, the humanists emphasized the primacy of moral philosophy. Also the
more metaphysical humanists recognized that Plato taught the
scientia bene beateque vivendi, the knowledge of how to live well
and blessedly, which forms the basis of piety. This strong emphasis on moral philosophy rather than on purely aesthetic experience
clearly accounts for the continued presence of many nice but dull
medieval authorities longer in Germany than among the Italian
humanists.

In November 1499, Erasmus was John Colet's dinner guest in

Oxford. Seated at the table together with serious theologians the young *poeta*, as he then referred to himself, told a whimsical after-dinner yarn about Cain's agrarian enterprise. Cain had often heard his parents speak of the wondrous plants in paradise. One day he approached the angel guarding the gates and by telling him that on earth dogs had been trained to do such jobs, he misled him into carelessness and then stole seeds from the garden. But when God saw the wonderful products of Cain's farming, he became very angry with him, for He realized what Cain had done. This prome-thean myth symbolized Erasmus' conception of the great natural ability, daring, independence, and resourcefulness of man.

In the *Hyperaspistes* and elsewhere Erasmus rhapsodized ecsta-tically on the infinite resources of the human genius, much to the delight of Rabelais, who quoted him years later. He constantly stressed the liberty of the spirit and the freedom of the will. This sovereignty of the will he extended beyond the natural and ethical realm to the area of Christian faith. Erasmus revealed his theologi-cal uncertainty by alternately speaking of the restoration through grace of original human nature, created good, and of the self-propelled and self-activated human nature capable of fulfilling whatever spiritual task it sets for itself. "What else is the *philoso-phia Christi*," he asks in the *Paraclesis*, "which he himself calls a rebirth, than the restoration of nature created good?" Again, in the *Enchiridion* he declares that "the human spirit has never de-manded anything of itself with vigor that it did not accomplish. A large part of Christianity is to wish to be a Christian with the whole heart." Since Erasmus was writing within the received tra-dition one can perhaps assume that he presupposed at least a measure of antecedent grace, although the passage sounds as hete-rodox as some statements in the *De libero arbitrio*. In this view of man Erasmus saw himself as a descendant of Clement of Alexan-dria, Origen, and Jerome. Origen, Erasmus' favorite Greek father, saw man as a free creature of reason, ἑκούσιον and λογικόν ζῷόν. God's relation to man was not basically one of undeserved love, ἀγάπη but of the divine education of man to be god-like, παίδ-ευσις.[10] With his Stoic-Platonic psychology of the *duplex* and even *triplex homo*, it was almost inevitable that Erasmus should read St. Paul's *Epistle to the Romans* as referring to the battle of the soul and spirit against the flesh as the sensate corporal part of man.

The *Devotio Moderna* had derived from its synergistic medieval ancestry and from its "safe classics" a certain conception of the *dignitas essendi*. For all its self-abnegations, German mysticism contained a strong subjective element. From its medieval Neoplatonic component it derived the conception of the divine essence in man. Manetti and Pico had been the most eloquent admirers of the dignity of man which the Italian humanists nearly all acclaimed in varying degrees. The German humanists with such intellectual ancestry did what they could be expected to do in lauding the grandeur of the human spirit and the "incredible power of the human mind." Antique poetry, Florentine Neoplatonism, and Cabalism in Celtis, Mutian, and Reuchlin developed a more elaborate metaphysical anthropology than is to be found in Agricola or other less philosophical humanists. But their conception of man was that of man as a little god, the mid-point, the microcosm. Man's flesh wars against the spirit, but through the life of virtue spirit can prevail. Man is ethically a free agent and the restoration of his original condition requires only the free development of his individual personal potential. The extent to which the infusion of divine grace is a necessary preliminary and indispensable component varies considerably among the humanists from Wimpfeling to Celtis and often from poem to poem or page to page. On the question of the nature of man, the rhetorical and metaphysical humanists were in essential agreement.

Luther, the reformer, answered very differently the question, "What is man?" He recognized that within the order of creation beauty, truth, and the morally good mirror the Eternal. But the image of God reflected there is external and does not reveal His heart. Luther shared to a larger degree than is often realized the high regard of his age for man's reason, his qualities as the loftiest creature, his learning and natural wisdom. In the world beautiful flowers and pretty butterflies are smiles of the Almighty. But in the realm of religion, man's relation to God, Luther saw man as fallen man, sinful man, whose only exit from this splendid, suffering world is death. The humanists believed in the religious educability of man, but Luther found no divine seed in the soul which he could unfold. He saw man whole, *totus homo*, not as a dualism in which spirit and flesh or soul and body war. Conscience and heart are as much a part of man as reason and the senses. Man as a unitive essence either in an unregenerate state, as flesh, wills and seeks the things of self or as a reborn person, as spirit, wills and seeks the things of God. This spiritual rebirth, which reconciles unworthy man to God, is the work of the Holy Spirit and the forgiveness of sin and reconciliation are a gift of God. Man can not, as Erasmus put it, wish to be a Christian and thus become one. Man first really becomes man when God's deed is done in him. With elemental force, though in elementary language, Luther expounded his position in the catechetical explanation of the third article: "I believe that I cannot of my own reason or strength believe on Jesus Christ my Lord, or come to him. But the Holy Ghost has called me by the gospel, enlightened me with his gifts, sanctified and kept me in the one true faith."

If the humanists preferred to dwell upon the great harmonies of beauty, truth, and goodness in the world and in man, Luther confronted the disharmonies of sin, ugliness, suffering, doubt, and death with a triumphant faith. His dialectic was that, though man's will is bad, God's will is good and his love infinite. Luther's ethic was theonomous. Religion to him was a matter of sin and grace, death and life. He saw spiritual man's life in the world as entirely a service to God and not in the first instance as a development of the individual potential. If Celtis could recommend the life of virtue as security against the fears of hell and others oppose a phrenetically active life against the fear of death, Luther first faced death, saw the Christian triumph over death, and then turned back to see man's life in this perspective. The freedom of the Christian man, he believed, was qualitatively different from the freedom that the study of the arts and sciences bestows.

An interesting counterpoint to this theme of humanist and reformer anthropology is to be found in the melancholy of the humanists, and the soul-struggles (*Anfechtungen* or *tentationes*) of the reformer. The phenomenon of humanist melancholy appears on the individual physchological level already in Petrarch, who suffered all the agonies of *Weltschmerz*, ἀκήδεια. Perhaps this was the price which had to be paid for new and broader cultural horizons. Aristotle had distinguished the higher melancholy of the gifted intellectual from the mean and crude variety. The German humanists in varying degrees suffered this trauma though less intensely than had Petrarch. Ficino had described its anatomy in his *De triplici vita*, where Dürer read of it. Dürer's "Melancholia I" was the only completed artistic portrayal of it. Luther's depressions, in contrast, were due not to a general *malaise de l'univers*, but to his spiritual feeling of unworthiness in the eyes of a righteous God. If religion was an aid to the humanists in making their way through personal crises, for Luther religious faith was the only salvation. Once faith was his, no reason remained for flight from the world, such as flight into antiquity. The Christian is not melancholy. Faith is existential and immediate, not historical and mediated. Nothing prevented Luther's robust acceptance of life, even though the struggle with *Anfechtungen* recurred until his dying day.

The enthusiasm of the German humanists for natural philosophy is of special interest in view of the vehement dispute among present-day scholars over the significance of the Renaissance for the rise of modern science. As in the case of moral philosophy, there is once again a large measure of agreement among the more literary and the more metaphysical humanists on the importance of a knowledge of nature, on cosmology, in the approach to the study of nature, and in the place of natural philosophy within the religious system. Agricola set the pace with his insistence that the knowledge of things human called for encyclopedic learning also about the world of nature. This *cognitio rerum*, knowledge of things, should be acquired both from the books of the ancients and by experience. One should make things one's own possession by the study of the lay of the lands, seas, mountains, rivers, the peculiarities of peoples, the empires, trees, and herbs, and all the things that Aristotle had explored. Though Wimpfeling and Erasmus, the moralists, were least concerned with natural philosophy, the others, like Pirckheimer, were wildly enthused over the Ciceronian program of learning the causes of things, *causas rerum cognoscere*.

Celtis, under the spell of antique-naturalistic philosophy, set as his goal nothing less than learning how to know the inner essence of the universe. Mutian's mystic way had much in common with Reuchlin's cosmology, the *Opus de Breshith*. They adopted a kind of panpsychism, conceived of the universe as a living organism, believed in the animated nature of matter, with powers of attraction and repulsion, the light metaphysic, the complete harmony of macrocosm and microcosm, and the immanence of God and his involvement in the processes of nature. The humanists under the heady influence of Florentine Neoplatonism and Cabalism were intoxicated with the feeling of the unity of the cosmos and the divinity of the natural. Although through an appeal to the creation story, which since the days of the Maccabees had come to mean *creatio ex nihilo*, they managed to preserve the idea of God as transcendent and *ultramundanus*, they came close to becoming involved in the same allegedly pantheistic difficulties which had engulfed their Cusanus.

The natural philosophy of all the German humanists shared certain common features. In the first place, they all began with a priori notions about the world of nature which were derived more from a Platonic than from an Aristotelian cosmology, although their syncretism embraced something of everything. Secondly, their natural philosophy was related to certain medieval scholastic assumptions, such as the notion that matter is seeking its own fulfillment and completion. Thirdly, they proceeded deductively rather than inductively and methodologically never went beyond experience to experiment. In all this they were very traditional. Beyond their poorly directed enthusiasm for the "book of nature" they had little to offer to modern science. Their attempts to control nature sometimes took a completely unscientific turn. One need only think of Trithemius' book of magic, Pirckheimer's fascination with the occult and secret arts, Celtis' preoccupation with astrology, Reuchlin's Pythagorean and Cabalistic formulas, or the fantastic Hermetic world which so intrigued Maximilian and his court circle.

The Neoplatonic theosophy had been present in the stream of Western thought throughout the Middle Ages. The church had limited it dogmatically and had rendered it theologically harmless. In these decades it threatened as a form of lay natural theology to get completely out of hand. The boast of Paracelsus that he was the first really original philosopher was not entirely unfounded. The age was hungry for the power which comes with knowledge and thirsty for fresh springs of the spirit. Next to the moral and spiritual solution of the humanists and the high theological response of the reformers, Paracelsus announced redemption through initiation into the secret formulas of nature. He represented the attempt, as C. G. Jung once observed, to find man's salvation in his harmonious adjustment to the right proportion of things in nature. Like Agrippa of Nettesheim, whose early work *De occulta philosophia* reflected Reuchlin's influence and who sought to unite all secret learning in one grand system, Paracelsus was completely taken by the Renaissance Neoplatonic cosmology. He revealed Reuchlin to be one of his major sources.

The humanists, due in part to their preoccupation with late antique sources and in part to the easy application of the light metaphysic to astral influences, by and large took astrology more seriously than had the scholastics even though it necessarily limited the freedom and dignity of man. Pirckheimer's and Celtis' "yes" to astrology is not so surprising as Reuchlin's qualified "no." Luther, like his spiritual ancestor Augustine, rejected it on theological and experiential grounds. Astrology, he held, with its determinism and stress on secondary causes, militates against the rule of God and the freedom and responsibility of man.

Hutten left the famous Renaissance debate over fate undecided, but he and other humanists were inclined more to the activist solution than to determinism. Luther believed that creation was an arena provided by God for man's responsible action and would have none of the poet's talk of Tyche Fortuna's tyranny. None of them proposed a solution so preposterous as the medieval pseudo-Thomas who ventured to suggest that fate operates through the general agency of the triune God.

Beyond the individual and the cosmos there is God. Besides moral and natural philosophy there is theology in the proper sense of the term. Classical antiquity had produced both an irreligious and a religious form of humanism. Next to the radical anthropocentrism of Protagoras' man the measure, *homo-mensura*, the skepticism of the radical sophists, or the atheism of the atomists, there was also a religious humanism of thinkers like Heraclitus, Parmenides, Plato, Aristotle perhaps, Cicero, and the Neoplatonists. But very naturally no uniform theology in the narrow sense of the word emerged out of classical philosophy. In Christian antiquity the statements about God in Revelation were refined into credal definitions which were designed more to indicate what conceptions of God were not compatible with the Christian understanding of God than to exhaust the totality of what God is in a few brief statements. Christian *traditio* preserved this vision of God as ineffable and his revelation in Christ as a *mysterium tremendum* throughout its long history. Aquinas, the prince of the scholastics, retained a sense of religious awe before the numenous and a feeling of wonder at the incarnation. Undeniably, late medieval theological practitioners, the *epigoni* in the Occamist tradition, tended to make an abstraction of God and reduce Him to a factor in an equation, a symbol in a dialectical proposition. In addition to the general theological uncertainty of the waning Middle Ages, several ecclesiastical developments tended to render God more remote from the experience and direct recourse of the common man. Sacerdotalism implied the interposition of the priest in such a way as to reduce God's immediate religious availability for the individual. The widening gap between laity and clergy and between secular and regular clergy became increasingly damaging to the religious life. Sacramentalism in its caricatured form of a mechanical act efficacious *ex opere operato* reduced the element of personal engagement. The endless multiplication of saints, shrines, and relics erected further intermediate objects between man and his God. On the theoretical and on the practical level the time was ripe for rethinking theology itself.

Once again mysticism and humanism moved in the same direction, this time toward a conception of God as the *deus tremendus et absconditus*. Celtis, Mutian, and Reuchlin took recourse to the *via negativa* in seeking a knowledge of God, whose real nature and essence it is ultimately impossible to understand. They were taken with the idea of God's immanence in nature. God is *duplex*, both far above all things and yet present everywhere. This view of God is clearly generically related to the Neoplatonic theosophy of Dionysius, Cusanus, Ficino, and the Cabala, the same theosophy which recurred in Wessel Gansfort and other mystics in this tradition. Luther found God to be the *deus absconditus sub contrario*, whom he learned to understand only through the paradox that God's righteousness is also his grace imparted to man through Christ. It must be emphasized again that Luther's *theologia crucis* with its recognition of the paradoxical manner in which the revealed God acts has nothing to do with the abscondite nature of God according to Neoplatonic negative theology, nor the incarnation with any generalized theory of His immanence. Zwingli, indeed, fused the Neoplatonic and New Testament picture of God with curious dogmatic results, as in his sacramental teachings. But to associate Luther's theology with the Neoplatonic mystic or humanist theosophy can only lead to misunderstanding. The other major German humanists may all be described as "correct" in their credal statements about God. From their fresh contacts with the fathers humanists such as Erasmus moved beyond static Trinitarian formulas to more dynamic patristic conceptions, a trend evident already in Cusanus.

Near the conclusion of his *Methodus*, Erasmus writes dramatically: "Who teaches Christ purely is the truly great teacher!" Erasmus was himself consistently Christocentric. The same is more or less true of all the German humanists. Their Christian humanism was neither anthropocentric nor undogmatic, but was based upon the *humanitas et benignitas Christi* [Titus 3:4]. Whether moralist or speculative, each, when writing theologically, stressed the unique importance of Christ. Christ seemed to them to be the model or example to be imitated, the archetype of perfect humanity, the "first teacher of the heavenly philosophy," the "author of wisdom," wisdom itself, or the "unique author of right feeling and blessed living." The dogmatic and the sacramental receded into the background, while Christ the teacher of ethics came to the fore. The stress was on piety, spiritual understanding, and devotion. If Erasmian humanism was poor in mystical experience, the speculative humanists compensated for the lack. But Christ remains a spiritual teacher, even when Reuchlin casts him in a cosmological role.

From the point of view of Pauline theology, none of the humanists, including Erasmus, took the incarnation seriously or radically enough. They left to Luther, the *homo religiosus*, the dramatic rediscovery of the historical core of Christianity. If the humanists delighted in the *bonae litterae*, Luther immersed himself in theology, which he called the *meliora studia*, the better studies. He did not do Erasmus justice in the famous letter to Oecolampadius in which he compared Erasmus with Moses, who died in the land of Moab without entering the promised land. And yet, neither Erasmus nor any other Christian humanist compared with Luther as an evangelist of the Word made flesh, the unique self-disclosure of God in Christ. Ecclesiastical institutionalism, mysticism, and moralism tend in different ways to minimize the historical singularity of Christ. Luther struggled free from all three limitations upon the completeness of God's redemptive act in Christ. In his understanding of the incarnation, crucifixion, and resurrection, he was Christological as well as Christocentric. This Christology determined his doctrine of justification through God's grace alone. The person of Christ was important to Luther, not only his teachings and the spiritual qualities which he represented. His death on the cross and the resurrection were as meaningful to him as they were to pristine Christianity and in the same way.

One cannot escape the impression that many "descents from the cross' done by Renaissance artists lament the death of Christ as a hero laid low by the forces of evil. The contrast with the grim agony of Mathias Grünewald's crucifixion scene is always instructive. Again, for the Renaissance artists the resurrection seemed to mean primarily the victory over death, immortality, the transcendence over the natural.[11] The artists illustrated the stress also of the German humanists on the death of Christ as a tragedy and his resurrection as a pledge of immortality. Celtis' doubts about life after death were not final even for him. Luther believed that the theological meaning of both the cross and the resurrection lay at a much deeper level. Luther saw Christ's death on the cross as the divine sacrifice of reconciliation. The resurrection demonstrated the all-sufficiency of the satisfaction for man's sin won by Christ's death. It was not the resurrection as a symbol of immortality, but the encounter of the risen Lord with his disciples which was central for Luther. First in order is the reconciliation with God and from this follows the gift of eternal life. "For," he wrote in the small Catechism, "where there is forgiveness of sins, there is also life and salvation." Celtis, Mutian, Pirckheimer, and Reuchlin, drawing upon Platonic sources could celebrate *Eros* as that divine love which is the bond of the whole universe. Luther proclaimed *Agape*, that undeserved love which God bestows upon man, a love which proceeds from that boundless mercy which endures forever.

The humanists' criticism of ecclesiastical ceremonies and sacramentalism was based on genuine religious considerations. It was a truly skeptical streak in Celtis that made him doubt the reality of transubstantiation. But the general objection of Mutian and the rest was to the externalization, crass formalism, and mechanical performance without personal religious involvement. They wished to respiritualize the sacraments, for, said Mutian, the essence of the sacrament is love. Luther's criticism and correction ran parallel to that of the humanists. But his sacramental teaching was once again more Christological. Not only was the Sacrament of the Altar a sweet and mystic communion with Christ, but the very Word of promise made of the Sacrament itself a means of grace. The Sacrament for him was not a symbol, as Zwingli the humanist reformer understood it, but a real communion with Christ, who is truly present.

The assertion of the absolutely unique historical role of Christ more than any other single consideration kept Luther from approving humanist theories about natural religion. The humanists drew on two main sources in developing universalist theses. The one source was the Alexandrine fathers, especially Clement's apologetic argument that the wisdom of the ancients had been a *praeparatio evangelica* and Justin Martyr's theory of the inspiration of ancient philosophers by the Spermatic Logos. The other source was Florentine Neoplatonism, not Italian literary humanism, for there is no good evidence of real religious universalism among the Italian humanists before Ficino. Cusanus represented a late medieval spiritualism which tended toward universalism. He wrote a treatise on the one true religion in a variety of rites, but he gave the Christian religion absolute primacy. All other religions must coincide with it to the extent to which they wish to meet the demands of reason. He reserved only religious questions of secondary or tertiary importance to the realm of *varietas*.[12] Dante was more typical of the medieval point of view for he put the noble ancients into the limbo. Medieval theology had developed the notion of the "beautiful bond of the light of nature and of grace," which served as a good point of departure for the theology of the humanists.

In stressing moral philosophy, good practical Christian living, and personal religious experience, thereby weakening the hold of dogma and priesthood, the *Devotio Moderna* and mysticism reduced the absoluteness of the received tradition and threatened the religious monopoly of the medieval church. They thereby indirectly contributed to a greater receptiveness toward universalism. There was no universal theism in Agricola, Wimpfeling, Hutten, or even in Pirckheimer, who asserted that the highest level of theology does not need ancient philosophy and is open to all without the benefit of Plato and Aristotle. The case of Erasmus is more complicated than that of the others. His attitude suggests that the direction of Northern piety may have been toward a conditional universalism, for he was personally not given to metaphysical speculation and had only circuitous connections with the Florentine doctrine on this subject. Erasmus was very much in earnest with his references to the divine inspiration of the *vera philosophia* of Socrates, Plato, Cicero, and Seneca. Nevertheless, he always assigned preeminence to Christianity on the grounds of revelation. When the Reformation was well under way Erasmus vigorously denied ever having equated pagan philosophy and Christian theology.

The evidence of religious relativism and conditional universalism is more obvious in the case of those German humanists like Celtis, Reuchlin, and Mutian who were affected by the *Theologia Platonica*. Celtis, writing at times with an almost Wagnerian flourish offered primitive Teutonic religion as an alternative to corrupt Christianity. The idea of the noble savage, like that of the sufficiently wise pagan philosopher, introduces an element of religious relativism. Reuchlin's association of the Cabalists' Messiah with the Johannine Logos, his image of this Messiah as revealer rather than redeemer, his emphasis on gnosis rather than on atonement put a non-Christian source and mystic knowledge at the side of revelation and grace. Mutian was really echoing Ficino with his sentences about the spiritual nativity of Christ before all ages and the inspiration of the philosophers through this pre-existent Logos.

Mutian once posed the following question to Georg Spalatin, who later became a close associate of Luther and a prominent reformer, "If Christ is the way, the truth, and the life, how then were people saved before the birth of Christ?" [13] If Mutian, Erasmus, or, for that matter, Zwingli, could with ease appeal to the patristic theories, Luther was as restrained as the Scriptures on this point. He began a university disputation with this problem in 1542 and, using Hebrews 13:8 (Jesus Christ is the same yesterday and today and for ever) as the basis, he related it to the doctrine of justification by faith alone.[14] Unlike the more metaphysical humanists, the reformer held that the Scriptures teach that those who lived before the time of Christ were saved by faith in God's promised seed, and that all theories as to the inspiration and salvation of the noble pagans are speculations about matters on which the Word has not enlightened us. Luther allowed a place for natural theology, but he distinguished sharply between the natural knowledge and the saving knowledge of God. What God is really like can be known only through his self-disclosure in Christ, which was an offence to the Greeks as well as a stumbling block to the Jews. Luther's biblical realism was a thing apart from humanist idealism. There was no hint of relativism in Luther's reply to Erasmus: "The Holy Spirit is not a skeptic!," nor in his catechetical refrain: "This is most certainly true!"

The humanists obviously did not develop a total *Weltanschauung* independent from the Catholic and Reformation view of life. But it is evident that there was a nascent tendency toward that absolutizing of culture which in its first phase of development set culture up as an area of primary concern and in its second phase of development subsumed religion itself as a part of general culture. This tendency reached its culmination in the secular Enlightenment, when religion was even abused by some savants as being antithetical to culture, a thing to be crushed. The humanists placed an independent, human, classical culture next to the medieval ecclesiastical culture. They thereby created the possibility of a shift in categories, which Aristotle would call a μετάβασις εἰς ἄλλο γένος. Culture might become a substitute for religion or a religion itself. The German humanists, except for Celtis now and then, or Mutian, escaped this form of deviation. They all had an undeniable inclination, however, in utilizing non-Christian sources, in spiritualizing and moralizing, in personalizing religion, to free religion from the historical restrictions imposed by dogma and the old forms of church life. This inclination was complemented further by their sharp and all too justified criticisms of conditions in the church. The historical situation was such that even Christocentric Erasmian spiritualism, to say nothing of the more radical Neoplatonism, could become dangerous to orthodoxy.

Erasmus' stress on things invisible, on the spirit which maketh alive, could lead the less cautious and conservative to make things visible either of secondary importance or of no importance at all. Carried to this extreme the incarnation, the Scriptures, the sacraments, the visible church on earth, the material basis of Christianity might no longer be taken seriously. During the Enlightenment John Solomon Semler, sometimes called the "father of German rationalism," asserted that "everything which the newer theology has painfully won for itself was already to be found in the great and admirable Erasmus." Thinking historically was not a strong point with the men of Enlightenment. Semler was wrong, and yet it is easy to see how he could read Erasmus according to his own lights. Semler was not entirely wrong.

A number of reasons may be suggested why German humanism failed to develop into a major historical force. The easiest, most common, but least satisfactory, explanation is that it was an aristocratic movement which could not reach the masses as did the evangelical Reformation. Ideas can filter down and become historically effective even in an altered form. A second reason was the lack of an economic or social base for humanism. But humanism was more widespread in the princely and ecclesiastical courts than has up to now been held by historians. This argument is also not so convincing as it might seem on first glance in view of the fact that the Reformation won all classes of people. More cogent is the intellectual and spiritual consideration that the religious renaissance of the humanists failed to develop or to rediscover a theological principle which could serve as a weapon in assaulting the work-righteousness which lay at the root of many, if not most, of the worst abuses in need of reform. The religion of humanism was itself too moralistic and synergistic to be religiously radical. As Jacob Burckhardt once observed, "to seek good works is only natural for man." Reform required a superhuman effort. A fourth and even more subtle reason is that German humanism was pulling in two different directions, tending to cancel out its own gains. There was the inclination in men as much alike as Agricola and Erasmus to the reasonable, the humane, the measured, the logical, the learned, the methodological, the wise, the witty. On the other side, there was the inclination in men as different as Reuchlin and Celtis to the mysterious, the transcendent, the occult, the ecstatic, the theosophic, the enigmatic, the luminous, the enthused (Plato's ἔνθεος). In spite of the many areas of correspondence in the anthropology, cosmology, and theology of the humanists, they were unconsciously tugging in two culturally divergent directions, a conflict never resolved. Finally, humanism failed to satisfy the deepest longings of the people for a religious renewal coming from the heart of Christianity. Really deepening the religious dimension was left to Luther, a prophetic type.

The Reformation was a young man's movement. It is almost possible to say that without the younger generation of humanists there could have been no Reformation. Certainly there would not have been a Reformation such as the one that did take place. The rejection of the Reformation by many of the older humanists was neither simply a dismissal of renewed Christianity by enlightened humanists nor simply hostility to radical religious change by men of a medieval mentality. The motives were in each case mixed, but the basic reason was their commitment to a program of ecclesiastical and religious renewal not inwardly compatible with the basic theological emphases of the Reformation. The old church, conversely, knew very well why it kept them in the fold, while expelling Luther. The younger humanists, less conditioned by long habit and emotional attachment to the familiar or moderate, but with a thorough intellectual appreciation of the new wealth of classical culture, turned to the renewed evangelical faith which satisfied their need for an ecclesiastical reform effort and for a more intense inner religious certainty.[15] In 1517 Luther was only thirty-four years old. All of his Catholic opponents excluding Eck were older than he, and almost all of his followers were younger. Most of the reformers were thirty years of age or younger. The new University of Wittenberg had the youngest faculty in Europe. Each year humanists were becoming increasingly important in the city councils, in chancelleries, in princely and ecclesiastical courts, strategic power centers during the Reformation struggle. These young humanists became activists, for they learned from Luther that the liberty of the Christian man means that, having received God's pardon for sin, he is free for action in the church and in society. It is astonishing to see how many of the younger humanists, *sodales* of Mutian, Hutten, Reuchlin, and Celtis, as well as many young Erasmians, changed their professions to take up theology and enter the parish ministry. In the year of the Augsburg Confession (1530) the leading two dozen intellectual leaders of the young church were young humanists turned reformer, from the precocious Melanchthon on down. It is also true beyond Germany that the reformers almost to a man came from the ranks of the young humanists. One need only think of Vadian, Zwingli, Servetus, Oecolampadius, or Calvin.

What became of their classical humanism as form and norm when they turned to serve the evangelical church? They kept the program of classical studies, which has remained the basis of the *gymnasium* curriculum down to the present day. Many of them also brought along those moralizing and spiritualizing tendencies characteristic of German humanism. The result was a gradual reversion in later years to synergism and a spiritualized view of the Sacrament, so that both Luther's teaching on justification and of the real presence in the Sacrament encountered resistance due in no small part to the early conditioning of many churchmen in the religious thought of the German humanists. The leaven of humanism in the Catholic church, continued also there by a younger generation, could be seen at work in the first session of the Council of Trent where humanist theologians with conciliatory inclinations kept discussions sufficiently open to allow a dialogue with Protestants to continue for a while. The Jesuits continued the classical tradition in secondary education. If Protestantism really appropriated humanist learning and brought it into the culture of the people, the Catholicism of the younger generation was more successful in fusing humanism and scholastic theology than had been that of the older generation. They used it in the Counter Reformation.

Luther rejected the Renaissance synthesist solution of the problem of religion and culture. He was a conversionist who insisted that faith active in love must change human society and culture. He clarified the theological picture by commissioning regenerate man to build a truly Christian culture as a work of love, not as an exaltation of self nor as a work of justification before God. Faith alone first makes man whole. Only the man who has been spiritually restored can build a wholesome, that is, a God-pleasing culture. Though many young humanists left the university to serve the church, Luther remained a university professor and, as he once put it, "sent out his books into all the world."

NOTES

I INTRODUCTION

1. Wilhelm Dilthey, "Auffassung und Analyse des Menschen im 15. und 16. Jahrhundert," *Gesammelte Schriften*, II (Leipzig, 1923), 1–89.

2. Johannes Janssen, *Geschichte des deutschen Volkes seit dem Ausgang des Mittelalters*, 8 vols. (Freiburg i. B., 1879–1894).

3. Paul Joachimsen, "Der Humanismus und die Entwicklung des deutschen Geistes," *Deutsche Vierteljahrsschrift für Literaturwissenschaft und Geistesgeschichte*, VIII (1930), 419f. Werner Näf, "Aus der Forschung zur Geschichte des deutschen Humanismus," *Schweizer Beiträge zur Allgemeinen Geschichte*, II (1944), 214, called Joachimsen's definition the first clear formulation of the concept of humanism and observed that discussion of the conceptual problem has since its publication very much subsided.

4. Heinrich Hermelink, *Die religiösen Reformbestrebungen des deutschen Humanismus* (Tübingen, 1907).

5. Gerhard Ritter, *Studien zur Spätscholastik*, 2 vols. (Heidelberg, 1921–1922); *Die Geschichte der Heidelberger Universität*, I, *Das Mittelalter, 1386–1508* (Heidelberg, 1936). In a brilliant study of late medieval thought entitled significantly *The Harvest of Medieval Theology* (Cambridge, Mass., Harvard University Press, 1963), Heiko A. Oberman sees the theology of the closing centuries of the Middle Ages as the fruition and culmination of the preceding centuries in many respects, not as the dregs of a better age or denouement following the climax of the thirteenth century, the pattern familiar from the works of Étienne Gilson and other medievalists.

6. Gerhard Ritter, "Romantische und revolutionäre Elemente in der deutschen Theologie am Vorabend der Reformation," *Deutsche Vierteljahrsschrift für Literaturwissenschaft und Geistesgeschichte*, V (1927), 342–380, especially 373ff. On Wessel's influence on German humanism, see Dr. M. Van Rhijn, *Wessel Gansfort* ('S-Gravenhage, 1917), pp. 248–263: Wessel's Invloed.

7. The most recent study of the religious side of Italian humanism is Michael Seidlmayer, "Religiös-ethische Probleme des italienischen Humanismus," *Germanisch-Romanische Monatsschrift*, N.F. VIII (1958), 105–126. See also August Buck, "Das Problem des christlichen Humanismus in der italienischen Renaissance," *Sodalitas Erasmiana*, I, *Il Valore Universale Dell' Umanesimo* (Naples, 1949), pp. 181ff. For detailed bibliography on this whole question, see Carlo Angelieri, *Il Problema Religioso del Rinascimento. Storia della critica e bibliografia* (Florence, 1952), especially pp. 178ff.

8. Henry Hart Milman, *History of Latin Christianity*, VIII (New York, 1871), 287: "the age to end in direct rebellion, in the Italian philosophers, against Christianity itself."

9. *Opera*, II, 1438, cited in André Chastel, *Marsile Ficin et l'art* (Geneva, 1954), p. 15.

10. See the brief study, Lewis W. Spitz, "The *Theologia Platonica* in the Religious Thought of the German Humanists," *Middle Ages-Reformation Volkskunde. Festschrift for John G. Kunstmann* (Chapel Hill, 1959), pp. 118–133, used here by permission of the publisher.

11. See, e.g., the recent studies by Giuseppe Saitta, *Nicolò Cusano e L'Umanesimo Italiano* (Bologna, 1957).

12. Ludwig Geiger, ed., *Johann Reuchlins Briefwechsel* (Tübingen, 1875), ep. 238, p. 269. On Vergenhans, Prenninger, Biel, and Reuchlin, see Johannes Haller, *Die Anfänge der Universität Tübingen 1477–1537* (Stuttgart, 1927), pp. 14ff., 143ff., 153ff., 239ff. Henri Johan Hak, *Marsilio Ficino* (Amsterdam, 1934), pp. 143–153, documents in detail Ficino's many personal contacts with the Germans. See also Raymond Marcel, *Marsile Ficin (1433–1499)* (Paris, 1958), pp. 534ff., L'Europe a l'école de Ficin.

13. *Epistolae, liber* V, fol. 783: Ego certe malo divine credere, quam humane scire. Giuseppe Saitto, *Il Pensiero Italiano nell' Umanesimo e nel Rinascimento*, I (Bologna, 1949), 509ff., presents a high idealist interpretation of the *religio docta*.

14. Ivan Pusino, "Ficinos und Picos religiös-philosophische Anschauungen," *Zeitschrift für Kirchengeschichte*, XLIV, N.F. VII (1925), 504ff., perhaps overemphasizes the universalist element but it is clearly there. Cf. *Marsilii Ficini Florentini, insignis philosophi Platonici, Medici atque Theologie clarissimi, Opera*, etc. (Basel, n.d.), p. 98: "Unity, truth, goodness are the same, and beyond these there is nothing."

II   AGRICOLA — Father of Humanism

1. Nichols, Francis M., ed., *The Epistles of Erasmus*, I (New York, 1901), 20; II (New York, 1904), 165, 609; Erasmus regrets the long delay in the publication of his works. Erasmus, *Opera*, I (Leyden, 1703), front matter, Letter to Joannus Botzhemius: Rodolphus Agricola primus omnium aurulam quandam melioris litteraturae nobis invexit ex Italia, quem mihi puero ferme duodecim annos nato, Daventriae videre contigit, nec aliud contigit.

2. Erasmus, *Dialogus cui titulus est Ciceronianus* (Basel, 1529), p. 169, where the sentence is spoken by Nosoponus, the author's protagonist at this point. Cf. also *Adagia*, 339, *Quid cani & balneo, Opera*, II, cols. 166f.

3. *Corpus Reformatorum*, XI, cols. 439ff., hereafter referred to as *CR*, with the volume and column number following.

4. Alard II, 215f., To Brother John, July 23, 1484: Difficile est mihi seruitutem discere iam increscente aetate . . . *Rudolphi Agricolae Phrisii De inventione dialectica libri omnes et integri & recogniti, etc., per Alardum Aemstelradamum* (Cologne, 1539), will be referred to simply as Alard with the volume and page number following.

5. Alard II, 178f., Agricola to Langen, Oct. 26, (1470?): Aude sapere ita ut facis, et quamvis magnam indoctorum manum aude contemnere. Nihil te multitudo mouerit . . . Agricola flattered Ercole, duke of Ferrara, and Galeazzo Maria at Pavia in the conventional manner. References to the *vulgus* are common in Agricola. Friedrich von Bezold, *Rudolf Agricola, ein deutscher Vertreter der italienischen Renaissance* (Munich, 1884), in a sparkling essay depicted Agricola's personality. Paul Joachimsen, "Loci

Communes," *Lutherjahrbuch*, VIII (1926), 27–97, overvalues his importance for the Heidelberg reform effort and gives Agricola's ideas too profound a meaning.

6. Alard II, 184, To Brother John: Itaque malui adhuc retinere quietem meam, et in libertate hac permanere. Alard II, 208, To James Barbirian, March 27 (1482): Quid ergo? Libera studijs quies . . .

7. Alard II, 181, To Johannes Reuchlin, Feb. 4 (1485): Ipse quoque in priori aetate id facturum me destinaueram, sed postea quam iam incepi diligentia me ipse introspicere, auersus sum ab eo consilio . . . sed deterruit me potius genus uitae meae.

8. *Vita Petrarchae illustrata per eruditissimum virum Rudolphum Agricolam Phrisium ad Antonium Scrofinium Papiensem. Anno salutis 1477* (*1473*) *Papiae*, Ludwig Bertalot, "Rudolf Agricolas Lobrede auf Petrarcha," *La Bibliofilia*, XXX (1928), 382–404. See Johannes Janssen, *Geschichte des deutschen Volkes*, I (Freiburg i. B., 1897), 50ff. Ludwig Geiger describes the *Declamatio* in the *Zeitschrift für Kulturgeschichte*, N.F. III (1874), 224. See also L. Geiger, "Die erste Biographie Petrarcas in Deutschland," *Magazin für die Literatur des Auslandes*, XLII (1873), 613f. J. Lindeboom, "Petrarca's Leven, Beschreven door Rudolf Agricola," *Nederlandsch Archief voor Kerkgeschiedenis*, XVII (1924), 81–107, edited the text of the *Vita* with a brief summary of the contents. Theodore E. Mommsen, "Rudolph Agricola's Life of Petrarch," *Traditio*, VIII (1952), 367–386, discusses the manuscript, texts, literary predecessors and sources, scholarly value, and special emphases.

9. In a letter of 1489 Erasmus cited the men who in his German fatherland seemed to represent true culture and eloquence, Alexander Hegius, Rudolf Agricola, Antonius Lieber, Rudolf von Langen, Friedrich Morman, Bartholomäus von Köln, Wilhelm Herman; P. S. Allen, *Opus Epistolarvm Des. Erasmi*, I (Oxford, 1906), 105–107, ep. 23. Of this group nearly no one can compare with Agricola in his appreciation for antique culture. P. S. Allen's edition of Erasmus' correspondence will hereafter be referred to as Allen, *Epistolae*, with the volume, page, and letter numbers following.

10. The best modern biography is that of H. E. J. M. van der Velden, *Rodolphus Agricola (Roelof Huusman) een nederlandsch Humanist der vijftiende Eeuw* (Leiden, 1911). The four earliest sources of biographical material, besides Trithemius' brief notice, Alard II, intro., are: 1. Dietrich von Pleningen's biography, Württembergische Landesbibliothek, *Cod. Poet. et Philol.*, no. 36, published by Franz Pfeifer, *Serapeum*, X (1849), 97–113; 2. Gerhard Geldenhauer's *vita* for Johannes Fichardus' *Viri Illustres* (Frankfort, 1536); 3. Melanchthon, *Epistola ad Alardum*, Alard II, CR, III, cols. 673–676, and *Oratio de vita Rodolphi Agricolae Frisii*, presented in 1539 in Wittenberg, ed. C. G. Bretschneider, *Philippi Melanthonis Opera, Corpus Reformatorum*, XI (1843), cols. 439ff.; 4. Wiener Nationalbibliothek, Hs. 9058: *Vitae Weszeli Groningensis, Rodolphi Agricolae, et Erasmi Roterodami hactenus non vulgatae*, presumed to be the letter of Goswin de Halen to Melanchthon in reply to his request for information, although the absence of certain materials contained in Melanchthon's essays and of positive evidence makes this identification somewhat uncertain; published in I. B. Kan, *Erasmiani Gymnasii Programma Litterarium* (Rotterdam, 1894). The

three main sources for Agricola's correspondence are: Peter Gilles, ed., *Rodolphi Agricolae Opuscula* (Louvain, 1511); Alard II, *Lucubrationes*; Karl Hartfelder, ed., "Unedierte Briefe von Rudolf Agricola," *Festschrift der Badischen Gymnasien* (Karlsruhe, 1886). P. S. Allen, "The Letters of Rudolf Agricola," *English Historical Review*, XXI (1906), 302–317, orders the letters chronologically.

11. There is no verification for the old tradition that Agricola studied with Thomas à Kempis at Zwolle, Adolphe Bossert, *De Rodolpho Agricola Frisio Litterarum in Germania restitutore* (Paris, 1865), p. 10. Of little value is the naive pioneering biography of Tjalling P. Tresling, *Vita et merita Rodolphi Agricolae* (Groningen, 1830). Georg Ihm, *Der Humanist Rudolf Agricola, sein Leben und seine Schriften* (Paderborn, 1893), while containing some factual errors, includes an anthology of some of Agricola's best passages.

12. J. C. Hermann Weissenborn, ed., *Acten der Erfurter Universität*, III. Theil (Halle, 1899), 174, 255, no. 15. There is no documentary evidence of the granting of his A. B. degree.

13. A. Polet, "Les Origines et les Débuts de l'Humanisme à l'université de Louvain," *Les Études Classiques*, VI (1937), 28ff., relates the appointment of the first rhetorician in 1444 and the subsequent fortunes of the classics at Louvain. Melanchthon recounts that, at Louvain, Agricola preferred reading good books to the study of traditional philosophy, *CR*, XI, col. 440. Plenningen wrote: . . . cui ne deesset Lovanium ad litteratorum conventum laudatissimum profectus est; Pfeifer, *Serapeum*, X, 101.

14. Hermann Keussen, ed., *Die Matrikel der Universität Köln 1389 bis 1559*, I (Bonn, 1892), 517: 292. rector, no. 62, May 1462.

15. Hartfelder, "Unedierte Briefe," ep. 2; Allen, "Letters of Rudolf Agricola," *E. H. R.*, XXI, 310, ep. 2, To John Vredewolt, winter [1469?], Pavia.

16. Melanchthon, *CR*, XI, col. 441. The three occasions were the rectorship of Matthias Richilus in 1471, Alard II, 138ff., of Paul von Bänst in 1473, and of Johannes von Dalberg, July 1474. On Agricola and Dalberg, see K. Morneweg, *Johann von Dalberg* (Heidelberg, 1887), pp. 29–41, 44–46, 60–63, 79–103, 351–353.

17. Alard II, 187–191; Allen, "Letters of Rudolf Agricola," *E. H. R.*, XXI, 312, ep. 21, To Alexander Hegius, Sept. 20, 1480, Groningen.

18. Alard II, 208; Allen, "Letters of Rudolf Agricola," *E. H. R.*, XXI, 313, ep. 29. To J. Barbirian, Nov. 1, 1482 (Cologne).

19. *CR*, XI, col. 442. Horawitz and Hartfelder, eds., *Der Briefwechsel des Beatus Rhenanus* (Leipzig, 1886), pp. 61f., ep. 36, Beatus Rhenanus Io. Rusero Novientano, Schlettstadt, Feb. 18, 1514; Rhenanus recalls Agricola's preoccupation with Pliny.

20. Alard II, 215f.; Allen, "Letters of Rudolf Agricola," *E. H. R.*, XXI, 314, ep. 39, To John Agricola, July 23, 1484, Heidelberg.

21. Alard II, 178; Allen, "Letters of Rudolf Agricola," *E. H. R.*, XXI, 310, ep. 3, To Rudolf von Langen, Oct. 26 (1470?), Ziloe.

22. Alard II, 177; Allen, "Letters of Rudolf Agricola," *E. H. R.*, XXI, 314, ep. 37, To Antonius Vrye, April 7, 1484, Deventer.

23. Alard I, 179; II, chap. 1., 180: . . . Istam uero miseram & cauillosam

loquendi solicitudinem, quam tu doces, certum est, non modo reliquis artibus discendis non prodesse, sed etiam obesse plurimum. *De Formando Studio*, Alard II, 194: Plerique etiam loquaces has, et inani strepitu crepitantes, quas ulgo artes iam vocamus, sibi uendicant . . .

24. In the *Exhortatio ad clerum wormatiensen*; Stuttgart ms., *Cod. Poet. et Philol.*, no. 36, fol. 186.

25. *CR*, XI, col. 442; Alard II, intro., letter of Melanchthon to Alard.

26. Alard I, 41; 37–41. Justus Velsius edited a separate edition of Agricola's comments, *Rodolphi Agricolae Phrisii eximia de universalibus disputatio* (Antwerp, 1543).

27. Alard II, 193–201, text; Allen, "Letters of Rudolf Agricola," *E. H. R.*, XXI, ep. 38, May 26, 1484, Heidelberg. The best treatment of Agricola's significance for education is still William H. Woodward, *Studies in Education during the Age of the Renaissance 1400–1600* (Cambridge, 1906), preferable to Karl Hartfelder's older *Erziehung und Unterricht im Zeitalter des Humanismus* (Stuttgart, 1889).

28. In the rectoral address for J. von Dalberg, July 1474, Agricola associated philosophy with the arts of justice and equity, Stuttgart codex, folios 328 and 328ᵛ.

29. Hain, no. 8128.

30. Alard I, 1–461. It even rated an Italian translation, *Rodolfo Agricola Frisio della invention dialettica; tradotto da oratio Toscanella della Famiglia di maestro lvca Fiorentino* . . . (Venice, 1567). Another interesting edition is *Rodolphi Agricolae Phrisij de inventione dialectica libri tres, cum scholijs Ioanni Matthaei Phrissemij* (Cologne, 1523), in which the editor defends Agricola vociferously against all who say his work contained nothing which was not to be found in Petrus Hispanus. The work was adapted to student purposes in the *Epitome commentariorum Dialecticae inuentionis Rodolphi Agricolae per Bartolomeum Latomum Arlunensem* (Cologne, 1530). By far the most excellent analysis of Agricola's "place-logic" is that of Walter Ong, S.J., *Ramus, Method, and the Decay of Dialogue* (Cambridge, Mass., 1958), pp. 92–130. Ong assesses Agricola's position and unique importance in the dialectical tradition, comparing his work with the *Summulae logicales* of Petrus Hispanus, and describing his great contribution to Ramism. See pp. 94–96 on Agricola's influence also in France and England. In a second work, *Ramus and Talon Inventory* (Cambridge, Mass., 1958), pp. 534–558, Ong supplies a preliminary short title check list of some printed editions and compendiums of the *De inventione dialectica*. Neal W. Gilbert, *Renaissance Concepts of Method* (New York, 1960), pp. 117 *et passim*, places Agricola's work within the general context of Renaissance discussions of method.

31. Alard I, 2. Valla, D. D., preface to the first book.

32. August Faust, "Die Dialektik Rudolf Agricolas," *Archiv für die Geschichte der Philosophie*, XXXIV (1922), 118–135. Carl Prantl, *Geschichte der Logik im Abendlande*, IV (Leipzig, 1870), 167ff., discusses Agricola's conception of logic as dialectic, in the "manner of the sophists." For criticisms of scholasticism, cf. Alard I, 17, 180. Paul Joachimsen, "*Loci communes*. Eine Untersuchung zur Geistesgeschichte des Humanismus und der Reformation," *Lutherjahrbuch*, VIII (1926), 27–97, analyzes Melanchthon's

use of *Loci* in theology and relates this to Agricola and Erasmus' use of *Loci* or τόποι in rhetorical dialectic.

33. *Rodolphi Agricolae Phrisij de inuentione dialectica libri tres, cum scholijs Ioannis Matthaei Phrissemij* (Cologne, 1523), 78, 149, presents tables collating the topics of Agricola with those of Cicero and Themistius and the terminology on syllogisms in Agricola, Aristotle, Cicero, Quintilian, and Boethius.

34. The idea of Agricola as a promoter of a "purified Aristotle" is widespread. See, e.g., Wilhelm Dilthey, *Gesammelte Schriften*, II (Leipzig and Berlin, 1940), 154. Melanchthon reported Agricola's constant preoccupation with Aristotle, *CR*, XI, col. 443.

35. Alard I, 14, 15.

36. *Ibid.*, 17.

37. Alard I, 78f., on efficient and final causes.

38. Alard II, 198.

39. Alard I, 454. Although Agricola is reported to have engaged in Heidelberg disputations on questions of chance, cause, soul-body problem, the entelechy, etc., the poverty of his speculative power is illustrated by his discussion of fate and his justification of an activist solution, Alard II, 181f. Quintilian, book 7, final chapter, discusses the glories of human reason.

40. Alard I, 254f., *Orationis ex uaria struendi ratione diuisio*. Aristotle's definition reads: "Rhetoric may be defined as the faculty of observing in any given case the available means of persuasion," *Rhetorica*, I, 7.

41. A brilliant, if somewhat ecstatic, discussion of this interpretation of Italian humanism is Ernesto Grassi, *Verteidigung des individuellen Lebens* (Bern, 1946).

42. . . . aliud est esse rationalem, aliud esse sapientem.

43. *De Officiis*, II, ii, 5: Sapientia autem est, ut a veteribus philosophis difinitum est, rerum divinarum et humanarum causarumque, quibus eae res continentur, scientia.

44. Alard II, 227ff.; Allen, "Letters of Rudolf Agricola," *E. H. R.*, XXI, 312, ep. 15, To John Agricola, Nov. 30, 1478, Ferrara.

45. Alard II, 231.

46. Alard II, 175; Allen, "Letters of Rudolf Agricola," *E. H. R.*, XXI, 310, ep. 4, To Antonius Vrye (Liber), Feb. 5, 1471 [Groningen].

47. *CR*, XI, col. 444; *CR*, IV, col. 929; Alard II, intro., D. Alardo Aemstelredamo Philippus Melanthon.

48. Alard II, 144–159.

49. Alard II, 150.

50. Alard II, 151f.

51. Hartfelder, "Unedierte Briefe," p. 4.

52. Agricola's *opuscula* consisted of a brief commentary on Boethius' *De Consolatione*, incorporated by Murmellius into his longer commentary, a translation of pseudo-Plato's *Axiochus*, that death is not to be feared, translations of Isocrates' *Paranesis* and *De regno*, political science in a moralistic key, a commentary on Aphthonius' *Progymnasmatum*, containing the elements of rhetoric, a commentary on the grammarian Priscian's translation of the pseudo-Hermogenes' *Praeexercitamenta*, a rhetorical exercise, translations of orations and declamations by Aescinus, Demosthenes, and Seneca,

notes on Cicero's oration *pro lege Manilia*, and, finally, Lucian's *Gallus*, on the vanity of human affairs, and *De non Facile credendis Delationibus*, on accusations which must not easily be believed. A comparison of Agricola's *Paranesis* with the earlier version of the Italian Lapo da Castiglionchio shows it to be an independent translation. Cf. K. Müllner, "Zur humanistischen Übersetzungsliteratur," *Wiener Studien. Zeitschrift für Klassische Philologie*, XXIII (1902), 276ff.

53. Hartfelder, "Unedierte Briefe," 18, ep. 10, Agricola an Adolf Occo; Allen, "Letters of Rudolf Agricola," *E. H. R.*, XXI, 312, ep. 18, August 24 [1479], Dillingen. Agricola reiterated his determination to study theology to Hegius and Reuchlin and began the study of Hebrew with a Christianized Jew supported by Bishop Dalberg. Wimpfeling reported that he actually completed a new translation of the Psalter into Latin. Alard II, 185; Allen, "Letters of Rudolf Agricola," *E. H. R.*, XXI, 315, ep. 43, To Alexander Hegius, Tuesday [c. January 1485], Worms. Alard II, 179f.; Allen, "Letters of Rudolf Agricola," *E. H. R.*, XXI, 315, ep. 41, To John Reuchlin, Nov. 9 [1484], Heidelberg.

54. Hartfelder, "Unedierte Briefe," 24f., ep. 12; Allen, "Letters of Rudolf Agricola," *E. H. R.*, XXI, 313, ep. 26, To Adolphus Occo, Oct. 11 [1482], Heidelberg: Ab usu medendi desciuit, perpetuo solus est in cubiculo et totos dies studijs sacris impendit. Albert Hyma, *The Christian Renaissance* (Grand Rapids, n.d.), p. 228.

55. Alard II, intro., Letter to Alard.

56. Stuttgart ms., *Cod. Poet. et Philol.*, no. 36, folios 182–190; *Exhortatio ad clerum wormatiensen in sinodo publica dicta*. Allen, "Letters of Rudolf Agricola," *E. H. R.*, XXI, 314.

57. Alard II, 163ff., *Oratio gratulatoria dicta Innocentio VIII.*

58. Alard II, 313f. In a poem on the death of Count Moritz von Spiegelberg he found comfort in the thought that Spiegelberg would at last see the divine being and that his drive toward all knowledge would now be satisfied.

59. Alard II, 118ff. *De Nativitate Sive immensa natalis diei iesv Christi Laetitia.* The *Oratio* was published separately as well in Tübingen, 1527.

60. *CR*, XI, col. 444. Melanchthon similarly reports Agricola's argument that ceremonies are not necessary, but it is wrong to spurn the decrees of the councils against the heretics, *CR*, XI, col. 443.

III   WIMPFELING — Sacerdotal Humanist

1. *Iacobi Vuimphelingii Selestensis, ad Iacobum Spiegel ex sorore nepotem expurgatio contra detractores.* 1512. G. Manacorda, *Della Poesia Latina in Germania Durante il Rinascimento* (Rome, 1907), p. 8, characterized Wimpfeling as a man, not of superior intelligence, but of good will; of variegated culture, but superficial; honest, but sordid.

2. *Oratio ad clerum Wormatiensem*, April 15, 1477; in the manuscript of the University of Upsala (C. 687), according to Hugo Holstein, *Iacobus Wimphelingivs Stylpho* (Berlin, 1892), p. vi.

3. *Jacobi Vimpfelingij Schletstattensis Theosophi Oratio de sancto spiritu* (Phorce, 1507). The oration was delivered May 26, 1482.

4. The best biography is still Joseph Knepper, *Jakob Wimpfeling (1450–*

1528) *Sein Leben und Seine Werke* (Freiburg i. B., 1902), written from a conservative Catholic point of view, citing the older literature, pp. xvii-xxx. See especially Gustav Knod, "Wimpfeling und die Universität Heidelberg," *Zeitschrift für die Geschichte des Oberrheins*, N. F. I, 317-335, and Charles Schmidt, *Histoire Littéraire de L'Alsace*, 2 vols. (Paris, 1879), I, 1-188, II, 317-340, listing ninety-eight of Wimpfeling's publications, not quite a complete roster. Heinrich Hermelink, "Jakob Wimpfeling, humanistischer Theologe," *Realencyklopädie für protestantische Theologie und Kirche*, XXI (Leipzig, 1908), 350-357, gives a useful summary. Richard Newald, *Elsässische Charakterköpfe aus dem Zeitalter des Humanismus* (Colmar [1944]), pp. 55-84, sketches his life and personality. Of interest is a letter of Erasmus describing the life of Wimpfeling, one of his "most faithful friends," *Praestantissima hanc in rem est Des. Erasmi Roterodami epistola, quam an. 1529, die 24. Ian. Basil, exarauit ad Io. Vlattenum*, in *Amoenitates Literariae Friburgenses* (Vlmae, 1776), pp. 161-165.

5. *Stylpho*, preserved in the Upsala University Manuscript (c. 687), was published in 1494. Cf. Holstein, *Stylpho*, the best critical text of the drama. Even the name Stylpho was taken from Terence.

6. J. Knepper, *Wimpfeling*, pp. 288-289.

7. *Ex Argentoraco, prima Septembris 1514*, in *Amoenitates Literariae Friburgenses*, p. 369, pp. 368-378, Wimpfeling and Erasmus' letters following the visit. Cf. Allen, *Epistolae*, II, 7-9, ep. 302; 17-24, ep. 305.

8. *Isidoneus*, chapter XXI.

9. *Amoenitates Literariae Friburgenses*, p. 223, Wimpfeling to Thomas Wolff, Jr., 1503.

10. *Opera Ioannis Pici Mirandule . . . novissime accurate revisa . . . quarumcunque facultatum professoribus tam iuncunda, quam proficua . . . AE.: Impressit Industrius Ioannes Priis civ. Argentinens. a. salut. 1503*; in *Amoenitates Literariae Friburgenses*, pp. 232-234. See *Apologia pro Republica Christiana*, chapter XXXI: Ionnis Pici Mirandvlani exemplo sacra pagina foret amplectenda.

11. *Amoenitates Literariae Friburgenses*, p. 223, reply to Thomas Wolff, Jr., who had written how much his edition of the *Eclogues* (*Bucolica*) would mean to the youth.

12. Schmidt, *Histoire Littéraire*, I, 154-155. Wimpfeling's works are replete with references to and citations from Mantuanus, e.g., *Jacobi Wimpfelingij Apologia pro Republica Christiana*, 1505, chapter XXI; *Germania Jacobi Wimpffelingij . . . Oratio Ia. Wimpfe. S. de annuntione angelica*, 1500, fol. g iiiᵛff.

13. *Isidoneus*, chapter XIII.

14. Wimpfeling to Brant, 1503, cited in Schmidt, *Histoire Littéraire*, I, 150.

15. *Isidoneus*, chapter XXI. In the *De Integritate*, chapter XIII, Wimpfeling recommends as the third remedy for lust the reading of sacred letters, including works by Cicero, Petrarch, Albertus Magnus, Gerhard Zutphen, Jean Gerson, Jacobo Phillippus, and Baptista Mantuanus.

16. *Diatriba iacobi Wimphelingij Seletstattini: sacre pagine licentiati.; De proba institutione puerorum in trivialibus . . .* fol. xivᵛ: *De ordine vitę sacerdotalis*. In the letter to Gemmingen, March 23, 1494, in *De nuntio*

angelico, Wimpfeling observes that men learn the knowledge of God from Christian writings and that of themselves from philosophy, rating Origen, Jerome, Augustine, and Rabanus Maurus especially high.

17. *Contra turpem libellum Philomusi*, fol. d, i and ii, cited in Knepper, *Wimpfeling*, p. 223.

18. Maximilian Buchner, "Ein Jugendgedicht Jakob Wimpfelings auf Bischof Mathias Ramung von Speier. Beitrag zur Geschichte des Humanismus in Heidelberg, "*Zeitschrift für die Geschichte des Oberrheins*, N. F. XXII (61. Band, 1907), 478–485. On the cathedral, *Laudes ecclesiae Spirensis . . .*"

19. See especially *Iacobi Wimphelingi Catalogus Episcoporum Argentinensium* (Argentorati, 1660). In chapter XXXIII of the *Apologia pro republica Christiana* Wimpfeling gives a winsome description of the ideal theologian.

20. *Germania Jacobi Wimpffelingij . . . Oratio Ia. Wimpfe. S. de annuntione angelica*, fol. giii^v ff., citing Hermes Trismegistus together with the prophets. See also Wimpfeling's preface to Rabanus Maurus' *De Laudibus sanctae Crucis opus*, in *Amoenitates Literariae Friburgenses*, pp. 228–229. Paul Wiskowatoff, *Jakob Wimpfeling, sein Leben und seine Schriften* (Berlin, 1867), p. 94, regarding the *Oratio* quite rightly concludes: 'In diesem Sinne fährt er fort, von der Beschäftigung mit den Wissenschaften zu reden, *immer ist es die moralische Heilkraft in ihnen, die er zur Geltung bringen will.*"

21. *Contra turpem libellum Philomusi. Defensio theologię scholasticę & neotericorum.* The controversy between Mellerstadt and Wimpina on the same theme is an even more renowned parallel.

22. *Expurgatio*, in *Amoenitates Literariae Friburgenses*, p. 420.

23. *Pro concordia dialecticorum et Oratorum inque philosophia diversas opiniones sectantium quos modernos et anti quos vocant. Oratio habita ad gymnosophistas Heydelbergenses Anno domini MCCCCXCIX. Pridie jdus Augusti.*

24. *Moriae encomium Erasmi Roterodami declamatio . . . Libello huic Iac. Wimphelingii epistola ad Des. Er. Rot . . .*, in *Amoenitates Literariae Friburgenses*, pp. 333–334. Cf. Allen, *Epistolae*, I, 462–465, ep. 224.

25. *Oratio in licentia viae modernae*, cited in Knepper, *Wimpfeling*, pp. 29–30.

26. *Memorabiles in hac editione est epistola Jacobi Wimphelingii ad Ioaannem Harstium, & Cosmam Wolfium, incitans eos ad studium philosophiae & sacrarum literarum, & ad honestatem praecipue in vestitu . . .*, in *Amoenitatis Literariae Friburgenses*, pp. 201–203.

27. *Diatriba*, chapter XIV, cited in Schmidt, *Histoire Littéraire*, I, 124.

28. *De Integritate Libellus*, chapters XXIX–XXX.

29. *Contra turpem libellum Philomusi*, chapter 3. See Schmidt, *Histoire Littéraire*, I, 125–128, and Knepper, *Wimpfeling*, pp. 221–227, on the controversy. Interestingly, Wimpfeling admired Bernard very much and edited some of his writings, *Divus Bernardus in Symbolum Apostolorum . . . (Argentoraci*, 1507), cited in Knepper, *Wimpfeling*, p. 240, note 1.

30. *De integritate*, chapter XXII.

31. Wimpfeling's programmatic academic speeches and addresses to the

clergy are all in the same vein. See, e.g., the *Oratio querulosa contra invasores sacerdotum*, c. 1493, or the *Immunitatis et libertatis ecclesiasticae statusque defensio*, about the same time, or the *Epistola de miseriis curatorum aut plebanorum*.

32. *Isidoneus germanicus*, 1497, chapter XVII. Of the thirty chapters, twenty are on grammar; the remaining are on the classic and Christian literature which the youth should learn to know.

33. Wimpfeling reiterates this theme in his *Diatriba de proba institutione puerorum in trivialibus et adolescentium in universalibus gymnasiis*, 1514, a handbook for teachers in the trivial schools. He prepared many other aids to learning, as his *Elegantię maiores*, 1509, or the *Elegantiarum medulla*, a selection from Valla's book on Latin eloquence. Wimpfeling was not a systematic pedagogue, but his principles were generally sound.

34. *Adolescentia Jacobi Wimphelingii cum nouis quibusdam additionibus per Gallinarium denuo reuisa ac elimata*, 1505.

35. See Walter Sohm, *Die Schule Johann Sturm und die Kirche Straszburgs in ihrem gegenseitigen Verhältnis 1530–1581*. (Munich, 1912); Herman Gumbel, "*Humanitas Alsatica*. Straszburger Humanismus von Jakob Wimpfeling zu Johann und Jakob Sturm," *Elsasz-Lothringisches Jahrbuch*, XVII (1938), 1–36.

36. *De triplici candore Marię*, cited in Knepper, *Wimpfeling*, p. 56.

37. *De vita et miraculis Ioannis Gerson. Defensio Wimphelingij p. diuo Ioanne Gerson: et clero seculari: qui in libro (cui titulus supplementum celifodine) grauiter taxati et reprehensi*, 1506; republished in *Amoenitates Literariae Friburgenses*, pp. 278ff. The mendicant had accused Gerson of being anti-monastic and irreverent to his superiors. Wimpfeling edited with Brant the *Hortulus animae* and in 1507 the *Speculum vitae humanae*. Wimpfeling everywhere recommends readings in Gerson, for example, in *Diatriba*, fol. xiv^v, etc.

38. See, for example, *Epistola Ja. Wymphelingi de inepta et superflua verborum resolucione in cancellis*, etc., 1503.

39. See the two interesting letters showing Wimpfeling's struggle for the income, Joseph Knepper, "Kleine Funde zum elsässischen Humanismus," *Zeitschrift für die Geschichte des Oberrheins*, N. F. XXI (1906), 40–49.

40. *Jacobi Wimpfelingij Apologia pro Republica Christiana* (Phorcae, 1506). With the *Orationis Angeli Anachoritę Vallis vmbrosę Ad Iulium. II. super Concilio Lateraneni* he reemphasized that many abuses had been tolerated too long.

41. *Apologia*, chapters XI, XII, XXVII ff., XXV, XLIV, *et passim*. See his *De actionibus & astutiis quorundam Curtisanorum*, in *Amoenitates Literariae Friburgenses*, pp. 499–515.

42. *Apologia*, chapter XLIII.

43. *Apologia*, XIII. See also *Iac. Wimphel.: eremita syluae hercyniae peccator angelo anacheritae Vallis vmbrosae S.*, in *Amoenitates Literariae Friburgenses*, pp. 325–331.

44. *Jacobi Wimphelingi de Integritate Libellus cum epistolis prestantissimorum virorum in hunc libellum approbantium & confirmantium*.

45. *Expurgatio contra F. Schatzer*, fol. iii, cited in Schmidt, *Histoire Littéraire*, p. 115.

46. See, for example, his *De Fide Concubinarum in suos Pfaffos*; Arnold von Tongern's *Avisamentum de concubinarijs*, which Wimpfeling republished in 1507; Nikolaus Paulus, "Wimpfelingiana," *Zeitschrift für die Geschichte des Oberrheins*, N. F. XVIII (1903), 46–57; *Carmina Prosae et Rithmi* in Gustav Knod, "Zwei anonyme Schriften Wimpfelings," *Vierteljahrsschrift für Kultur und Litteratur der Renaissance*, II (1887), 267–270.

47. *Erasmus in epistola ad Paulum Volsium*, in *Amoenitates Literariae Friburgenses*, p. 510, note 3, a.

48. *Appologetica declaratio Wymphelingij in libellum suum de integritate*. The *Ad Julium II. Pontificem Max* was in the form of an elegiac poem. In the defense to Julius, Wimpfeling asserted that the Augustinians had received their rule from a secular bishop.

49. See, for example, Gustav Knod, "Neun Briefe von und an Jakob Wimpfeling," *Vierteljahrsschrift für Kultur und Litteratur der Renaissance*, I (1886), 229ff., eps. V, IX, etc.

50. *Contra quendam qui se Franciscvm Schatzer appellat* . . . , in *Amoenitates Literariae Friburgenses*, pp. 281–282. *Oratio querulosa contra invasores sacerdotum*, in *Amoenitates Literariae Friburgenses*, p. 394, addressed to Alexander VI.

51. On Sixtus IV, Knepper, *Wimpfeling*, p. 50; on Alexander VI, *ibid.*, p. 62; on Julius II, *De integritate*, chapter II (fol. Aiiij), *Soliloquium Wimphelingij Pro pace Christianorum et pro Heluecijs vt resipiscant, epistola ad Jacobum*; Wimpfeling hopes for progress under Julius; on Leo X, *Ad Leonem X. pontificem maximum carmen*, in *Amoenitates Literariae Friburgenses*, pp. 426–430.

52. See Joseph Knepper, *Nationaler Gedanke und Kaiseridee bei den elsässischen Humanisten* (Freiburg i. B., 1898), *passim*; Emil von Borries, *Wimpfeling und Murner im Kampf um die ältere Geschichte des Elsasses* (Heidelberg, 1926), *passim*. Paul Joachimsen, *Geschichtsauffassung und Geschichtsschreibung in Deutschland unter dem Einfluss des Humanismus* (Leipzig and Berlin, 1910), pp. 64–79. On Charles VIII, *Iac. Wimphelingii Carmina de Arma Britannica per Carolum VIII. Francorum regem rapta*, in *Amoenitates Literariae Friburgenses*, pp. 575–577; on noblemen, *Tetrastichon contra bellisequaces*, R. Priebsch, "A case of Collaboration between Jakob Wimpfeling and Sebastian Brant," *The Modern Language Review*, XXV (1930), 192–194. The history is the *Epithoma Germanorum Jacobi Wympfelingij et suorum opera contextum*.

53. *Apologia pro republica christiana*, chapter 44. The *Agatharchia* describes the good prince who protects his land from exploitation. The *Responsa et replice* . . . reveals resentment against the cultural aspersions of Aeneas. The *Oratio querulosa contra Inuasores Sacerdotum* calls on the princes to defend the priests.

54. See H. Ulmann, "Studie über Maximilian's I. Plan einer deutschen Kirchenreform im Jahre 1520," *Zeitschrift für Kirchengeschichte*, III (1879), 199–219. Wimpfeling's memorandum was the *Gravamina Germanicae Nationis cum remedijs et avisamentis ad Caesaream Maiestatem*, 1518. It is republished in *Amoenitates Literariae Friburgenses*, pp. 515–533. In 1520 Jakob Spiegel published an edition in Schlettstadt, *Diuo Maximiliano iubente Pragmaticę sanctionis Medulla excerpta*. On Wimpfeling's interest in re-

newing the concordat of princes, see his *Concordata Principum Nationis Germaniae* and the discussion of its relation to Maximilian's reform plan, Gustav Knod, "Zwei anonyme Schriften Wimpfelings," *Vierteljahrsschrift für Kultur und Litteratur der Renaissance*, II (1887), 227–280.

55. *D. Erasmi epistola . . .* , in *Amoenitates Literariae Friburgenses*, pp. 540–541. On Wimpfeling and the Reformation, see Knepper, *Wimpfeling*, pp. 315–321. It seems possible that Wimpfeling was the author of an anonymous tract, *Apologia Christi pro Luthero*, sent to Spalatin at the time of the diet in 1521, ridiculing Leo's citation of Luther to Rome and recounting vicious anecdotes of papal immorality, Edward Böcking, *Drei Abhandlungen über reformations-geschichtliche Schriften* (Leipzig, 1858), pp. 51–64; E. Böcking, *Opera Ulrichi Hutteni*, II (Leipzig, 1854), pp. 35ff. Kalkoff argues for Wimpfeling's authorship largely on the basis of similarities of anecdotes and like evidence, Paul Kalkoff, "Wimpfelings letzte lutherfreundliche Kundgebung," *Zeitschrift für die Geschichte des Oberrheins*, N. F. XXXV (1920), 1–35. The evidence, largely internal, is inconclusive, however, and the piece seems out of character with Wimpfeling's usual respect for the papacy. He must have been in a rare temper indeed to have written such a tract! The authorship must most likely be assigned to some younger man, perhaps Hermann von dem Busche.

56. See P. Kalkoff, "Jakob Wimpfeling und die Erhaltung der katholischen Kirche in Schlettstadt," *Zeitschrift für die Geschichte des Oberrheins*, N. F. XII (1897), 577–619, XIII (1898), 84–123, 264–301. The defection of Strassburg, where Luther's writings were printed as early as 1519, grieved Wimpfeling particularly. See Willy Andreas, *Strassburg an der Wende vom Mittelalter zur Neuzeit* (Leipzig, 1940), pp. 42–45. Timotheus Röhrich, *Geschichte der Reformation im Elsass und besonders in Strassburg*, 3 vols. (Strassburg, 1830–32) is still of value, though containing some highly dubious material.

57. *Canonis missae contra Huldricum Zuinglivm Defensio*, 1524, in *Amoenitates Literariae Friburgenses*, pp. 541–543.

58. A copy of Wimpfeling's letter of May 8, 1521, *Ja. Wimphelingus Ja. Spiegel iureconsulto, imperiali secretario, nepoti charissimo S. D.*, is, in fact, still in Rome, Cod. Vat. 6199, fol. 42: *Epistola excusatoria Jacobi Wimpfelingi de Luthero*. See Paul Kalkoff, "Wimpfelings kirchliche Unterwerfung," *Zeitschrift für die Geschichte des Oberrheins*, N. F. XXI (1906), 262–270.

IV   REUCHLIN — Pythagoras Reborn

1. *De accentibus et orthographia* (Hagenau, 1518), *praefatio;* Ludwig Geiger, ed. *Johann Reuchlins Briefwechsel* (Tübingen, 1875), ep. 250, pp. 282ff., hereafter cited as *Reuchlins Br.*, with the letter and page number following. The standard biography of Reuchlin is still Ludwig Geiger, *Johann Reuchlin, Sein Leben und seine Werke* (Leipzig, 1871). In English there is little of independent value aside from William Lilly, *Renaissance Types* (London, 1901), chapter IV, previously published in *The Quarterly Review*, CLXXXVIII, no. 375 (1898), 1–30.

2. *Reuchlins Br.* 5, pp. 7f.

3. Karl Christ, *Die Bibliothek Reuchlins in Pforzheim* (Leipzig, 1924), pp. 6, 24.

4. *Reuchlini consilium pro libris iudaeorum non abolendis*, cited in Wilhelm Dilthey, *Gesammelte Schriften*, II (Leipzig and Berlin, 1940, 4th ed.), 44, n. 2. Similarly in the dedication of the *De arte cabalistica* to Leo X, Reuchlin reminded the pontiff: ". . . ego primus omnium Graeca in Germaniam reduxi et primus omnium ecclesiae universalis artem et studia sermonis Hebraici condonavi atque tradidi." *Reuchlins Br.* 238, p. 275. Reuchlin is quoting from Horace, *Q. Horati Flacci Carminvm, Liber tertivs*, XXX, 1: *Exegi monumentum aere perennius*.

5. *Reuchlins Br.* 115, p. 123, *De verbo mirifico* (Tübingen, 1514), fol. dv^vff., hereafter cited as *D.V.M. De accentibus et orthographia*, fol. LXX: *Moyses, scriptor antiquissimus. De arte cabalistica* in *Opera omnia ioannis Pici Miriandvlae* (Basel, 1557), p. 870, hereafter cited as *D.A.C. Reuchlins Br.* 102, p. 105, Reuchlin urges the need of Hebrew for Old Testament studies.

6. J. G. Herder, "Zu Reuchlins Bilde" (1777), *Herders Sämmtliche Werke*, ed. Bernhard Suphan, IX (Berlin, 1893), 516.

7. Carl Krause, *Der Briefwechsel des Mutianus Rufus* (Kassel, 1885), Br. 289, p. 353. On Erasmus' inglorious role in the Reuchlin controversy, see Manfred Krebs, "Reuchlins Beziehungen zu Erasmus von Rotterdam," *Johannes Reuchlin. 1455–1522* (Pforzheim, 1955), pp. 140ff.

8. *Reuchlins Br.* 182, p. 213, *Reuchlins Br.* 130, pp. 137ff., Reuchlin assured Tungar, Cologne professor, that he always loved sacred theology. *Reuchlins Br.* 131, pp. 140ff., Reuchlin conceded to Kollin that he, too, opposed Jewish writings harmful to the Christian religion. *Reuchlins Br.* 138, pp. 154ff., Reuchlin avows his desire to avoid scandal and declares his faith in Christ. *Reuchlins Br.* 143, p. 165, Reuchlin asks for peace. Cf. L. Geiger, *Johann Reuchlin*, pp. 162ff.

9. *Reuchlins Br.* 280, p. 313. *Reuchlins Br.* 175, pp. 200ff. *Reuchlins Br.* 127, p. 135. *Reuchlins Br.* 253, pp. 290ff. In the dedication of the *D.A.C.* to Leo X, Reuchlin wrote: ". . . quare spero me non frustra speare, posteritatem ecclesiasticam meritis meis futuram non ingratam teque praesentem . . ." On his wishes for old age, see *De accentibus et orthographia*, fol. LIX^v, preface to the second book.

10. *Rudimenta hebraica*, pp. 123, 223.

11. *Reuchlins Br.* 134, p. 150. *Reuchlins Br.* 130, p. 139.

12. Geiger, *Johann Reuchlin*, pp. 157f. *Reuchlins Br.* 15, pp. 15f.

13. Geiger, *Johann Reuchlin*, p. 146, shows his liberal verve in overemphasizing Reuchlin's daring nonconformity. In reference to Reuchlin's respect for truth, he writes: "Damit war aller Autoritätsglaube gebrochen, waren alle Schranken niedergerissen, die eine freie, von Rücksichten unbeirrte Erklärung der Bibel hinderten." *D.V.M.*, fol. diiii^v and fol. diiii. For typical criticisms of scholasticism, see *D.A.C.*, p. 743: Eo quod longo iam tempore a malis praeceptoribus delusi nondum prudentes pueri tenera in aetate relictis optimarum literarum studijs, ad sordida sophismata compelluntur, etc.; p. 778 . . . nostro aeuo sophistarum . . . ; p. 863 . . . quorsum quisque uellet, quem admodum accepimus uulgarios quosdam Sophistas

agere, ut hac aetate uideant suis syllogismis illa sanctissima diuini spiritus oracula prope in publicum contemptum adduxisse.

14. *D.V.M.*, fol. eiii, fol. ev. Joseph Blau, *The Christian Interpretation of the Cabala in the Renaissance* (New York, 1944), p. 44.

15. *Rudimenta hebraica*, p. 548.

16. *Reuchlins Br.* 215, p. 245f. At the end of his treatise of 1505, *Dr. Johann Reuchlins tütsch missive warumb die Juden so lang im ellend sind*, he invited any Jew who wanted instruction in Christianity to come to him and promised to care for his needs during the period of study. This spirit is reminiscent of the missionary outreach of William Postel in the sixteenth century as depicted in the fascinating book by William J. Bouwsma, *Concordia Mundi. The Career and Thought of Guillaume Postel (1510–1581)* (Cambridge, Mass., 1957).

17. Pico, *Opera* (Basel, 1557), p. 107, Conclusiones Cabalisticae numero LXXI (sic) secundum opinionem propriam, ex ipsis Hebreorum sapientum fundamentis Christianam religionem maxime confirmantes. P. 166, Apologia: Nulla est scientia, quae nos magis certificet de diuinitate Christi, quam Magis & Cabala. Reuchlin credited Pico with introducing the Cabala to Christians, *D.A.C.*, p. 758 . . . ac nostra aetate a Latinis, authore Joanne Pico . . . Two studies of the Cabala of special value for scholars who wish to examine it in greater detail than is here possible, especially from the point of view of comparison with Gnosticism, Neoplatonism, or Pythagoreanism, are S. Karppe, *Étude sur les origines et la nature du Zohar* (Paris, 1901), and Gershon G. Scholem, *Major Trends in Jewish Mysticism* (Jerusalem, 1941), by far the best book on the subject.

18. *Reuchlins Br.* 87, pp. 83f. Blau, *Christian Interpretation of the Cabala*, pp. 17ff., 31ff., discusses Pico as the "phoenix of his age," who first attracted his fellow humanists in any considerable number to the Cabala. Christ, *Bibliothek Reuchlins*, p. 32, names Pico's works in Reuchlin's library. *D.A.C.*, p. 835, Reuchlin cites Pico's importance as an interpreter of Cabala. Reuchlin read Ficino's *De religione christiana* and other works and so understood their apologetic intent. It is interesting that Reuchlin's major cabalistic work was published in several sixteenth-century editions of Pico's *Opera*, Basel, 1557 and 1572, for example. Cecil Roth, *The Jews in the Renaissance* (Philadelphia, 1959), pp. 112ff., discusses the contacts of Pico and the humanists of Florence with Jewish learning. Chapter VII, The Christian Hebraists, pp. 137ff., offers an interesting account of Egidio da Viterbo, Cardinal Domenico Grimani, Fra Francesco Giorgi, and others interested in Hebrew scholarship and Jewish mysticism.

19. *D.A.C.*, p. 734.

20. *D.A.C.*, pp. 734ff.: Id tamen absque Hebraeorum Cabala fieri non potuit, eo quod Pythagorae philosophia de Cabalaeorum praeceptis initia duxit, quae patrum memoria discendens e magna Graecia rursus in Cabalistarum volumina incubuit. *Reuchlins Br.* 215, pp. 245f.: Nam idem studium, aequalis opera, par exercitium Pythagorei et Cabalistae, ars etiam eadem et consimilis scientia. His friends nourished this thought by continually writing about his Pythagorean books. In the dedication of *De accentibus et orthographia*, fol. lxxxiii, he wrote: Pythagoreo more citharam nostram docemus divina Hebraeorum carmina resonare, quorum symphoniam hic sub

jungimus. *D.A.C.*, p. 777: . . . nisi forte unus Pythagoras ille meus, philosophiae pater. *D.A.C.*, p. 835: Quo animadvertimus Pythagorae philosophiam fere omnem esse a Cabalaeis ortam, qui pari modo symbolicum tradendi morem ad Graecos transtulit . . . Already the *Rudimenta hebraica*, p. 4, was to serve "ad arcanae Pythagorae disciplinam et artem Cabalisticam." Reuchlin showed an interest in Pythagorean symbolism as early as 1477, *Oratio, Reuchlins Br.*, Appendix Ia, p. 341.

21. *D.A.C.*, pp. 787, 835, 893.

22. Cf. Hans Rupprich, "Johannes Reuchlin und seine Bedeutung im Europäischen Humanismus," ed. Manfred Krebs, *Johannes Reuchlin*, pp. 15f. The whole article is very excellent and suggestive. On Reuchlin's Cusanus manuscripts, see Karl Preisendanz, "Die Bibliothek Johannes Reuchlin," *ibid.*, p. 42.

23. Philolaus speaks of "us Christians," *D.A.C.*, p. 791. Reuchlin may have chosen the name from Philolaus, the wandering prophet of Pythagoreanism in the generation before Plato. For a brief summary of Reuchlin's works, see Christian Ginsburg, *The Kabbalah* (London, 1920), pp. 206ff. There is a difficulty, of course, in extrapolating Reuchlin's own thought from works in dialogue. It seems satisfactory, however, to assume that ideas which the protagonists use to advance the argument toward the author's conclusion represent his point of view.

24. *D.A.C.*, p. 746. *Reuchlins Br.* 106, pp. 109f.: . . . altissima speculationum . . . Geiger, *Johann Reuchlin*, pp. 173ff., discusses Reuchlin's cabalistic sources. Gerhard Scholem, *Bibliographia Kabbalistica* (Leipzig, 1927), numbers 937 and 938, cites the various editions of Reuchlin's two major works.

25. *D.A.C.*, p. 835. *D.A.C.*, p. 834, citing the second chapter of Gikatilia's *Porto lucis*. Reuchlin borrows the whole symbolic mechanism such as the fifty portals of understanding, the great Jubilee, the one thousand generations, and the kingdom of all centuries, which had impressed Pico as well, *D.A.C.*, pp. 838f.

26. Blau, *Christian Interpretation of the Cabala*, pp. 8f.

27. *D.A.C.*, pp. 738f. *D.A.C.*, p. 874 . . . seculum elementorum, & in eo est homo qui appellatur עולם הקטן, id est, seculum paruum, quod Graeci dicunt, μικρόκοσμος, hoc est, minor mundus, seu rectius paruus mundus.

28. *D.A.C.*, p. 820. *D.A.C.*, p. 773: Idcirco etiam nunc magis sine iniuria dici arbitror, quod homo Microcosmus & mundus sensibilis ille magnus, communicant in mente. *D.V.M.*, fol. biiii, Reuchlin cites Ovid: Est deus in nobis. *D.A.C.*, p. 740, Reuchlin describes the parts of man, body, life, reason, mind, whence he is named a god, according to the oracle: I have said you are gods.

29. *D.A.C.*, p. 805. Marranus introduced Mohammed as an unusual witness to the effect that God will lead good men to paradise, *D.A.C.*, pp. 814f.

30. *D.A.C.*, pp. 801f. With less urgency Reuchlin defends Pythagoras also against charges of vegetarianism, *D.A.C.*, p. 806. Wilamowitz-Moellendorff, among other modern scholars, also praised Pythagoras for recognizing in the human soul the immortal element of life. Alister Cameron, *The Py-*

thagorean Background of the Theory of Recollection (Menasha, Wisc., 1938), p. 5.

31. *D.A.C.*, p. 831: Nam quid aliud intendit . . . ; p. 836: Exequar igitur primum . . .

32. *D.A.C.*, p. 825: Proinde affectiones in nobis . . .

33. *D.A.C.*, p. 814: Si recta ratione uixeris . . .

34. *D.A.C.*, p. 893: Tota namque philosophia . . .

35. *D.A.C.*, p. 739: Haec illa est . . . *D.A.C.*, p. 740: Cum igitur trium regionum duo interualla sensus & iudicium duplicantur secundum inferius & superius, & utraque ad binos reducuntur terminos, restant decem scalae gradus, per quos ad cognitionem omnium quae sunt uere aut sensu, aut scientia, aut fide ab imo ad summum ascendere possumus.

36. *D.A.C.*, p. 747: Sed nobilior quaedam notitia . . . *D.A.C.*, p. 765, discusses the "Speculatio illuminans," the intuitive knowledge of God. *D.A.C.*, p. 782: Mens quidem et sensus non syllogissant.

37. *D.V.M.*, fol. ci: Posuit igitur hominem in medio universi. *D.V.M.*, fol. bvff.: Faciam facile quia iubetis Capnion ait. Capnion discusses *scientia* and *sapientia*. He concludes that certain knowledge of human things is not possible. *D.V.M.*, fol. biiii: Atque divina scire . . . Sidonius argues we cannot know divine things from men.

38. *D.V.M.*, fol. cviv: Sola enim recta fides . . . *D.A.C.*, p. 891: Plotinus, Porphyry . . .

39. *D.A.C.*, p. 849: Verba composita loquimur . . . *D.A.C.*, p. 762: Estque Thalmudistarum . . .

40. *D.A.C.*, p. 783: Quoniam & simplicitatis fides melior . . . *D.A.C.*, p. 884: Inveniuntur & alij Cabalistae . . . *D.A.C.*, pp. 784f.: . . . quae sola fide constant . . . *D.V.M.*, fol. cii: Nos uero siue hominis . . .

41. *D.A.C.*, pp. 762ff.: Ita quicquid de sacra scriptura . . . *D.V.M.*, fol. av: Nam omnem ago uitae meae cursum in contemplatione rerum naturalium consummare statui . . .

42. *D.A.C.*, p. 821: Mundum igitur hunc . . . *D.A.C.*, pp. 763f.: Deinde coelum quoque . . . *D.A.C.*, p 788: Nam mundus superior . . .

43. *D.A.C.*, p. 789. *D.A.C.*, p. 840: Ab initio cum non . . .

44. Sebastian Brant, *Ship of Fools*, trans. E. Zeydel (New York, 1944), p. 216.

45. *D.A.C.*, p. 775: Semper enim . . . *D.V.M.*, fol. diii: Non igitur nos . . . *D.A.C.*, p. 883: Hinc illud extat Mirandolani . . . *Reuchlins Br.* 81, pp. 75f.; *Reuchlins Br.* 90, p. 86. Geiger, *Johann Reuchlin*, pp. 176ff.

46. *D.A.C.*, p. 812: Atqui Deus ipso . . .

47. *D.A.C.*, p. 865, God as the Aleph, Tetragrammaton, and so forth. The Cabala provides the best tool for understanding revelation. The Tetragrammaton, because of its four letters, refers to the four elements and the four basic geometrical concepts. The first letter, a point ('), and at the same time a sign for the number ten, signified the beginning and end of all things. The second letter (ה), the number symbol for five, signified the Trinity of the Godhead and nature, which Pythagoras took to be a duality, etc. Cf. *D.A.C.*, pp. 853f., a Hebrew poem using the Tetragrammaton in each line.

48. *D.V.M.*, fol. dv: . . . homo migret in deum et deus habitet in homine.

49. *D.V.M.*, fol. f.: Fundatrix causa et opifex entis . . . Reuchlin distinguished between the names Jah, benevolence, and El, power and virtue, but made no critical use of this distinction, *D.A.C.*, p. 851.

50. *D.V.M.*, fol. hviv: Sicut autem solis est . . .

51. *D.A.C.*, pp. 751–757: Haec est illa reuelatio . . . expectatio salutis universae.

52. *D.A.C.*, p. 773: Id circo etiam . . .

53. *D.V.M.*, fol. vv: Deus logos dicitur . . . *D.V.M.*, fol. hvff.: Est ergo filius uerbum. *D.V.M.*, fol. hiivff.: Quoniam deum nemo . . . ; fol. hiiiv: Habetis igitur tres status verbi, Est deus, est filius, est incarnatus. *D.V.M.*, fol. i iiiff.: Fac serpentem aeneum . . . Deus enim erat . . . *D.V.M.*, fol. kiiff.: Jesus homo natus . . . *D.A.C.*, p. 862: Est enim Messiha uirtus Dei . . . The possibility on the basis of the Dead Sea Scrolls of the Gospel of John proving to be basically Jewish in Background rather than Hellenistic would make Reuchlin's association of the Logos idea and the Cabala all the more interesting.

54. *D.A.C.*, pp. 767f.: Nos contra, meo arbitratu . . . He cites also the suffering servant theme from Isaiah.

55. *D.V.M.*, fol. hvv: . . . ut homines illuminaret . . . *D.A.C.*, p. 842: Tandem porta quinquagesima . . .

56. *D.V.M.*, fol. iv: Nomen miraculosum & mirificum . . . *D.A.C.*, pp. 791f.: Sed ut receptui canam . . . *D.V.M.*, fol. giiv: Tetractyn uocant . . .

57. Dilthey, *Gesammelte Schriften*, II, 45: Already Erasmus and Reuchlin were strongly influenced by the religious universal theism of the Italian humanists. *D.A.C.*, p. 792: . . . tum rogatus a nobis quidnam illud esset quod praecipuum diuinitatis reuelatum fuisse putaret, ad quod generatim omnes diuinorum revelationes reducerentur.

58. This tradition persisted in such older biographies as Francis Barham, *The Life and Times of John Reuchlin or Capnion, the Father of the German Reformation* (London, 1843), based upon Ernst Mayerhoff, *Johann Reuchlin und seine Zeit* (Berlin, 1830). Reuchlin is viewed as "the originator of that religious amelioration which the reformers so gallantly carried forward."

59. *Reuchlins Br.* 227, p. 311, Luther to Reuchlin, Dec. 14, 1518. Geiger, *Johann Reuchlin*, pp. 353ff., an excellent discussion of Luther and Reuchlin.

60. *Reuchlins Br.* 297, pp. 326f. Reuchlin was estranged also from Melanchthon, withdrawing the promise of his library. Melanchthon, in turn, ignored his death and did not relent until thirty years later when he published his *Oratio continens historiam Joannis Capnionis Phorcensis*, CR, XI, 999. L. Geiger, *Über Melanchthons Oratio continens historiam Capnionis* (Frankfurt, 1868).

61. Frank Rosenthal, "The Rise of Christian Hebraism in the Sixteenth Century," *Historia Judaica*, VII, no. 2 (October 1945), 173ff. Rosenthal lists Melanchthon, Oekolampadius, J. Gnostopolitanus, J. Forster, Jacob Ceporinus, C. Pellican, and R. Wakefield. Geiger, *Johann Reuchlin*, pp. 196ff. Pistorius, one of the Lutheran deputies at the Diet of Augsburg,

attacked the superstitions of the Cabala which had been introduced into Christendom, A. E. Waite, *The Holy Kabbalah* (London, 1929), p. 460.

62. *Reuchlins Br.* 299, pp. 327ff., February 22 (1521).

63. *D.A.C.*, p. 807: At de fabis . . . ; p. 808: Sola imitantes ad corticem . . . Geiger, *Johann Reuchlin*, pp. 149f., like a true liberal argues that the Reformation took over the liberating function of humanism and differed only in its appeal to the masses.

64. Arthur O. Lovejoy, "The Meaning of Romanticism for the Historian of Ideas," *Journal of the History of Ideas*, II, no. 3 (June 1941), 257 ff. There is something to Giuseppe Toffanin's argument for the orthodoxy of the humanists, *Che cosa fu l'umanesimo* (Florence, 1929), and *Storia dell' umanesimo* (Naples, 1933). Reuchlin's case shows, however, what extraneous religious ideas could be fitted over an orthodox framework. Hiram Haydn, *The Counter-Renaissance* (New York, 1950), would be hard pressed to classify Reuchlin as either a classical Renaissance or a counter-Renaissance man. Paul Joachimsen, "Der Humanismus und die Entwicklung des deutschen Geistes," *Deutsche Vierteljahrsschrift für Literaturwissenschaft und Geistesgeschichte*, VIII (1930), 447f., associates Reuchlin with "the phantastic and mystic drives of the German spirit," referring to Cusanus' mathematical preoccupations and the reflections of this mentality in Dürer's *Melancholia*. Though Reuchlin read Cusanus, it is quite difficult to isolate distinctively Cusan ideas in him. *Reuchlins Br.* 111, pp. 114ff.; *Reuchlins Br.* 116, p. 124, Beatus Rhenanus returns the works of Cusanus borrowed from Reuchlin.

65. Paul Wernle, *Die Renaissance des Christentums im 16. Jahrhundert* (Tübingen, 1904), emphasized the Florentine influence on Reuchlin. Heinrich Hermelink, *Die religiösen Reformbestrebungen des deutschen Humanismus* (Tübingen, 1904), stressed the independent Northern sources of German humanism. In Reuchlin's case there is clearly the influence of both Northern piety and of Italian philosophy. But the Italian influence was demonstrably more constructive and religious than many nineteenth-century historians imagined.

66. Hansmartin Decker-Hauff, "Bausteine zur Reuchlin-Biographie," ed. Krebs, *Johannes Reuchlin*, p. 101.

V CELTIS — The Arch-Humanist

1. The early biography of Celtis, Engelbert Klüpfel, *De Vita et Scriptis Conradi Celtis Protucii Praecipui Renascentium in Germanis Literarum Restauratoris Primique Germanorum Poetae Laureati*, 2 vols. (Freiburg i. B., 1827), contained many errors. An excellent analysis of his personality and cultural ideals deserves special mention, Friedrich von Bezold, "Konrad Celtis, der deutsche Erzhumanist," *Historische Zeitschrift*, XLIX (1883), 1–45, republished in *Aus Mittelalter und Renaissance* (Munich, 1918), and separately again in Darmstadt, 1959. See also Friedrich Moth, *Conradus Celtis Protucius: Tysklands förste laurbaerkronede Digter* (Copenhagen, 1898), a Danish dissertation, and two more recent publications, Harald Drewinc, *Vier Gestalten aus dem Zeitalter des Humanismus* (St. Gallen, 1946), and Leonard Forster, *Selections from Conrad Celtis, 1459–1508* (Cam-

bridge, England, 1948), the first book in English on Celtis. Of the various articles which appeared in 1959 commemorating the five-hundredth anniversary of Celtis' birth, the best is Michael Seidlmayer "Konrad Celtis," *Jahrbuch für Fränkische Landesforschung*, XIX (1959), 395–416, which, while bringing no new materials, succeeds in a fine brief characterization. The latest biography of Celtis is Lewis W. Spitz, *Conrad Celtis, The German Arch-Humanist* (Cambridge, Mass., 1957).

2. *Quattuor Libri Amorum* II, 9, lines 153f., hereafter referred to as *Am.* with the book and poem number following.

3. *Fünf Bücher Epigramme*, Karl Hartfelder, ed. (Berlin, 1881), *Ep.* 1, 63, line 12, hereafter referred to as *Ep.* with the book and epigram number following.

4. *Am.* II, 10, lines 53f.

5. *Am.* I, 3, lines 61f. See Ludwig Sponagel, *Konrad Celtis und das deutsche Nationalbewusztsein* (Bühl-Baden, 1939), on the theme of Celtis' cultural nationalism. The importance of Celtis' patriotic feeling for his interest in the geography of the fatherland is evident from an older work by Th. Geiger, *Conrad Celtis in seinen Beziehungen zur Geographie* (Munich, 1896). An excellent recent work by Gerald Strauss, *Sixteenth-Century Germany. Its Topography and Topographers* (Madison, Wisc., 1959), pp. 19–25 *et passim*, places Celtis into the whole phase of German humanism concerned with "illustrating" the German past and the German lands through a combination of narrative history and descriptive geography.

6. Hans Rupprich, ed., *Der Briefwechsel des Konrad Celtis* (Munich, 1934), Nr. 335, p. 597, lines 25f., hereafter referred to as *Br.*, with the number of the letter and page following.

7. *Ep.* III, 40.

8. *Ep.* II, 48. Cf. also *Ep.* II, 47: *De manu Syllae et pede papae; Ep.* II, 46: *Ad Romam, dum illam intraret.*

9. Repeated as *Ep.* V, 78.

10. Hans Rupprich, ed., *Conradus Celtis Protucius Oratio in Gymnasio in Ingelstadio publice recitate* (Leipzig, 1932) contains also this *Ode to Fusilius*. The version included in the 1513 edition as *Ode* I, 11, is reprinted in F. Pindter, ed., *Conradus Celtis Protucius Libri Odarum Quattuor* (Leipzig, 1937), hereafter referred to as *Ode*, with the book and ode number following. Celtis himself republished the ode for the benefit of his Vienna students under the title *Protrepticus ingeniorum puerorum.*

11. *Ode* II, 23, lines 97ff.

12. *Ep.* I, 6: *Ad Jovem.* See also *Ode* II, 2 lines 77ff.; *Ode* II, 14.

13. *Br.* 160, pp. 267ff.

14. *Epod.* 13. The *Liber Epodon* was published with the *Odes.*

15. *Ode* III, 1, lines 85ff.

16. *Am.* IV, 15, lines 39f.

17. *Ode* II, 22, lines 33ff.

18. *Ep.* II, 81: *De Patria et doctrina Alberti Magni; Ep.* II, 44: *De praestigiis Alberti Magni.*

19. *Ep.* V, 79.

20. *Lucij Apulei Platonici et Aristotelici philosophi Epitoma diuinum de mundo seu Cosmographia ductu Conradi Celtis Impressum Uienne.* J.

Winterburger was the publisher. Two epigrams announcing Celtis' lectures on Apuleius are *Ep.* IV, 44: *Archigymnasio Viennensi* and *Ep.* IV, 50: *Celtis Academiae*. The *editio princeps* of Apuleius' works was edited by Andreas in 1469.

21. *Br.* 179, pp. 294, the dedication of the Apuleius edition to Fuchsmagen and Krachenberger.

22. *Am.* I, 11, lines 49ff.; cf. also *Ode* I, 29, lines 1ff.; *Proseuticum ad diuum Fridericum tercium pro laurea Appollinari* (Nuremberg, 1487); *Am.* IV, 14, lines 29f.: Sive ingens animal, totum quod dicimus orbem,/Spiramenta suis faucibus illa vomit. Cf. *Ode* I, 27, lines 78: rerum cognoscere causas.

23. *Br.* 275, pp. 494–503. For representative passages in Ficino parallel to Celtis' effusions, cf. *Opera* (Basel, 1576), I, 659, *Epistolarum Liber I*; I, 978, *Liber de lumine*; I, 529, *Liber de unita coelitus comparanda*, etc. On the relation of the idea of the sympathetic bonds, the whole light metaphysics, and astrology in medieval and Renaissance Platonism, cf. Clemens Baeumker, "Mittelalterlicher und Renaissance-Platonismus," *Beiträge zur Geschichte der Renaissance und Reformation* (Munich, 1917), pp. 5ff.

24. *Norimberga*, chapter 6, published in 1502 with the *Amores*. The modern edition was edited by Albert Werminghoff, *Conrad Celtis und sein Buch über Nürnberg* (Freiburg i. B., 1921).

25. *Ep.* II, 35: *De fati ordine ex septem stellis, ex sententia Macrobii.* Cf. also *Ep.* 11, 34: *De operatione siderum.* All bodies are altered by sidereal causation is the argument. See also *Ode* II, 11, lines 45ff.; *Ep.* III, 70–76; *Ep.* IV, 78; *Ep.* IV, 66.

26. *Ode* I, 17.

27. *Ep.* IV, 64: *Ad astrologos.*

28. *Ep.* I, 59: *De mendaciis astrologorum; Ep.* I, 60: *De imperito astrologo; Ep.* IV, 7: *De cano, gallo et culina: astrologis.*

29. *Ep.* III, 7: *Ad Saturnum*, is one of the few references to Saturn and it is little more than an aside. See Erwin Panofsky, *Albrecht Dürer*, I (Princeton, 1948), 157.

30. *Am.* I, 14: *De exclusione; necromanticas et magicas artes commemorat.*

31. *Br.* 275, pp. 494ff., lines 121ff. *Br.* 101, pp. 165ff., line 22.

32. *Ode* I, 5, lines 137ff.

33. *Ode*, I, 19.

34. *Ode* I, 16.

35. *Am.* IV, 4, lines 89ff.

36. Schedel's manuscript is in Munich in the Bayerische Staatsbibliothek Clm 24848. Celtis' edition of the Propositions was republished by Michael Zimmermann, *Propositiones Domini Cardinalis Nicolai Cusae de ly non aliud* (Vienna, 1556). Cf. *Nicolae de Cusa, Opera Omnia, XIII, Directio Speculantis seu de non aliud*, eds. Ludwig Baur and Paulus Wilpert (Leipzig, 1944), p. xi. The theses are to be found in a German translation in Paul Wilpert, *Vom Nichtanderen* (Hamburg, 1952), pp. 87–95, together with a good introduction to the dialogue, pp. v–xxviii, used above. Johannes Uebinger, who discovered the Schedel manuscript in 1888, published the

text in *Die Gotteslehre des Nikolaus Cusanus* (Münster and Paderborn, 1888), pp. 194–198: *Propositiones . . . de virtute ipsius non aliud.*

37. *Br.* 2, p. 4, line 43; *Ep.* I, 6; *Ep.* I, 19, etc.

38. *Ode* IV, 9; *Br.* 3, p. 7, lines 26 ff.; *Am.* IV, 3, lines 6off.; *Ep.* V, 40.

39. *Ep.* II, 38; *Ode* III, 6, lines 57ff.; *Ode* IV, 2, lines 3ff., 41ff.; *Epod* 7, lines 31ff.; *Ep.* V, 60; *Ars versificandi et carminum* (Leipzig, 1487): *Ad lectorem.*

40. *Ode* I, 29.

41. *Am.* III, 14.

42. *Am.* III, 12, lines 53–62; *Ode* III, 15.

43. *Ode* I, 29, lines 13ff.

44. *Ode* IV, 6, lines 15–18; *Am.* IV, 3, lines 6off.; *Am.* IV, 4, lines 56ff.

45. *Ode* I, 5: *Ad Andream Pegasum de fato et felicitate.*

46. *Ode* II, 22, lines 45ff.

47. *Ep.* IV, 16: *In Fortunae vultum ex sententia philosophorum.* In *Ode* III, 1, lines 77f., virtue opposes fortune; in *Epod* 9, lines 23f., fortune through various perils makes a way to virtue.

48. *Ode* II, 2, lines 77f. In *Ode* II, 14 Celtis warns against inquiring into the counsels of the gods. Apollo and poetry raise man above concern for the fates.

49. *Ep.* I, 6: *Ad Jovem optimum maximum.* Cf. also *Am.* IV, 4, where Celtis ponders the imponderable, God, fate, nature.

50. *Br.* 79, pp. 131f., lines 26f. Cf. *Ep.* II, 2: *Ad Germanos.* In *Ep.* V, 5, Celtis repeats the fiction of the papess Joan. In *Br.* 313, p. 566, Augustinus Moravus asks the suppression of his anecdotes about the Pope.

51. *Ep.* IV, 17: *De sacerdote capum pro pisce comedente.*

52. *Ode* III, 15, lines 29ff.; *Ep.* IV, 23; *Am.* III, 9, lines 47ff.

53. *Am.* III, 9.

54. *Am.* III, 10, lines 49ff.

55. *Oratio inauguralis*, sentence 79, published with the *Panegyris ad Duces Bauarie* (Augsburg, 1492), as well as in a modern edition by Hans Rupprich, *Conradus Celtis Protucius Oratio* (Leipzig, 1932), in the "Bibliotheca Scriptorum" series. The *Oratio* is included with the text and translation in Forster, *Conrad Celtis Selections*, pp. 36ff. In *Br.* 32, p. 56, lines 11f., Celtis complains of the bad Latin of the clamoring scholastics. Gregor Nitsch, a humanist canon at the Cathedral of Olmütz, observes that poets and theologians have been at odds also in preceding centuries (*Br.* 251, p. 424, lines 39ff.).

56. *Vita, Br.* 339, pp. 609ff., lines 132f., Scripsit Parnasum bicipitem, in quo poetas et theologos concordat. *Br.* 110, pp. 184ff., may be a reference to this work.

57. *Br.* 5, p. 10, line 79; *Br.* 306, pp. 552ff., line 14; *Epod* 14; *Br.* 305, pp. 549ff.; *Br.* 210, pp. 348ff.

58. *Br.* 312, pp. 465ff.

59. *Ep.* I, 20, 21; *Ep.* III, 24; *Ep.* V, 19; *Br.* 325, p. 581, lines 2ff. Bayerische Staatsbibliothek Clm codex 782; *Ad divinam Catherinam; Ad divam Virginem.*

60. *Ep.* I, 19; *Ep.* II, 37; *Ep.* III, 1; *Ep.* V, 14; *Ode* II, 8. Clm codex 6007 or Ebersberg 2071, p. 112; "Chunradus Celtes, laureatus poeta sic dicit de

beata Maria virgine in carmine suo saphico," in Franz Leitschuh, *Studien und Quellen zur deutschen Kunstgeschichte des XV.-XVI. Jahrhunderts* (Fribourg, 1912), p. 145. *Ars versificandi,* p. 46.

61. *Am.* III, 13, lines 7ff. *Ode* II, 30: *De tumba divae Valpurgis in Archstadio* . . .

62. "In aede divae genitricis . . ."; *Ep.* V, 4; *Ep.* IV, 36, 37. In December 1502, Celtis visited Alt-Oetting, where he was met by Aventine and taken to the latter's home in Abensberg on December 7; Johannes Turmair (Aventinus), *Sämmtliche Werke* (Munich, 1881–1908), IV, 8.

63. *Br.* 343, pp. 619f.

64. *Br.* 345, p. 622, line 9.

65. *Br.* 308, pp. 556, note 2.

66. *Index librorum damnatorum Matriti,* Bernhard de Sandoval (Madrid: Lud. Sanchez, 1612, appendix 1614), 194: Conradus Celtes, seu Celtis Protussius, seu Protuncius Francof. German. poeta, et cosmographus. E Klüpfel, *De Vita et Scriptis,* I, 223, goes to great lengths to defend Celtis' orthodoxy.

67. *Br.* 252, pp. 425ff., specifically line 84.

VI HUTTEN — Militant Critic

1. Edvardvs Böcking, *Vlrichi Hvtteni Eqvitis Germani Opera,* 7 vols. (Leipzig, 1859–1864), I, 38, hereafter cited as Böcking with volume and page number following. The best work on Hutten by far is Hajo Holborn, *Ulrich von Hutten and the German Reformation* (New Haven, 1937) based on a German edition of 1929, containing Holborn's valuable bibliographical notes, pp. 203–209. Holborn repaints the picture left by David Friedrich Strauss, *Ulrich von Hutten,* 2 vols. (Leipzig, 1858), of Hutten as the carrier of a happy optimistic dawn spirit. He also effectively corrects the jaundiced views of P. Kalkoff, *Ulrich von Hutten und die Entscheidungsjahre der Reformation* (Leipzig, 1920) and *Ulrich von Huttens Vagantenzeit und Untergang* (Weimar, 1925). It must be conceded to Kalkoff, however, that he made a real contribution in refuting the accepted notion of Hutten and Luther as two great figures with the same reform program. Otto Flake, *Ulrich von Hutten* (Berlin, 1929) adds little of essential novelty. Harald Drewinc, *Vier Gestalten* (St. Gallen, 1946), provides an interesting brief sketch. The basic monograph for the present problem is the thorough study by Paul Held, *Ulrich von Hutten. Seine religiös-geistige Auseinandersetzung mit Katholizismus, Humanismus, Reformation* (Leipzig, 1928). A very helpful guide to Hutten's publications, supplementing Böcking's "Verzeichnis der Schriften Ulrichs von Hutten" of 1858, is Josef Benzing, *Ulrich von Hutten und seine Drucker* (Wiesbaden, 1956).

2. Böcking II, 145.

3. Böcking I, 5.

4. Böcking I, 217.

5. Olga Gewerstock, *Lucian und Hutten* (Berlin, 1924), pp. 14ff., demonstrates the formal influence of Lucian on Hutten's dialogues and to a lesser extent his influence on Hutten's satires.

6. Böcking I, 166.

7. Böcking I, 182.

8. Böcking I, 180.

9. Böcking III, 416ff.

10. Böcking I, 237.

11. Böcking I, 193; I, 125, Hutten to Richardus Crocus Anglus; *Epistolae Obscurorum Virorum*, part II, ep. LV. Erasmus, too, cited Horace's *Ridentem dicere verum, Quid vetat?* with approval, *Opera*, IX, col. 3.

12. Böcking I, 110.

13. *Vlrichi de Hvtten Eqvitis Germani ad Caesarem Maximilianvm Epigrammatvm Liber vnus*, Böcking III, 205ff.

14. Böcking III, 260, ep. 134, *De ivlio II. Pontifice Maximo Orbem Christianvm in arma concitante*; III, p. 261, ep. 135, *De Gladio Ivlii*; III, p. 262, ep. 136, *De eodem*; III, p. 263, ep. 137, *De Ivlii Perfidia*; III, p. 265, ep. 142, *De Ivlio Allvsio*; III, p. 266, ep. 145, *De Indvlgentiis Ivlii*; III, p. 269, *In tempora Ivlii Satyra, et alii.*

15. *Ulrichi De Hutten ad Crotvm Rvbianvm De Statv Romano Epigrammata ex vrbe missa*, Böcking III, pp. 278ff., eps. 1–8.

16. Böcking IV, 145ff. Julius Freund, *Huttens Vadiscus und seine Quelle* (Marburg, 1899), concludes that Crotus Rubeanus probably wrote fifty-eight German triads in Italy and they formed the basis of Hutten's work, another instance of Crotus' influence.

17. Böcking I, 155ff.

18. Böcking I, 325ff., 331. Hutten runs through the history of the controversies of German emperors with the popes in the little piece *Herr Ulrichs von Hutten anzoig Wie allwegen sich die Römischen Bischöff, oder Bäpst gegen den teütschen Kayszeren gehalten haben, vff dz kürtzst usz Chronicken und Historien gezogen, K. maiestät fürzubringen*, Böcking V, 363ff.

19. Böcking I, 431f.

20. Böcking V, 386ff., *Vergleichung der Bäpst satzung gegen der leer Christj Jesu.*

21. Böcking III, 470ff., *Das teutsch Requiem der verbranten Bullen und Bebstlichen Rechten.*

22. Böcking II, 219.

23. Böcking I, 135.

24. Holborn, *Ulrich von Hutten*, pp. 57f., 69, citing Böcking I, 183.

25. Böcking I, 146, 147, 216.

26. Böcking I, 146.

27. Böcking I, 103.

28. In a letter to the Archbishop of Mainz, December 21, 1518, at any rate, Erasmus praised Hutten: hunc animum meum literis significorum iuveni non minus eruditione quam imaginibus claro, Udalricho Hutteno, sed hoc unice nobili, quod tua dignitas illum inter praecipuos ac interiores officiarios complectitur.

29. Böcking I, 151.

30. Böcking I, 248.

31. Böcking I, 270.

32. Böcking I, 368.

33. Böcking I, 368; I, 423; II, 178ff., Erasmus writes of Hutten's estrange-

ment; II, 180, Hutten's reply. See Werner Kaegi, "Hutten und Erasmus. Ihre Freundschaft und ihr Streit," *Historische Vierteljahrschrift*, XXII (1924), 200–278, 461–514, an account of their friendship, an analysis of the deeper reasons for their friendship, a comparison of their personalities, and a description of the break between them under the pressures of the Reformation.

34. Böcking II, 216ff.

35. Böcking II, 277ff.

36. Böcking II, 258f.

37. Böcking II, 379, October 1, 1523.

38. Böcking II, p. 409.

39. Held, *Ulrich von Hutten*, p. 89.

40. *Ibid.*, 83, 86, 89, 91, 94.

41. *Ibid.*, 94.

42. *Ibid.*, 100, citing Böcking IV, 395.

43. *Ibid.*, 100, citing Böcking I, 326.

44. *Ibid.*, 100, citing Böcking IV, 153.

45. Böcking I, 146.

46. Held, *Ulrich von Hutten*, pp. 95–98.

47. Böcking V, 332, Hutten declares that the pope should feed the sheep, etc.

48. Böcking I, 374.

49. Held, Ulrich von Hutten, p. 103, citing Böcking IV, 178.

50. Böcking V, 323, Hutten attacked Leo for calling an appeal to a council a crime.

51. Held, *Ulrich von Hutten*, p. 102, citing Böcking I, p. 397.

52. F. G. Stokes, ed., *Epistolae Obscurorum Virorum* (London, 1909), ii, xliii, 223. D. F. Strauss, *Ulrich von Hutten* (London, 1874), p. 128, was so insensitive to theology as to claim that Hutten's strictures against indulgences in the *Epistolae Obscurorum Virorum* contained Luther's doctrine.

53. Ipsa suas Fortuna rotas pro tempore versat/Et levibus nostras axibus ambit opes. *Querelae*, Böcking III, 45. The *Ad Caesarem Maximilianum epigrammatum liber unus* exploits the theme of *Fortuna* at least nine times, Böcking, III, 229, 230, 231, 232, 233, 234, 235, 236, 239. On *Virtus*, Böcking III, 208.

54. Holborn, *Ulrich von Hutten*, p. 85; Drewinc, *Vier Gestalten*, p. 254.

55. Böcking IV, 75–100; Gewerstock, *Lucian und Hutten*, pp. 78ff., 84, 87.

56. Holborn, *Ulrich von Hutten*, p. 133, citing Böcking I, 99.

57. Böcking I, 167, April 3, 1518, letter to Count Newenar.

58. Böcking I, 355, Mainz, June 4, 1520, Hutten to Luther.

59. Böcking I, 370, Luther to Spalatin, September 11, 1520. Böcking I, 420, In a letter to Spalatin, October 3, 1520, Luther wrote: Huttenus ingenti spiritu accingitur in Romanum pontificem armis et ingenio rem tentans.

60. Böcking V, 301ff.

61. Böcking IV, 309ff.; IV, 330, Hutten attacks Roman venality, avarice, rapacity, insatiability.

62. Böcking IV, 337ff., 342, 347.

63. Böcking IV, 398.

64. Böcking I, 324

65. Böcking III, 473ff., cited in Holborn, *Ulrich von Hutten*, p. 158. Maurice Gravier, *Luther et l'opinion publique* (Paris, c. 1942), chapter II: Hutten et Luther à l'assaut de l'Église romaine (1520), described Hutten's key role in the war of the pamphlets.

66. Böcking I, 383ff.

67. Böcking I, 405, September 28, 1520, *Ein Clagschrift des Hochberümten und Eernuesten herrn Ulrichs von Hutten gekröneten Poeten und Orator an alle stend Deutscher nation* . . . In an open letter, November or December 1520, Hutten decried the bull of Leo X for trying to suppress Christian truth and German liberty, Böcking I, 430. He affirmed repeatedly that Luther's cause was that of truth and of Christ, Böcking I, 435.

68. Böcking I, 450. At the end of the *Gesprächbüchlein* Luther and Hutten are pictured with appropriate verses on their common defense of truth, Böcking I, 451ff.

69. Böcking II, 15; II, 21ff. *Invectiva in Lvtheromastigos Sacerdotes*: Luther — praedicatorem veritatis et evangelicae doctrinae dispensatorem fidelissimum; II, 38ff., the exhortation to Charles, March 27, 1521, 40: *pro Christi doctrina, pro patria libertate*; II, 43, *ad Carolvm Imperatorem pro Lvthero Exhortatoria: Spes fuit Romanum te a nobis iugum ablaturum, istam pontificum tyrannidem demoliturum*; the Litany to the Germans, Böcking II, pp. 52ff.; Böcking II, 98, a letter identifying Luther and Hutten as fighters for Christian and German liberty. See Wilhelm Reindell, *Luther, Crotus und Hutten* (Marburg, 1890), on this subject of Luther and the young Erfurt humanists.

70. Böcking II, 55, April 17, 1521, *Martino Lvthero Theologo Evangelistae Invictissimo amico sancto*.

71. Böcking II, 59ff. In his *Endtschuldigung wider etlicher unwahrheiten*, Hutten repeated that the priests had made of Christianity a tyrannous suppression, Böcking II, 141.

72. Mea humana sunt, tu perfectior iam totus ex divinis dependes.

73. Holborn, *Ulrich von Hutten*, p. 193.

74. Böcking III, 223, cited in Holborn, *Ulrich von Hutten*, p. 192.

75. Flake, *Ulrich von Hutten*, p. 289, February 9, Luther to Staupitz.

76. *Ibid.*, p. 265.

77. Böcking II, 277ff., the *Spongia*. Paul Kalkoff was correct, then, in denying the inner identification of Hutten with the basic religious and ethical content of the evangelical message. He was entirely wrong in minimizing the importance of Hutten to the Reformation and completely unfair in accusing him of abandoning Luther's cause for imperial money and dissipating his waning strength in a futile "priest war," "Erasmus und Hutten in ihrem Verhältnis zu Luther," *Historische Zeitschrift*, CXXII, 2. Folge, XXVI, 2. Heft (1920), 260ff. Hutten had long looked to the princes and emperor and war on the Romanists was always central to his reform program of attack on abuse. See Fritz Walser, *Die politische Entwicklung Ulrichs von Hutten während der Entscheidungsjahre der Reformation* (Munich, n.d.). Gerhard Ritter, "Ulrich von Hutten und die Reformation," *Die Weltwirkung der Reformation*, 2d ed. (Darmstadt, 1959), p. 109, shows

that Hutten was proud of his independence from Luther, but that he never betrayed Luther or his cause, as Kalkoff asserted.

78. Böcking II, 34, *Hutteni invectiva in Lutheromastigos sacerdotes, Mart., 1521.*

79. Böcking II, 130ff., 133, *Entschüldigung Ulrichs von Hutten Wyder etlicher vnwarhafftiges auszgeben, von ym, als solt er wider alle geystlichkeit vnd priesterschafft sein.*

80. Böcking II, 142, *Entschüldigung Ulrichs von Hutten Wyder etlicher unwarhafftiges auszgeben* [1522?]: Christus hat zwen ständ, darinnen wir sälig werden mügen, angezeigt, eynen volkomlichen, darinnen er vns heist, was wir haben verkauffen und es den armen geben, wer uns den mantel nympt, jm auch den rock volgen lassen, wer vns auf einen backen schlägt, im den andern darwenden. Sol disser stand von yemant, solt er fürwar von den geistlichen vortreten werden, dann sy söllen uns mit güten beyspilen vorgehen, und was an uns gebrechen, so an yn erfült werden.

81. Böcking II, 142f. Hutten quotes Luther on this point as well as Isaiah, Ezekiel on the sword, in a mood of prophetic denunciation. Held, *Ulrich von Hutten*, p. 36, cites the *Exhortatio ad Principes Germanos, ut bellum Turcis inferant*, 1518, as illustrating Hutten's objection to papal interference in the affairs of the princes, Böcking, V, 103.

82. Böcking I, 331, cited in Held, *Ulrich von Hutten*, p. 37. His conventional double standard for clergy and laity was evident even in the *Vadiscus* where he said that if the heads of the Christian faith live so wrongly the unbeliever must wonder how the other members of the same body live, *Böcking* IV, pp. 196, 221. In *Monitor I* Luther, the model of sacerdotalism, explains the difference between Christian and civil virtue, showing again Hutten's failure to comprehend Luther. Similarly in the preface to his edition of Valla's *De Donatione* he looked to the pope for needed reform, criticizing papal political commitments, Held, *Ulrich von Hutten*, p. 38.

83. Böcking II, 245, cited in Held, *Ulrich von Hutten*, p. 38.

84. Böcking I, 154.

85. Böcking V, 100ff., 102.

86. Böcking III, 245ff., *Exclamatio in sceleratissimam Ioannis Pepericornis vitam.*

87. Ernst Borkowsky, *Aus der Zeit des Humanismus* (Jena, 1905), p. 175: "Hutten war Rationalist in religiösen Dingen . . ."

88. Böcking IV, 49, *Missulus S. Avla. Dialogvs*, 1518.

89. See, for example, the many references to the *Respublica Christiana* and the *orbus Christianus* in his oration against the Turks, Böcking V, 100ff., *Ulrichi de Hvtten Eqvitis ad Principes Germanos vt Bellvm in Tvrcas Concorditer svscipiant exhortatoria.*

90. Cf. Hans Keller, *Ulrich von Huttens Tod auf der Ufenau* (Stäfa, 1948), pp. 1–8.

VII MUTIAN — Intellectual Canon

1. Carl Krause, *Der Briefwechsel des Mutianus Rufus* (Kassel, 1885), Letter 89, p. 99. Citations from Krause will hereafter read, e.g., Krause 89, p. 99. See Ludwig Geiger, "Mutian," *Allgemeine Deutsche Biographie*, XXIII (Leipzig, 1896), 108.

2. Georg Kaufman, *Die Geschichte der Deutschen Universitäten*, II (Stuttgart, 1896), 501ff.

3. For his registration, cf. *Acten der Erfurter Universität*, ed. J. C. H. Weissenborn, I (Halle, 1881), 41.

4. Krause 71, p. 77, Urban describes his respect and admiration for Mutian ever since his study under him at Erfurt.

5. F. W. Kampschulte, *Die Universität Erfurt in ihrem Verhältnisse zu dem Humanismus und der Reformation*, 2 vols. (Trier, 1858), was the most influential of the earlier studies. Gustav Bauch, *Die Universität Erfurt im Zeitalter des Frühhumanismus* (Breslau, 1904), has supplied the major corrective to Kampschulte's excessive enthusiasm and false emphases. On Bauch, see G. v. Orterer, "G Bauch, *Die Universität Erfurt*," *Historisches Jahrbuch*, XXVI (1905) 439ff. See also Werner Schnellenkamp, *Baugeschichte des "Collegium Majus" der Universität Erfurt* (Erfurt, 1936); Friedrich Paulsen, "Die Gründung der deutschen Universitäten im Mittelalter," *Historische Zeitschrift*, XLV (1881), 251ff. Friedrich Benary, "*Via antiqua* und *via moderna* auf den deutschen Hochschulen des Mittelalters mit besonderer Berücksichtigung der Universität Erfurt," *Zur Geschichte der Stadt und der Universität Erfurt am Ausgang des Mittelalters* (Gotha, 1919), compares previous studies on Erfurt and criticizes them all for basing their conclusions on the position of individuals rather than on the structure of the faculty as a whole.

6. *Acten der Erfurter Universität*, p. xii.

7. Theodor Kolde, *Martin Luther*, I (Gotha, 1884), 39. Theodor Kolde, *Das religiöse Leben in Erfurt beim Ausgange des Mittelalters* (Halle, 1898), p. 40, holds that in the city itself the ideal of medieval piety persisted so that as late as 1518 new brotherhoods were organized in Erfurt. Similarly Paul Kalkoff, *Humanismus und Reformation in Erfurt (1500–1530)* (Halle, 1926), p. 16, believes that the spirit of dissent in the University has been overemphasized. While individuals may have expressed critical sentiments, the faculty of theology was not anti-curial, but conformed even in the crisis of 1520.

8. Kampschulte, *Die Universität Erfurt*, pp. 30 *et passim*, argues that scholasticism was not so dominant here as elsewhere, there were no tourneys of disputation, more stress on biblical knowledge and the like.

9. *Acten der Erfurter Universität*, p. viii; G. Kaufmann, "Die Universitäts-Privilegien der Kaiser," *Deutsche Zeitschrift für Geschichtswissenschaft* (1889), p. 150. Gray Cowan Boyce, "Erfurt Schools and Scholars in the Thirteenth Century," *Speculum*, XXIV (1949), 1ff.; on the *Carmen satiricum*, pp. 12ff.

10. Nicolai de Bibera, "Carmen satiricum," *Erfurter Denkmäler, Geschichtsquellen der Provinz Sachsen*, I (Halle, 1870), 5ff.

11. Krause 636, pp. 654f.

12. Krause 174, p. 223.

13. Krause 32, p. 39; Krause 59, p. 65.

14. For publications of the classics in Erfurt, see Martin Wähler, "Die Blütezeit des Erfurter Buchgewerbes, 1450–1530;" *Mitteilungen des Vereins für die Geschichte und Altertumskunde von Erfurt*, XLII (1924), 5ff.

15. Kampschulte, *Die Universität Erfurt*, p. 118.

16. On the revolution, see Friedrich Benary, "Über die Erfurter Revolution von 1509 und ihren Einfluss auf die Erfurter Geschichtschreibung," *Mitteilungen des Vereins für die Geschichte und Altertumskunde von Erfurt*, XXXIII (1912), 125ff. He does not discuss the role of the humanists in the affair, however.

17. Friedrich Zarncke, *Aufsätze und Reden zur Kultur-und Zeitgeschichte* (Leipzig, 1898), p. 163. See Friedrich Paulsen, *The German Universities, their character and historical development* (New York, 1895), p. 40.

18. Georg Ellinger, *Die neulateinische Lyrik Deutschlands in der ersten Hälfte des Sechzehnten Jahrhunderts* (Berlin, 1929), p. 3. Kalkoff, *Humanismus und Reformation*, p. 13, maintains, however, that the opposition to scholasticism demonstrated real strength only after the Leipzig debate, when Justus Jonas assumed the leadership in the University and the influence of Mutian receded.

19. Léon Dorez and Louis Thuasne, *Pic de la Mirandole en France, 1485–1488* (Paris 1897), p. 28.

20. *Marsilii Ficini Florentini, insignis Philosophi Platonici, Medici atque Theologi clarissimi, Opera, etc.* (Basel, n.d.), p. 79, *Theologia Platonica*, p. 98, "unity, truth, goodness are the same, and beyond these there is nothing"; p. 119, "the soul is the mid-level of things and all superior and inferior levels are connected in it, while it itself ascends to those above and descends to those below." An excellent epitome by Josephine Burroughs is contained in *The Renaissance Philosophy of Man*, ed. Ernst Cassirer *et al.* (Chicago, 1948), pp. 185ff.

21. Adolph Harnack, *Lehrbuch der Dogmengeschichte*, III (Leipzig, 1897), 597ff. See also Charles Elsee, *Neoplatonism in Relation to Christianity* (Cambridge, 1908), pp. 138ff.; C. Bigg, *Chief Ancient Philosophies: Neoplatonism* (London, 1895), pp. 334ff.

22. Cf. Krause 85, p. 93; Krause 137, p. 175; Krause 392, p. 460; Krause 548, p. 616; Krause 557, p. 626; Krause 311, p. 385: "At quoniam sine sacris et Christo philosopharis, stulto stultior esse et ab academia Platonicisque meis aberrare videris neque nostrae Musae Congruis."

23. Krause 233, p. 289.

24. Krause 558, p. 626.

25. Krause 269, p. 331.

26. Krause 5, p. 5; Krause 19, p. 21 *et passim*.

27. Krause 8, p. 10.

28. Krause 120, pp. 150f.

29. Krause 596, p. 636; text in Karl Gillert, *Der Briefwechsel des Conradus Mutianus, Geschichtsquellen der Provinz Sachsen und angrenzender Gebiete*, XVIII (Halle, 1890), ep. 163, p. 233. This reply was worthy of Poggio, who believed that *studium* and *virtus* would overcome the power of the stars and the goddess Fortuna. Ernst Walser, *Poggius Florentinus* (Leipzig and Berlin, 1914), pp. 196, 236.

30. Krause 73, p. 79.

31. Krause 373, p. 445; Krause 553, p. 621.

32. Krause 140 and 141, pp. 180–188.

33. Krause 142, p. 189 (1510). On the significance of Mantuanus for

English literature, especially Spenser, see Lewis Einstein, *The Italian Renaissance in England* (New York, 1902), p. 348.

34. Anton Störmann, *Die städtischen Gravamina gegen den Klerus am Ausgange des Mittelalters und in der Reformationszeit* (Münster i. W., 1916), pp. 1ff. Ernst Troeltsch, *Die Soziallehren der christlichen Kirchen und Gruppen* (Tübingen, 1912), pp. 418ff., interprets this phenomenon as a result of lay culture rising in opposition to the ecclesiastical world of ideas.

35. Krause 125, p. 157.

36. Krause 233, p. 291.

37. Krause 10, p. 11.

38. Dante Alighieri, *The Divine Comedy* (New York, 1948), p. 135, *Paradiso*, canto 4.

39. Krause 357, pp. 427f.

40. Krause 85, pp. 93f.

41. *Documents of the Christian Church*, ed. Henry Bettenson (New York, 1947), p. 50. See also the reply of Irenaeus to Syrian gnosticism.

42. Krause 83, p. 89.

43. Krause 85, p. 93.

44. Krause 27, p. 35.

45. Krause 85, p. 93.

46. Krause 52, p. 57.

47. Krause 69, p. 75; Krause 52, p. 57.

48. Krause 147, p. 195.

49. Krause 85, p. 94.

50. Krause 553, p. 621: "Religiosus salutandum erat numen." Krause 120, p. 150.

51. Karl Hasse, *Von Plotin zu Goethe* (Leipzig, 1909), p. 156; Walter Moench, *Die italienische Platonrenaissance und ihre Bedeutung für Frankreichs Literatur-und Geistesgeschichte (1450–1550)* (Berlin, 1936), pp. 151ff.; *Marsilii Ficini, insignis Philosophi, Platonici, Medici atque Theologi clarissimi, Opera, etc.*, p. 1013, developed from Dionysius the Areopagite the idea of man as *lumen divinum*. It is a curious fact that astrology, related to the microcosm idea from antiquity and seemingly its natural consequence, played no part in Mutian's thinking. Perhaps he rejected it on ethical grounds, following Pico's lead, as being inconsistent with the creative autonomy of the individual.

52. Krause 223, p. 278.

53. Krause 49, p. 53.

54. Krause 331, p. 403.

55. Krause 11, p. 12.

56. *Marsilii Ficini, insignis Philosophi, Platonici, Medici atque Theologi clarissimi, Opera, etc.*, p. 1082.

57. Krause 52, p. 57; Krause 89, pp. 97ff.

58. Krause 75, p. 80.

59. Krause 25, p. 28; Krause 488, pp. 551ff.

60. Edmond Vansteenberghe, "Autour de la docte ignorance, une controverse sur la théologie mystique au XVe siecle," *Beiträge zur Geschichte der Philosophie des Mittelalters*, XIV (1915), 11. Nicolas Cusanus, *De Possest*, fol. 174b. in Joh. Uebinger, "Die philosophischen Schriften des

Nikolaus Cusanus," *Zeitschrift für Philosophie und philosophische Kritik, CVII* (1895), 53, on the relation of the Godhead to the visible creation.

61. Edmond Vansteenberghe, "Le 'De Ignota Litteratura' de Jean Wenck de Herrenberg contre Nicolas de Cuse," *Beiträge zur Geschichte der Philosophie des Mittelalters,* VIII (1910), 16ff. See Paul Shorey, *Platonism, Ancient and Modern* (Berkeley, 1938), pp. 31, 94, 107; Richard Falckenberg, *Geschichte der Neueren Philosophie von Nikolaus von Kues bis zur Gegenwart* (Berlin, 1927), p. 21.

62. See J. Lewis McIntyre, *Giordano Bruno* (London, 1903), pp. 122ff.; Albert Stöckle, *Geschichte der Philosophie des Mittelalters,* III (Mainz, 1866), 106ff.

63. Krause 373, p. 445; "Due ex nihilo cuncta creavit."

64. Krause 2, p. 3.

65. Krause 25, p. 28: "There is but one God and one Goddess, but there are many names: Jupiter, Sol, Apollo, Moses, Christ, Luna, Ceres, Proserpina, Tellus, Mary . . . In religious matters we must employ fables and enigmas as a veil. Thou who hast the grace of Jupiter, the best and greatest God, shouldst despise the little gods. When I say Jupiter, I mean Christ and the true God."

66. Krause 268, pp. 33f.

67. Krause 488, p. 552.

68. Krause 26, p. 32.

69. Paul Mestwerdt, *Die Anfänge des Erasmus, Humanismus und "Devotio Moderna"* (Leipzig, 1917), p. 84.

70. *Marsilii Ficini Florentini, insignis Philosophi Platonici, Medici, atque Theologi Clarissimi, Opera, etc.,* p. 1ff. For the patristic idea of philosophy as a "school master" bringing the Greek mind to Christ, see Clement of Alexandria, *Christ the Educator, The Fathers of the Church,* XXIII (New York, 1954). On Moses and the Hebrews as teachers of the Greek philosophers, see such representative selections as Clement's *Stromata* I, chapter 25: Plato an imitator of Moses in framing laws; chapter 29: The Greeks but children compared with the Hebrews; II, chapter 5: He proves by several examples that the Greeks drew from the sacred writers, etc.; *The Ante-Nicene Fathers* II (Grand Rapids, Mich., 1951), pp. 338, 341, 351f.

71. *Plotini Enneades cum Marsilii Ficini interpretatione castigata* (Paris, 1845), p. 16, de beatitudine, Ennead IV, III, p. 207: "Lex divina animis insita ducit eos tam sponte quam necessario ad terminos affectioni eorum convenientes."

72. Krause 11, p. 13.

73. Krause 137, p. 174.

74. *Marsilii Ficini Florentini, insignis Philosophi Platonici, Medici, atque Theologi Clarissimi, Opera, etc.,* p. 459: "Justitia quidem, quae satisfacit Deo, qua iustificatur apud Deum anima, comparatur per ipsam fidem, Christo Evangelio Praestitam. Per fidem, inquam, uiuam, id est, charitatem formatum, et operantem."

75. Jean Festugière, *La Philosophie de l'amour de Marsile Ficin* (Coimbra, 1923), pp. 22, 25ff.

76. Cf. Krause 266, p. 328; Krause 362, p. 432.

77. Krause 628, p. 647; Krause 658, p. 665.

78. Krause 371, p. 441; Krause 171, p. 220: ". . . dialecticum Augustininum cum interprete Hieronymo, romanis scriptoribus associa."

79. Krause 634, p. 651. Eoban dedicated to Erasmus his *Carmen Heroicum*, Erfurt, 1519.

80. Krause 29, pp. 36f.

81. Krause 25, p. 28.

82. Krause 85, pp. 91f.; Krause 498, p. 563.

83. Krause 349, p. 419.

84. Krause 178, p. 228.

85. Krause 137, p. 174.

86. Krause 201, p. 256.

87. Krause 137, p. 175.

88. Geiger, *Johann Reuchlin*, p. 351.

89. Krause 96, p. 112.

90. Cf. Krause 592, p. 635.

91. Krause 11, p. 13.

92. Krause 287, p. 353.

93. Krause 335, p. 408.

94. David Friedrich Strauss, *Ulrich von Hutten* (London, 1874), p. 365.

95. Krause 585, p. 634.

96. Krause 287, p. 353; cf. also Krause 146, p. 194.

97. Krause 120, p. 151.

98. Julius Köstlin, *Martin Luther*, I (Berlin, 1903), 132; Krause 622, p. 645, text in Gillert, *Briefwechsel*, ep. 560, p. 224.

99. Compare Krause 633, p. 650 and Krause 636, p. 657, for example.

100. *Dr. Martin Luthers Werke, Tischreden*, II (Weimar, 1913), 627.

101. Krause 644, pp. 660f.; cf. *Vorrede*, p. ix.

102. Carl Krause, *Helius Eobanus Hessus*, I (Gotha, 1879), 316.

VIII PIRCKHEIMER — Speculative Patrician

1. Cochläus an Pirckheimer, June 9, 1517; Paul Drews, *Wilibald Pirckheimers Stellung zur Reformation* (Leipzig, 1887), p. 16.

2. Emil Reicke, ed., *Willibald Pirckheimers Briefwechsel*, II (Munich, 1956), ep. 371, p. 573, Von Erasmus [Basel], Oct. 16 [1515]. This volume of correspondence will hereafter be referred to as *Br.* with the volume, letter, and page numbers following.

3. C. J. Burckhardt, "Willibald Pirckheimer," *Neue Schweizer Rundschau*, N. F. IV, no 10 (February 1937), 577ff., 582. The essay is reprinted in Burckhardt's *Gestalten und Mächte* (Zürich, 1941), 47–69. M. Herrmann, *Die Reception des Humanismus in Nürnberg* (Berlin, 1898), describes the slow progress of humanism in the imperial city. See Hans von Schubert, *Lazarus Spengler und die Reformation in Nürnberg, Quellen und Forschungen zur Reformationsgeschichte*, XVII (Leipzig, 1934), 1ff.

4. Émile Offenbacher, "La Bibliothèque de Wilibald Pirckheimer," *La Bibliofilia*, XL (1938), 241–263. In 1512, Cochlaeus characterized Pirckheimer's library as "Tam dives librorum, ut similis bibliotheca utriusque linguae nusquam per Germaniam reperiri queat." See Erwin Rosenthal, "Dürers Buchmalereien für Pirckheimers Bibliothek," *Jahrbuch der Preu-*

szischen Kunstsammlungen. Beiheft zum Neunundvierzigsten Band (Berlin, 1929), arguing that Dürer was the artist of a series of book illustrations in Pirckheimer's library.

5. There is as yet no adequate modern biography of Pirckheimer or edition of his works. A lengthy biography prefaced each of the two earliest editions, Hans III. Imhoff, *Theatrum Virtutis et Honoris; oder Tugend Büchlein* (Nuremberg, 1606), containing a selection of Pirckheimer's German writings, and Konrad Rittershausen and Melchior Goldast, *Opera politica, historica, philologica et epistolica* (Frankfort, 1610). The manuscript sources are to be found primarily in the Nürnberger Stadtbibliothek, *Pirckheimerpapiere, Nachlasz*; the Bayerisches Staatsarchiv Nürnberg, the *Briefbücher*; the British Museum, the Arundel Manuscripts; and the Library of the College of Arms. Until recently only scattered selections of Pirckheimer's letters were made available by J. B. Riederer, G. Th. Strobel, Th. Freytag, F. Thurnhofer, M. Spahn, and T. Kolde. The most extensive collection was that of Johann Heumann, *Documenta literaria* (Altdorf, 1758). This was the first and only volume of a projected three-volume edition of the correspondence and it included letters found in a most romantic manner. Around the year 1750 the house of Pirckheimer's descendants, the Imhoffs, on Egidienberg became the property of Christoph Joachim Haller von Hallerstein. During the process of remodeling, a mason struck a hidden space behind a wall in which was found a chest containing priceless Pirckheimer manuscripts, outlines, final copies, translations, astrological notes, medicinal recipes, accounts of his gout, confessions of his faith and moral opinions, and many letters. His correspondence is at last appearing in a scientific edition, Émil Reicke, ed., *Willibald Pirckheimers Briefwechsel* I (Munich, 1940), II (Munich, 1956), vols. IV and V of the *Humanisten-Briefe*, published under the auspices of the *Veröffentlichungen der Kommission zur Erforschung der Geschichte der Reformation und Gegenreformation*. These two volumes include the correspondence to 1515 and two additional volumes are promised in the near future.

6. Arnold Reimann, *Die älteren Pirckheimer: Geschichte eines Nürnberger Patriziergeschlechtes im Zeitalter des Frühhumanismus (bis 1501)* (Leipzig, 1944) reveals Willibald's debt to his learned forebearers. Also of great value are Reimann's *Pirckheimer-Studien I. und II. Buch* (Berlin, 1900), drawn from his Berlin dissertation exploring the *Nachlasz* and the family library. Paul Lehmann, "Grundzüge des Humanismus deutscher Lande, zumal im Spiegel deutscher Bibliotheken des 15. und 16. Jahrhunderts," *Aevum*, XXXI (1957), 263, reports that the study of the library of Johannes Pirckheimer, Willibald's father, shows a rejection and exclusion of scholasticism. Karl Hagen undertook an ambitious study of Pirckheimer as a major figure of his epoch, *Deutschlands literarische und religiöse Verhältnisse im Reformationszeitalter. Mit besonderer Rücksicht auf W. Pirkheimer* (Erlangen, 1841ff., 2nd ed., Frankfort a.M., 1868). Although he presented useful translations of important passages, the synthesis was only partially successful. Friedrich Roth, *Willibald Pirkheimer, ein Lebensbild aus dem Zeitalter des Humanismus und der Reformation* (Halle, 1887), was popular and too brief to do justice to the deeper problems. He asserted (p. 18) that in his theological standpoint Pirckheimer was thoroughly humanistic, always an

Erasmian. Emil Reicke, *Willibald Pirckheimer. Leben, Familie und Persön-lichkeit* (Jena, 1930) is brief and popular, pointing up the colorful rather than wrestling with the more difficult intellectual problems. Three studies to date are concerned specifically with the problem of Pirckheimer's re-lation to the Reformation. Rudolf Hagen, *Willibald Pirckheimer in seinem Verhältnis zum Humanismus und zur Reformation* (Nuremberg, 1882), held that Pirckheimer remained loyal to the Reformation even though con-fessionalism was distasteful to him. Hagen therein reflects the older in-terpretation of Heinrich Erhard, *Die Geschichte des Wiederaufblühens der wissenschaftlichen Bildung*, III (Magdeburg, 1832), 1–61, that Pirckheimer increasingly favored the Reformation during his last years. P. Drews, *Willibald Pirckheimers Stellung zur Reformation* (Leipzig, 1887) was writ-ten with certain Whiggish prejudices. Drews saw Pirckheimer as a man of sharpest contradictions and discrepancies. But he believed his basic view-point to have been humanistic-aesthetic on religious and ethical questions so that he attempted a basic impartiality toward both parties. Franz Kirner, "Willibald Pirckheimer's Verhältnis zur Reformation" (Vienna disserta-tion, 1950) seeks to demonstrate that Pirckheimer was much more deeply rooted in the Christian tradition than one would expect of a humanist. The most recent, very excellent analysis of Pirckheimer's spiritual essence is that of Hans Rupprich, "Willibald Pirckheimer. Beiträge zu einer Wesens-erfassung," *Schweizer Beiträge zur Allgemeinen Geschichte*, XV (1957), 64–110. Done with Professor Rupprich's usual meticulous care, the essay is particularly valuable for its treatment of Pirckheimer's work as a philologist and translator. He believes that Pirckheimer basically in heart and soul always remained within the realm of the late medieval ecclesiastical faith and jurisdiction, although after his Reformation encounter he was too complicated, critical, and skeptical to embrace the old again completely.

7. Hans Rupprich, *Wilibald Pirckheimer und die erste Reise Dürers nach Italien* (Vienna, 1930), pp. 5–22. In this earlier work Rupprich still agreed with Dilthey's analysis of the Stoic core in Pirckheimer's religious character and believed that he preferred a Platonic text to the Scriptures.

8. *Br.* I, ep. 51, p. 166.

9. *Br.* II, ep. 173, p. 8.

10. *Bilibaldi Pirckheimeri Patritii Norinbergensis et Praefecti Copiarum eiusdem Reip. Bellum Suitense sive Helveticum cum Maximiliano Imp. atque Dynastis et civitatibus suevicis feliciter gestum anno MCCCCXCIX. Tiguri Helvetiorum: Typis Conradi Orelli et Sociorum, MDCCXXXVII.* See Ernst Münch, *Bilibald Pirkheimers Schweizerkrieg und Ehrenhandel mit seinen Feinden zu Nürnberg* (Basel, 1826); Otto Markwart, *Wilibald Pirckheimer als Geschichtsschreiber* (Zürich, 1886), who cites the pattern of classic history in the *Bellum Suitense* and agrees with Ranke that from the de-parture of the troops from Nuremberg on the account is good; and Karl Rück, *Wilibald Pirckheimers Schweizerkrieg* (Munich, 1895). Emil Reicke denies Rück's assumption that Pirckheimer wrote his account during his last years of life. On the basis of archival research, Reicke attempted to determine Nuremberg's real role in the Swiss or Swabian war, "Willibald Pirckheimer und die Reichsstadt Nürnberg im Schwabenkrieg," *Jahrbuch für Schweizerische Geschichte*, XLV (1920), 138ff.

11. Wilhelm Dilthey, *Gesammelte Schriften*, II, 49f. The most damning judgment of Pirckheimer's character is that of Drews, *Pirckheimers Stellung*, p. 13. Drews expresses disappointment in Pirckheimer's patent unfaithfulness to his own strong ethical idealism so eloquently articulated. A man of the sharpest contradictions, Pirckheimer was not a solid, earnest character, which can be explained on the basis of his humanist direction which became part of his flesh and blood. As a humanist he loved lofty phrases, but did not apply them to his own life. He had, Drews held, merely an aesthetic appreciation of ethics and of religion.

12. The shrill charges of Hans Schütz, for example, that Pirckheimer was guilty of rascally and mischievous conduct is typical of the kind of charges brought against him before the Council: cf. Pirckheimer, *Br.* II, ep. 302, pp. 340ff.; *Br.* II, ep. 310, pp. 376ff.; *Br.* II, ep. 311, p. 413. See also *Br.* II, ep. 193, pp. 83ff., for charges made to the Council. E. Mummenhoff recounts his strife with Kraft Vetter, *Mitteilungen des Vereins für die Geschichte der Stadt Nürnberg*, XXVI (1926), 311ff.

13. Dürer's Venice letters are to be found in Pirckheimer, *Br.* I, ep. 91, pp. 298ff. to ep. 129, p. 440, *passim*. Erwin Panofsky, *The Life and Art of Albrecht Dürer* (Princeton, 1955), pp. 108f., speaks of the very delightful tone and flavor of Dürer's communications, giving some charming excerpts. See Emil Reicke, "Der Bamberger Kanonikus Lorenz Beheim, Pirckheimers Freund," *Forschungen zur Geschichte Bayerns. Vierteljahrsschrift*, XIV (1906), 30, 34, on Pirckheimer's syphilis and mistresses. Pirckheimer's *Nachlasz* contains a number of frivolous love poems, some rather cynical. Compare, for example, Nürnberger Stadtbibliothek, *Nachlasz*, no. 149, *Gedicht von verschmähter Liebe; Br.* I, pp. 55–56, *Sprichwörter*, etc.

14. Goldast, ed., *Opera*, pp. 386–388. Pirckheimer's *Nachlasz*, no. 288, contains a brief outline of the dialogue. E. Mummenhoff, "War Willibald Pirckheimer ein Verleumder? Ein Beitrag zu seiner Charakteristik," in "Zeitungsauschnitte aus dem Fränkischen Kurier," Bibliothek des Germanischen Nationalmuseums, Bg. 7527 cm, defends Pirckheimer against the charges of Moriz Thausing that he slandered Dürer's wife and other strictures against his morality.

15. *Apologia seu Podagrae Lavs. Biblibaldo Pirckeymhero authore. Ex officinia Foederici Peypus. Nurenbergae. MCXXII.* Goldast, ed., *Opera*, pp. 204–211. William Est did an English translation under the title: *The Praise of Gout, Or, the Gouts Apologie. A paradox both pleasant and profitable* (London, 1617).

16. Pirckheimer, *Br.* I, ep. 42, pp. 128ff. The original account is in the British Museum under the title: *Colloquium de animae post mortem statu.*

17. Pirckheimer, *Br.* I, ep. 154, p. 499, March 1, 1507.

18. Pirckheimer, *Br.* I, ep. 5, pp. 6off. [1496?].

19. Pirckheimer, *Br.* I, ep. 61, pp. 202f., after Dec. 20, 1503.

20. Pirckheimer, *Br.* I, ep. 62, pp. 204f.; ep. 102, pp. 337f., ep. 103, pp. 342f.; ep. 147, pp. 488f.; ep. 148, p. 490, etc.

21. Goldast, ed., *Opera*, p. 26. Hans Rupprich, *Pirckheimers Elegie auf den Tod Dürers* (Vienna, 1956), *Sonderabdruck aus dem Anzeiger der phil.-hist. Klasse der Österreichischen Akademie der Wissenschaften* (1956), nr. 9, analyses the poem and comments on its excellence.

22. The *Brief an . . . über Astrologie* is no. 95 of the *Nachlasz*, Nürnberger Stadtbibliothek; edited, Pirckheimer, *Br.* I, ep. 141, pp. 460–464. Examples of the astrological diagrams, charts, and horoscopes are to be found in the *Nachlasz*, no. 356, 25 folios; no. 87, a letter to Pirckheimer on horoscopes; no. 202, a very comprehensive work on nativity prognostications. The *Briefwechsel* is replete with astrological references.

23. Pirckheimer, *Br.* II, ep. 347, pp. 508 [beginning of 1515?].

24. In a letter to Andreas Imhoff, Goldast, ed., *Opera*, p. 35, Pirckheimer claimed credit for accurate predictions of events in the mid-twenties, according to the assured principles of astrology and added: ". . . iam tamen vident et agnoscunt, *quantas res Deus Opt. Max. per sidera efficiat . . .* tamen scio, me non fuisse hariolatrum, sed meas praedictiones *ex certis Astrologiae principiis desumpsisse.* Atque vtinam non tam certus meis prognosticis respondisset euentus. Deus omnia ad sui nominis gloriam dirigat."

25. The *Oesterreichische Nationalbibliothek*, codex 12466: Pirckheimer über Chiromantie [palm reading] und Rezepten gegen Podagra. The *Nachlasz* has material such as no. 361 on *Chiramancia*, explaining the significance of the lines. The *Nachlasz*, no. 203, contains an item on dream interpretation: "Incipiunt expositiones visionum quae fiunt in Somnis secundum Magistrum Arnoldum de villa nova, etc." Pirckheimer, *Br.* I, ep. 114, pp. 371ff., Beheim writes that he does not know the precise formula for the *aurum potabile* with curative power. *The Briefwechsel*, pp. 375–378, reproduces five recipes from the *Nachlasz*.

26. Pirckheimer, *Br.* II, ep. 362, pp. 555f., to Trithemius, Nuremberg, June 13, 1515. He expressed himself on demons and miracles in his first writing on the Lord's Supper.

27. *Belli Helvetici Bilibaldo Pirckheimero descripti*, Goldast, ed., *Opera*, p. 64.

28. *Geographicae enarrationis libri octo*, 2 vols. (Strasbourg, 1525). Rupprich, "Wilibald Pirckheimer. Beiträge," pp. 97–99, describes Pirckheimer's relation to Regiomontanus, Bernhard Walther, and Johannes Werner and their interests in Ptolemy. The *Nachlasz*, no. 235, refers to the *Cosmography*. Pirckheimer's work was the *Germaniae ex variis scriptoribus per breuis explicatio. Norembergae apud Io. Petreium, anno MDXXX.* It was republished in Antwerp, 1585, in the *Descriptio Germaniae utriusqve Tam superioris quam inferioris: auctoribus Bilibaldo Pirckheimero et caeteris quorum nomina sequenti pagina continentur.* See M. Weyrauther, *Konrad Peutinger und Willibald Pirkheimer in ihren Beziehungen zur Geographie* (Munich, 1907).

29. This description dates from 1528 and was edited for publication by his secretary Andreas Rüttel, *Priscorum numismatum ad Nurembergensis Monetae valorem facta aestimatio* (Tübingen, 1533).

30. This judgment is precisely the reverse of the very common opinion held, for example, by Roth, *Willibald Pirkheimer*, p. 18, who says even of his editions of the Greek church fathers that they were "sicher mehr durch das Gefallen an der Sprache der Alten und durch historisches Interesse als durch religiöse Impulse veranlaszt." Rupprich, "Willibald Pirckheimer. Beiträge," pp. 81–89, *et passim*, presents the best arrangement and discussion of the translations yet to appear.

31. Pirckheimer, *Br.* II, ep. 243, pp. 231ff.

32. Pirckheimer, *Br.* I, ep. 60, pp. 200f. According to a letter to Celtis, September 17, 1503, Pirckheimer had already completed the *Ad Demonicum* and wished to publish it, Pirckheimer, *Br.* I, ep. 60, pp. 197ff.

33. Franz Xaver Thurnhofer, *Bernhard Adelmann von Adelmannsfelden, Humanist und Luthers Freund* (Freiburg i. B, 1900), p. 145.

34. Goldast, ed., *Opera*, p. 231.

35. *Gregorii Nazianzani orationes XXX, Bilibaldo Pirckheimero interprete, nunc primum editae, quarum catalogum, cum alijs quibusdam, post epistolam Des. Erasmi Roter(odami) euidebis* (Basileae, 1531). Erasmus' preface is republished in Goldast, ed., *Opera*, pp. 43f.

36. Goldast, ed., *Opera*, pp. 247f., *Praefatio*.

37. Hans Imhoff, ed., *Theatrum virtutis et honoris*, fol. a, pp. 11–13. Cf. *Br.* II, ep. 377, pp. 596f. *Beatiss. Patris Nili Episcopi Et martyris Theologi antiquisz. Sententiae morales e graeco in latinum versae . . . Fridericus Peypus Nurembergae iterum impressit.*

38. *Sententia* 236.

39. Marsiglio Ficino, *Opera Omnia* (Basel, 1576), p. 1768, cited in E. H. Gombrich, "Icones Symbolicae," *Journal of the Warburg Institute*, XI (1948), 172, a most lucid discussion of the Neoplatonic presuppositions basic to the vogue of the hieroglyph, emblem, and pictorial symbolism.

40. George Boas, *The Hieroglyphics of Horapollo* (New York, 1950), pp. 28, 39.

41. *Hori apollinis Niliaci hieroglyphica quae ipse lingua edidit Aegyptiaca, Philippus autem in Graecum transtulit idiomo.* Rupprich, *Wilibald Pirckheimer und Dürer*, p. 103, refers to an earlier Egyptian interest of Pirckheimer, his *Corographia Historialis Aegipti* based on Orosius and modern travel accounts. The starting point for all later research into the problem of the hieroglyphic lore of humanism will remain Karl Giehlow, "Die Hieroglyphenkunde des Humanismus in der Allegorie der Renaissance," *Jahrbuch der Kunsthistorischen Sammlungen des Allerh. Kaiserhauses*, XXXII (1915), 170ff. Karl Dannenfeldt, "Egypt and Egyptian Antiquities in the Renaissance," *Studies in the Renaissance*, VI (1959), 10, relates how the revival of Neoplatonism enhanced the role of Egypt as the original land of theologians and philosophers through Ficino's translation of the *Corpus Hermeticum*, for example, and the many editions of Horappollon's *Hieroglyphica*.

42. Letter to Bernhard Adelmann, Sept. 1, 1521, Goldast, ed., *Opera*, p. 234. From his father Pirckheimer had Ficino's translation of Plato of 1483–84 and a manuscript translation by Ficino of *Pymander*, Hermes Trismegistus' work on the power and wisdom of God. Cf. *Br.* I, ep. 1, p. 1: Opus Marsilii Ficini affinibus dedi, qui id se transmissuros dixerunt. Theologiam Marsilii seu Platonis non reperio. *Br.* I, ep. 2, p. 13: Nullum Marsilii opus reperio. Florenciae imprimuntur, ideo rara hic sunt. Cf. *Br.* I, pp. 10f.: Exkurs III: Pirckheimer und Marsilius Ficinus.

43. Nationalbibliothek Handschriftensammlung, Bibl. Pal. Vind., Codex 12466.

44. *Br.* I, p. 208, a book list.

45. *Br.* II, ep. 204, p. 132.

46. An example would be the verse: "In deum: O νοῦς enim nobis est in singulis deus; Omnino est omniaque aspiciens deus."

47. *Br.* I, ep. 60, p. 202. The lines were written on the reverse side of a draft of a letter to Kilian Leib, c. Dec., 1503.

48. *Br.* I, p. 196, Poem on the virtues of the quiet heart. W. Dilthey, "Auffassung und Analyse," *Gesammelte Schriften*, II, 49f.: "Auch bei ihm finden wir als Kern die Person zusammenhaltenden Überzeugungen die römische Stoa und deren in sich gefasztes männliches Lebensgefühl." This judgment and the few select quotations presented leave an unbalanced picture of Pirckheimer.

49. Goldast, ed., *Opera*, pp. 220–222. Protestants later used Pirckheimer's essay in criticizing an error typical of those who favor the Roman pontiff and his infallibility, *Illvstris Bilibaldi Pirckheimeri Consiliarij Caesarei et Particij Norimbergensis Dissertatio De Maria Magdalena, Quod falso à quibusdam habeatur pro illa peccatrice seu πόρνῃ. Accessit de eadem Quaestione Uberior Disquisitio Nicolai Baringii, S. Theol. Doctorandi, & Ecclesiastae Hannoverani.* (Hannover, 1644). The traditional association of the three Marys with one person is made in the *Legenda aurea*, c. 96, and in late medieval art, where Mary Magdalene regularly appears at the feet of the crucified Christ as a reminder that she once anointed his feet. See Hans Rupprich, "Willibald Pirckheimer. Beiträge," p. 89, n. 58. In a letter to Erasmus, Pirckheimer explained that he preferred an opinion closer to piety in such an uncertain manner, Goldast, ed., *Opera*, p. 403. Cf. Allen, *Epistolae*, IV, 244–250, ep. 1095, dated April 30 [1520]; an improved text.

50. Goldast, ed., *Opera*, p. 222.

51. *Ibid.*

52. *Br.* I, ep. 52, pp. 172f. [Nuremberg, summer 1502?]. In *Br.* I, ep. 54, pp. 177ff., a letter to Kilian Leib [Nuremberg, 1502?], he repeats sentence by sentence in improved form these strictures against scholasticism itemized to Lang.

53. *Br.* II, ep. 204, pp. 131ff.; *Br.* II, ep. 244, pp. 245ff.

54. *Br.* II, ep. 366, pp. 564f.

55. Goldast, ed., *Opera*, p. 403.

56. Cited from letter to Lorenz Beheim, prefacing the *Piscator seu Reviviscentes*.

57. *Br.* II, ep. 234, pp. 210ff., Dec. 1, 1512. That he followed the controversy closely is evident from his letter to Spalatin, Oct. 25, 1513, *Br.* II, ep. 272, p. 281.

58. Goldast, ed., *Opera*, p. 401: *Bilibaldi epistola ad amicvm de conviciatoribus et criminatoribus ferendis: & de Io. Reuchlini adversariis iniquissimis, Ex Nurenberga Kal. Dec. M. D. XVI.*

59. Goldast, ed., *Opera*, p. 270, Letter to Erasmus, Dec. 31, 1517. Cf. Allen, *Epistolae*, III, 179–181, ep. 747.

60. *Ibid.*, p. 261.

61. Roth, *Willibald Pirkheimer*, pp. 28f. Pirckheimer also exchanged letters with Staupitz.

62. Siegfried Szamatólski, *Eckivs Dedolatus* (Berlin, 1891), vii, marshals various evidences for Pirckheimer's authorship. Paul Merker, *Der Verfasser*

des Eccius Dedolatus und anderer Reformationsdialoge (Halle/Saale, 1923), argued for Nikolaus Gerbelius as author. Hans Rupprich, *Der Eckius dedolatus und sein Verfasser* (Vienna, 1930) made a case for Fabian Gorteler (Fabius Zonarius) of Goldberg in Silesia. Perhaps Bernhard Adelmann might be considered as a possibility. It may at this late date be impossible without the discovery of new evidence to establish the authorship definitely, since the internal evidence has been exhausted without definitive results.

63. Nürnberger Stadtbibliothek, *Nachlasz*, no. 141: *Conceptio prima dialogi ludicri de Ioanne Eckio bibulo.* Cf. Joseph Schlecht, "Pirkheimers zweite Komödie gegen Eck," *Historisches Jahrbuch*, XXI (1900), 402–413.

64. Goldast, ed., *Opera*, pp. 199–201: Bilibaldus Pirckheimeri et Lazari Spengleri Scheda Appelationis ad Leonem, X. P. M. See Paul Kalkoff, *Pirkheimers und Spenglers Lösung vom Banne 1521* (Breslau, 1898), and P. Roth, *Die Einführung der Reformation in Nürnberg, 1517–1528* (Würzburg, 1885). When Pirckheimer was threatened with excommunication he disavowed any commitment to Luther's doctrine and denied any acceptance of Luther beyond that of most men. See Drews, *Pirckheimers Stellung*, p. 45.

65. Offenbacher, "La Bibliothèque," p. 249.

66. Franz Xaver Thurnhofer, "Willibald Pirkheimer und Hieronymus Emser," *Beiträge zur Geschichte der Renaissance und Reformation. Joseph Schlecht Festgabe* (Munich, 1917), pp. 335–347, traces Pirckheimer's relations with Emser, relating the divergent ways in which Luther and Emser interpreted his dedication of Lucian's rhetoric to Emser.

67. Goldast, ed., *Opera*, pp. 372–374: *Bilibaldi Pirckheimeri Epistola ad S. D. N. Adrianvm P. M. de Motibvs in Germania, per Dominicanos, & horum complices excitatis, & de occasione Lutheranismi.*

68. *Ibid.*, pp. 385f.: *De perseqvvtoribvs evangelicae vertitatis, eorvm consiliis et machinationibvs.*

69. *Eyn missyve odder Sendbrieff so die Ebtissche von Nürnberg an den hochberümptenn Bock Emser geschrieben hatt. D., M., xxiii. Ex Nurnberga Sexta Junij Anno. M. D. xxij.*

70. Roth, *Willibald Pirkheimer*, p. 58.

71. *Epistola Bilibaldi ad Philippvm Melanchthonem, continens qverelas de Monialium vexatione*, Goldast, ed., *Opera*, pp. 374f. The letter is incomplete and it is not certain that Pirckheimer actually sent it to Melanchthon.

72. *Wie alle Closter vnd sonderlich Junckfrawen Clöster in ain Christlichs wesen möchten durchs gottes gnadengebracht werden.* Noricus Philadelphus, MDxxiiii.

73. Roth, *Willibald Pirkheimer*, pp. 64f.

74. *Oratio Apologetica, Monialivm Nomine Scripta a Bilibaldo*, Goldast, ed., *Opera*, pp. 375–385. The oration was translated into German by Conrad Vetter, a German Jesuit, under the definitive title *Schutzschrifft und Rettung Bilibaldi Pirckheimers Geschlechters vnnd Rhatsherrens zu Nürnberg, an den löblichen Stattrhat daselbsten, im Namen der Klosterfrawen bey S. Clara zu Nürnberg, darinnen Rechnungschafft ihres Lebens vnnd Glaubens, dann auch Antwort auff die Nachreden ihrer Miszgönner gegeben, und endtlich begehrt wirdt, man sie nicht mit Gewalt ausz ihrem Kloster herausz wolle* (Ingolstadt, 1614).

75. Oecolampadius' treatise was entitled *De genuina verborum Domini*:

"*Hoc est corpus meum*" *iuxta vetustissimos authores expositione liber* (Strassburg, 1525). Pirckheimer's reply was *De vera Christi carne et vero eius sanguine ad Joannem Oecolampadium responsio* (Nuremberg, 1526). The most detailed account of the controversy remains Drews, *Pirckheimers Stellung*, pp. 89–106, who, however, does Pirckheimer an injustice in simply accepting the Zwinglian aspersions on his motives as vanity and desire for attention in the theological arena. Pirckheimer's *Nachlasz*, no. 182, for example, contains many bitter assaults on the "radicals" linking the names of Zwingli and Oecolampadius with those of Carlstadt and Münzer. Oecolampadius also attempted to show that the church fathers favored a spiritualistic interpretation of Christ's presence in the sacraments, Ernst Staehelin, *Das theologische Lebenswerk Johannes Oekolampads* (Leipzig, 1939), pp. 607–618.

76. Goldast, ed., *Opera*, pp. 320, 286. Luther commented on the raucous reaction of Oecolampadius and the Zwinglians to Pirckheimer's treatise in his sacramental treatise "Das diese wort Christi (Das ist mein leib etce) noch fest stehen widder die Schwermgeister. 1527," *D. Martin Luthers Werke*, XXIII (Weimar, 1901), 77.

77. Oecolampadius' tract was entitled *Responsio ad Bilibaldum Pyrkaimerum de re eucharistiae* (Zurich, 1526). The reply was *Bilibaldi Pirckheymeri de vera Christi carne et vero eius sanguine, adversus convicia Ioannis, qui sibi Oecolampadii nomen indidit, responsio secunda* (Nuremberg, 1527).

78. Oecolampadius, *Responsio posterior ad Bilibaldum Pyrkaimerum de Eucharistia* (1527). Pirckheimer's tract was entitled, *Bilibaldi Pirkheymeri de convitiis Monachi illius, qui graecolatine Caecolampadius, germanice vero Ausshin nuncupatur, ad Eleutherium suum epistola* (Nuremberg, 1527).

79. *28 Propositiones contra digamiam episcoporum.* Pirckheimer knew the arguments of the pseudo-Ulrich, eleventh century, against clerical celibacy, *Epistola de continentia clericorum.*

80. Cochlaeus refers to the manuscript *De votivo coelibatu*, to the five hundred theses, and proposed attack on Luther, *Ioan. Cochlei ad Bilibaldvm*, Goldast, ed., *Opera*, pp. 395f. The *Nachlasz, Nürnberger Stadtbibliothek*, no. 89: *Sacrae literae ideo a Deo hominibus datae sunt, ut saluti eorum conferant*, 10 folios, argues against Luther's interpretation of 1 Timothy 3:2. No. 90: *Responsio adversus propositiones Andreae Osiandri theologicas ac inridicas plane Christiana modestia refertas*, folios 1–6, contains 150 theses against Osiander. Folios 6–11 contain 147 theses against Linck: *Responsio adversus impias et blasphemas conclusiones Wenceslai Linck et collaboratorum suorum pro bigamice defensore confictas.* On the whole controversy, see Gustav Kawerau, "Der Nürnberger Streit über die zweite Ehe der Geistlichen," *Beiträge zur bayerischen Kirchengeschichte*, X (1903), 119–129.

81. Drews, *Pirckheimers Stellung*, p. 122. Drews documents Pirckheimer's vacillation with many excerpts from the correspondence, *ibid.*, pp. 110–123.

82. Goldast, ed., *Opera*, pp. 238ff.

83. Münch, *Pirkheimers Schweizerkrieg*, pp. 48–54.

84. Venatorius to Erasmus, Allen, *Epistolae*, IX, 342, ep. 2537.

85. Goldast, ed., *Opera*, p. 43.

IX   ERASMUS — Philosopher of Christ

1. Allen, *Epistolae*, V, 129, ep. 1314, to Zwingli [3?] September 1522.

2. Ephraim Emerton, *Desiderius Erasmus of Rotterdam* (New York, 1899), pp. 1f.

3. "Erasmus Reuchlino suo," Aug. 27, 1516, L. Geiger, ed., *Johann Reuchlins Briefwechsel*, Br. 221, p. 254: Germaniae nostrae decus. Paul Mestwerdt, *Die Anfänge des Erasmus* (Leipzig, 1917), p. 81, reports that in 1489 Erasmus named Dutchmen and Germans together as men of his fatherland with culture and eloquence.

4. See Gerhard Ritter, *Erasmus und der deutsche Humanistenkreis am Oberrhein* (Freiburg i. B., 1937), emphasizing Erasmus' Freiburg years.

5. Erasmus, *Opera*, IX, col. 1. On Froben's scholar, see P. S. Allen, *Erasmus. Lectures and Wayfaring Sketches* (Oxford, 1934), p. 9. On Reuchlin, see L. Geiger, ed., *Johann Reuchlins Briefwechsel*, Br. 265, p. 304. On Beatus Rhenanus, see P. S. Allen, *The Age of Erasmus* (Oxford, 1914), p. 267.

6. Lucien Febvre, *Au Coeur Religieux du XVIᵉ Siècle* (Paris, 1957), p. 86.

7. H. R. Trevor-Roper, "Desiderius Erasmus," *Men and Events* (New York, 1957), p. 35. Myron P. Gilmore, *Erasmus: The Scholar and the World*, Henry Wells Lawrence Memorial Lectures, IV (New London, 1959), 27–43, examines three episodes in the career of Erasmus in each of which may be seen a variation of the general problem of the duty of the scholar in the world.

8. Erasmus retained his fascination for Valla, doing an epitome of his *Elegantiae*, and himself following the pattern of the *Annotationes*, and the like in later years. Erasmus, *Opera*, I, cols. 1065–1126: *Desiderii Erasmi Roterodami in Laurentii vallae elegantiarum libros epitome*. On Erasmus' early years, see Albert Hyma, *The Youth of Erasmus* (Ann Arbor, 1930) and Paul Mestwerdt, *Die Anfänge des Erasmus; Humanismus und "Devotio moderna"* (Leipzig, 1917). For bibliography on the *Devotio Moderna*, see J. M. E. Dols, *Bibliographie der moderne devotie* (Nimwegen, 1941).

9. Erasmus, *Opera*, V. cols. 1239–1262.

10. Erasmus, *Opera*, IV, cols. 617–624. The Colloquy *Conflictus Thaliae et barbariei, Opera*, I, cols. 889–894, dating from Erasmus' Deventer days, inveighed against the barbarity at Zwolle.

11. Margaret Mann, *Érasme et les débuts de la réforme française (1517–1536)* (Paris, 1934), recounts the details of Erasmus' sojourn in Paris and the nature of his influence in three phases on French humanism and the Reformation until Calvin made plain the great chasm between the two in 1536. Otto Schottenloher, *Erasmus im Ringen um die humanistische Bildungsform* (Münster, 1933), studies Erasmus' inner development through the early years during which his mystical piety is shattered and replaced by classic aesthetic norms which, in turn, give way to moral and religious concerns enriched by contact with Christian antiquity. The significance of the *Antibarbari* as a clue to the young Erasmus' intellectual development is discussed in an article by the well-known Reformation scholar K. A. Meissinger, "Erasmus entdeckt seine Situation: Gedanken über die Antibarbari," *Archiv für Reformationsgeschichte*, XXXVII (1940), 188–198.

12. Eugene F. Rice, "Erasmus and the Religious Tradition, 1495–1499," *Journal of the History of Ideas*, XI, no. 4 (1950), 387–411, in an excellent study analyzes the effects of this pervasive secularism upon Erasmus' views of 1. various religious practices such as the veneration of saints; 2. monasticism; 3. scholasticism; and 4. the ethical character of the classics. He tends, however, to overemphasize somewhat the conventional nature of Erasmus' religious positions as mere conformity.

13. Ernest Hunt, *Dean Colet and His Theology* (London, 1956), and Eugene Rice, "John Colet and the Annihilation of the Natural," *Harvard Theological Review*, XLV (1952), 141–163, both argue for the Pauline character of Colet's anthropology and soteriology, reversing the former position that Colet followed Ficino in exegesis and religious philosophy. Ivan Pusino, "Ficinos und Picos religiös-philosophische Anschauungen," *Zeitschrift für Kirchengeschichte*, XLIV (1928), 540, exaggerates very much the influence of the Florentine Platonists on Colet and through him on Erasmus. Similarly, Leland Miles, *John Colet and the Platonic Tradition* (LaSalle, Ill., 1961) exaggerates Colet's Platonism and fails to differentiate thoroughly and consistently the medieval Platonic component and the Renaissance Platonism in Colet leading to a false impression as to the importance of the latter in Colet's intellectual make-up. Lamberto Borghi, *Umanesimo e concezione religiosa in Erasmo di Rotterdam* (Florence, 1935), convinced of the complete immanentist nature of Renaissance humanism, completely exaggerates the influence of Florentine Platonism on Erasmus and his "universal religious theism." His thesis is more applicable, as we have seen, to Mutian. Albert Hyma, *Renaissance to Reformation* (Grand Rapids, 1951), pp. 209–249, minimizes the influence of Colet on Erasmus' attitude toward scholasticism, monasticism, and Neoplatonism and stresses more the influence of Jean Vitrier. See his articles, "Erasmus and the Oxford Reformers," *Nederlandsch Archief voor Kerkgeschiedenis*, n. s. XXV (1932), 69–92, 97–136; "Erasmus and the Oxford Reformers (1503–1519)," *ibid.*, n. s., XXXVIII (1951), 65–85.

14. An important text is the letter to John Colet, Allen, *Epistolae*, I, no. 108, pp. 245–249. *Epistolae*, I, 248: "Res ista non tyronem sed exercitatissimum requirit imperatorem."

15. Erasmus, *Opera*, III, cols. 95ff.

16. Erasmus, *Opera*, V, cols. 1265–1292; cols. 1291–1294: Responsio ad argumenta Erasmiana. Karl Bauer, "John Colet und Erasmus von Rotterdam," *Festschrift für Hans von Schubert*, ed. Otto Scheel (Leipzig, 1929), pp. 176–186, discusses these two debates.

17. In 1515 he did a translation for the school at Colet's request, *Libellus de octo orationis partium constructione*, Erasmus, *Opera*, I, cols. 165–180. As a thank-you to England, Erasmus presented to Colet the *De Dvplici Copia Verborum ac Rerum, Opera*, I, cols. 1f. He praised the Christian piety of life, his public-service-mindedness, and service to the fatherland. Even more touching is his sermon, 1513–1515, to the boys of St. Paul's on the virtues of the child Jesus, *Concio de pvero iesv a puero in schola coletica . . . , Opera*, V, cols. 599–610. The Huntington Library has what may be the only copy in existence. A glance at the *Short Title Catalogue* reveals the amazing number of sixteenth-century English editions of Erasmus'

works. Margaret Mann Phillips, *Erasmus and the Northern Renaissance* (New York, 1950) is a popular summary, but it is based on the best scholarship available.

18. Erasmus, *Opera*, II. Theodore Appelt, *Studies in the Contents and Sources of Erasmus' Adagia* (Chicago, 1942), pp. 41–47, analyzes the moralistic contents of the adages. Margaret Mann Phillips believes they reflect Erasmus' positive religious philosophy, "La *Philosophia Christi* reflétée dans les *Adages* d'Erasme," *Courants religieux et humanisme à la fin du XVᵉ et au début du XVIᵉ siècle* (Paris, 1957), pp. 53–71. Two works of major importance cover Erasmus and Italy, Pierre de Nolhac, *Érasme en Italie* (Paris, 1888) on the journey and events, and Augustin Renaudet, *Érasme et L'Italie* (Geneva, 1954) on his interior development and influence.

19. Erasmus, *Opera*, IV, cols. 85–380. *The Parabolae sive Simila, Opera*, I, cols. 557ff. are of a similar nature and are drawn from Plutarch, Seneca, Lucian, Aristotle, Pliny, and Theophrastus in the manner of the medieval *Florilegae*.

20. Antonio Corsano, *Il Pensiero Religioso Italiano* (Bari, 1937), p. 11, n. 2. For an example of Erasmus' use of *philosophia evangelica*, cf. *Opera*, VI, front matter: *Epistola de Philosophia Evangelica*. Josef Bohatec, *Budé und Calvin* (Graz, 1950), p. 251, n. 68, asserts that the term *christiana philosophia*, the only true philosophy, occurs for the first time in Augustine, *Contra Jul. Pelag.* 4, 14, 72. The Oratorian, Louis Bouyer, *Antour d'Erasme* (Paris, 1955), p. 127; English trans., *Erasmus and His Times* (Westminster, Md., 1959), p. 142, in a very general statement argues that Erasmus borrowed it from the ordinary usage of the Greek fathers, particularly of those he liked best, the Alexandrians and the Cappadocians.

21. *D. E. R. venerabili collegio Virginum Machabaeiticarum, apud coloniam Agrippinam* . . . (Basel, 1524); *Opera*, V, cols. 589–600.

22. Cf. the *Epistola apologetica de interdicto esu carnium deque similibus hominum constitutionibus*, April 21, 1522, to Bishop Christoph of Basel, *Opera*, IX, col. 1197. A. Renaudet, *Études Érasmiennes (1521–1529)* (Paris, 1939), p. 41. In his *Christiani Matrimonii Institutio, Opera*, V, cols. 613–766, Basel, 1526, Erasmus includes with the positive aspect also an elaborate consideration of the impediments of matrimony, cols. 633–634. On the whole subject of marriage and celibacy, see Émile Telle, *Érasme de Rotterdam et le Septième Sacrament* (Geneva, 1954), together with the highly critical review by Albert Hyma, *Archiv für Reformationsgeschichte*, 48 (1957), 145–164.

23. Allen, *Epistolae*, II, 586.

24. Allen, *Epistolae*, V, 1403.

25. Erasmus, *Opera*, I, cols. 728ff. *Colloquium Inquisitio de fide;* col. 731: Qui consentiunt in fide evangelica, qui colunt unum Deum patrem, qui totam suam fiduciam collocant in eius Filio, qui eodem huius spiritu aguntur.

26. *Ibid.*, col. 731: Extra ecclesiam est, quisquis non agnoscit pontificem romanum.

27. Preface to *De ratione conscribendi, Opera*, I, cols. 343–344: Verum haud scio quo pacto sit, ut Pontificum auctoritas longe plus valeat ad excitandum inter Principes bellum, quam ad componendum.

28. Erasmus, *Opera*, I, cols. 311–312: *Hieronymo Buslidiano, praeposito*

ariensi, consiliario regio, D. E. R. . . . Bononiae XV Calendas Decembres.
MDVI. Carl Stange, *Erasmus und Julius II eine Legende* (Berlin, 1937),
argues convincingly that the *Julius Exclusus*, ascribed to Erasmus by P. S.
Allen, P. Smith, and other scholars, was actually a polemical piece done for
the French King. In an article, "Girolamo Rorario und Julius II," *Zeitschrift für systematische Theologie*, XVIII (1941), 535–588, Stange refutes
the effort of Pio Paschini to ascribe the authorship to Girolamo Rorario of
Pordenone, "L'autore del dialogo satirico contro Giulio II," *Atti dell' Ac-
cademia degli Arcadi e Scritti dei Soci*, n. s. XIII-XIV (1934–35), 85–98.
Stange holds Faustus Andrelinus to have been the author, with the possible
assistance of Stephen Poncher. Karl Schätti, *Erasmus von Rotterdam und
die Römische Kurie* (Basel, 1954), pp. 47f., remarks that in so far as this
dialogue really does not substantially change the picture of Erasmus' relation to the curia, the question of authorship is not vital to his theme, a
remark a propos also to this present summary presentation.

29. Erasmus, *Opera*, V, col. 49: Apostolus, Pastor, Episcopus officii sunt
vocabula non dominatus. Papa, Abbas, caritatis cognomina sunt, non po-
testatis.

30. *Responsio ad Notationes Edvardi Lei in Lvcam, Opera*, IX, col. 163.

31. *Opera*, VI, front matter, *De dvabus postremis editionibus qvarta et
qvinta*.

32. R. C. Jebb, *Erasmus* (Cambridge, 1897), p. 27.

33. *Opera*, V, col. 1097, in *De Ratione Concionandi Liber IV*. Étienne
Gilson is quite right in holding that Erasmus did not criticize scholasticism
because he despised sacred knowledge, but only desired to return that
knowledge to its first purity. É. Gilson, *Moyen âge et naturalisme* (Paris,
1938), pp. 187–195. On Erasmus' condemnation of the distortion of liberal
arts training by the dialecticians, cf. *Opera*, I, col. 522: *De Ratione Stvdii*:
Ad haec si quis Dialecticen addendam statuet, non admodum refragabor,
modo ab Aristotele eam discat, non ab isto loquacissimo Sophistarum genere,
neque rursum ibi desideat, et velut ad Scopulos (ut inquit Gellius) Sirenaeos
consenescat. On Erasmus' views on Aquinas and scholastic philosophy in
general, see A. Renaudet, *Érasme, sa pensée religieuse* (Paris, 1926), pp. 6f.:
Études Érasmiennes, pp. 124f.

34. *Opera*, IV, cols. 381–504. The *Stultitiae Laus* was completed in More's
house in 1509, published in 1511.

35. Preserved Smith, *A Key to the Colloquies of Erasmus* (Cambridge,
1927), p. 39. *Colloquia Familiaria, Opera*, I, cols. 625–908.

36. Bailey, *Colloquies of Erasmus*, I, p. xiii.

37. *Exorcismus, sive spectrum, Opera*, I, cols. 749–752; *Alcumista, Opera*,
I, cols 752–756, a colloquy which influenced Ben Jonson's *The Alchemist*.

38. 'Ιχθυοφαγία, *Opera*, I, cols. 787–810, especially col. 809; *convivium
profanum, Opera*, I, cols. 659–672.

39. *Convivium Religiosum, Opera*, I, col. 683. Smith, *Key to the Colloquies*, p. 10, comments on the *Convivium*.

40. *Naufragium, Opera*, I, cols. 712–720. The *Perigrinatio Religionis
ergo, Opera*, I, cols. 774–787, recounts superstitions associated with the
shrines of St. James of Compostela, the tomb of Thomas à Becket, and

others. Cf. also Ἰχθυοφαγία, *Opera*, I, col. 809, against the invocation of Mary and the saints in preference to Christ.

41. *De utilitate Colloquiorum*, *Opera*, I, col. 903. *Alia in Congressu*, *Opera*, I, cols. 639–640, of superstitious pilgrimages to Jerusalem and elsewhere.

42. Smith, *Key to the Colloquies*, pp. 14f.

43. *Virgo* Μισόγαμος, *Opera*, I, cols. 697–701; *Virgo poenitens*, *Opera*, I, cols. 701–702.

44. This theme is recurrent and recalls Erasmus' later reconstruction of his own experience. Cf. *Militis et Carthusiani*, *Opera*, I, cols. 708–710.

45. ΠΤΩΧΟΠΛΥΣΙΟΙ, *Opera*, I, cols. 739–744; *Exsequiae Seraphicae*, *Opera*, I, cols. 866–873. *Funus*, *Opera*, I, cols. 810–817, describes the true Christian death of one who trusts in the mercy of God rather than in various fictions.

46. *Abbatis et Erudite*, *Opera*, I, cols. 744–746.

47. *Adolescentis et Scorti*, *Opera*, I, cols. 718–720. Smith, *Key to the Colloquies*, pp. 21f. In another piece on benefice-hunting, Erasmus remarks that many who run to Rome for benefices hazard loss of morals and money, *Opera*, I, cols. 640–641.

48. *Cyclops, sive evangeliophoras*, *Opera*, I, cols. 831–833.

49. *Epicureus*, *Opera*, I, cols. 882–890. The *Confabulatio Pia*, *Opera*, I, cols. 648–653, defined pure religion as the pure worship of God and the observing of his commandments. It requires four things: that man have a true and pious apprehension of God himself and the Holy Scriptures, loving Him as a beneficent Father; that he keep himself blameless; that he exercize charity; and that he practice patience.

50. *De utilitate Colloquiorum ad lectorem*, *Opera*, I, cols. 901–908; Bailey, *Colloquies of Erasmus*, II, p. 374.

51. *Opera*, V, col. 1263; *Opera*, IX, col. 1101, *Ad Albertum Pium*.

52. Renaudet, *Érasme et l'Italie*, p. 5.

53. See Rudolf Pfeiffer, *Humanitas Erasmiana* (Leipzig, 1931).

54. Richard McKeon, "Renaissance and Method in Philosophy," *Studies in the History of Ideas*, III (New York, 1935), 80ff.

55. *De Ratione Concionandi*, *Opera*, V, cols. 849–858, *passim*. Erasmus placed grammar first in the *De Ratione Studii* as well, *Opera*, I, cols. 517–530, especially col. 521. On the way in which Erasmus humanized Christian education while Christianizing classical learning, see Otto Schottenloher, *Erasmus im Ringen um die humanistische Bildungsform* (Münster, 1933).

56. *Convivium Religiosum*, *Opera*, I, cols. 681–682. Bailey, *Colloquies of Erasmus*, I, p. 182.

57. *Opera*, X, col. 1742: Prometheus est nobis imitandus: qui illi suo luteo, vitam ex astris ausus est petere, sed tum demum ubi quicquid humano artificio praestari potuit, adhibuisset.

58. *Antibarbarorum Liber I*, *Opera*, X, col. 1730. An excellent discussion of Erasmus and the Thomistic doctrine of the *gentiles salvati* is contained in Hans Baron's brief study, "Erasmus-Probleme im Spiegel des Colloquium Inquisitio de fide'," *Archiv für Reformationsgeschichte*, XLIII (1952), 254–263.

59. Renaudet, *Études Érasmiennes*, pp. 31f., presents this order and offers

evidence of Erasmus' detailed knowledge of the fathers. In *Opera*, V, col. 432, Erasmus cites the fathers who lapsed into error. Citing Erasmus' use of the fathers, especially Jerome, for the renewal of theology, Denys Gorce hails him as the "father of positive theology," "La Patristique dans la réforme d'Érasme," *Festgabe Joseph Lortz*, I (Baden-Baden, 1958), 233–276.

60. *De Ratione Concionandi Liber I, Opera*, V, col. 772. Erasmus used this Logos conception also in the "Preface to Luke," *Paraphrases of Erasmus on the New Testament* (London, 1551), fol. ccccbi.

61. *Apologia de in Principio erat sermo, Opera*, IX, cols 111–122.

62. Renaudet, *Études Érasmiennes*, p. 24, finds this change in title significant in that Erasmus left the traditional term and adopted a word which better expressed the Greek διαθήκη, implying a convenant or pact between God and man. Erasmus reëdited the text four times. On the two editions see August Bludau, "Die beiden ersten Erasmus-Ausgaben des Neuen Testaments und ihre Gegner," *Biblische Studien*, VII, no. 5 (1902), 12ff., 27ff.

63. *Opera*, VI, front matter: *Dilecto Filio Erasmo Roterodamo Sacrae Theologiae Professori Leo* . . . Rome, 1518.

64. *Ratio verae theologiae, Opera*, V, col. 92.

65. Renaudet, *Érasme et l'Italie*, p. 6; *Études Érasmiennes*, xiii–xvi, virtually makes Erasmus another Marcion rejecting the whole Old Testament and keeping only the Gospels and Paul's Epistles in the New. That Renaudet should deny Erasmus' high regard for the prophets is incredible in view of his extensive use of them not only for social ethics but for Messianic prophecy. This is an unfortunate distortion of Erasmus' attitude toward the Scriptures and the discussion of the Scriptural principles of the Reformers is also very inadequate.

66. *Enarratio in Psalmum XXXVIII, Opera*, V, col. 432: Atque haud scio an ex universo mortalium genere, praeter unum Christum, quisquam inveniatur, qui nusquam lapsus sit verbo: aut inter omnia Scriptorum genera sit ullus liber absque naevo erroris, praeter Scripturam Canonicam, quae tam nescit fallere, quam ipse Spiritus diuinus cujus afflatu prodita est.

67. On the *Quadriga*, see Harry Caplan, 'The Four Senses of Scriptural Interpretation and the Mediaeval Theory of Preaching," *Speculum*, IV (1929), 282–290.

68. *De Amabile Ecclesiae Concordia, Opera*, V, col. 470: Nec oportet historicum sensum rejicire, quo locus fiat allegoriae, quum ille sit hujus basis et fundamentum, qui cognitus facit, ut aptius tractetur intelligentia retrusior ac mystica.

69. *De Ratione Concionandi, Opera*, V, col. 1066.

70. *Ibid.*, col. 1037.

71. *Enchiridion*, chapter II, *Opera*, V, cols. 5–10.

72. *De Ratione Concionandi Liber III, Opera*, V, cols. 1055–1056.

73. *Ibid.*, col. 1026.

74. Beryl Smalley, *The Study of the Bible in the Middle Ages* (New York, 1952), p. 14.

75. *De Ratione Concionandi, Opera*, V, cols. 1033–1934. In col. 1061 he explains that Augustine used these four senses: historical, aetiological, analogical, allegorical.

76. *Ibid.*, cols. 1048–1049. Cf. *Enchiridion*, chapter XIII, on the necessity for allegory without which Scripture is barren, *Opera*, V, col. 29.

77. *Ibid.*, cols. 1029–1030.

78. *Ibid.*, cols. 1041–1045.

79. *Enarratio Primi Psalmi, Opera*, V, cols. 171–232.

80. *Concio in Psalmvm IV, Opera*, V, col. 261.

81. *Enarratio Psalmi XIV, Opera*, V, cols. 291–312. The exposition of Psalm XV also applies the psalm to the Christian church.

82. *In Psalmum XXII, Opera*, V, cols. 311–346. In the *De Amabili Ecclesiae Concordia, Enarratio Psalmi LXXXIII, Opera*, V, cols. 469ff. Erasmus found Christ signified by three names in the more hidden meaning.

83. *Enarratio in Psalmum XXXIII, Opera*, V, cols 369ff.

84. *The Paraphrases of Erasmus Upon the Newe Testament*, II, Dedicated to Edward VI by Miles Coverdale (London, 1552), fol. ii, spelling modernized.

85. *Annotationes Novi Testamenti, Opera*, VI, col. 562, notes 38 and 39.

86. *Paraphrases*, fol. vii; *Annotationes*, to Rom. 3:21, note 21, *Opera*, VI, cols. 575f.

87. Allen, *Epistolae*, no. 181, To John Colet, Paris [c. December] 1504, p. 405. Alfons Auer, *Die vollkommene Frömmigkeit des Christen. Nach dem Enchiridion militis Christiani des Erasmus von Rotterdam* (Düsseldorf, 1954), sees the *Enchiridion* as the key to Erasmus' entire work, marking the transition from a literary-aesthetic humanism to religious humanism and pointing up the basic formula in his whole system of piety: from things visible to things invisible.

88. *Enchiridion*, chapter II, *Opera*, V, col. 7.

89. *Ibid.*, chapter VI, col. 16.

90. Hajo Holborn, ed., *Desiderius Erasmus Roterodamo Ausgewählte Werke* (Munich, 1933), pp. 3–21. Cf. Pierre Mesnard, "Un texte important d'Érasme touchant sa 'Philosophie Chrétienne,' " *Revue Thomiste*, XLVII, no. 3 (1947), 524–549.

91. *Paraclesis, Opera*, V, cols. 137–144; Holborn, ed., *Erasmus Werke*, pp. 139–149.

92. *Ratio seu Methodus, Opera*, V, col. 75–138; Holborn, ed., *Erasmus Werke*, pp. 177–305.

93. Renaudet's statement that Erasmus' Jesus was similar to Renan's is simply incredible and can be explained only in the light of Renaudet's intense desire to prove the "modernism" of Erasmus. Cf. A. Renaudet, *Études Érasmiennes*, p. xxix. Renaudet is a little closer to the real picture when he says that in the course of a controversy with Lefèvre d' Étaples on a text from Hebrews, it appeared that the Christ of Erasmus remained the *Ecce Homo* crowned with bloody thorns, the God of pity of the workshops of Flanders and Burgundy, whereas the Christ of Lefèvre remained the metaphysical God of Ficino, *Érasme et L'Italie*, p. xi. But even this is not an adequate analysis. On the Lefèvre-Erasmus debate, see Margaret Mann, *Érasme et les débuts de la réforme française* (Paris, 1934), chapter III: Érasme et Lefèvre d'Étaples, pp. 47ff. Erasmus' Christ was the dogmatic and not the historical Christ of nineteenth-century criticism.

94. *De Ratione Concionandi, Opera*, V, cols. 1056–1057. *Opera*, V, col. 1156: Jesum Christum esse verum Deum ex Deo, et eundem verum hominem natum ex homine virgine, citra virilem operam, sed actu divini Spiritus. In the colloquium *Inquisitio de fide* Erasmus subscribed to the doctrine of the two natures of Christ.

95. Preface to Lucian's *Toxaris, Opera*, I, cols. 213–214.

96. *Opera*, IV, 578: "[Christus] solus est totus imitandus . . . At in hoc absolutum est omnis virtutis ac sapientiae exemplar.

97. J. B. Pineau, *Érasme, sa pensée religieuse* (Paris, 1924), p. 269. Pineau's conclusions on this universalistic aspect of Erasmus' thought are, however, too relativistic to be applicable to sixteenth-century Erasmus. For him, as for the fathers, the revelation in Christ remained the instrument by which the influence of the Spirit on pagan philosophers is detected and the criterion by which they are judged.

98. *Opera*, V, col. 1183.

99. *De Immensa Misericordia Dei*, 1524, or *De Magnitudine misericordiarum Domini, Opera*, V, cols. 557–588. In the introduction to the English translation, *The Immense Mercy of God* (San Francisco, 1940), E. M. Hulme is guilty of a typical liberal misreading when he identifies this as "a specific plea for tolerance."

100. *Opera*, V, col. 558; ed. Hulme, *Immense Mercy*, pp. 6f.

101. *Opera*, V, col. 560; ed. Hulme, *Immense Mercy*, p. 10.

102. *Opera*, V, col. 561; ed. Hulme, *Immense Mercy*, p. 12.

103. *Symboli Catechesis VI, Opera*, V, col. 1181.

104. *Symboli Catechesis III, Opera*, V, col. 1155.

105. *De Ratione Concionandi, Opera*, V, col. 820. On the Eucharist, a favorite term of the Eastern fathers, cf. his *An Epistle of the famous clerke Erasmus of Roteredame, concernyng the veryte of the Sacrament of Christes body and bloude, which Epistle is set before the excellent bokke, instituted D. Algeri De veritate corporis et sanguinis dominici in Eucharistia*, 1530. Renaudet's assertion that Erasmus wanted the Eucharist returned to a simple commemoration is simply mistaken.

106. *Exomologesis sive modus confitendi, Opera*, V, cols. 145–170. See also the colloquy *Confabulatio Pia, Opera*, I, cols. 651–652, in which he has Gaspar reply: ". . . whether He appointed Confession as it is now used in the church I leave to be disputed by the divines."

107. A few of his many writings directed toward a pedagogical end are the *Declamatio de pueris ad virtutem ac literas liberaliter instituendis idque protinvs a nativitate, Opera*, I, cols. 485–516; *De civilitate morum puerilium libellus, Opera*, I, cols. 1029–1044; *Epostulatio Jesu cum Homine Suapte Culpa Pereunte, Opera*, V, cols. 1319–1320; *Precationes Aliqvot Novae*, etc., sample prayers for the young, *Opera*, V, cols. 1197–1206; *Modus Orandi Deum, Opera*, V, cols. 1099–1132.

108. *Institutio, Opera*, IV, cols. 559–612. Renaudet, *Érasme et l'Italie*, p. 9, holds that his ideal remained that of a small city republican. Fritz Caspari, *Humanism and the Social Order in England* (Chicago, 1954), p. 45, presents an intelligent and documented discussion of Erasmus' political views. F. Caspari, "Erasmus on the Social Functions of Christian Humanism," *Journal of the History of Ideas*, VIII (1947), 78–106, finds the unity of purpose in

Erasmus' thought in his high esteem of reason, his sole interest in moral behavior, coupled with his lack of concern for the practical needs of social organization and the realities of political power. Guido Kisch, *Erasmus und die Jurisprudenz seiner Zeit* (Basel, 1960), a highly original study, shows how Erasmus' whole concept of law from the *Aequitas naturalis* down to positive laws was determined by his *philosophia christiana*, pp. 108–132, especially, pp. 120f. He sees his thought as derived more from the general concept of the just and suitable, Plato's καλὸν καὶ δίκαιον, rather than from the more technical Aristotelian concept of equity, ἐπιείκεια. In a brief essay, pp. 457–461, *Zu Erasmus' Christi Philosophia*, Kisch discusses some recent scholarly opinion of Erasmus' religious thought.

109. *Querela Pacis, Opera*, IV, cols. 625–642. Cf. the *Colloquy* on the life of a soldier, *Militaria, Opera*, I, cols. 641–643. The comparison of war and peace is of the same order, *Ad Philippvm Panegyricvs, Opera*, IV, cols. 536–538. On the Turkish wars, cf. *Utilissima Consultatio de Bello Turcis Inferendo et obiter enarratus Psalmus XXVIII, Opera*, V, cols. 345–368. Joseph Lecler, S.J., *Histoire de la tolérance au siècle de la Réforme*, I (Paris, 1955), pictures Erasmus' struggle for true tolerance and peace. A suppressed edition of the *Querela Pacis*, hitherto unnoticed, is referred to in a letter from Tunbridge in Kent to Edward Jeningham in London, Nov. 8, 1801, in which he says he translated and printed (1795) Erasmus' *Querela Pacis*, but added: "Party rage running high, I never published it — not a single copy was offered for sale; nor to my knowledge given away. The whole impression was locked up or cancelled. I have only two copies. But as you, Sir, appear to be an admirer of Erasmus, I will, if you should favor me with a line signifying that it could be acceptable, lend you one of the copies bound up with the *Antipolemas* in an Octavo volume . . . You may rest assured that it is a translation from Erasmus and not an original piece as some have falsely and ignorantly asse [rted] *Antipolemas* to be." Henry E. Huntington Library, ms. JE 542.

110. *Ciceronianus, Opera*, I, cols. 969ff. Erasmus had not actually traveled far from his early preference for Baptista Mantuanus among the modern poets. Cf. Dr. C. Reedijk, *The Poems of Desiderius Erasmus* (Leiden, 1956), pp. 79, 99.

111. Henri J. Hak, *Marsilio Ficino* (Amsterdam, 1934), pp. 156–159, cites Erasmus' contacts with Neoplationism, although not always with convincing documentation.

112. *Catechesis III, Opera*, V, 1150. *De Ratione Studii, Opera*, I, col. 523: Philosophiam optime docebit Plato, & Aristoteles, atque hujus discipulus Theophrastus, tum utrinque mixtus Plotinus.

113. *Enarratio in Psalmum XXXVIII, Opera*, V, col. 432. Renaudet, *Érasme et l'Italie*, p. 7.

114. *Opera*, I, col. 1014.

115. Manfred Krebs, "Reuchlins Beziehungen zu Erasmus von Rotterdam," *Johannes Reuchlin 1455–1522* (Pforzheim, 1955), pp. 139–155. In the *De arte cabalistica* Reuchlin had praised Erasmus extravagantly.

116. *De incomparabili heroe Johanne Reuchlino in divorum numerum relato, Opera*, I, cols. 689–692. See Giulio Vallese, *L'Apoteosi di Reuchlin* (*Apotheosis Capnionis*) *di Erasmo da Rotterdam* (Naples, 1949), which,

after an introductory chapter on the *Colloquies*, discusses Erasmus and Reuchlin, the composition and fortune of the *Apotheosis*.

117. P. S. Allen, *Erasmus. Lectures and Wayfaring Sketches* (Oxford, 1934), pp. 25f. Jacques Étienne, *Spiritualisme érasmien et théologiens louvanistes* (Louvain, 1956), presents a summary analysis of Erasmian spiritualism.

118. *Dilucida et pia explanatio Symboli; quod apostolorum dicitur, Decalogi Praeceptorum, et Dominicae Precationis, Opera*, V, cols. 1133–1196; citation, col. 1135; done at Freiburg, 1533, one of Erasmus' many theological writings in his later years. See also his definition of faith, *Symboli Catechesis*, II, *Opera*, V, col. 1147: 1. to believe that there is a God; 2. to give credence to His words; 3. to cast all thought and mind upon Him with full confidence and trust. See also the discussion of his exegesis of Rom. 1: 17 and Rom. 3: 21 above. In the *Inquisitio de fide, Opera*, I, cols. 728–732, the inquiry has to do with faith as the acceptance of orthodox dogma. Smith, *Key to the Colloquies*, p. 24, cites Erasmus to the effect that the two participants in the dialogue were Luther and Erasmus. Erasmus complained that the masses understood that man being justified by faith meant that there was no righteousness from his works. It is pious to reject faith in works, especially which do not proceed from faith and love, *De Ratione Concionandi*, Liber III, *Opera*, V, col. 1070. See Craig R. Thompson, *Inquisitio de Fide, A Colloquy by Desiderius Erasmus Roterodamus, 1524* (New Haven, 1950).

119. *Enchiridion, Opera*, V, cols. 38–39. Jean-Daniel Burger, *Érasme en Face de la Réforme* (Geneva, 1956), pp. 33–36, is mistaken in holding that, with Luther, Erasmus had professed the three fundamental doctrines of the Reformation: the sovereign authority of the Scriptures, salvation by grace, and the invisible character of the true church. Heinrich Bornkamm, "Erasmus und Luther," *Luther-Jahrbuch*, XXV (1958), 3–22, believes that Luther achieved a much deeper understanding of the relation of theology to philosophy than did Erasmus with his uncomplicated *philosophia Christi*.

120. R. E. Allen, "The Socratic Paradox," *Journal of the History of Ideas*, XXI (1960), 256–265. Joseph Lortz, *Die Reformation*, I (Freiburg i. B., 1939), 50, believes that Erasmus was guilty of the Socratic fallacy that who knows is also good.

121. The views of Dilthey, who called Erasmus the Voltaire of the sixteenth century, and of Harnack, who declared Erasmus to be too many-sided and uncertain in principles, are by now *passé*. Cf. Arthur Schröder, *Der moderne Mensch in Erasmus* (Leipzig, 1919), pp. 12, 68. Schröder calls him more a man of reason than a religious man. J. Janssen, *History of the German People*, III (London, 1900), p. 24, pronounced the *philosophia Christi* nothing but moralism. A recent book by an anticlerical and non-professional historian, Siro Attilio Nulli, *Erasmo e il Rinascimento* (Turin, 1955), pp. 25ff: "Il pensiero religioso di Erasmo," resurrects the image of a radical Erasmus. According to Nulli, he did not have a system, but a state of mind, a liberal, critical temperament. Émile Telle, *Érasme de Rotterdam et le Septième Sacrement*, p. 11, speaks of the *Philosophia Christi* as anti-monastic, epicurean, anti-Christian, and Paulinian without St. Paul. But in contemporary scholarship the views of the great scholar A. Renaudet de-

serve more serious attention. A man who has followed Erasmus' religious development almost day by day through more than a decade of his life, Renaudet believes that "Erasmian modernism" was based essentially on the foundation of a new theology, that much of his program was essentially heretical and heterodox, and that Erasmus actually favored the appearance of a third church, the Roman church completely reformed. Renaudet, *Érasme et l'Italie*, pp. xi, 8, 200; *Études Érasmiennes*, p. 23, Erasmianism defined. Some of his views are summarized in his article, "Le Message Humaniste et Chrétien d'Érasme," *Sodalitas Erasmiana*, I, *Il Valore Universale dell'umanesimo* (Naples, 1949), pp. 44ff. Bouyer, *Autour d'Erasme*, is Renaudet's severest critic and the most ardent defender of Erasmus' orthodoxy. Bouyer's work, however, while bright and suggestive, shows signs of haste, ex parte writing, and lack of thorough scholarship. Its special merit lies in its emphasis upon the importance of the patristic literature for the religious thought of Erasmus.

122. An irenic Catholic historian, Joseph Lortz, *Die Reformation*, I, 126–135, decries Erasmus' indifference, his personal ethical shortcomings, his rationalism, relativism, theological unclarity, and optimistic moralism which left little room for sin, grace, redemption, and deeper religious concern. Louis Gardet, "Actualité d' Érasme," *Revue Thomiste*, XLVII, no. 3 (1947), 550–560, agrees with Lortz, arguing that Erasmus lacked good theological sense, so that on the pretext of putting the accent on the essence of Christianity he subverted the means to that end, and thus he unwillingly risked subverting or minimizing the end itself. A liberal Protestant, Paul Joachimsen, "Der Humanismus und die Entwicklung des deutschen Geistes," *Deutsche Vierteljahrsschrift für Literaturwissenschaft und Geistesgeschichte*, VIII (1930), 419–480, agreed that "the Erasmian philosophy thus became the most dangerous enemy of the contemporary church." Albert Hyma, a conservative Protestant, consistently classifies Erasmus with the more-or-less pagan rationalists like Valla and Voltaire; see "The Continental Origins of English Humanism," *Huntington Library Quarterly*, IV (1940), 17. Fritz Caspari, "Erasmus: Leistung und Forderung," *Deutsche Beiträge zur Geistigen Überlieferung*, ed. Arnold Bergsträsser (Chicago, 1947), p. 74, speaks of Erasmus' effort to realize a humanistic, liberal Christianity.

123. Compare for example, how extensively Erasmus appeals to the authority of the fathers in defending his *Annotationes* against Edward Lee, *Opera*, IX, cols., 123–200. On the church fathers as Christian humanists, see R. R. Bolgar, *The Classical Heritage and Its Beneficiaries* (Cambridge, 1954), pp. 49ff.

124. *De Praeparatione ad Mortem, Opera*, V, cols. 1293–1318, col. 1318. On the question as to whether Erasmus himself received the last rites in Basel from a priest, cf. V. De Caprariis, "Qualche precisazione sulla morte di Erasmo," *Rivista Storica Italiana*, LXIII, 100–108, who concludes in the negative. R. G. Villoslada, "La muerte de Erasmo," *Miscellanea Giovanni Mercata*, IV (Rome, 1946), claims on the basis of a late unsubstantiated report that Lambert Coomans, Erasmus' *famulus*, as an ordained priest attended Erasmus in his final hours. It is virtually certain, however, that Coomans was not yet ordained at that time. Karl Heinz Oelrich, *Der späte Erasmus und die Reformation* (Münster, 1961), *Reformationsgeschichtliche*

Studien und Texte, no. 86, depicts Erasmus in his final lustrum as very conservative, particularly after the crisis year 1529.

X LUTHER — The Reformer

1. Wilhelm Pauck, "The Historiography of the German Reformation during the Past Twenty Years," *Church History*, IX (1940), 15, mentions that the problem of Luther's relation with humanism requires a new investigation. The two scholars who are archetypes of the opposing viewpoints on the relation of the Renaissance and Reformation are Wilhelm Dilthey, *Gesammelte Schriften*, II, *Weltanschauung und Analyse des Menschen seit Renaissance und Reformation* (Leipzig/Berlin, 1940), 53ff., and Ernst Troeltsch, *Protestantisches Christentum und Kirche in der Neuzeit, Kultur der Gegenwart*, I, *Teil* IV (1906); *Die Bedeutung des Protestantismus für die Entstehung der modernen Welt* (Munich, 1906); *Renaissance und Reformation*, 1911. The question medieval or modern is formulated too simply and is meaningless without refinement and careful definition. Of interest is the M.A. dissertation by Milton Zagel, "Martin Luther and the Embryonic Stage of the Cultural Reformation," University of Iowa, 1936, which I have been unable to consult. Carl Stange, "Luther und der Geist der Renaissance," *Zeitschrift für systematische Theologie*, XVIII (1941), 3–27, while overestimating the extent of Luther's humanist connections, makes some perceptive observations on the similarities and differences between Luther and the humanists. Friedrich Schenke, "Luther und der Humanismus," *Luther. Zeitschrift der Luther-Gesellschaft*, XXXIII, no. 2 (1962), 77–85, examines once again the theological issues involved in the Luther-Erasmus debate, argues against Friedrich Heer's criticisms of Luther in his volume *Die dritte Kraft* (Frankfort, 1959), and holds that Luther showed merely human *humanitas* unrelated to God's sovereign majesty to be an illusion. Luther probes the problem more deeply, wishes to warn, but by no means desires to destroy the human image or the responsibility of man.

2. *D. Martin Luthers Werke, Kritische Gesamtausgabe*, I (Weimar, 1883), 355: *Disputatio Heidelbergae habita, conclusio 36*: "Aristoteles male reprehendit ac ridet platonicarum idearum meliorem sua Philosophiam." Although Bucer reported in a letter on the discussion of the theological theses, it seems that the philosophical theses were not disputed. Père Daniel Olivier, a careful student of the Heidelberg Disputation, has expressed some doubts as to whether the *probatio* actually came from Luther himself. The philosophical theses were not debated. The Weimar edition will hereafter be cited as *WA*, with volume and page number following.

3. Rudolf Kekow, *Luther und die Devotio Moderna* (Hamburg, c. 1937) studies in detail Luther's relation with the Brethren. See Albert Hyma, *New Light on Martin Luther* (Grand Rapids, Mich., 1958), pp. 44, 119.

4. Kenneth Strand, *A Reformation Paradox: The Condemned New Testament of the Rostock Brethren of the Common Life* (Grand Rapids, Mich., 1960). The Rostock Brethren persisted in publishing a translation of the New Testament with Cochlaeus' notes, arousing Luther's opposition.

5. Fr. Ludger Meier, O.F.M., "Research that has been made and is yet to be made on the Ockhamism of Martin Luther at Erfurt," *Archivum Francis-*

canum Historicum, XLIII (1950), 56–67, sees no evidence for the direct influence of Occam on Luther at Erfurt since Occam was not important in that center as yet. Bengt Hägglund, *Theologie und Philosophie bei Luther und in der occamistischen Tradition* (Lund, 1955) clarifies Luther's relation to the Occamist tradition, demonstrating how far Luther's conception of faith differed from that of Occam. Certainly in his stress on God's immanence, the nature of the church, the problem of authority, and other questions the variance of Luther's views from those of Occam was very great.

6. Unfortunately the major monograph on this subject by Burgdorf is unreliable in drawing conclusions far beyond what the evidence warrants. Martin Burgdorf, *Der Einflusz der Erfurter Humanisten auf Luthers Entwicklung bis 1510* (Leipzig, 1928) attempted to establish close connections between Luther and Crotus' circle at Erfurt. Köstlin and Kawerau believed humanism had an important influence. Otto Scheel minimized it, as did Hans von Schubert, "Reformation und Humanismus," *Lutherjahrbuch*, VIII (1926), 1–26. Hyma, *New Light on Martin Luther*, pp. 21f., is very severe in his criticism of Burgdorf. Hans Tümmler, *Luther und Erfurt* (Erfurt, 1943), 84pp., is a popular, nicely illustrated book on the Erfurt that Luther knew.

7. Cf. William E. Painter, "Baptista Mantuanus," unpublished dissertation, University of Missouri (Columbia, 1961), for a survey of Mantuanus' extensive influence in the North.

8. Hans von Schubert, "Reformation und Humanismus," pp. 16f.

9. Cited in Albert Hyma, *Renaissance to Reformation* (Grand Rapids, Mich., 1951), p. 275.

10. *WA*, I, 379.

11. *WA*, *Tischreden*, III, 619.

12. The value of the old monograph, Oswald G. Schmidt, *Luthers Bekanntschaft mit den alten Klassikern* (Leipzig, 1883), is very limited, but it still has not been replaced by a more complete modern work using the Weimar edition for references.

13. See Charles Edward Trinkhaus, Jr., "Introduction to Valla," ed. Ernst Cassirer *et al*, *The Renaissance Philosophy of Man* (Chicago, 1948), p. 153.

14. E. Harris Harbison, *The Christian Scholar in the Age of the Reformation* (New York, 1956) has a beautiful chapter showing that it is impossible to separate Luther the man of faith from Luther the man of scholarship.

15. *CR*, I, col. 613, cited in James MacKinnon, *Luther and the Reformation*, III (London, 1929), p. 212.

16. *WA, Br.* III, no. 596, p. 512; St. Louis ed., *Luthers Sämmtliche Schriften*, XXI^a, no. 596, col. 492, German text. Enders, *Briefwechsel*, IV, 119–120, cited in MacKinnon, *Luther and the Reformation*, III, 216. This letter was first published in a collection of letters addressed to Eobanus Hessus under the title: *De non contemnendis studiis humanioribus futuro theologo maxime necessariis*, etc.

17. *WA*, XV, 48.

18. *Gesammelte Schriften*, II, 61.

19. Ronald G. Smith, "A Theological Perspective of the Secular," a paper given at the Ecumenical Institute Conference, Bossey, Switzerland,

1959, p. 10. H. Richard Niebuhr, *Christ and Culture* (London, 1952), p. 177, correctly commented: "More than any great Christian leader before him, Luther affirmed the life in culture as the sphere in which Christ could and ought to be followed; and more than any other discerned that the rules to be followed in the cultural life were independent of Christian or church law. Though philosophy offered no road to faith, yet the faithful man could take the philosophic road to such goals as were attainable by that way." In underestimating the importance of the *ordo creationis* for Luther, however, his emphasis upon the positive function of the state and worldly orders as instruments of God's love, not merely as negative curbs *de ratione peccati*, and the activist nature of faith working in love also in the realm of culture, Niebuhr classified Luther too decisively as a dualist without in this essay bringing out adequately his conversionist concerns.

20. *WA*, 30^{II}, 554.

21. *WA*, 30^{II}, 562. See Ernst Lichtenstein, "Luther und die Humanität, *Evangelische Theologie*, X (1951), 393.

22. *WA*, 42, 486. Reason can to be sure say something about the *causa materialis et formalis*, but nothing about the *causa efficiens et finalis, WA*, 42, 93.

23. *WA, Br.* no. 499 [1522]; Lichtenstein, "Luther und die Humanität," p. 393.

24. Philippians 4: 8, cited from the RSV.

25. *WA*, XV, 37.

26. *WA*, XV, 31, 36, 52, cited in Lichtenstein, "Luther und die Humanität," p. 395. Kurt Aland, "Die Theologische Fakultät Wittenberg und ihre Stellung im Gesamtzusammenhang der Leucorea während des 16. Jahrhunderts," *450 Jahre Martin Luther Universität Halle-Wittenberg*, I (Wittenberg, 1952), 155–237, argues that it was Luther's personal initiative which won over his colleagues to give the coup to scholasticism and introduce a humanist curriculum.

27. *WA*, 39^{I}, 175–180; *Luther's Works*, American Edition, XXXIV (Philadelphia, 1960), 137. See Paul Drews, *Disputationen D. Martin Luthers* (Göttingen, 1895), pp. 90–96.

28. Brian Albert Gerrish, *Grace and Reason; a Study in the Theology of Luther* (Oxford, 1962), originally a Columbia University Dissertation, 1958, provides a very intelligent discussion of the problem together with some choice illustrations of Luther's own intellectual achievements. Bernhard Lohse, "Luthers Antwort in Worms," *Luther. Mitteilungen der Luthergesellschaft*, 1958, no. 3, 124–134, objects to the older interpretation of *ratio evidens* as simply the logical processes and argues that it is actually man's regenerate reason. B. Lohse, *Ratio und Fides. Eine Untersuchung über die ratio in der Theologie Luthers* (Göttingen, 1958), traces the development of Luther's conception of *ratio* from his notes on Augustine and Peter Lombard (1509–1510) to his lectures on Hebrews (1517–1518) and then presents a brilliant systematic analysis of the concept in his theology.

29. Luther an Spalatin, Feb. 22, 1518, *WA, Br.*, I, no. 61, 149–150, cited in Richard McKeon, "Renaissance and Method in Philosophy," *Studies in the History of Ideas*, III (New York, 1935), 98. The text is rendered in German, ed., Walch, St. Louis ed. *Luthers Sämmtliche Schriften*, XV,

Anhang, no. 10, cols. 2400–2401. On this problem of philosophy and theology, see the study by Wilhelm Link, *Das Ringen Luthers um die Freiheit der Theologie von der Philosophie* (Munich, 1940), in which he contrasts Luther's theology with four constructions of theological metaphysics. Proceeding from Luther's *simul justus et peccator*, Link argues that this formula is to be understood theologically and not psychologically or morally. In Luther the kerygmatic content of the gospel is preserved, although it is spoiled in the Augustinian and Thomistic syntheses as well as in nominalism and mysticism.

30. See the very fine book on Luther's social ethic, George Forell, *Faith Active in Love* (New York, 1954). A charming discussion of Luther as a professor is Theodore G. Tappert, "Luther in His Academic Role," *The Mature Luther* (Decorah, Ia., 1959), pp. 3–55, on Luther and his students, and his attitudes toward history and theology.

31. Ernest G. Schwiebert, "The Reformation from a New Perspective," *Church History*, XVII (1948), 3–31; *Luther and His Times* (St. Louis, 1951), a comprehensive account emphasizing the key role played by the University of Wittenberg as a nursery for the Reformation. In his exciting little book *Die Reformation. Einführung in eine Geistesgeschichte der deutschen Neuzeit* (Frankfurt/Main, 1936), the late Herbert Schöffler stressed the decided advantage to Wittenberg of being free from the heavy weight of tradition which kept the older universities bound by inertia. Schöffler's work has been reprinted together with three other studies of his under the title *Wirkungen der Reformation* (Frankfurt/Main, 1960).

32. *An die Ratherren aller Städte deutschen Landes, dasz sie christliche Schulen aufrichten und erhalten sollen. 1524. WA*, XV, 49.

33. Enders, *Briefwechsel*, IV, 328, cited in MacKinnon, *Luther and the Reformation*, III, 216.

34. *WA*, XV, 46.

35. These paragraphs follow very closely the résumé of the *Appeal* in MacKinnon, *Luther and the Reformation*, III, 216–222.

36. *Ibid.*, p. 222. See Franklin Painter, *Luther on Education* (Philadelphia, 1889), a strongly pro-Luther essay; Emil Zweynert, *Luthers Stellung zur humanistischen Schule und Wissenschaft* (Leipzig, dissertation, 1895); and John Alfred Faulkner, "Luther and Culture," *American Society of Church History Papers*, VIII (New York, 1928), 147–168. In view of the reorganization of the educational system and the founding of reformed schools at Magdeburg, Nuremberg, Nordhausen, Halberstadt, Gotha, Eisleben, and many other places in the year following the publication of the *Appeal*, the judgment of Leonard Elliott-Binns sounds quite ridiculous when he writes, *Erasmus the Reformer* (London, 1929), p. 52: "Another weakness of the Reformation was that it had no real sympathy with learning. Luther, it is true, was exceedingly anxious that education should be fostered in order that all might be able to read their Bibles, but his denial of the freedom of the will took away the desire for study, since direct inspiration, as with the Theosophists of our own day, was a quicker, and less burdensome method of arriving at the truth, etc." Hans-Bernhard Kaufman, "Grundfragen der Erziehung bei Luther," *Luther. Mitteilungen der Luthergesellschaft*, XXV, no. 2 (1954), 60–76, documents Luther's own amazing insights into educa-

tional psychology and method. Kaufmann's dissertation under the same title is Kiel University, 1955. Harold J. Grimm in his excellent lectures on "Luther and Education," *Luther and Culture* (Decorah, Ia., 1960), pp. 73–142, discusses Luther's impact on the schools, Luther as a teacher in the pulpit, and Luther's catechisms as textbooks.

37. Bolgar, *The Classical Heritage*, p. 342.

38. *WA, Tischreden*, I, 439 (Veit Dietrich, 1533).

39. Caplan, "The Four Senses of Scriptural Interpretation," *Speculum*, IV (1929), 286.

40. Robert M. Grant, *The Bible in the Church* (New York, 1954), p. 101. I wish to express my appreciation to my student, Rev. Robert Smith, for bringing this passage to my attention.

41. Karl Holl, *Gesammelte Aufsätze zur Kirchengeschichte*, I (Tübingen, 1927), 545.

42. Frank Rosenthal, "The Rise of Christian Hebraism in the Sixteenth Century," *Historia Judaica*, ed. Guido Kisch, VII, no. 2, 174–177. In the *Dictata*, Luther's first major exegetical lectures on the Psalms, 1513–1515, Luther used the best Vulgate editions of Froben (1498 and 1509) and Amerbach (1498–1502). He also used Reuchlin's *Septem psalmi poenitentiales*, 1512, and the *Rudimenta linguae hebraicae*, 1506, containing the *Lexicon hebraicum*, which Luther owned from 1506 or 1509 on and used very often. Hans Volz, "Luthers Arbeit am lateinischen Psalter," *Archiv für Reformationsgeschichte*, XLVIII (1957), 44ff., 53, describes Luther's progress with Hebrew to his *Operationes in Psalmos* in which he was able to do independent work directly from the text and went well beyond his predecessors like Lefèvre. See also Walter Koenig, "Luther as a student of Hebrew," *Concordia Theological Monthly*, XXIV (1953), 845–853.

43. *WA*, XLᴵ, 663; English trans., Philip S. Watson's revision of the Middleton edition of 1575, *Luther's Commentary on Galatians* (London, 1953), p. 421. For general background reading, see D. P. Lockwood and R. H. Bainton, "Classical and Biblical Scholarship in the Age of the Renaissance and the Reformation," *Church History*, X (1941), 3–21.

44. *WA*, XLᴵ, 657; ed. Watson, *Commentary on Galatians*, p. 417.

45. *WA*, XIV, 499–500, *Deuteronomion Mosi cum annotationibus*, 1525, trans. Richard R. Caemmerer, *Lectures on Deuteronomy, Luther's Works*, IX, 6, 8.

46. *WA*, XLᴵ, 302; et illorum errorem approbat et confirmat hodie Erasmus. Gerhard Ebeling, *Evangelische Evangelienauslegung. Eine Untersuchung zur Luthers Hermeneutik* (Munich, 1942), pp. 44–49, recounts Luther's break with allegory. See also Ebeling's article, "Die Anfänge von Luthers Hermeneutik," *Zeitschrift für Theologie und Kirche*, XLVIII (1951), 172–229. Walter von Loewenich, *Luther und das Johanneische Christentum* (Munich, 1935) and *Luther als Ausleger der Synoptiker* (Munich, 1954), shows that Luther lived in the world of the gospels, despite his Pauline orientation. He had a keen sense of the differences between the autoptic and synoptic gospels, Christ as "vermenschender Gott" or as "vergötterter Mensch." Loewenich sees an astonishing freedom in Luther toward his own formulas and a tendency toward the existential interpretation of the Scriptures.

47. Holl, *Gesammelte Aufsätze*, I, 546; Gordon Rupp, *The Righteousness of God* (London, 1953), p. 135. According to Rupp, Erich Vogelsang believes that the combination of the christological (literal) and tropological interpretation precipitated Luther's discovery of the evangelical meaning of *justitia Dei*. See the bright little study by Peter Sandstrom, *Luther's Sense of Himself as an Interpreter of the World to the World* (Amherst, Mass., 1961), especially the second chapter on the theme of the Word of God both spoken and written. P. 25: The teacher must preach, and the preacher teach.

48. A recent study available in microfilm compares Luther's early and later commentaries on the Psalms, J. Hilburg, "Luther und das Wort Gottes in seiner Exegese und Theologie, dargestellt auf Grund seiner *Operationes in psalmos* 1519/21 in Verbindung mit seinen frühen Vorlesungen" (Marburg dissertation, 1948). Luther's later work quite naturally showed greater clarity and precision. The Old Testament references to Christ were comprehended in the concept of *sensus literalis propheticus*, but such extensions of this sense to include the children of Israel as the Christian church was tropological in nature.

49. Heinrich Bornkamm, *Luther und das alte Testament* (Tübingen, 1948), p. 75. Fritz Hahn, "Faber Stapulensis und Luther," *Zeitschrift für Kirchengeschichte*, LVII (1938), 356–432, discusses Lefèvre's influence on Luther in individual passages in the determination of the literal-spiritual sense of Scriptures, in the idea that only the Holy Ghost can correctly interpret Scriptures, that the existential moment lies outside of Scripture, and in the demand for humility on the part of the exegete. Jean de Savaignac, "Un nouveau progrès dans la redécouverte de Luther," *Scriptorium. International Review of Manuscript Studies*, IX, no. 2 (1955), demonstrates anew the influence of Lefèvre on Luther between 1513 and 1519, showing the traces of his Pauline commentaries in Luther's *Dictata*, as well as in the commentaries on Romans, Hebrews, and Galatians. A. Brandenburg, *Iudicium und Evangelium* (Paderborn, 1960), an investigation of the *Dictata* from the point of view of systematic theology stresses Luther's tropological application to the individual believer, but unfortunately is tendential in overemphasizing the existential over the ontological element in Luther's theological interpretation of the Psalms.

50. Ragnar Bring, *Luthers Anschauung von der Bibel* (Berlin, 1951), pp. 6f., comments that the humanists' religious presuppositions colored their approach to the Scriptures. Fritz Hahn, "Die Heilige Schrift als Problem der Auslegung bei Luther," *Evangelische Theologie*, X (1951), 407–424, documents Luther's basic concern with the literal interpretation, p. 418: the *sensus germanus et proprius* (*WA*, V, 75, 22, 122), the *einfache, deutliche* sense (*WA, V*, 490, 580, 633), the *klare, duerre, helle Wort* (*WA*, XXIII, 93, 161), the *sensus historicus* (*WA*, XLII, 172). Jaroslav Pelikan, *Luther the Expositor* (St. Louis, 1959), analyzes Luther's exegesis in terms of four main components, the Word of God, tradition, the Church, and the role of polemics, and adds a case study of Luther's exegesis on various aspects of the Sacrament.

51. *WA*, XLI, 120; ed. Watson, *Commentary on Galatians*, pp. 70f. Wilhelm Maurer, "Die Anfänge von Luthers Theologie. Eine Frage an die

lutherische Kirche," *Theologische Literaturzeitung*, LXXVII (1952), cols. 1-12, is quite mistaken in his contention that Luther arrived at his doctrine of justification through his creative reproduction of the dogma of the ancient church through Augustine, for it is clear that in this central question the Scriptures were his source as well as his norm.

52. Heinz Zahrnt, *Luther deutet Geschichte* (Munich, 1952), pp. 14ff. Zahrnt's book is a good summary statement, although it is not very original in its own right. Paul Joachimsen, *Geschichtsauffassung und Geschichtsschreibung in Deutschland unter dem Einflusz des Humanismus* (Leipzig, 1910), provides a detailed account of cultural nationalism and humanist historiography. Hans Walter Krumwiede, *Glaube und Geschichte in der Theologie Luthers* (Göttingen, 1952), explains the origin of historicism and concludes that there is no direct line from it to Luther. E. Kohlmeyer, "Die Geschichtsbetrachtung Luthers," *Archiv für Reformationsgeschichte*, XXXVII (1940), 150-170, stresses that Luther saw divine power at work throughout all creation and that interpretations of Luther which separate God from the whole realm of natural and historical events are false. Luther acknowledged a natural ethical law anterior to revelation running through all human orders and history. But it is the gospel which reveals the true meaning of history. Hans Pflanz, *Geschichte und Eschatologie bei Martin Luther* (Stuttgart, 1939), 54 pp., believes that Luther contrasted the kingdom of the world as the stage of history with the kingdom of grace as the place of eschatological expectation. Paul Althaus, "Luthers Wort vom Ende und Ziel der Geschichte," *Luther. Mitteilungen der Luthergesellschaft*, 1958, no. 3, 98-105, stresses the eschatological element in Luther's view of history as culminating in the immanent second coming of Christ. This is, of course, in contrast to the humanists' lack of any sense of urgency.

53. See the discussion of history in Karl Holl, *The Cultural Significance of the Reformation* (New York, 1959), a translation of the German original of 1911. Georg Wünsch, *Luther und die Gegenwart* (Stuttgart, 1961), pp. 156ff., suggests some points of contact between modern historical thought and that of Luther, specifically in Hegel, Bismarck, Nietzsche, and historicism.

54. *WA*, XLIII, 418. On Luther's references to ancient history, see Karl Dannenfeldt, "Some observations of Luther on pre-Greek history," *Archiv für Reformationsgeschichte*, XLII (1951), 49-63.

55. *WA*, LI, 214-215, cited in Heinrich Bornkamm, *Luther's World of Thought* (St. Louis, 1958), pp. 199-200.

56. *WA*, L, 383-385; *Luther's Works*, American ed., XXXIV (Philadelphia, 1960), 275-278. Heinrich Bornkamm, *Gott und die Geschichte nach Luther*, 2nd ed. (Lüneberg, 1947), provides a beautiful interpretation of Luther's theological understanding of history, of the *deus absconditus* in history, and of history seen through the eyes of faith. P. 14: God speaks with us and indeed not with words but with acts, that is the meaning of history. Another commendable study is Hans Frh. von Campenhausen, "Reformatorisches Selbstbewusztsein und reformatorisches Geschichtsbewusztsein bei Luther, 1517/22," *Archiv für Reformationsgeschichte*, XXXVII (1940), 128-150. Luther, he says, knew nothing of an autonomous history free from

God. Rather, God's command is to promote public righteousness and, above all, the world needs the humility of faith.

57. Hans Lilje, *Luther Now* (Philadelphia, 1952), pp. 176f. See also Holl, *The Cultural Significance of the Reformation*, on poetry and art. Heinz Burger, "Luther als Ereignis der Literaturgeschichte," *Luther Jahrbuch*, XXIV (1957), 86–101, discusses Luther's work as a translator and hymn-odist, finding his translating to be more in the tradition of Albrecht von Eyb's free rendition than Nicholas von Wyle's literal translations.

58. Erwin Panofsky, *The Life and Art of Albrecht Dürer* (Princeton, 1955), pp. 198ff. The relation of Dürer's art to humanist themes is documented in the monograph, Georg Weise, *Dürer und die Ideale der Humanisten* (Tübingen, 1953). Dürer's opposition to the anti-aesthetic or iconoclastic tendencies of radical Protestantism is related in the brief study of Hans Rupprich, *Dürers Stellung zu den agnoetischen und Kunstfeindlichen Strömungen seiner Zeit* (Munich, 1959).

59. *WA, Br.*, V, 635ff., no. 1727. On the new Protestant congregational singing, see L. D. Reed, *Luther and Congregational Song*. Hymns Society of America, 1947.

60. On this whole subject, see the very excellent article, Walter E. Buszin, "Luther on Music," *The Musical Quarterly*, XXXII, no. 1 (January 1946). Of less value and apologetic in tone is Paul Nettl, *Luther and Music* (Philadelphia, 1948). Nettl traces the rise of music in Lutheran church services and the influence of Luther on later composers such as Bach. Also of interest is R. Stevenson, "Luther's Musical Achievement," *Lutheran Quarterly* (1951). Theodore Hoelty-Nickel in his lectures "Luther and Music," *Luther and Culture* (Decorah, Ia., 1960), pp. 145–211, discusses the philosophy of Lutheran church music, Lutheran hymnody, and Luther's *Deutsche Messe*. Cf. *WA, Tischreden*, III, 3815: "Musica est insigne donum Dei et theologiae proxima . . . et juventus assuescenda est huic arti; sie macht fein, geschichte leut"; *WA, Tischreden*, VI, 7034: "Die Musika ist eine Gabe und Geschenk Gottes, nicht ein Menschengeschenk. So vertreibt sie auch den Teufel und macht die Leut fröhlich, man vergiszt dabei alles Zorns, Unkeuschheit, Hoffart und andrer Laster." Walter Blankenburg, "Luther und die Musik," *Luther. Mitteilungen der Luthergesellschaft*, 1957, no. 1, 14–27, discusses three problems, music and creation, music and theology, and music and speech. Arnold Schmitz, *Die Bildlichkeit der Wortgebundenen Musik Johann Sebastian Bachs* (Mainz, 1950), pp. 15ff., the historical background of Bach's musical oratory in terms of the relation of music and rhetoric from antiquity to the eighteenth century.

61. *WA*, II, 436.

62. *WA*, XIII, 242–243, cited in Pelikan, *Luther the Expositor*, pp. 75–76.

XI Conclusion

1. From a considerable literature on this subject a representative title is Herbert Grundmann, *Religiöse Bewegungen im Mittelalter* (Hildesheim, 1960; reprint of the 1935 Berlin thesis). Contemporary evidence for the increase of popular religious feeling during these centuries is plentiful. For example, in his *Exhortation to the Clergy Assembled at Augsburg, 1530*,

Luther cited the endless multiplication of religious novelties, like new relics and pilgrimages, all designed to quench the religious thirst of Christian people. An excellent summary article on the difficulties of the church as a traditional institution in an age of transition in economics, politics, and culture is Wallace K. Ferguson, "The Church in a Changing World," *American Historical Review*, LIX (1953), 1–18.

2. The net result of these studies on this question of origins, then, is really to document the suggestions of Hans Baron's brilliant *Jugendarbeit* done many years ago, "Zur Frage des Ursprungs des deutschen Humanismus und seiner religiösen Reformbestrebungen," *Historische Zeitschrift*, CXXXII (1925), 413–446, especially 436ff.

3. *Individuum und Kosmos in der Philosophie der Renaissance* (Leipzig and Berlin, 1927), p. 4.

4. *Renaissance und Humanismus in Italien und Deutschland* (Berlin, 1882), pp. 332–337.

5. See the article by Franz Schnabel, "Humanismus und bürgerliches Denken," *Neue Rundschau*, LIII (1942), 547–554. The role of the city councils in the proprietary church arrangements before and during the Reformation would make a challenging and important subject for a full-length study. A good beginning in the study of the rising urban centers and the Reformation has been made by Harold Grimm, "The Social Basis of the German Reformation," *Church History*, XXXI (March 1962), 3–13; "The Relations of Luther and Melanchthon with the Townsmen," ed. Vilmos Vajta, *Luther and Melanchthon* (Philadelphia, 1961), pp. 32–48.

6. Paul Joachimsen, "Loci Communes," *Lutherjahrbuch*, VIII (1926), 54, described Erasmus' special importance for humanism as follows: "Seine Bedeutung für den Humanismus liegt darin, dasz er den Begriff der humanitas von der italienischen Renaissance Kultur, auf denen die ganze Entwicklung von Petrarca bis Pico bezogen hatte, loslöst und auf das Christentum als solches bezieht; er entdeckt die christliche Antike als eine Welt religiöser Ideale und entnimmt aus ihr die Absicht einer *restitutio Christianismi*, einer Wiederherstellung des Christentums."

7. Erwin Metzke, "Die 'Skepsis' des Agrippa von Nettesheim," *Deutsche Vierteljahrsschrift für Literaturwissenschaft und Geistesgeschichte*, XIII (1935), 407ff. Metzke disagrees with Rudolph Stadelmann's stress on Agrippa's skepticism in his book *Vom Geist des ausgehenden Mittlelalters* (Halle, 1929), arguing that the very title of Agrippa's main work continues with a reference to the *Verbum Dei*. See also the excellent article by Charles G. Nauert, Jr., "Magic and Skepticism in Agrippa's Thought," *Journal of the History of Ideas*, XVIII (1957), 161–182.

8. *WA, Br.* I, Nr. 235, p. 602, Luther an Hieronymus Dringersheim, Ende Dezember 1519. The letter of May 18, 1517, Luther to his friend Lang, is to be found in *WA, Br.* I, Nr. 41, p. 99.

9. Otto Herding, "Probleme des frühen Humanismus in Deutschland," *Archiv für Kulturgeschichte*, XXXVIII (1956), 368ff. Herding has some interesting pages on Agricola's opinion of Boethius as a Christian-colored Platonist, not merely a half-Stoic.

10. Rudolf Pfeiffer, "Erasmus und die Einheit der klassischen und der christlichen Renaissance," *Historisches Jahrbuch*, LXXIV (1955), 186.

11. Carl Stange, "Luther und der Geist der Renaissance," *Zeitschrift für systematische Theologie*, XVIII (1941), 21–27.

12. Michael Seidlmayer, " 'Una religio in rituum varietate.' Zur Religionsauffassung des Nikolaus von Cues," *Archiv für Kulturgeschichte*, XXXVI (1954), 168.

13. Irmgard Höss, *Georg Spalatin 1484–1545* (Weimar, 1956), p. 31.

14. *WA*, XXXIX[II], 187–203; *Luther's Works*, XXXIV, 301–321: The Licentiate Examination of Heinrich Schmedenstede.

15. See the outstanding article, Bernd Moeller, "Die deutschen Humanisten und die Anfänge der Reformation," *Zeitschrift für Kirchengeschichte*, LXX (1959), 47–61. Although he exaggerates somewhat, Schöffler, *Die Reformation*, gives the data on the ages of the young reformers and points out that it was a new university with the youngest faculty, in territory last of all converted, that led in the Reformation. The older article by Gerhard Ritter is still of considerable value, "Die geschichtliche Bedeutung des deutschen Humanismus," *Historische Zeitschrift*, CXXVII (1923), 393–453, reprinted separately in 1962. Ritter sought to free the picture of German humanism from the Italian Renaissance conception and from the liberal interpretation represented by Strauss' work on Hutten, and emphasized the religious components of humanist thought. It hardly seems necessary to add that German Renaissance humanism has little in common with the so-called second humanism of Wilhelm von Humboldt and his contemporaries, which made reason and experience the sole touchstones of truth. It has almost nothing whatsoever in common with the new or third humanism, militantly anthropocentric and not infrequently antireligious. With Heidegger's "humanism of being" and Sartre's claim that existentialism is a humanism, as well as the communist Orwellian use of the term Progressive Humanism, the historian will very shortly have to reckon with as many humanisms as there have been French republics.

Index

troversy, 175–176; Luther, the Reformation and, 177–196, 243, 286; Sacramentarian controversy, 189–192, 326n6; second marriage controversy, 192–193; death and burial, 195–196, 267; summary evaluation of, 272; on natural philosophy, 281; no universalism in, 288

Piscator seu Reviviscentes, 169, 175

Pistoris, Maternus, 134

Pius III, 135

Platina, 47

Plato: von Tepl familiar with, 6; Egidio da Viterbo on, 12; Ellenbogen student of, 13; cited by Ficino, 13; harmonized with Aristotle, 16; Wimpfeling cautions against, 47; *Kratylos* influences Reuchlin, 68; Reuchlin cites, 76; Dürer woodcut, 90; on soul returning to star, 100; scholastics unfamiliar with, 103; Hegius opposed to, 132; Florentine revival of, 136–137; natural law in, 143; Mutian on, 146, 154; pupil of Moses, 147; Gabriel Zerbus lectures on, 158; Pirckheimer and, 167, 170–171, 172, 173, 288; used hieroglyphic expression, 169; Erasmus and, 211, 212, 213, 224, 229, 288; Luther and, 238; replaces Boethius, 277; enthusiasm, 291

Platonic: tradition, Cusanus and, 11; philosophy, 13, 16; ideas of Niphus, 158; view of God, 285

Platonism: influence on humanists, 7; Neoplatonism of Florentines, 12–15, 136–137; influence in North, 16; Reuchlin's thought, 18, 71–76 *passim*; Agricola not influenced by Florentine, 39; Celtis', 106–107; Pirckheimer's, 158, 170–171; Erasmus and, 213; Luther and, 238; medieval form of, 275; religious emphasis of, 283; theosophy of, 284–285

Plautus, 47, 89, 133, 240

Pletho, Gemisthos, 13, 165

Pliny, 24, 103, 210, 246, 249

Plotinus, 13, 14, 72, 147

Plutarch, 165, 166, 167, 178, 210, 211

Poggio Bracciolini, G. F., 6, 12, 39, 209, 322n29

Pole, Reginald, 7

Polich, Martin, 104

Politian, 5, 44, 65, 133

Polybius, 33

Pomponazzi, 158

Pomponio Laetus, 45, 90

Porphyry, 29, 72, 151

Porst, Nicolaus, 160

Postillae perpetuae in universam S. Scripturam, 66

Praedones, 123

Praefatio in Harmonias de Passione Christi, 264

Praise of Folly, 108, 120, 203, 204, 207–208, 228

Preface to Galeatius Capella's History, 260

Prenninger, Martin, 13

Prescriptions Against Heretics, 237

Prierias, 179

Prince, The, 101

Priscian, 249

Pro concordia dialecticorum, 48

Proclus, 10, 97, 166

Prodicus, 27

Prometheus, 213, 338n58

Propertius, 47

Propositiones reverendissimi Domini Nicolae cardinalis de virtute ipsius non aliud, 98

Protagoras, 27, 283

Protagoras, 233

Prudentius, 43, 214

Pseudo-Hermogenes, 35

Pseudo-Plato, 35

Pseudo-Thomas, 283

Ptolemy, 90, 164, 167

Pythagoras: Cabala and, 67–80 *passim*; natural law in, 143; humanist name for Benedict, 146; used hieroglyphic expression, 169; Valla praises, 206; Erasmus on, 222, 229; Luther favors, 238; Reuchlin defends, 309n30

Querela Pacis, 228, 342n109

Querelae, 111

Quintilian: Agricola learns from, 23, 29; glories of reason, 31, 300n39; apostle of eloquence, 32; rhetoric of, 38; Whittenberg offers lectures on, 246, 249

Quintus Curtius, 210

Raimund von Gunk, 133

Ramus, Peter, 29

Ranke, Leopold von, 258

Rashi, Salomo ben Isaac, 66

Ratio seu methodus compendio, 224–225

Reformatio Poetarum, 104

Regiomontanus, 90, 156, 162, 164